THE GOOD
Web Site
GUIDE 2003

D1510371

THE GOOD
Web Site
GUIDE 2003

GRAHAM EDMONDS

ORION

First published in 2002 by Orion Media
An imprint of Orion Books Ltd
Orion House, 5 Upper St Martin's Lane,
London WC2H 9EA

A CIP catalogue record for this book is
available from the British Library.

ISBN 0 75284 636 1

Designed by Staziker Jones, Cardiff

Printed by Clays Ltd, St Ives plc

Introduction

This is the third edition of the *Good Web Site Guide* and we've sold over 100,000 copies of the first two, this edition is fully updated, all the sites have been checked and rechecked and I've added several hundred more.

I review the very best sites in each category, then look for those sites that offer something unique or have features that make them stand out and recommend those too. I also list alternatives, especially in the popular genres such as music, shopping or finance. Essentially I concentrate on what's really useful and I would like to encourage people to see the Internet as a tool like any other and not be intimidated by it.

So what's changed in a year since the last edition? Generally, sites have improved in speed and design and in ease of use, more thought and care is being taken. Quality is still a big issue, the costs and time involved in maintaining a good site is sometimes prohibitive so that many sites don't seem to be updated as frequently as they should be, while others just die through lack of interest and funding. Still hundreds of sites go live every day showing that creativity and entreprenurialism are alive and kicking on the Net.

Lack of time and resource often results in site names (URLs) being turned over to directories,

search engines or even adult entertainment
sites. I got caught out in the last guide when a
couple of sites ceased to exist, their ownership
lapsed and annoyingly, they were rented out to
an adult entertainment company while awaiting
re-sale. This was particularly irresponsible
considering that one was a site that children
were likely to access. Orion acted fast and
purchased it, but was unable to buy the other
one which had a more adult oriented URL.
Thank you to those people who wrote in to let
us know.

*Please do let me know if you find any major
changes to the sites recommended in this book, I
can assure you that all the reviews are accurate at
the time of writing this book. Send comments to:*
goodwebsiteguide@hotmail.com

It's also become obvious that there will be
less free information in the future with more
sites charging subscription fees for access to
the information they hold. There's more pressure on sites to become more commercial now
as shareholders and investors demand a return.

It is disappointing that there are relatively
few really well designed web sites. Most sites
are informative and do the job but really
entertaining sites, those that make you want to
go back for more, are rare. Surprisingly, even as
web design becomes more sophisticated, few
have that genuine 'wow' factor, and it's as if

they all come from one or two web site making machines.

On a positive note, the Internet does allow a great deal of freedom; you can really indulge your interests, be informed, up-to-date and experience things maybe you've not experienced before, and it will save you time and money.

The best sites are brilliant. Here's my top ten of the best designed and most useful and user-friendly sites (in no particular order of merit):

www.2020shops.co.uk – outstanding shop directory site

www.cd-wow.com – the best value music shop, great for the latest CD's

www.eyestorm.com – beautiful contemporary art shop

www.google.co.uk – an excellent search engine and directory

www.mapblast.com – useful maps and route finder service

www.metmuseum.org – the Metropolitan Museum in New York

www.skyscrapers.com – this is a labour of love

www.unmissable.com – brilliant travel site

www.whitecube.com – truly original site design from an art gallery

www.xrefer.co.uk – look up anything, a great reference tool

Web site designers who want our loyalty and custom should take note and make their own sites similarly impressive.

KEEPING SAFE

Some people are worried about using their credit card to shop on the Net. In theory it's safer than giving credit card details over the phone, because on most sites the information is encrypted. Before giving out card details, check that you are on a secure line, a small padlock icon will appear on your toolbar, and the **http://** prefix will change to **https://** Providing you shop from UK sites you are fully covered by the same fair trade laws that cover every form of shopping in the UK, but buying from abroad could have some risks attached. If in doubt, shop from reputable firms and known brand names.

There's also a great deal of concern about cookies. A cookie is the popular name of a file which holds some information about your machine and, only if you give it out, about you. They have a sinister reputation but they enable web site owners to monitor traffic and find out who is visiting their sites. In theory, this means they can tailor their content to their customers or provide a better service. If you're worried about cookies, you can easily delete them or set your computer to not receive them. Be aware however, that many sites do need cookies to function, especially shopping sites.

If you are concerned about security and viruses there are several free programs you can download:

Zonelabs (**www.zonelabs.com**) offer a free security system for home users including a firewall, it's relatively easy to use and set up.

Grisoft (**www.grisoft.com**) offer a free virus checker which is reliable. See also Housecall (**http://housecall.antivirus.com**).

At Lava Soft (**www.lavasoftusa.com**) you can down load a free program that roots out spyware and other nasties.

USING THE LIST

Ratings

ORIGIN UK
SPEED ✓✓✓✓✓
INFO ✓✓✓✓✓
VALUE ✓✓✓✓✓
EASE ✓✓✓✓✓

✓ = slow/poor   ✓✓✓✓✓ = fast/good

Speed – some sites take ages to download and use. This gives an indication of what you can expect from the site in question. During the course of preparing the book I visited each reviewed site several times. All the work was done on the same PC using the same service provider.

Info – this gives you a gauge of how much information is available, with respect to how much you are entitled to expect. It's also a measure of the number and quality of links they provide.

Value – value for money. The higher the score the better value you can expect. In some cases this is not relevant.

Ease – this is intended to give an indication of how easy the site is to use. Is it logical, easy to navigate or well signposted?

Origin – a site's country of origin is not always obvious. This can be important, especially if you are buying from abroad. There may be restrictions or taxes that aren't obvious at the time of purchase. Also information that is shown as general may apply to one part of the world and not another. For instance, gardening advice on a US site may not be appropriate in the UK.

I don't pretend to be a judge and jury, my ratings are just my opinion, that of a customer and consumer.

If you have any suggestions as to how I can improve the *Good Web Site Guide* or have a site you think should be included in the 2004 edition then please e-mail me at **goodwebsiteguide@hotmail.com**

Acknowledgements

I'd just like to end in thanking a few important people:

Firstly, a big thank you to all those people who have written in with suggestions and sites for me to check out, over 100 sites have been included in the book as a result of people e-mailing me.

Orion, especially the sales team and Jo Carpenter who did a great job with the other books and I know will with this one.

In particular to Deborah Gray for great patience and excellent advice and ever increasing contributions to the book.

All my many friends and colleagues for their support and suggestions.

Anyone who bought the first books and the booksellers who supported them.

Lastly to Michaela for all else that matters.

Aircraft and Aviation

www.flyer.co.uk

AVIATION IN THE UK

ORIGIN UK

SPEED ✓✓✓

INFO ✓✓✓✓✓

EASE ✓✓✓✓

Comprehensive news, views and information about the world of aviation from the *Flyer Magazine* site. There's a good section on aviation links, a club and school guide and info on how to buy and sell an aircraft, classified ads and even free Internet access.

www.aeroflight.co.uk

AVIATION ENTHUSIASTS

ORIGIN UK

SPEED ✓✓✓

INFO ✓✓✓✓✓

EASE ✓✓✓✓

This site attempts to offer an 'information stop' for all aviation enthusiasts. It has details on international air forces, a section on the media including specialist books and bookshops, a discussion forum, as well as details of air shows and museums.

www.f4aviation.co.uk

AIR SCENE UK

ORIGIN UK

SPEED ✓✓✓

INFO ✓✓✓✓

EASE ✓✓✓✓

A weekly e-zine provided by F4 aviation, a group of enthusiasts, this site has lots of information, nostalgia, links to related sites and personal flying accounts. It's also got an air show listing with reports and previews.

www.landings.com

THE BUSIEST AVIATION HUB IN CYBERSPACE

ORIGIN US

SPEED ✓✓✓✓

INFO ✓✓✓✓✓

EASE ✓✓✓

A huge amount of information on offer from this site with everything from the latest news to history and masses of links with plenty of new features promised for 2002.

www.raf.mod.uk
ROYAL AIR FORCE

ORIGIN UK

SPEED ✓✓✓

INFO ✓✓✓✓

EASE ✓✓✓✓

This site features lots of information on the RAF, the history section is particularly good with data on the very first planes to the latest, with a good gallery of pictures to complement the information, although the time-line section isn't quite up-to-date at time of writing. You can also find out what the Red Arrows are up to, get career advice and technical information.

http://theaerodrome.com
WW1

ORIGIN UK

SPEED ✓✓

INFO ✓✓✓✓

EASE ✓✓✓✓

Devoted to the aircraft and aces of the First World War, this site offers lots of background information, personal experiences and details about the pilots who fought above the trenches.

www.wpafb.af.mil/museum
US AIR FORCE MUSEUM

ORIGIN US

SPEED ✓✓✓

INFO ✓✓✓✓✓

EASE ✓✓✓✓

A superbly detailed site with masses of data on the aircraft and their history from the first planes to space flight, the archive section is particularly good with features on particular types of aircraft and weapons, with information on how they were developed.

www.thunder-and-lightnings.co.uk
BRITISH POST WAR MILITARY AIRCRAFT

ORIGIN UK

SPEED ✓✓✓✓

INFO ✓✓✓✓

EASE ✓✓✓✓

You won't find Spitfires here, but you will learn about great British military planes produced since the war, each has a linked page which is very detailed. There's also a spotter's guide, links, events and a photo quiz. If you do want to know about Spitfires try the excellent site **www.spitfiresociety.demon.co.uk**

http://cloud.prohosting.com/hud607

THE UGLY AND UNCOMMON AIRCRAFT

ORIGIN UK
SPEED ✓✓✓
INFO ✓✓✓✓
EASE ✓✓✓✓

We couldn't resist this one, with its devotion to uncommon and ugly aircraft, each with a page devoted to why it existed in the first place. You can contribute to the annual survey too.

www.airdisaster.com

NO.1 AVIATION SAFETY RESOURCE

ORIGIN US
SPEED ✓✓✓
INFO ✓✓✓✓✓
EASE ✓✓✓✓

A rather macabre site that reviews each major air crash, and looks into the reasons behind what happened. It's not for the squeamish, but the cockpit voice recordings and eyewitness accounts make fascinating, if disturbing, reading. See also www.aaib.gov.uk for the Air Accident Investigation Branch which has a monthly bulletin with details of crashes and current investigations.

http://catalogue.janes.com/jawa.shtml

JANES DEFENCE INFORMATION

ORIGIN UK
SPEED ✓✓✓
INFO ✓✓✓✓✓
VALUE ✓✓✓
EASE ✓✓✓

Janes are the authority on military information, and you can download (with monthly updates) their *All the World's Aircraft* list for £950 annually, or buy it on CD-Rom for £865. For their homepage go to www.janesonline.com

www.gliderpilot.net

GLIDER PILOT NETWORK

ORIGIN UK
SPEED ✓✓✓✓
INFO ✓✓✓
EASE ✓✓✓✓

Weather, news, links and information on all forms of gliding, plus chat and classified ads.

www.iac.org

AEROBATICS

ORIGIN	UK
SPEED	✓✓✓✓
INFO	✓✓✓
EASE	✓✓✓✓

The site of the International Aerobatic Club and the place to go for information on the sport. See also **www.aerobatics.org.uk** for the British Aerobatic Association.

www.airshows.co.uk

UK AIRSHOWS

ORIGIN	UK
SPEED	✓✓✓✓
INFO	✓✓✓
EASE	✓✓✓✓

A slightly messy site with a guide to air shows in Britain with maps, dates and plenty of pictures.

Antiques and Collectibles

The Internet is a great place to learn about antiques, it's also full of specialist sites run by fanatical collectors. If you want to take the risk of buying over the Net, then the best prices are found on the big auction sites such as Ebay and icollector.

www.antiques.co.uk

FIND AND BUY ONLINE

ORIGIN	UK
SPEED	✓✓✓✓
INFO	✓✓✓✓
VALUE	✓✓
EASE	✓✓✓✓

An attractive and well-designed site, which is basically an online showroom dedicated to most aspects of art and antiques. The emphasis is on quality and experts vet all items and you can arrange viewings too. There's also a news and reviews section with interesting articles on the latest fashionable antiques.

www.antiquesbulletin.co.uk

INTERACTIVE WORLD OF ANTIQUES

ORIGIN UK
SPEED ✓✓✓✓
INFO ✓✓✓✓✓
VALUE ✓✓✓
EASE ✓✓✓✓

A well laid out site with loads of information and links to more specialist sites and dealers. It aims to cover every aspect of antiques and does a great job, there are details on auctions, advice on how to buy and sell and a bookshop. You can also buy and sell from the site. To access the articles archive, you need to purchase a site licence.

www.antiquegems.net

ANTIQUE JEWELLERY

ORIGIN UK
SPEED ✓✓✓
INFO ✓✓✓✓
VALUE ✓✓✓
EASE ✓✓✓✓

A fine site from a Birmingham dealer and restorer with a good selection of gems and jewellery as well as watches and a selection of bargains. You can't buy online but there's a contact service for the pieces that you're interested in.

www.invaluable.com

ART MARKET INTELLIGENCE

ORIGIN UK
SPEED ✓✓✓✓
INFO ✓✓✓✓✓
EASE ✓✓✓

Get the latest word on antiques, plus contact details and links to hundreds of dealers, catalogues and auction houses world-wide. The links section is particularly good.

www.antiquesworld.co.uk

FOR EVERYONE WITH AN INTEREST IN ANTIQUES AND COLLECTIBLES

ORIGIN UK
SPEED ✓✓✓✓
INFO ✓✓✓✓✓
EASE ✓✓✓

Catch up on the latest news, obtain details on major and local fairs and events, book a course or indulge your interests by linking to a specialist online retailer or club. You can't buy from this site but the links and information are very good.

www.dmgantiquefairs.com

FOR THE LARGEST ANTIQUES FAIRS

ORIGIN UK
SPEED ✓✓✓
INFO ✓✓✓✓
EASE ✓✓✓✓

DMG run the largest fairs in the UK. Their attractive site gives details of each fair, including dates, location and local tourist information. For a site that simply lists antiques and collectors fairs in date order with links to organiser's web sites go to www.antiques-web.co.uk/fairs.html

www.collectiques.co.uk

COLLECTIBLES

ORIGIN UK
SPEED ✓✓✓✓
INFO ✓✓✓✓✓
EASE ✓✓✓✓

Despite its fairly naff name, Collectiques is a good resource if you're searching for information or that elusive piece for your collection. It covers an impressive array of areas of interest from toys to models, kits and architectural antiques, it's easy to use and it's great for background info and links.

www.collectorcafe.com

ONLINE COLLECTING COMMUNITY

ORIGIN UK
SPEED ✓✓✓✓
INFO ✓✓✓✓
EASE ✓✓✓✓

A portal site which is great for classified ads links, articles and chat covering most of the major areas of collecting.

www.worldcollectorsnet.com

BY COLLECTORS FOR COLLECTORS

ORIGIN US
SPEED ✓✓✓✓
INFO ✓✓✓
VALUE ✓✓✓
EASE ✓✓✓✓

Great for discussion groups, collector's message boards and general chat about collecting. There's also a good online magazine plus plenty of advice and links.

www.finds.org.uk

THE PORTABLE ANTIQUITIES SCHEME

ORIGIN UK
SPEED ✓✓✓✓
INFO ✓✓✓
EASE ✓✓✓✓

A surprisingly interesting site devoted to volunteered archaeological and antiquity finds made by individuals who offer to register them so that they can be researched properly.

Ceramics

www.ukceramics.org

A CERAMICS SHOWCASE

ORIGIN UK
SPEED ✓✓✓
INFO ✓✓✓
EASE ✓✓✓✓✓

An excellent showcase site for new and established artists. It has beautiful pictures of the ceramics with good biographical information. The site enables you to contact artists to buy their work.

www.studiopottery.com

THE POTTERY STUDIO

ORIGIN UK
SPEED ✓✓✓
INFO ✓✓✓✓✓
EASE ✓✓✓✓

Divided into 3 sections: pots, potters and potteries, this site gives information on the history of studio pottery. It's a huge site with over 3,700 pages and it's continually being updated. Everything is cross-referenced with good explanations and photographs.

www.claricecliff.com

THE FIRST LADY OF CERAMIC DESIGN

ORIGIN UK
SPEED ✓✓✓
INFO ✓✓✓✓✓
VALUE ✓✓
EASE ✓✓✓✓

A must for fans of Clarice Cliff pottery. There is information on auctions, biographical details, patterns, shapes; also a newsletter and forum for related chat. The site offers reproductions and related merchandise for sale.

Apple Mac Users

The following sites specialise in Apple Mac technology and programs. See also the general sections on Computers, Software and Games which may also have relevant information.

www.apple.com or www.uk.euro.apple.com
HOME OF THE ORIGINAL

ORIGIN US	Get the latest information and advances in Apple
SPEED ✓✓✓	computers at this beautifully designed site. You can
INFO ✓✓✓✓	buy from the Applestore but don't expect huge
VALUE ✓✓✓	discounts, although they do offer finance deals.
EASE ✓✓✓✓	

www.cancomuk.com
APPLE MAC HARDWARE AND SOFTWARE

ORIGIN UK	A well-designed site offering a wide selection of
SPEED ✓✓✓✓	hardware, peripherals and software all developed
INFO ✓✓✓✓	for Apple computers. There are plenty of deals and
VALUE ✓✓✓✓	free delivery on all orders over £100 before VAT.
EASE ✓✓✓✓	

www.macwarehouse.co.uk
GREAT PRICES ON MACS

ORIGIN UK	Part of the Microwarehouse group, they specialise in
SPEED ✓✓✓✓	mail order supply with a reputation for excellent
INFO ✓✓✓✓	service. Good prices and a wide range make this a
VALUE ✓✓✓✓	good first port of call if you need a new PC or an
EASE ✓✓✓	upgrade.

www.macintouch.com

THE ORIGINAL MAC NEWS AND INFORMATION SITE

ORIGIN US
SPEED ✓✓✓
INFO ✓✓✓✓✓
EASE ✓✓

If you have a Mac then this is the site for you. It has lots of information, bug fixes and software to download, but it is a little overwhelming and it takes a while to get your bearings. Once you've done that, for the Mac user this is invaluable. In the unlikely event that you can't find what you're looking for here try **www.macaddict.com** or the Mac News network at **www.macnn.com**

www.macinsearch.com

APPLE SEARCH

ORIGIN US
SPEED ✓✓✓✓
INFO ✓✓✓✓✓
EASE ✓✓✓✓

A search engine devoted to all things Macintosh with access to masses of links and relevant articles. See also **www.macinstein.com** which is pretty comprehensive.

www.macassist.co.uk

APPLE HELP

ORIGIN UK
SPEED ✓✓✓✓
INFO ✓✓✓✓
EASE ✓✓✓✓✓

A great looking site from a British company that specialises in Macintosh computers with advice on the latest hardware, plus forums, classified ads and virus information.

www.ihateapple.com

IF YOU REALLY DON'T LIKE APPLE

ORIGIN US
SPEED ✓✓✓✓
INFO ✓✓✓✓
EASE ✓✓✓

An entertaining anti-Apple web site devoted to 'debunking' and exposing Apple faults – it's actually quite informative and funny too.

Games for Macs

Here are three great sites to help you if you feel restricted by having an Apple Mac.

www.macgamer.com
MAC GAMER MAG

ORIGIN	US	A great looking online magazine with all the usual
SPEED	✓✓✓	features we've come to expect: news, reviews, links
INFO	✓✓✓✓	and even a few giveaways. It's all neatly packaged
EASE	✓✓✓✓	on an attractive website.

www.macgamefiles.com
MAC GAME FILE LIBRARY

ORIGIN	US	To quote them 'Macgame files.com is the one-stop
SPEED	✓✓✓	source for Macintosh game files. The web site
INFO	✓✓✓✓✓	features lively libraries of Macintosh demos, share-
EASE	✓✓✓✓	ware, updaters, tools, add-ons, and more'. And
		they're right; it's a very good site with some really
		good games and useful stuff.

www.insidemacgames.com
IMG MAGAZINE

ORIGIN	US	A magazine devoted to Mac games where you can
SPEED	✓✓✓	find the latest demos, updates for the games, loads
INFO	✓✓✓✓	of shareware games, news and reviews.
EASE	✓✓✓✓	

Architecture

www.greatbuildings.com

ARCHITECTURE ONLINE

ORIGIN US
SPEED ✓✓✓
INFO ✓✓✓✓
EASE ✓✓✓

This site shows over 1,000 buildings and features hundreds of leading architects, with 3D models, photographic images and architectural drawings, commentaries, bibliographies and web links. It's all well packaged, easy to use and you can search by architect, building or location.

www.skyscrapers.com

SKYSCRAPERTASTIC!

ORIGIN US
SPEED ✓✓✓
INFO ✓✓✓✓
EASE ✓✓✓✓

This really entertaining and award-winning site has many thousands of images of skyscrapers and major buildings from around the world, and more are being added constantly. There are also features, chat and you can search by region as well as by architect or building.

www.architecture.com

THE ROYAL INSTITUTE FOR BRITISH ARCHITECTS

ORIGIN UK
SPEED ✓✓✓
INFO ✓✓✓✓✓
EASE ✓✓✓✓

A massive site from the RIBA with some 250,000 pages on all aspects of architecture including history, jobs, events and features on great buildings. Also check out www.architectureforall.com which is a collaborative venture between the Victoria & Albert museum and the RIBA to promote understanding of architecture.

Art and the Arts

One of the best things about the Internet is the ability to show-case things that otherwise would be quite obscure or inaccessible. Now working artists can show their wares to excellent effect and we can view their art before we buy. In addition, we can now 'visit' some of the world's great galleries and museums. Here are the best sites for posters, online galleries, museums, cartoons, exhibitions, showcases for new talent and how to get the best clip-art for your own use.

Art – resources, shops, museums, galleries and exhibitions

www.artlex.com

THE VISUAL ARTS DICTIONARY

ORIGIN US
SPEED ✓✓✓✓
INFO ✓✓✓✓
EASE ✓✓✓

From abbozzo to zoomorphic, there are over 3,000 definitions of art-related terms with links to related articles other sites; however, some of the links aren't reliable.

www.artcyclopedia.com

THE FINE ART SEARCH ENGINE

ORIGIN CANADA
SPEED ✓✓✓
INFO ✓✓✓✓✓
EASE ✓✓✓✓✓

A popular resource for finding out just about anything to do with art, it's quick, nicely designed and informative. At time of writing they had indexed 1200 leading arts sites, and offer more than 32,000 links directly to an estimated 100,000 works by 7,500 different artists. See also the economically designed **www.artincontext.com** and **www.artswire.org** home of the New York Foundation of the Arts.

www.accessart.org.uk

MAKING ART ACCESSIBLE

ORIGIN UK
SPEED ✓✓✓✓
INFO ✓✓✓✓
EASE ✓✓✓✓

A really good, colourful site dedicated to helping students, children and teachers get to grips with the art world and the meaning behind art. There are good online workshops on topics such as sculpture, use of colour and photography.

http://wwar.com

THE WORLD-WIDE ART RESOURCE

ORIGIN US
SPEED ✓✓✓
INFO ✓✓✓✓✓
EASE ✓✓✓✓✓

This is an effective search vehicle with links to artists, exhibitions, galleries and museums, it is now much better designed and easier to use as a result.

www.design-council.org.uk

PROMOTING THE EFFECTIVE USE OF DESIGN

ORIGIN UK
SPEED ✓✓✓
INFO ✓✓✓
EASE ✓✓✓✓

This good looking site effectively promotes the work of The Design Council through access to their archives of articles on design and details of their work with government; also gives feedback on design issues.

www.artguide.org

THE ART LOVER'S GUIDE TO BRITAIN AND IRELAND

ORIGIN UK
SPEED ✓✓✓
INFO ✓✓✓✓
EASE ✓✓✓✓

Organised by artist, region, exhibition or museum with more than 4,500 listings in all. This site is easy to navigate with a good search engine and cross-referencing making it simple to find out about events in a particular region, aided by annotated maps.

www.thegallerychannel.com
WORLD'S MOST COMPREHENSIVE ARTS LISTING

ORIGIN UK
SPEED ✓✓✓
INFO ✓✓✓✓
EASE ✓✓✓✓

The Gallery Channel provides information on exhibitions, with online cross-referencing for over 16,000 artists, 13,000 exhibitions at 5,000 venues in the UK. The site is continually updating and there's always something new to look at along with plenty of articles, news and previews.

www.24hourmuseum.org.uk
OPEN ALL HOURS

ORIGIN UK
SPEED ✓✓✓✓
INFO ✓✓✓✓✓
EASE ✓✓✓✓

Run by the Campaign for Museums, this site aims to give high quality access to the UK's galleries, museums and heritage sites, and it succeeds. The graphics are clear, it's easy to use and really informative. There's a museum finder, links, a magazine, resources for research and they're completing a kids' section at the time of going to press. See also the rather pretentious www.artmuseum.net which is supported by Intel.

www.artchive.com
MARK HARDEN'S ARTCHIVE

ORIGIN UK
SPEED ✓✓✓
INFO ✓✓✓✓✓
EASE ✓✓✓✓

Incredible, but seemingly the work of one art fanatic, this superb site not only has an excellent art encyclopaedia, but also the latest art news and galleries with special online exhibitions. The quality of the pictures is outstanding. There's also a section on theory and good links.

www.surrealism.co.uk

ONLINE GALLERY

ORIGIN UK	Not as way out as you'd expect, this site gives an
SPEED ✓✓✓✓	overview of surrealism and features contemporary
INFO ✓✓✓	artists. The online gallery is OK without being that
EASE ✓✓✓✓	exciting, but as a showcase it works.

www.graffiti.org

THE WRITING ON THE WALL

ORIGIN UK	If you're fascinated by graffiti then here's the place
SPEED ✓✓✓✓	to go – it's got a gallery of the best examples, history
INFO ✓✓✓✓	and links to other graffiti sites.
EASE ✓✓✓✓	

www.the-artists.org

20TH CENTURY ART

ORIGIN UK	This site is easy to use, with minimalist design and
SPEED ✓✓✓✓	details of every major artist of the last century.
INFO ✓✓✓✓	
EASE ✓✓✓✓	

The major museums and galleries

www.tate.org.uk

THE ARCHETYPAL GALLERY SITE

ORIGIN UK	A real treat with good design and quality pictures,
SPEED ✓✓	the site is divided into these sections:
INFO ✓✓✓✓	
VALUE ✓✓✓	
EASE ✓✓✓✓	

1 One for each Tate gallery, including what's on and what's coming.
2 The collection, which can easily be browsed or searched by artist.
3 The shop sells art related merchandise.
4 A forum for art chat and a feedback feature.
5 Notes about the sponsors.
6 Future plans for the galleries.
7 Details about touring exhibitions.

www.nationalgallery.org.uk

THE NATIONAL COLLECTION

ORIGIN UK
SPEED ✓✓✓✓
INFO ✓✓✓✓✓
EASE ✓✓✓✓✓

A very comprehensive site, similar in style to the Tate but without a shop. Divided into five major sections:

1 The collection, very good quality pictures with notes on each one.
2 What's on and when.
3 Information on the gallery, how to get there etc.
4 What's new and coming.
5 A good search facility.

For access to the all the Scottish National Galleries on a similar site, go to **www.natgalscot.ac.uk** who have a similarly informative and enjoyable site.

www.thebritishmuseum.ac.uk

ILLUMINATING NEW CULTURES

ORIGIN UK
SPEED ✓✓✓✓
INFO ✓✓✓✓
VALUE ✓✓✓
EASE ✓✓✓✓

Whether you explore the world's cultures with interactive mapping, understand and educate yourself or just browse the collection, this is a beautifully illustrated site. The online shop stocks a selection of gifts and goods based on museum artefacts. Delivery in the UK starts at £3.95. They also arrange museum tours.

www.npg.org.uk

THE NATIONAL PORTRAIT GALLERY

ORIGIN UK
SPEED ✓✓✓✓
INFO ✓✓✓✓✓
VALUE ✓✓
EASE ✓✓✓✓

With over 10,000 works on view, this is one of the biggest online galleries. It shows the most influential characters in British history portrayed by artists of their time. You can search by sitter or artist, and buy the print. The online shop offers gifts plus pictures with options on print size, framing and delivery, including overseas.

www.royalacademy.org.uk

WHERE ART IS MADE, SEEN AND DEBATED

ORIGIN UK
SPEED ✓✓✓
INFO ✓✓✓✓
EASE ✓✓✓✓

A well-designed and modern gallery site with all the information you need on the Royal Academy as well as ticket information and live waiting times for the exhibitions. There's support for schools, colleges and teachers, plus previews of exhibitions, although they've yet to put the collection online.

www.vam.ac.uk

VICTORIA & ALBERT MUSEUM

ORIGIN UK
SPEED ✓✓✓✓
INFO ✓✓✓✓
VALUE ✓✓
EASE ✓✓✓✓

The world's largest museum has a plain functional web site, with information on visiting, learning and how you can help support the museum. The online shop offers gifts, reproductions and books. You can also explore the museum virtually, visiting most of the galleries with back-up information explaining their exhibits with details of what they contain.

www.moma.org

THE MUSEUM OF MODERN ART IN NEW YORK

ORIGIN US
SPEED ✓✓✓
INFO ✓✓✓✓✓
VALUE ✓✓
EASE ✓✓✓

This attractive site is split into six major areas:

1 The collection, with a selection of the best paintings.
2 What's on.
3 Education resources, for teachers and pupils.
4. Details on becoming a member.
5 Visiting information.
6 The online store which is excellent for the unusual.

You need to install Shockwave for features such as the audio commentary on the paintings. Do browse the store as some products on sale are exclusive; members get discounts on items sold in the store. Delivery to the UK is expensive.

www.metmuseum.org

THE METROPOLITAN MUSEUM OF ART IN NEW YORK

ORIGIN US
SPEED ✓✓✓✓
INFO ✓✓✓✓
VALUE ✓✓✓
EASE ✓✓✓✓

A beautiful and very stylish site, featuring lots of great ideas, with quality illustrations and photographs, you can view any one of 3,500 exhibits, become a member, or visit a special exhibition. The shop offers a great range of products, many exclusive, and there's a handy gift finder service. Delivery costs to the UK depend on how much you spend.

www.uffizi.firenze.it/welcome.html

THE UFFIZI GALLERY IN FLORENCE

ORIGIN ITALY
SPEED ✓✓✓
INFO ✓✓✓
EASE ✓✓✓✓

It's the quality of the images of the paintings that make this site stand out. They are superb and it's a shame that there are not more of them to view. Navigating is easy and quicker than most. There is also gallery information and a tour.

www.louvre.fr

FRANCE'S TREASURE HOUSE

ORIGIN FRANCE
SPEED ✓✓✓
INFO ✓✓✓✓
VALUE ✓
EASE ✓✓✓✓

Similar to the UK's National Gallery site:
1 You can take a virtual tour.
2 View the collection.
3 Learn about its history.
4 Check out the latest exhibitions and buy advance tickets.
5 The shop has interesting items and delivery to the UK is about £7.

www.guggenheim.org

VANGUARDS OF ARCHITECTURE AND CULTURE

ORIGIN US
SPEED ✓✓✓
INFO ✓✓✓✓
VALUE ✓✓
EASE ✓✓✓✓

There is the promise of a unique virtual museum, but while we wait, the other four – Berlin, Bilbao, Venice and New York can be visited here.

1 You can find out about exhibitions and collections, projects, tours, events and developmental programs.
2 Join. Membership entitles you to free entry and a store discount.
3 The store is stocked with a wonderful selection of unusual goods and gifts, and is not bad value. Delivery to the UK is around £20.

www.artgalleries-london.com

GUIDE TO LONDON'S TREASURES

ORIGIN UK
SPEED ✓✓✓✓
INFO ✓✓✓✓
EASE ✓✓✓✓

An attractive site that offers a directory of the capital's museums, galleries and relevant links to related sites.

Sites featuring the top artists:
www.daliuniverse.com – Dali
www.mos.org/leonardo/ – Da Vinci
www.norfacad.pvt.k12.va.us/project/degas/degas.htm – Degas
www.lucidcafe.com/library/96jun/gauguin.html – Gauguin
http://arthistory.about.com/library/blartist_matisse.htm – Matisse
www.marmottan.com – Monet
www.tamu.edu/mocl/picasso – Picasso
www.chez.com/renoir/indexe.html - Renoir
www.mark-rothko.com – Rothko
www.vangoghgallery.com – Van Gogh.

Clip–art

www.clipart.com
THE PLACE TO START IF YOU NEED CLIP-ART

ORIGIN US
SPEED ✓✓✓✓
INFO ✓✓
EASE ✓✓✓✓

Links to over 500 clip-art sites but using the very good search facility, you should quickly find the perfect image. Although huge, this site is low on information. Many linked sites have free art for use, otherwise cost varies enormously depending on what you want. You can also try the very similar www.clipart.net as well. Photographs can be found on page 309.

Cartoons

www.cartoonbank.com
WORLD'S LARGEST CARTOON DATABASE

ORIGIN US
SPEED ✓✓✓
INFO ✓✓✓
EASE ✓✓✓✓

Need to find a cartoon for a particular occasion? Then there's a choice of over 20,000, mostly from *New Yorker* magazine. You can send e-cards, but they only supply products to the USA. For a massive set of links to cartoon and humorous sites then try the excellent Norwegian search site www.cartoon-links.com

www.cartoon-factory.com
BUYING CARTOON CELS

ORIGIN US
SPEED ✓✓✓✓
INFO ✓✓✓✓
VALUE ✓✓
EASE ✓✓✓✓✓

Buy cartoon cels, mainly from Disney and Warner cartoons; you can search by subject or artist. Delivery is expensive, although they are flexible about payment.

Buying art

www.artrepublic.co.uk

BOOKS, POSTERS AND WHAT'S ON WHERE

ORIGIN UK
SPEED ✓✓✓✓
INFO ✓✓✓✓
VALUE ✓✓✓
EASE ✓✓✓✓✓

A nicely designed, easy-to-use site which features four sections:

1 Posters – choose from over 1,500 posters, use the glossary of art terms or peruse artist's biographical data. Free shipping world-wide.
2 Books – read reviews or select from over 30,000 books. Delivery costs £3 for anywhere.
3 Details of their store in Brighton.
4 What's on worldwide – details of the latest exhibitions, competitions and travel information for over 1,200 museums around the world.

www.onlineposters.com

POSTER SHOPS ONLINE

ORIGIN UK
SPEED ✓✓✓✓
INFO ✓✓✓✓
EASE ✓✓✓✓

Simply a ranked list of shops that sell posters, from the generalist to the very specialised retailers.

www.barewalls.com

INTERNET'S LARGEST ART PRINT AND POSTER STORE

ORIGIN US
SPEED ✓✓✓✓
INFO ✓✓✓✓
VALUE ✓✓
EASE ✓✓✓✓✓

This site backs its claim with a huge range, it's also excellent for gifts and unusual prints and posters but be aware that the shipping costs are high – $29 for the UK. There's also a gift voucher scheme.

www.postershop.co.uk
FINE ART PRINTS AND POSTERS

ORIGIN UK
SPEED ✓✓✓✓
INFO ✓✓✓✓
VALUE ✓✓✓
EASE ✓✓✓✓✓

There are over 22,000 prints and posters available to buy, covering the work of over 3,000 artists. There's also a framing service and a good user-friendly search facility where you can search by subject as well as artist. In the museum shop there's a range of art-related gifts to choose from. Delivery costs £5 for the UK.

www.totalposter.com
GET THE BIG PICTURE

ORIGIN UK
SPEED ✓✓✓✓
INFO ✓✓✓✓
VALUE ✓✓✓
EASE ✓✓✓

Excellent poster store, specialising in photographic posters with a very wide selection. Extra services include: printing up your own photos to poster size, plus pictures of recent key sporting and news events in their 'Stop Press' section. Delivery costs vary.

www.easyart.com
FINE ART PRINTS AND POSTERS

ORIGIN UK
SPEED ✓✓✓✓
INFO ✓✓✓✓
VALUE ✓✓✓✓
EASE ✓✓✓✓

Excellent art shop selling posters, limited editions, photographs and etchings. They provide inspiration too with advice on the best place to hang art in your home and a custom art section where you can turn pictures of your friends into pop icons.

www.eyestorm.com
BUYING CONTEMPORARY ART

ORIGIN UK
SPEED ✓✓✓✓
INFO ✓✓✓
VALUE ✓✓✓
EASE ✓✓✓✓✓

A really attractive and well-designed site, which showcases contemporary art and photography, you can buy online as well.

www.whitecube.com

WHITE CUBE GALLERY

ORIGIN UK
SPEED ✓✓✓✓
INFO ✓✓✓✓
VALUE ✓✓✓
EASE ✓✓✓✓

Outstanding design makes this site stand out, it showcases top artists in an original way and highlights what can be done when web site development technology is used at its best. Although influential in developing the careers of some of the best artists working today, you can buy art here at reasonable prices too.

Other online art showcase sites and stores worth visiting:

www.artandparcel.com – messy site that boasts the largest gallery on the web.

www.art4deco.com – attractive site offering 3,000 works for sale; good search facility.

www.britart.com – good looking site concentrating on the work of 400 British artists.

www.artlondon.com – well designed art store with an emphasis on the UK, value for money and quality.

www.countereditions.com – slow site with a mixture of American and British artists.

www.insidespace.com – clutter free design, original prints and photographs from contemporary artists for sale.

www.hangingfriedeggs.com – a gallery offering a broad range of work with a percentage of sales going to the charity Shelter.

Creating art

www.kurzweilcyberart.com

CYBER ART

ORIGIN US
SPEED ✓✓✓
INFO ✓✓✓✓
EASE ✓✓✓✓

Once you download the program, watch in fascination as art is created for you as a screen saver. It's free and great fun too.

www.arthouse.uk.com

WATERCOLOURS ON THE WEB

ORIGIN UK
SPEED ✓✓✓
INFO ✓✓✓✓
VALUE ✓✓
EASE ✓✓✓

Learn about watercolour techniques, go on a course, find out about exhibitions, seek out designers or book an artistic holiday. There are also several galleries devoted to artists with work for sale and many pictures to view.

www.simplypainting.com

FRANK CLARK

ORIGIN UK
SPEED ✓✓✓
INFO ✓✓✓✓
VALUE ✓✓✓
EASE ✓✓✓

Learn how to paint with leading art teacher Frank Clark, the site has free lessons, tips plus a shop and gallery.

Astrology

www.astrology.com
ALL ABOUT ASTROLOGY

ORIGIN UK	A very comprehensive site offering free advice from
SPEED ✓✓✓	the stars, you can buy a personalised reading and
INFO ✓✓✓✓✓	chart or just browse the more general horoscopes.
EASE ✓✓✓✓	You can find celebrity horoscopes too, and learn

about the history and techniques of astrology. See
also **www.horoscope.co.uk** home of *Horoscope Magazine*.

www.live-astro.com
RUSSELL GRANT

ORIGIN UK	Now is your chance to buy a horoscope from a real
SPEED ✓✓✓	celebrity, costs range from £3.99 upwards. This site
INFO ✓✓✓✓	has been expanded to include dream interpretations,
VALUE ✓✓	tarot and other astrological resources as well as the
EASE ✓✓✓✓	various horoscopes.

www.easyscopes.com
ASTROLOGY SEARCH ENGINE

ORIGIN US	Here you can get as many different free horoscopes
SPEED ✓✓✓✓	as you can handle, the site contains direct links to
INFO ✓✓✓✓✓	the daily, weekly, monthly and yearly horoscopes
EASE ✓✓✓✓	for each zodiac sign. You just have to select your

zodiac sign and you are presented with a large list
of horoscopes to choose from. It's amazing how
different they all are for the same sign!

www.lovetest.com

ARE YOU COMPATIBLE?

ORIGIN	US
SPEED	✓✓✓
INFO	✓✓✓✓✓
EASE	✓✓✓✓

It's a bit long winded to use but enter your birthday and your partner's and you get a compatibility score based on the star signs. There are also quizzes, chat, classified ads, links, not forgetting the love test thermometer.

Auctions and Classified Ads

Before using these sites be sure that you are aware of the rules and regulations surrounding the bidding process, and what your rights are as a seller or purchaser. If they are not properly explained during the registration process, then use another site. They should also offer a returns policy as well as insurance cover.

Whilst there are plenty of bargains available, not all the products on offer are cheaper than the high street or specialist vendor, it's very much a case of buyer beware. Having said that, once you're used to it, it can be fun, and you can save a great deal of money.

www.ebay.co.uk

YOUR PERSONAL TRADING COMMUNITY

ORIGIN	UK
SPEED	✓✓✓
INFO	✓✓✓✓
VALUE	✓✓✓
EASE	✓✓✓✓

With over 3 million items you are likely to find what you want here. The emphasis is on collectibles and it is strong on antiques of all sorts, although there's much, much more. There is a 24-hour support facility and automatic insurance cover on all items up to £120. Previous clients have reviewed each person who has something to sell, that way you can check up on their reliability.

www.ebid.co.uk

NO CHARGE TO LIST AN ITEM

ORIGIN UK	Divided into auctions, wanted and swap sections.
SPEED ✓✓✓	The auctions can easily be accessed and browsed; its
INFO ✓✓✓✓	strengths are in computing, electronics and music,
VALUE ✓✓✓	although there has been a great increase in the
EASE ✓✓✓✓	number of collectibles available.

www.icollector.com

REDEFINING THE ART OF COLLECTING

ORIGIN US	An attractive site bringing together the wares of
SPEED ✓✓✓	some 950 auction houses and dealers, icollector is
INFO ✓✓✓✓	an ambitious project that works well. The emphasis
VALUE ✓✓✓	is on art, antiques and collectibles. Be sure that
EASE ✓✓✓✓	the auction house you're dealing with ships outside
	the USA.

www.qxl.com

A PAN-EUROPEAN AUCTION COMMUNITY

ORIGIN UK/EUROPE	This wide-ranging site offers anything from airline
SPEED ✓✓✓	tickets and holidays to cars, collectibles and elec-
INFO ✓✓✓✓	tronics (in several languages). The quality of
VALUE ✓✓✓✓	merchandise seems better than most sites. Another
EASE ✓✓✓✓	site worth checking out is **www.CQout.co.uk** it has
	over 20,000 lots, a wide selection of categories and
	a nice design.

www.sothebys.com

QUALITY ASSURED, BUT JUST FOR THE CONNOISSEURS

ORIGIN UK/US	You can bid in their online auctions, find out about
SPEED ✓✓✓	their normal auctions or enlist their help with one of
INFO ✓✓✓✓	the many extra services they offer. The emphasis
VALUE ✓✓	here is on high quality and the arts and you can buy
EASE ✓✓✓✓	catalogues too.

www.christies.com

FOR THOSE WITH DEEP WALLETS

ORIGIN UK
SPEED ✓✓✓
INFO ✓✓✓
VALUE ✓✓
EASE ✓✓✓

Christies have a slowish site with info on their programme of auctions and on how to buy and sell through them, but you can't carry out transactions from the site. The 'LotFinder' service searches their auctions for that special item – for a fee. There's also a good specialist bookstore and lots of information on how to buy and sell.

www.ad-mart.co.uk

AWARD WINNING

ORIGIN UK
SPEED ✓✓✓✓
INFO ✓✓✓✓
VALUE ✓✓✓✓
EASE ✓✓✓✓✓

Excellent design and ease of use makes this site stand out; there are fourteen sections, all the usual suspects plus personal ads, boating and pets. There's also a section for announcements of upcoming events such as auctions and car boot sales. See also **www.nettrader.co.uk** which is also really well designed and easy to use.

www.exchangeandmart.co.uk

EXCHANGE & MART

ORIGIN UK
SPEED ✓✓✓✓
INFO ✓✓✓✓
VALUE ✓✓✓✓
EASE ✓✓✓✓✓

Everything the paper has and more, great bargains on a massive range of goods found with good search facility, all packaged in a bright easy-to-use site. It is split into five major sections:

1 Motoring – including cars, vans, number plates and finance.
2 Home – including DIY and gardening.
3 Travel and holidays.
4 Products – for small businesses including computers.
5 Property.

You can place an ad, or get involved with their online auctions.

www.loot.com

FREE ADS ONLINE

ORIGIN UK	Over 100,000 ads and over 3,000 auctioned items
SPEED ✓✓✓	make Loot a great place to go for a bargain. It's an
INFO ✓✓✓✓	interesting site to browse with seventeen sections
VALUE ✓✓✓✓	covering the usual classified ad subjects supple-
EASE ✓✓✓	mented by areas featuring students, jobs, accommo-
	dation and personals. Go to Loot café for a chat.

Beauty

Beauty product retailers have now cottoned on to the Internet so we've featured a few of the best ones for advice help and shopping!

www.beautyconsumer.com

COMPLETE GUIDE TO SKIN CARE

ORIGIN UK	An excellent web site with help and information
SPEED ✓✓✓	on all forms of skin care as well as beauty tips
INFO ✓✓✓✓✓	and product information, there's even a section
EASE ✓✓✓✓✓	especially for men. Two people experienced in
	the field put it together and the information is
	very easy to access.

www.lookfantastic.com

LOOK FANTASTIC

ORIGIN UK	Not as much fun as it was when it started, but it's
SPEED ✓✓✓	still a well-designed online retailer offering some
INFO ✓✓✓✓	really good discounts, while shipping costs start at
VALUE ✓✓✓✓	£2. It also offers advice guides on how to use make-
EASE ✓✓✓✓	up, shampoo and conditioners, in fact virtually
	everything a girl needs – it's war out there after all.

www.bodyshop.co.uk
ISSUES, SELF-ESTEEM AND COSMETICS

ORIGIN UK
SPEED ✓✓✓
INFO ✓✓✓✓✓
EASE ✓✓✓✓

Balancing the rights of the under-privileged with the demands of a commercial cosmetics company. There is good product information but you can't buy online.

www.fragrancenet.com
WORLD'S LARGEST DISCOUNT FRAGRANCE STORE

ORIGIN US
SPEED ✓✓✓✓
INFO ✓✓✓✓
VALUE ✓✓✓
EASE ✓✓✓✓

A massive range of perfumes for men and women, every brand is represented and there are some excellent offers. However, the site is American with shipping costs from $19 dollars and more depending on what you buy.

www.directcosmetics.com
WIDE RANGE AND THE BEST PRICES

ORIGIN UK
SPEED ✓✓✓✓
INFO ✓✓✓✓
VALUE ✓✓✓✓
EASE ✓✓✓✓

They claim to offer a wide range of perfumes with up to 90% off UK recommended retail prices plus the latest news from the big brand names. The site is quick and easy-to-use and the offers are genuine; however, delivery costs £3.95. See also www.perfumeshopping.com who offer 1,000 perfumes and fragrances from a well-designed site.

www.lush.co.uk
SOAP WITHOUT THE SCENT

ORIGIN UK
SPEED ✓✓✓✓
INFO ✓✓✓
VALUE ✓✓✓
EASE ✓✓✓✓

Lush offer a wide range of soaps and associated products from their site, it's easy to shop and if you like their soap but find the smell of the high street shops over powering, then it's perfect. Postage & packing is free on orders over £30, otherwise it is £4.

See also:

www.allbeautyproducts.com – excellent site from
the Allcures camp.

www.beauty4you.co.uk – slow and not very up to
date.

www.beautynaturals.com – attractive all round
beauty site.

www.wellbeing.com – strong offering from Boots,
easier to shop than the real store!

www.cosmetics.com – American skincare specialists.

www.folica.com – great site on hair care.

www.skinstore.com – good looking site selling
premium skincare products.

Books and Booksellers

*Books were the first products to be sold in volume over the
Internet, and their success has meant that there are many online
booksellers, all boasting about the speed of their service and how
many titles they can get. In the main, the basic service is the same
wherever you go, just pick the bookshop that suits you.*

www.bookbrain.co.uk

BEST PRICES FOR BOOKS

ORIGIN UK

SPEED ✓✓✓✓

INFO ✓✓✓✓

VALUE ✓✓✓✓✓

EASE ✓✓✓✓

All you do is type in the title of the book and
Bookbrain will search out the online store that is
offering it the cheapest (including postage). You
then click again to get taken to the store to buy the
book – simple. It's also worth checking out the
American site **www.bestbookbuys.com**

www.amazon.co.uk

MORE THAN JUST A BOOKSTORE

ORIGIN UK
SPEED ✓✓✓✓
INFO ✓✓✓✓
VALUE ✓✓✓
EASE ✓✓✓✓

Amazon is the leading online bookseller and most online stores have followed their formula of combining value with recommendation. Amazon has spent much on providing a wider offering than just books and now has sections for music, gifts, travel, games, software and DVD/video. It also offers an auction service, there's an excellent kids' section, aimed at parents and you can download e-books which can be read on your PC or handheld computer. There are also auctions and zshops where Amazon act as a guarantor for the stores it recommends. For books, there are better prices elsewhere. See also **www.waterstones.co.uk** who have abandoned their site in favour of Amazon, as has Borders **www.borders.com**

www.bol.com

THE EURO-BOOKSELLER

ORIGIN UK/EUROPE
SPEED ✓✓✓
INFO ✓✓✓✓✓
VALUE ✓✓✓
EASE ✓✓✓✓

Owned by Bertlesmann the German media giant, you can get access to books in seven European countries. Slightly dull, it appeals to the true book lover, with lots of recommendations but recently they've increased the number of offers. The 'Books in the Media' section provides day-by-day listing of books that were featured in TV programs, the press or on the radio. Like Amazon it has expanded to include music, video, DVD and games, and you can also download audio books.

www.bookshop.co.uk

THE INTERNET BOOKSHOP

ORIGIN UK
SPEED ✓✓✓✓
INFO ✓✓✓✓
VALUE ✓✓✓✓
EASE ✓✓✓✓

Owned by W.H.Smith, this follows the usual Internet bookshop pattern, but it is slightly clearer with a variety of offers. Also sells videos, CDs and games, with links to other magazines and, unusually, stationery.

www.ottakars.co.uk

RECOMMENDS ONLY

ORIGIN UK
SPEED ✓✓✓
INFO ✓✓✓✓
EASE ✓✓✓✓

Ottakars' site is clear and easy to use with some nice personal touches; it offers a mix of store information, recommendation, competitions and they offer free online magazines on a variety of genres. There's even a web page for each store giving information on the locale and events. There are no facilities to buy books from the site.

http://bookshop.blackwell.co.uk

FOR ACADEMICS AND THE SERIOUS MINDED

ORIGIN UK
SPEED ✓✓✓
INFO ✓✓✓✓
VALUE ✓✓✓
EASE ✓✓✓✓

Blackwells are best known for academic and professional books, but their site offers much more, with the emphasis on recommendation and help finding the right book rather than value for money. For more academic books, a good place to try is www.studentbookworld.com or www.swotbooks.co.uk

www.countrybookshop.co.uk

YOUR LOCAL BOOKSHOP

ORIGIN UK
SPEED ✓✓✓✓
INFO ✓✓✓✓
VALUE ✓✓✓
EASE ✓✓✓✓✓

A small bookseller attempting to take on the corporate giants and largely succeeding if this site is anything to go by. It's very comprehensive and although it may not offer the cheapest books it's easier and more enjoyable to use than many sites. Another triumph of content and good design is at the Book Pl@ce www.thebookplace.com who offer the usual online bookshop but with the addition of a magazine devoted to books and an 'Ask a Bookseller' facility if you can't decide what you want.

www.bn.com

THE WORLD'S BIGGEST BOOKSELLER

ORIGIN US
SPEED ✓✓✓✓
INFO ✓✓✓✓✓
VALUE ✓✓✓✓
EASE ✓✓✓✓

Barnes and Noble's site boasts more books than any other online bookseller. In style it follows the other bookshops with an American bias, and looks very similar to Amazon. It has a good out-of-print service; you can also buy software, prints and posters as well as magazines and music. Unusual features include an e-book shop and their online university where you can take courses in anything from business to learning a language.

www.alphabetstreet.com

STREETS AHEAD

ORIGIN UK
SPEED ✓✓✓✓
INFO ✓✓✓✓
VALUE ✓✓✓✓
EASE ✓✓✓✓

Part of the Streets Online group, this site follows the pattern for other bookshops. However, it offers a flat rate £1 delivery charge in the UK making it one of the cheapest booksellers. It also offers a cash back loyalty scheme in conjunction with its other sites that sell music, games and DVDs.

www.bookpeople.co.uk

INCREDIBLE DISCOUNTS

ORIGIN UK
SPEED ✓✓✓
INFO ✓✓✓
VALUE ✓✓✓✓✓
EASE ✓✓✓✓

Offers a limited range of discounted books with up to 75% off the r.r.p. it's strong on children's titles and certain types of fiction, but low on recommendations. Some books vary from shop editions – using cheaper paper or are paperback editions. Delivery is free if you spend over £25, plus point-based loyalty scheme.

www.powells.com

MASSIVE

ORIGIN US
SPEED ✓✓✓✓
INFO ✓✓✓✓✓
VALUE ✓✓✓
EASE ✓✓✓✓

A huge and impressive site which is well designed and relatively easy to use, Powells seems to occupy most of Portland in Oregon and for once the cost of shipping isn't prohibitive for UK customers. A good place to go if you're looking for something unusual.

www.abebooks.com

ADVANCED BOOK EXCHANGE

ORIGIN US
SPEED ✓✓✓✓
INFO ✓✓✓✓
VALUE ✓✓✓✓
EASE ✓✓✓✓

A network of some 9,000 independent booksellers from around the world claiming access to 27 million books, just use the excellent search engine to find your book and they'll direct you to the nearest bookseller.

http://classics.mit.edu

THE CLASSICS ONLINE

ORIGIN US
SPEED ✓✓✓✓
INFO ✓✓✓✓✓
VALUE ✓✓✓✓✓
EASE ✓✓✓✓

A superb resource offering over 440 free books to print or download, there's also a search facility and help with studying.

www.bibliomania.com

WORLD LITERATURE ONLINE

ORIGIN UK
SPEED ✓✓✓✓
INFO ✓✓✓✓✓
VALUE ✓✓✓✓✓
EASE ✓✓✓✓

A superb resource, Bibliomania has changed to a more commercial and attractive site. You can search the entire site for quotes, for a specific book, get help with research or subscribe to the magazine. There are also plans for a shop and a tie in with a specialist publisher.

www.shakespeare.sk

COMPLETE WORKS

ORIGIN US
SPEED ✓✓✓
INFO ✓✓✓✓
EASE ✓✓✓✓

This is a straightforward site featuring the complete writings of Shakespeare, including biographical details and a glossary explaining the language of the time.

www.booklovers.co.uk

QUALITY SECOND HAND BOOKS

ORIGIN UK
SPEED ✓✓✓✓
INFO ✓✓✓✓
VALUE ✓✓✓✓
EASE ✓✓✓✓

If you can't find the book you want, then this is worth a try. There is an excellent search facility or you can leave them a request. They give a quote if you want to sell a book or arrange a swap. There's also an events listing for book fairs. If you can't find what you're looking for here it's worth checking out three very good sites www.shapero.com www.bookfinder.com and www.bibliofind.com (part of Amazon) who all have very fast search facilities.

www.achuka.co.uk

CHILDREN'S BOOKS

ORIGIN	UK
SPEED	✓✓✓
INFO	✓✓✓✓
VALUE	✓✓✓
EASE	✓✓✓✓

Achuka are specialists in children's books and offer a comprehensive listing of what's available from a fairly boring site. There's plenty of information on the latest news and awards as well as reviews, author interviews, a chat section and links to booksellers.

Other children's book sites:
www.childrensbookshop.com – very traditional site from a shop based in Hay on Wye.
www.wordpool.co.uk – good advice on what to read.
www.ucalgary.ca/~dkbrown/ – home of the excellent Children's Literature web guide.
www.carolhurst.com – good design and great for book reviews.

www.audiobooks.co.uk

THE TALKING BOOKSHOP

ORIGIN	UK
SPEED	✓✓✓✓
INFO	✓✓✓✓
VALUE	✓✓✓
EASE	✓✓✓

Specialists in books on tape, they have around 6,000 titles in stock and can quickly get another 10,000. They also stock CDs but no MP3 yet. Search the site by author or reader, as well as by title. There are some offers, but most stock is at full price with delivery being £2 per order.
Also uses **www.talkingbooks.co.uk** See also **www.isis-publishing.co.uk** who offer thousands of unabridged audio books, and more in the way of CDs, but for a really unusual audio experience go to **www.totallyword.com**

Book specialists

The following sites specialise in one form or genre of book:

www.compman.co.uk – computer manuals.

www.crimeboss.com – crime comic books.

www.e-books.co.uk – download from a wide selection.

www.firstbookshop.com – one of the few to offer book tokens.

www.lotrfanclub.com – Lord of the Rings fanclub.

www.poems.com – home of *Poetry Daily*.

www.poetrybooks.co.uk – the poetry book society.

www.purefiction.com – features, links and advice for budding novelists.

www.stanfords.co.uk – excellent site from the UK's leading travel and map retailers.

www.swotbooks.co.uk – low cost books for clever dicks.

www.theromancereader.com – lots of romantic reviews and links.

Cars

Whether you want to buy a car, check out your insurance or even arrange a service, it can all be done on the Net. If you want to hire a car see page 471.

Information and motoring organisations

www.dvla.gov.uk

DRIVER AND VEHICLE LICENSING AGENCY

ORIGIN	UK
SPEED	✓✓✓✓
INFO	✓✓✓✓✓
VALUE	✓✓✓
EASE	✓✓✓

Excellent for the official line in motoring, the driver's section has details on penalty points, licence changes and medical issues. The vehicles section goes through all related forms and there's also a 'What's New' page. It's clearly and concisely written throughout and information is easy to find.

www.smmt.co.uk

SOCIETY OF MOTOR MANUFACTURERS & TRADERS

ORIGIN	UK
SPEED	✓✓✓✓
INFO	✓✓✓✓
EASE	✓✓✓✓

The SMMT support the British motor industry by campaigning and informing the trade and public alike. Here you can get information on topics like the motor show and the new tax regime based on exhaust emissions. There's also a good company car tax calculator on Lex Vehicle Leasing's site **www.lvl.co.uk** If you're scared of getting a company car now, it may be worth your while checking out the offers at **www.contracthireandleasing.com** who have a large number of options available.

www.theaa.co.uk

THE AA

ORIGIN UK
SPEED ✓✓✓✓
INFO ✓✓✓✓✓
VALUE ✓✓✓
EASE ✓✓✓✓

Now a more comprehensive motoring site with a route planner, new and used car info, travel information, insurance quotes, shop and a car data checking facility.

www.rac.co.uk

THE RAC

ORIGIN UK
SPEED ✓✓✓
INFO ✓✓✓✓✓
VALUE ✓✓✓
EASE ✓✓✓✓

A much clearer site than The AA's, with a very good route planner and traffic news service. There's also information about buying a car, getting the best finance and insurance deals and a small shop.

www.greenflag.co.uk

GREEN FLAG

ORIGIN UK
SPEED ✓✓✓✓
INFO ✓✓✓✓
EASE ✓✓✓✓

The usual route planner and car buying advice all packaged on a nice looking and very green site, there's a particularly good section on European travel and motoring advice from Sue Baker.

TV tie-in sites

www.topgear.beeb.com

TOP GEAR

ORIGIN UK
SPEED ✓✓✓
INFO ✓✓✓✓
EASE ✓✓✓✓

A functional site with a shopping guide and lots of features and reviews. There's a Formula 1 section, links and a good search facility. Somehow you expect more in the way of features and articles and less advertising – the Beeb at its most commercial.

www.4car.co.uk

DRIVEN

ORIGIN UK	News, sport, reviews, advice, chat and games – it's
SPEED ✓✓✓	all here, and you can find out what's been and is
INFO ✓✓✓✓✓	being featured on each of their main motoring
EASE ✓✓✓✓	programmes.

Traders, magazines and buying guides

www.parkers.co.uk

REDUCING THE GAMBLE

ORIGIN UK	The premier buying guide with a premier site, this
SPEED ✓✓✓✓	covers all the information you'll need to select the
INFO ✓✓✓✓✓	right car for you. There are five sections:
EASE ✓✓✓✓	**Pricing** – a complete list of cars from 1982 and what

you should be paying.

Choosing – advice on the right car for you.

Buying – with details of used cars and finance deals.

Owning – insurance, warranties and advice on how
to sell.

Advice – legal, important contacts and chat.

www.autoexpress.co.uk

THE BEST MOTORING NEWS AND INFORMATION

ORIGIN UK	Massive database on cars, with motoring news and
SPEED ✓✓	features on the latest models, you can check prices
INFO ✓✓✓✓✓	too. It also has classified ads and a great set of links.
EASE ✓✓✓✓	You have to register to get access to most of the

information; lots of advertising makes the site a bit
annoying to use.

www.whatcar.co.uk

BRITAIN'S NUMBER 1 BUYER'S GUIDE

ORIGIN UK
SPEED ✓✓✓
INFO ✓✓✓✓✓
VALUE ✓✓✓
EASE ✓✓✓✓

A neatly packaged, one-stop shop for cars with sections on buying, selling, news, features and road tests, the classified section has thousands of cars and an easy-to-use search facility.

www.carnet.co.uk

ONLINE CAR MAGAZINE

ORIGIN UK
SPEED ✓✓✓✓
INFO ✓✓✓✓
EASE ✓✓✓✓

Car Net is a well designed and fun site with the latest news and new car reviews as well as feature micro-sites and links to deals on cars and insurance, statistics (on over 6,000 cars) and the boring postcards section. You can also visit the specialist chat sections and have a go at the trivia quizzes.

www.hoot-uk.com

IT'S A HOOT!

ORIGIN UK
SPEED ✓✓✓
INFO ✓✓✓✓✓
EASE ✓✓✓✓

A fun, simple site with a marque-by-marque news listing and the latest headlines. There are also sections with car tests, some good writing and chat at the aptly named 'Gas Station'.

www.carkeys.co.uk

INFORMATION SERVICE STATION

ORIGIN UK
SPEED ✓✓✓
INFO ✓✓✓✓✓
EASE ✓✓✓✓

A wide-ranging magazine-style site with lots of data on current and new models as well as launch reviews and motoring news.

www.testcar.com

TEST REPORTS

ORIGIN	UK
SPEED	✓✓✓
INFO	✓✓✓✓✓
EASE	✓✓✓✓

With test reports on a large number of cars and free Internet access, this site is very useful if you're not sure what to buy. It's also got classified ads and an irreverent column called 'Let's be Frank'. See also the new car review site **www.new-car-net.co.uk** which is attractive and has a good car magazine. A good feature is that you can compare up to three car specifications at the same time.

www.motortrak.com

USED CAR SEARCH

ORIGIN	UK
SPEED	✓✓✓✓✓
INFO	✓✓✓
EASE	✓✓✓✓

A hi-tech site where, in theory, you can find the right used car. Just follow the search guidelines and up pops your ideal car! It's easy to use and very fast – turn off the sound though.

www.autobytel.co.uk

WORLD'S LEADING CAR BUYING SERVICE

ORIGIN	US/UK
SPEED	✓✓✓✓
INFO	✓✓✓✓✓
VALUE	✓✓✓
EASE	✓✓✓

The easy way to buy a car online, just select the model you want then follow the online instructions, they've improved information on used and nearly new cars and will get quotes from local dealers. All cars featured have detailed descriptions and photos. There's also financial information and aftercare service.

www.eurekar.com

SAVE MONEY BY IMPORTING FROM EUROPE

ORIGIN	UK
SPEED	✓✓✓
INFO	✓✓✓✓✓
VALUE	✓✓✓✓✓
EASE	✓✓✓

Eurekar is a venture set up by the ISP Totalise to import cheaper right-hand drive cars from Europe. They claim to save up to 40% off UK prices. The choice of cars is limited, but all are inspected by Green Flag and have a warranty. Totalise offer quotes inclusive of VAT, delivery and duties.

www.oneswoop.co.uk

SMART WAY TO BUY

ORIGIN	UK
SPEED	✓✓✓✓
INFO	✓✓✓✓✓
VALUE	✓✓✓✓
EASE	✓✓✓✓

A straightforward site that concentrates on making the process of importing and buying a car from Europe as painless as possible. You can choose a car through one of three methods: buy what's available quickly; have a bit more choice; or be really picky. There are also some good special offers and a finance section.

www.jamjar.com

DIRECT LINE

ORIGIN	UK
SPEED	✓✓✓✓
INFO	✓✓✓✓✓
VALUE	✓✓✓✓✓
EASE	✓✓✓✓

One of the most hyped sites for car buying, Jam Jar is a big investment for Direct Line Insurance and they want to make it work well. The design isn't that great though, but if you persevere there are some fantastic offers and they're also improving the service by branching into other merchandise related to driving.

For more car buying information and cars for sale try:
www.autolocate.co.uk – excellent for links, good new car guide and review section, also good for used cars.
www.autoseek.co.uk – thousands of cars for sale, great for links.

www.autotrader.co.uk – claiming to be Britain's biggest car showroom with 200,000 listed. Nice, clear design.

www.broadspeed.com – car import specialists with a nicely designed and fast site.

www.carseller.co.uk – free advertising if selling and good links.

www.carsource.co.uk – great for data and online quotes, lots of cars for sale.

www.fish4cars.co.uk – around 140,000 cars on their database, plus hundreds of other vehicles. Comprehensive.

www.importanewcar.co.uk – good site if you fancy importing a car from Europe, they help you all the way and there's the potential to save wads of cash in the process.

www.showroom4cars.com – bright, brash and fast.

www.tins.co.uk – sophisticated and with a large selection of new and used cars, not always the cheapest though.

www.topmarques.co.uk – luxury vehicles only, some 6,000 for sale.

www.vanbuy.co.uk – vans and more vans of all shapes and sizes.

www.virgincars.com – good savings and speedy delivery, nice design and good features such as a car servicing service.

www.carpricecheck.com

WHERE TO GET THE BEST DEAL

ORIGIN UK	If you can't be bothered with trawling around the
SPEED ✓✓✓✓	different car dealers, just put in the model you want
INFO ✓✓✓✓	and after you've given a few details 'Car price
EASE ✓✓✓✓	Check' will get back to you with the best deal. See
	also the car price checker at **www.uk.kelkoo.com**

Car registrations

www.dvla-som.co.uk
CHERISHED AND PERSONALISED NUMBERS

ORIGIN UK	Here's the first port of call if you want that special
SPEED ✓✓✓✓	number plate. They sell by auction but there's
INFO ✓✓✓✓	plenty of help and you search for un-issued,
VALUE ✓✓	select registrations in both new and old styles.
EASE ✓✓✓✓	Order over the phone using their hotline.

For more sites try:
www.newreg.co.uk – the first online directory
of cherished registration marks.
www.alotofnumberplates.co.uk – good search
engine, over 5 million combinations.
www.statreg.co.uk – lots of cheap plates.

Insurance

www.easycover.com
CAR INSURANCE

ORIGIN UK	Quotes from a large number of insurance suppliers,
SPEED ✓✓✓	you just fill in the form, and they get back to you
INFO ✓✓✓✓✓	with a quote. **www.insureyourmotor.com** specialises
VALUE ✓✓✓	in travel and car insurance and you can get a quote
EASE ✓✓✓	online.

See also:
www.cheapest-motor-insurance.co.uk
www.theaa.co.uk
www.swinton.co.uk
www.eaglestar.co.uk

Looking after and repairing your car

www.ukmot.com
M.O.T.

ORIGIN UK
SPEED ✓✓✓✓
INFO ✓✓✓✓
EASE ✓✓✓✓

Find your nearest M.O.T. test centre, get facts about the test and what's actually supposed to be checked, there's also a reminder service. You can also run an HPI check from the site and find out about the foibles of specific models.

www.carcareclinic.com
LOOKING AFTER YOUR CAR

ORIGIN UK
SPEED ✓✓✓✓
INFO ✓✓✓✓
EASE ✓✓✓

If you need advice with car repairs or faults, then help is at hand here. There are discussion forums on all sorts of problems and, if you post a message or ask for advice, there's always someone to answer. They also provide a glossary of terms and a good set of links.

www.haynes.co.uk
HAYNES MANUALS

ORIGIN UK
SPEED ✓✓✓✓
INFO ✓✓✓
VALUE ✓✓✓
EASE ✓✓✓✓

Unfortunately they've stopped the download service, so now you have to buy the books – there's almost 2,000 available so there should be one for you.

Specialist car sites

www.classicmotor.co.uk
FOR CLASSIC CARS

ORIGIN UK
SPEED ✓✓✓✓
INFO ✓✓✓✓✓
VALUE ✓✓✓✓
EASE ✓✓✓

By far the best classic car site. Design wise it's a mess, but it's comprehensive, including clubs, classifieds and books; here you can buy anything from a car to a headlight bulb. See also www.classic-car-directory.com which is a well categorised links site.

www.pistonheads.com

BEST OF BRITISH MOTORING

ORIGIN UK
SPEED ✓✓✓
INFO ✓✓✓✓✓
VALUE ✓✓✓✓
EASE ✓✓✓

Pistonheads is a British site dedicated to the faster side of motoring and is great for reviews of the latest cars and chat. It's passionate and very informative.

www.krbaker.demon.co.uk/britcars

HISTORY OF BRITISH CARS TO 1960

ORIGIN UK
SPEED ✓✓✓
INFO ✓✓✓✓✓
VALUE ✓✓✓
EASE ✓✓✓

An amateur site with a good make-by-make history of the British car industry, it includes a glossary and information on tax and other historical references. Unfortunately it's not well illustrated.

www.online-supercars.com

IF YOU LIKE FAST CARS

ORIGIN UK
SPEED ✓✓✓
INFO ✓✓✓
EASE ✓✓✓

A fairly sparse site that catalogues and discusses the fastest and most powerful cars. The design doesn't quite do justice to the subject matter; but speed freaks amongst us will be fascinated.

www.allcarsites.co.uk

ALL ABOUT CARS

ORIGIN UK
SPEED ✓✓✓
INFO ✓✓✓✓✓
EASE ✓✓✓✓

A good all-round motoring site. It's main strength is that it has a directory of over 6,400 sites covering all forms of motoring and information about cars.

Learning to drive

www.driving.co.uk

BSM TUITION

ORIGIN UK
SPEED ✓✓✓
INFO ✓✓✓✓✓
EASE ✓✓✓✓

A fairly sparse site from the British School of Motoring, with information and advice on taking the test, driving in general and funny stories that make you feel more relaxed.

www.learners.co.uk

LEARNER'S DIRECTORY

ORIGIN UK
SPEED ✓✓✓
INFO ✓✓✓✓
EASE ✓✓✓✓

The point of this site is to help you find the right driving school, just type in your postcode and the schools will be listed along with helpful additional information such as whether they have a female instructor or that they train for motorway driving. There is plenty of supplementary information on things like theory tests and how to buy a car.

www.2pass.co.uk

THEORY AND PRACTICAL TESTS

ORIGIN UK
SPEED ✓✓✓✓
INFO ✓✓✓✓✓
EASE ✓✓✓✓

A learner driver's dream, this site helps with your tests in giving advice, mock exams plus other interesting snippets of information such as why the British drive on the left. There are also articles on driving abroad, on motorbikes and driving automatics. There's also plenty of fun with top stories, even poems and crash of the month!

www.driving-tests.co.uk

THE DSA

ORIGIN UK
SPEED ✓✓✓✓
INFO ✓✓✓✓
EASE ✓✓✓✓

Get the official line from the Driving Standards Agency where you can book an online driving theory test, get advice for learners and instructors and learn about government schemes to promote better driving. For the Highway Code faithfully reproduced as a website go to www.roads.dtlr.gov.uk/roadsafety/hc/index.shtml

www.iam.org.uk

INSTITUTE OF ADVANCED MOTORISTS

ORIGIN UK
SPEED ✓✓✓✓
INFO ✓✓✓✓
EASE ✓✓✓✓

A site from IAM to give you all the encouragement you need to become an advanced driver.

Car miscellaneous

www.kitcars.org

BUILD YOUR OWN

ORIGIN UK
SPEED ✓✓✓
INFO ✓✓✓✓✓
EASE ✓✓✓✓

All you need to know about kit cars, this site is excellent for links, information, pictures and classified ads for all things to do with them.

www.autofashion.co.uk

ACCESSORISE YOUR CAR

ORIGIN UK
SPEED ✓✓✓✓
INFO ✓✓✓✓
EASE ✓✓✓

An entertaining site where you can buy body kits and accessories for many makes of car, including custom made. See also Motech at **www.motech.uk.com** who specialise more in performance enhancement.

www.caraudiocentre.com

IN CAR AUDIO SYSTEMS

ORIGIN UK
SPEED ✓✓✓
INFO ✓✓✓✓
VALUE ✓✓✓✓
EASE ✓✓✓✓

Here you can get loads of advice and offers on a wide range of stereos with a price promise and low delivery costs. See also **www.toade.com** who have a highly interactive site and can also supply security, multi-media and navigation equipment on top of audio.

Driving issues

www.speed-trap.co.uk

THE SPEED TRAP BIBLE

ORIGIN UK
SPEED ✓✓✓
INFO ✓✓✓✓✓
EASE ✓✓✓✓

While not condoning speeding, this site gives the low down on speed traps, the law and links to police forces. There's even data on the types of cameras used and advice on dealing with the courts and police. However, remember that they are sponsored by a speed trap detector company. See also www.ukspeedcameras.co.uk

www.parkingticket.co.uk

PARKING PROBLEMS

ORIGIN UK
SPEED ✓✓✓
INFO ✓✓✓✓
EASE ✓✓✓✓✓

An interesting site campaigning for fair parking charges. It details council policies on parking fines and gives information about where you can and can't park. The aim is to help motorists avoid parking tickets but there is also advice on what to do if you are unfortunate enough to get one.

www.abd.org.uk

CAMPAIGNING FOR THE DRIVER

ORIGIN UK
SPEED ✓✓✓
INFO ✓✓✓✓
EASE ✓✓✓✓

The Association of British Drivers aims to be the lobbying voice of beleaguered drivers in the UK. Here you can find out about their campaigns against speed traps speed limits, the environment and the road infrastructure.

www.rospa.co.uk/cms/

ROYAL SOCIETY FOR THE PREVENTION OF ACCIDENTS

ORIGIN UK
SPEED ✓✓✓✓
INFO ✓✓✓✓✓
EASE ✓✓✓✓

An excellent site from ROSPA with loads of information about road safety with fact sheets available on most issues and problems that affect every driver and pedestrian.

www.reportroadrage.co.uk

ROAD RAGE ISSUES

ORIGIN	UK	A site supported by the RAC that looks into every
SPEED	✓✓✓	aspect of road rage, including its causes and how to
INFO	✓✓✓✓✓	prevent it. There's lots of advice, stories and informa-
EASE	✓✓✓✓	tion to help you become a safer and calmer driver.

Celebrities

Find your favourite celebrities and their web sites using these sites. A word of caution though – there are many celebrity search engines available on the web and while it's easy to find your favourite, it's also easy to unwittingly access adult-orientated material through them.

www.celeblink.com

LINKS TO THE STARS

ORIGIN	US	Just about the best celebrity directory in terms of
SPEED	✓✓✓✓	lack of advertising and dodgy links. There's also
INFO	✓✓✓✓	some good articles, gossip and entertainment news.
EASE	✓✓✓✓	

www.celebhoo.com

FOR EVERYTHING CELEBRITY

ORIGIN	US	A very good fan site directory plus information
SPEED	✓✓✓✓	birthdays, chat and gossip.
INFO	✓✓✓✓✓	
EASE	✓✓✓✓	

www.celebrityemail.com

E-MAIL THE STARS

ORIGIN	US	E-mail addresses to over 15,000 of the world's most
SPEED	✓✓✓✓	famous people, it's quite biased towards Americans
INFO	✓✓✓	but give it a try anyway, you might get a reply.
EASE	✓✓✓	

www.debretts.co.uk

POSH CELEBRITY GOSSIP

ORIGIN UK
SPEED ✓✓✓✓
INFO ✓✓✓✓✓
EASE ✓✓✓✓

An excellent site from Debretts who have been tracking the lives of celebrities for many years longer than the likes of *OK* and *Hello*. There are sections on people in the news plus a good celebrity search engine. There are also sections on the royal family, a guide to the season, charities and a fun search section where you can match birthdays.

www.hello-magazine.co.uk

THE WORLD IN PICTURES

ORIGIN UK
SPEED ✓✓✓
INFO ✓✓✓✓
EASE ✓✓✓

Hello magazine's web site features pictures and articles from current and previous issues with loads of celebrities. You can't search by celebrity but you can have fun trawling through the pictures.

www.glamourmagazine.co.uk

LOSE YOURSELF IN GLAMOUR

ORIGIN UK
SPEED ✓✓✓
INFO ✓✓✓✓
EASE ✓✓✓

Gossip, fashion, beauty tips, chat, competitions and, of course, celebrities are the mainstay of *Glamour* magazine's site. Its main function though is to plug the real magazine.

www.famousnamechanges.com

WHO WAS WHO

ORIGIN US
SPEED ✓✓✓✓
INFO ✓✓✓
EASE ✓✓✓✓

Find out what name celebrities where born with and what they changed it to – great for trivia quizzes.

www.amiannoyingornot.com

VOTE FOR MOST ANNOYING CELEBRITIES

ORIGIN US
SPEED ✓✓✓✓
INFO ✓✓✓
EASE ✓✓✓✓

You can spend ages on this site; it's easy to vote and fun to use. Each celeb gets a page with biographical details and reasons why they could be annoying or not...

Charities

The Internet offers a great opportunity to give to your favourite charity or support a cause dear to your heart. There are so many that we're unable to list them all, but here are some top sites with directories to help you find the ones that interest you. For charity cards see page 208.

www.charitychoice.co.uk
ENCYCLOPAEDIA OF CHARITIES

ORIGIN UK	A very useful and well-put together directory of
SPEED ✓✓✓✓	charities with a good search facility and a list in over
INFO ✓✓✓✓✓	30 categories, there's also the excellent 'Goodwill
EASE ✓✓✓	Gallery' where you can post up a service or a
	donation you're willing to give to charity.

www.caritasdata.co.uk
CHARITIES DIRECT

ORIGIN UK	A support site for charities with information on how
SPEED ✓✓✓✓	to raise funds and run a charity, there's also a good
INFO ✓✓✓✓✓	directory of UK charities and you can rank them by
EASE ✓✓✓✓	expenditure, revenue and fund size.

www.charitycommission.gov.uk
THE CHARITY COMMISSION

ORIGIN UK	The Charity Commission's mission is to give the
SPEED ✓✓✓✓	public confidence in the integrity of charities in
INFO ✓✓✓✓✓	England and Wales, and their site lists over 180,000
EASE ✓✓✓✓	charities. There's also lots of advice for charities.

See also:
www.charitychallenge.com – raise money for your
  chosen charity by taking an adventure holiday
  through Charity Challenge.

www.bcconnections.org.uk – businesses can find out
    how they can get involved in charity donations
    and charities can find out how they can get busi-
    nesses involved in their work.

www.thehungersite.com – just one click and you'll
    donate a cup of food to the world's hungry via
    registered sponsors, a brilliant idea and one that
    works – over 200 million cups have been donated
    to date. There are now sister sites for breast
    cancer and saving rain forests.

Chat

There are literally thousands of chat sites and rooms on the web
covering many different topics. However, this is the area of the
Net that people have the most concerns about. There have been
loads of cases where people have been tricked into giving out
personal information and even arranged unsuitable meetings.
But at its best, a chat program is a great way to keep in contact
with friends, especially if they live miles away. So chat wisely by
following our top tips for keeping safe.

CHAT – OUR TOP TIPS

1 Be wary, just like you would be if you were visiting any new place.
2 Don't give your e-mail address out without
   making sure that only the person you're sending it
   to can read it.
3 People often pretend to be someone they're not
   when they're chatting; unless you know the
   person, assume that's the case with anyone you
   chat with online.

4 Don't meet up with anyone you've met online -
  keep your online life separate. Chances are they'd
  be a let down anyway, even if they were genuine.
5 If you like the look of a chat room or site, but
  you're not sure about it, get a recommendation
  first.
6 If you want to meet up with friends online,
  arrange a time and place beforehand.
7 If you don't like someone, just block 'em.
8 Check out the excellent **www.chatdanger.com** for
  more info on how to chat safely.

The following are the major chat sites and programs:

www.aim.com

AOL INSTANT MESSENGER

ORIGIN UK	One of the most popular, it's pretty safe and anyway
SPEED ✓✓✓✓	you can easily block people who are a nuisance, or
INFO ✓✓✓✓	just set it up so that only friends can talk to you.
EASE ✓✓✓✓	

http://web.icq.com/

ICQ — I SEEK YOU

ORIGIN US	There are lots of chat rooms here. It's quick and
SPEED ✓✓✓✓	easy to use combined with a mobile phone. There
INFO ✓✓✓✓	are lots of features such as games, money advice,
EASE ✓✓✓✓	music and lurve.

http://communities.msn.com/people

MICROSOFT MSN MESSENGER

ORIGIN US	Easy to use but it can be confusing as Microsoft are
SPEED ✓✓✓✓	so keen for you to use other parts of their massive site
INFO ✓✓✓✓	you'll often find yourself suddenly transferred. The
EASE ✓✓✓✓	best bet is to customise it so that there's no mistake.

www.mirc.com
IRC – INTERNET RELAY CHAT

ORIGIN US	Recently improved and updated, this remains a
SPEED ✓✓✓✓	straightforward chat program that is easy to use.
INFO ✓✓✓	Generally it's been overtaken by the likes of MSN
EASE ✓✓✓✓	and AOL but some web sites may opt to use it.

www.trillian.cc
COMMUNICATE WITH FLEXIBILITY AND STYLE

ORIGIN US	Trillian is a newish site that enables connections to
SPEED ✓✓✓✓	all the major chat programs through one interface.
INFO ✓✓✓✓	The reader looks good and you can personalise it
EASE ✓✓✓✓	too. An excellent idea that works well.

www.paltalk.com
VERSATILITY

ORIGIN US	A feature laden system with everything from video
SPEED ✓✓✓✓	conferencing to instant messaging – all free!
INFO ✓✓✓✓	
EASE ✓✓✓✓	

Children

There's been a continuing growth in the number of sites in this category. You can save pounds on children's clothes and toys by shopping over the Net; it's easy and the service is often excellent because the sites are put together by people who really care. The Internet is also an excellent way to educate and entertain children. They are fascinated by it and quickly become experts. Listed here are some of the best sites anywhere. For ideas for days out with children see the British travel listings page 461, for educational sites see page 104 and for parenting concerns see page 295.

Shopping for children

www.elc.co.uk

EARLY LEARNING CENTRE

ORIGIN UK
SPEED ✓✓✓
INFO ✓✓✓✓✓
VALUE ✓✓✓
EASE ✓✓✓✓✓

A well-designed and user-friendly site that offers a wide range of toys for the under-fives in particular, it's strong on character products and traditional toys alike. Delivery costs £2.95 per order and you can expect goods to arrive in 5 days.

www.toymania.com

RAVING TOY MANIAC

ORIGIN US
SPEED ✓✓✓✓
INFO ✓✓✓✓✓
VALUE ✓✓
EASE ✓✓✓✓

A toy magazine full of details and news on all the latest toys along with an online shop. It's an enjoyable site to browse, the selection is vast and it's a good place to start if you're looking for something you can't get in the UK. Shipping costs depend on the weight of your order.

www.hamleys.co.uk

FINEST TOY STORE IN THE WORLD

ORIGIN UK
SPEED ✓✓✓✓
INFO ✓✓✓
VALUE ✓✓✓
EASE ✓✓✓✓

Hamley's has improved its site and you can search for toys by gender, price or age. There's also an okay selection of character areas within the store as well as the more traditional range, which is their main strength. Delivery starts at £4.95.

www.toysrus.co.uk

NOT JUST TOYS

ORIGIN UK/US
SPEED ✓✓✓
INFO ✓✓✓✓
VALUE ✓✓✓✓
EASE ✓✓✓✓

Good site with all the key brands and 'in' things you'd expect – you can even buy a mobile phone. Has links to key toy manufacturer's sites and a sister site called **www.babiesrus.co.uk** which covers younger children. Delivery is £2.50 for the UK.

www.thetoyshop.com

THE ENTERTAINER

ORIGIN UK	The online spin-off from the Entertainer high street
SPEED ✓✓✓	stores; it offers much in the way of bargains and this
INFO ✓✓✓✓	bright and breezy site is easy to navigate. You can
VALUE ✓✓✓✓	search by toy, age, price or category. Shipping to the
EASE ✓✓✓✓	UK is £3.50 flat rate while international rates vary.

www.newcron.com

CHARACTER PRODUCTS

ORIGIN UK/US	Newcron has taken over the Character Warehouse
SPEED ✓✓✓	site to produce an online store that offers a wide
INFO ✓✓✓✓	range of mainstream and unusual character
VALUE ✓✓✓✓	products. You can search by character, product
EASE ✓✓✓✓	or price; delivery starts at £3.99. See also
	www.shop4toys.co.uk which has a similar offer.

www.dawson-and-son.com

FOR TRADITIONAL WOODEN TOYS

ORIGIN UK	Specialists in the art of making simple, traditional,
SPEED ✓✓✓	wooden toys, Dawson and Son offer a wide range of
INFO ✓✓✓	beautifully made items from rattles to sophisticated
VALUE ✓✓	games. Delivery depends on the value and weight of
EASE ✓✓✓✓	order.

www.outdoortoysdirect.co.uk

LOW PRICES ON OUTDOOR TOYS

ORIGIN UK	Excellent value for money with free delivery, a
SPEED ✓✓✓✓	money back guarantee, plus a wide range of goods.
INFO ✓✓✓✓✓	The selection consists of everything from trampo-
VALUE ✓✓✓✓✓	lines to swings, slides and play houses. To complete
EASE ✓✓✓✓	your outdoor experience you can always pay a visit
	to **www.kiteshop.co.uk** who offer a wide range of
	kites and advice from an excellent site.

www.krucialkids.com

ALL ABOARD THE KRUCIAL KIDS EXPRESS

ORIGIN UK
SPEED ✓✓✓
INFO ✓✓✓✓
VALUE ✓✓✓
EASE ✓✓✓✓

Annoying name, but not an annoying site. It specialises in developmental toys for children up to eight years old, providing detailed information on the educational value of each of the 200 or so toys. The prices aren't bad either. Delivery is free if you spend over £60. For educational toys see also www.ticktocktoys.co.uk and the well designed www.playbug.co.uk

www.airfix.com

AIRFIX KITS

ORIGIN UK
SPEED ✓✓
INFO ✓✓✓✓
VALUE ✓✓✓
EASE ✓✓✓✓

Some 50 current kits are available to buy with illustrations and background info on the real thing and an indication of how difficult they are to put together. There are also details of the modeller's club and parts replacement service. Delivery costs are dependent on the weight of the order.

Other toy stores worth a visit are:

www.huggables.co.uk – specialists in teddies and other cute soft toys.

www.theoldtoyshop.com – mainly vintage and collectible toys.

www.totalrobots.com – all sorts of robots, probably one for dads really.

www.toysforus.co.uk – good design, specialists in Brio among other things.

www.toys-n-ireland.com – excellent Irish store with some 20,000 lines available.

Other than toys

www.thepartystore.co.uk
SELLING FUN

ORIGIN UK
SPEED ✓✓✓
INFO ✓✓✓✓
VALUE ✓✓✓
EASE ✓✓✓✓

Great site, not just for children, but there is an excellent children's party section. They sell character outfits, themed tableware, masks, party boxes and all sorts of accessories. Delivery takes two to five working days and costs £3.50.

www.jojomamanbebe.co.uk
FASHIONABLE MOTHERS AND THEIR CHILDREN

ORIGIN UK
SPEED ✓✓✓✓
INFO ✓✓✓✓
VALUE ✓✓✓
EASE ✓✓✓✓

Excellent for everything from maternity wear and designer children's clothes to gifts for newborn babies. Also has sections on toys, maternity products and special offers. All the designs are tested and they aim to be comfortable as well as fashionable. Delivery costs £3.50, free if collected from the warehouse in Newport. For babywear go to www.overthemoon-babywear.co.uk who include a section on natural fibre clothing with free postage in the UK; while for older children www.tots2teens.co.uk is a good bet.

www.gltc.co.uk
THE GREAT LITTLE TRADING COMPANY

ORIGIN UK
SPEED ✓✓✓✓
INFO ✓✓✓✓✓
VALUE ✓✓✓
EASE ✓✓✓✓

A good looking site offering a wide range of child safety products, furniture and baby equipment, you can search the site by age and by product category. Delivery starts at £3.95.

www.urchin.co.uk

WORTH HAVING A BABY FOR

ORIGIN UK
SPEED ✓✓✓✓
INFO ✓✓✓✓
VALUE ✓✓✓
EASE ✓✓✓✓

Urchin has some 300 products available: cots and beds, bathtime accessories, bikes, clothes, for baby, travel goods, toys and things for the independent child who likes to personalise their own room. They boast a sense of style and good design, and they succeed. Also have a bargains section. Delivery is £3.95 per order with a next day surcharge of £3.

Things to do

www.mamamedia.com

THE PLACE FOR KIDS ON THE NET

ORIGIN US
SPEED ✓✓✓
INFO ✓✓✓✓
EASE ✓✓✓✓

This versatile site has everything a child and parent could want, there is an excellent selection of interactive games, puzzles and quizzes, combined with a great deal of wit and fun. Best of all it encourages children to communicate by submitting a message and gets them voting on what's important to them. There's a superb 'Grown-ups' section with information on getting the best out of the Net with your children.

www.bonus.com

THE SUPER SITE FOR KIDS

ORIGIN US
SPEED ✓✓✓
INFO ✓✓✓✓✓
EASE ✓✓✓✓✓

Excellent graphics and masses of genuinely good games make a visit to Bonus a treat for all ages. There are quizzes and puzzles, with sections offering a photo gallery, art resource and homework help. Access to the web is limited to a protected environment. Shame about the annoying pop-ups.

www.yucky.com

THE YUCKIEST SITE ON THE INTERNET

ORIGIN US
SPEED ✓✓✓✓
INFO ✓✓✓✓✓
EASE ✓✓✓✓

Find out how to turn milk into slime or how much you know about worms – yucky lives up to its name. Essentially this is an excellent, fun site that helps kids learn science and biology. There are guides for parents on how to get the best out of the site and links to recommended sites. Try this URL if you can't get access on the usual one **http://yucky.kids.discovery.com**

www.kidsonline.co.uk

FOR KIDS BY KIDS

ORIGIN UK
SPEED ✓✓
INFO ✓✓✓
EASE ✓✓✓✓

Excellent graphics make this site stand out and its content is very good too; however it can be a little slow. Split into two sections for younger and older kids, there are reviews of favourite books, films and web sites, what's on as well as a smattering of games.

www.wonka.com

THE WILD WORLD OF WONKA

ORIGIN UK
SPEED ✓✓✓✓
INFO ✓✓✓✓✓
EASE ✓✓✓✓

Ingenious site sponsored by Nestlé with great illustrations and a fun approach, it has several sections all with lots of interactivity, as well as an online club. There's the Invention Room with lots of trivia, Planet Vermes which is about space, Loompaland takes you into the animal kingdom and so on. You can also send postcards and get involved in competitions.

www.switcheroozoo.com

MAKE NEW ANIMALS

ORIGIN	US
SPEED	✓✓
INFO	✓✓✓
EASE	✓✓✓

Over 6,500 combinations of animals can be made at this very entertaining web site, you need Shockwave and a decent PC for it to work effectively.

www.magictricks.co.uk

THE UK'S LEADING ONLINE MAGIC TRICKS STORE

ORIGIN	UK
SPEED	✓✓✓✓
INFO	✓✓✓✓✓
VALUE	✓✓✓✓
EASE	✓✓✓✓

A site chock full of tricks, sets and accompanying equipment. You can send in suggestions for new tricks and even find a magician. There's also a section on TV magicians and a bookstore. See also www.magicweek.co.uk which is well-designed but more adult.

Other activity sites worth checking out:

http://web.ukonline.co.uk/conker – The Kids Ark – Join Captain Zeb gathering material on the world, strange animals, myths and facts – before it all disappears.

www.alfy.com – excellent for young children, with lots of games and plenty of things to do and see.

www.ex.ac.uk/bugclub – bugs and creepy crawlies for all ages.

www.hotwheels.com/kids – a good looking, but slow site from a model car maker that has some good features and games.

www.kiddonet.com – download the interactive play area for games and surfing in a safe environment. Masses to do and good links.

www.kids.warnerbros.com – a selection of popular activities at the Warner Brothers site, shame about the pop-up shop advertisements.

www.kidscom.com – play games, post a message on the message board and write to a pen friend (unfortunately the safe chat lines are open during our night-time). A bit dull.

www.kidsdomain.com – masses to download, from colouring books, music demos and homework help and games. Split into 3 age ranges.

www.kidskorner.net – great use of cartoons to introduce and play games – stealthily educational, the wizard school is good with lots to do.

www.kidsreads.com – an American site all about kids' books, with games and quizzes. Good for young Harry Potter fans.

www.kzone.com.au – excellent activity site from Australia.

www.lemonadegame.com – how much lemonade can you sell? Learn about market forces in this oddly fascinating game.

www.missdorothy.com – a good, wide-ranging site with plenty to do and see, linked to the Brownies.

www.neopets.com – look after a multitude of virtual pets, play games and even trade them.

www.planit4kids.co.uk – activities plus what to do when you're short of ideas. Good design.

www.zeeks.com – a very good American kids' magazine site.

www.24hourmuseum.org.uk/24kids.html – good quality online educational kids' content from the 24-hour Museum site with interactive journeys, a Harry Potter trail and arts activities.

TV, book and character sites

www.citv.co.uk
CHILDREN'S ITV

ORIGIN UK	Keep up-to-date with your favourite programmes
SPEED ✓✓✓✓	and talk to the stars of the shows. There's lots to
INFO ✓✓✓✓✓	occupy children here including chat with fellow
EASE ✓✓✓✓	fans, play games, find something to do, enter a
	competition, e-mail a friend and join the club.

www.nickjr.com

THE NICKELODEON CHANNEL

ORIGIN US	Ideal for under-eights, this has a good selection of
SPEED ✓✓✓	games and quizzes to play either with an adult or
INFO ✓✓✓	solo. The 'Red Rocket Store' has an excellent selec-
VALUE ✓✓	tion of merchandise, but beware of shipping costs.
EASE ✓✓✓✓	For activities aimed at a wider age range check out

www.nick.co.uk where there is chat, gossip, games
and plenty of background info on the shows.

www.sesamestreet.com

THE CHILDREN'S TELEVISION WORKSHOP

ORIGIN US	Enter Elmo's world which is very colourful, with
SPEED ✓✓✓	lots to do. There are games to play, art and music to
INFO ✓✓✓✓	create and friends to talk to. There's plenty for
VALUE ✓✓✓	parents too. Another site dedicated to the very
EASE ✓✓✓✓	young is www.funschool.com

www.bbc.co.uk/cbbc

CHILDREN'S BBC

ORIGIN UK	Lots of activities here, you can catch up on the latest
SPEED ✓✓✓	news, play games and find out about the stars of the
INFO ✓✓✓✓	programs. There are also web guide links to other
EASE ✓✓✓✓	recommended children's sites. See also

www.bbc.co.uk/cbeebies, which is for the very
young with printable colouring pages, stories and
games.

www.disney.com

WHERE THE MAGIC LIVES

ORIGIN US	A vastly improved site from the advert laden one
SPEED ✓✓	that existed before although it's still pretty slow.
INFO ✓✓✓✓	
EASE ✓✓✓✓	

There are seven sections:

Entertainment – details of films, activities and a Disney A–Z.

Kids Island Home – lots of games and music.

Playhouse – games and character sites for younger children.

Blast – the online kids' club.

Family fun – party planners, recipes and craft ideas.

Vacations – Information on the theme parks.

Shopping – the Disney store and auctions.

The British version **www.disney.co.uk** is more compact with less about vacations and more emphasis on activity. For young children a Disney colouring book can be found at **http://disney.go.com/kids/color/index.html**

www.cooltoons.com

RUGRATS, STRESSED ERIC AND MORE

ORIGIN UK
SPEED ✓✓✓✓
INFO ✓✓✓
EASE ✓✓✓✓

Each character has their own section where you can find lots to do and see. There's also an eight-step guide on how to become an animator. The store has all the related merchandise.

www.foxkids.co.uk

FOX TV

ORIGIN UK
SPEED ✓✓✓
INFO ✓✓✓✓
EASE ✓✓✓✓

All the characters and shows are featured on this bright and entertaining site with added extras like a games section, competitions, a sports page and a magazine. There's also a shopping facility where you earn Brix by using the site, they can then be spent on goodies in the 'Boutik'. The graphics can be a little temperamental.

www.aardman.com

HOME OF WALLACE AND GROMMIT

ORIGIN UK   This brilliant site takes a while to download but it's
SPEED ✓✓✓   worth the wait. There's news on what the team are
INFO ✓✓✓✓   up to, links to their films, a shop and an inside story
EASE ✓✓✓✓   on how it all began.

www.guinnessrecords.com

GUINNESS WORLD RECORDS

ORIGIN US   An outstanding site that offers much in the way of
SPEED ✓✓✓✓   entertainment with footage of favourite records and
INFO ✓✓✓✓✓   informative sections on key areas of record breaking
EASE ✓✓✓✓   such as sport, nature, the material world and human
   achievements.

Here's where the best children's characters hang out:

Action Man – www.actionman.com
Art Attack – www.artattack.co.uk
Artemis Fowl – www.artemisfowl.co.uk
Bagpuss – www.smallfilms.co.uk/bagpuss/
Barbie – www.barbie.com
Beano – www.beano.co.uk and www.dccomics.com
Bill and Ben –
     www.bbc.co.uk/cbeebies/characterpages/billandben/
Bob the Builder – www.bobthebuilder.org
Buffy – www.buffy.com and www.buffyguide.com
Danger Mouse – www.dangermouse.org
Dragonball Z – www.dragonballz.com
Goosebumps – www.scholastic.com/goosebumps/
Lemony Snicket – www.lemonysnicket.com/
Letter Land – www.letterland.com
Mary Kate and Ashley –
     www.marykateandashley.com
Mr Men – www.mrmen.com

Noddy – **www.noddy.com**
Paddington – **www.paddingtonbear.co.uk**
Pokemon – **www.pokeland.yorks.net/** or
   www.pokemon.com
Roald Dahl – **www.roalddahl.org** or
   www.roalddahlclub.com
Robot Wars – **www.robotwars.co.uk**
Sabrina – **www.paramount.com/television/sabrinatv/**
Teletubbies – **www.teletubbies.com**
Thomas the Tank Engine –
   www.thomasthetankengine.com
Tintin – **www.tintin.be**
Thunderbirds – **www.thunderbirdsonline.co.uk** and
   www.thunderbirdsonline.com
Tweenies – **www.bbc.co.uk/tweenies**
Winnie the Pooh – **www.winniethepooh.co.uk**
Yu-Gi-Oh – **www.yugiohkingofgames.com**

HARRY POTTER

Harry Potter deserves a special mention and with loads of web sites springing up, here are the official ones. You might want to keep checking the Warner Brothers site for information on the next film at **http://harrypotter.warnerbros.co.uk**

www.bloomsbury.com/harrypotter

WHERE IT ALL BEGAN

ORIGIN UK
SPEED ✓✓✓✓
INFO ✓✓✓✓
EASE ✓✓✓✓

You have to enter using a secret password known only to witches and wizards everywhere, then you get to find out all about the books, meet JK Rowling and join the Harry Potter club. 'Howlers and Owlers' – e-mail insults and compliments – is great, but don't worry if you're a 'Muggle', all is explained.

www.scholastic.com/harrypotter

HARRY AMERICAN STYLE

ORIGIN US	Here's wizard trivia, quizzes, screensavers, informa-
SPEED ✓✓✓	tion about the books and an interview with JK
INFO ✓✓✓✓	Rowling, all on a fairly boring web site.
EASE ✓✓✓✓	

Search engines and site directories

www.yahooligans.com

THE KID'S ONLINE WEB GUIDE

ORIGIN US	Probably the most popular site for kids, yahooligans
SPEED ✓✓✓✓	offers parents safety and kids hours of fun. There
INFO ✓✓✓✓	are games, articles and features on the 'in' charac-
EASE ✓✓✓✓	ters, education resources and sections on sport,
	science, computing and TV. It has an American bias.

www.ajkids.com

ASK JEEVES FOR KIDS

ORIGIN US	A search engine aimed at children, it's simple, safe
SPEED ✓✓✓✓	and is excellent for homework enquiries and games.
INFO ✓✓✓✓	
VALUE ✓✓✓✓	
EASE ✓✓✓✓	

www.beritsbest.com

SITES FOR CHILDREN

ORIGIN US	Over 1,000 sites in this directory split into six major
SPEED ✓✓✓	categories, fun, things to do during holidays, nature,
INFO ✓✓✓✓✓	serious stuff (homework), chat and surfing. Each site
EASE ✓✓✓✓	is rated for speed and content and you can suggest
	new sites as well.

www.surfmonkey.com

SURFING FOR KIDS

ORIGIN US   A very well designed site where you can download
SPEED ✓✓✓   the Surf Monkey browser, then your children can
INFO ✓✓✓✓   surf over 5,000 sites in safety, it's also great for
VALUE ✓✓✓   beginners, but it is $3.95 per month.
EASE ✓✓✓✓

Competitions

www.loquax.co.uk

THE UK'S COMPETITION PORTAL

ORIGIN UK   This site doesn't give away prizes but lists the web
SPEED ✓✓✓✓   sites that do. There are hundreds of competitions
INFO ✓✓✓✓✓   featured, and if you own a web site they'll even run
EASE ✓✓✓✓   a competition for you. There are daily updates and
special features such as 'Pick of the Prizes' which
features the best the web has to offer, with links to
the relevant sites. See also **www.theprizefinder.com**
who offer a wide range of prizes in lots of
categories, you have to register though, as you
have to at **www.myoffers.co.uk**, which is a slow
site, with as the name suggests lots of offers.

Computers

It's no surprise that the number one place to buy a computer is the Internet. With these sites you won't go far wrong, and it's also worth checking out the price checker sites on page 312 before going shopping and checking the software sites on page 353. Mac users should also check out the section on Apple Macs page 20.

www.itreviews.co.uk

START HERE TO FIND THE BEST

ORIGIN UK
SPEED ✓✓✓✓
INFO ✓✓✓✓✓
EASE ✓✓✓✓

IT Reviews gives unbiased reports, not only on computer products, but also on software, games and related books. The site has a good search facility and a quick visit may save you loads of hassle when you come to buy. For other excellent information sites try **www.zdnet.co.uk** or **www.cnet.com** both have links to good online stores, while **www.reviewbooth.com** have some 20,000 product reviews and guides.

www.pcadvisor.co.uk

EXPERT ADVICE IN PLAIN ENGLISH

ORIGIN UK
SPEED ✓✓✓✓
INFO ✓✓✓✓✓
EASE ✓✓✓✓

A derivative from *PC Advisor* magazine, the site offers much in the way of reviews and information on how to find the best PC. It also allows you to pick up advice from experts on technical queries. There's a games room, a place from which you can download programs and a consumer section where you can air your praises and gripes.

www.pcworld.co.uk

THE COMPUTER SUPERSTORE

ORIGIN UK
SPEED ✓✓✓
INFO ✓✓✓✓
VALUE ✓✓✓✓
EASE ✓✓✓✓

A very strong offering from one of the leading computer stores with lots of offers and star buys. They sell a wide range of electronics from cameras to the expected PCs and peripherals.

www.simply.co.uk

SIMPLY DOES IT

ORIGIN UK
SPEED ✓✓✓✓
INFO ✓✓✓✓
VALUE ✓✓✓✓
EASE ✓✓✓✓

An award-winning site and company that offers a wide range of PCs and related products, their strengths are speed, quality of service and competitive prices. They also sell mobile phones.

www.dabs.com

500,000 CUSTOMERS LATER...

ORIGIN UK
SPEED ✓✓✓✓
INFO ✓✓✓✓
VALUE ✓✓✓✓
EASE ✓✓✓

One of the most successful online computer product retailers, there are loads of offers and a wide range of goods. It's a big site and not that easy to navigate, but there are rewards for those who persevere in the guise of dabspoints which can be converted to airmiles.

www.tiny.com

LATEST TECHNOLOGY AT UNBEATABLE PRICES

ORIGIN UK
SPEED ✓✓✓✓
INFO ✓✓✓✓
VALUE ✓✓✓
EASE ✓✓✓✓

A businesslike site that includes all the details you'd need on their range of computers and peripherals for home and office use. Tiny are the UK's largest computer manufacturer and have a history of reliability and good deals. Shipping costs vary according to what you buy and where you live.

Other PC manufacturers' site addresses:
Apple – www.apple.com
Dan – www.dan.co.uk
Dell – www.dell.co.uk
Elonex – www.elonex.co.uk
Evesham – www.evesham.com
Gateway – www.gateway.com/uk
Hewlett Packard – www.hp.com/uk
Time – www.timecomputers.com
Viglen – www.viglen.co.uk

www.oink-oink.com

CARTRIDGES, REFILLS AND PAPER

ORIGIN UK	One of many sites specialising in supplying
SPEED ✓✓✓✓	peripheral products, we particularly liked this
INFO ✓✓✓	one because it's fun and some of the proceeds
VALUE ✓✓✓✓	go to supporting the RSPCA.
EASE ✓✓✓✓	

Crime

*We thought it would be a good idea to introduce this section,
as it may help victims of crime or it may even help solve one.
If you have a site you'd like us to include please contact us at
goodwebsiteguide@hotmail.com*

www.police.uk

THE POLICE ONLINE

ORIGIN UK	Here you can notify the police of minor crimes and
SPEED ✓✓✓✓	get essential information on the organisation and
INFO ✓✓✓✓	how it works. There are sections on specific crimes
EASE ✓✓✓✓	or appeals, recruitment and information on related
	organisations. The site is easy to navigate and use.
	See also www.nationalcrimesquad.police.uk

www.cjsonline.org

THE CRIMINAL JUSTICE SYSTEM

ORIGIN UK
SPEED ✓✓✓✓
INFO ✓✓✓✓✓
EASE ✓✓✓

A helpful site that tells what happens when someone gets arrested, and provides information about the trial procedure, how a court works and what you need to do if you're a witness. There's a guide to who does what in the legal profession and a section on related links.

www.crimestoppers-uk.org

KEEP 'EM PEELED

ORIGIN UK
SPEED ✓✓✓✓
INFO ✓✓✓✓✓
EASE ✓✓✓

Information on the Crimestoppers trust and how you can get involved in their fight against crime with information on the latest campaign and initiatives, links and, of course, their phone number 0800 555 111. See also www.crimereduction.gov.uk which has been set up by the government to become the number one resource for the crime prevention practitioner. It's not there yet, but the site is growing.

www.localhomewatch.co.uk

NEIGHBOURHOOD WATCH

ORIGIN UK
SPEED ✓✓✓✓
INFO ✓✓✓✓
EASE ✓✓✓✓

A directory of neighbourhood watch schemes by county with advice on preventing crime and how you can set up a neighbourhood watch scheme in your area.

www.victimsupport.com

VICTIM SUPPORT

ORIGIN UK
SPEED ✓✓✓✓
INFO ✓✓✓✓
EASE ✓✓✓✓

An independent charity that supports the victims of crime throughout the UK with help and advice. It also advises witnesses on the justice system and campaigns for equal opportunities. You can also find out about how you can help or give funds.

www.fraud.org

NATIONAL FRAUD INFORMATION CENTER

ORIGIN US	Find out about the many ways you can be defrauded
SPEED ✓✓✓✓	and how to spot a fraud on the Internet.
INFO ✓✓✓✓	
EASE ✓✓✓✓	

www.secureyourmotor.gov.uk

SECURITY TIPS FOR MOTORISTS

ORIGIN UK	Pretty straightforward site detailing the best steps to
SPEED ✓✓✓✓	guard against your car, bike or truck being stolen.
INFO ✓✓✓✓	You can take tests to see how secure your car is or
EASE ✓✓✓✓	test your security knowledge.

Cycles and Cycling

*See page 463 for cycling holidays and tours and page 368 for
information on cycling as a sport.*

www.cycleweb.co.uk

THE INTERNET CYCLING CLUB

ORIGIN UK	A great attempt to bring together all things cycling.
SPEED ✓✓✓✓	Aimed at a general audience rather than cycling as
INFO ✓✓✓✓✓	a sport, it has masses of sections and links on
VALUE ✓✓✓	everything from the latest news to clubs, shops
EASE ✓✓✓	and holidays.

www.bikemagic.com

BIKE MAGIC!

ORIGIN UK	There's plenty here on the world of bikes, it has
SPEED ✓✓✓	forums on hot bike topics, reviews of equipment,
INFO ✓✓✓✓	buying advice, classifieds, the latest news, links and
VALUE ✓✓✓	an events calendar.
EASE ✓✓✓	

www.bicyclenet.co.uk

UK'S NUMBER 1 ONLINE BICYCLE SHOP

ORIGIN UK	Great selection of bikes and accessories, there's also
SPEED ✓✓✓	good advice on how to buy the right bike and
INFO ✓✓✓✓	assembly instructions on all that they sell. Delivery
VALUE ✓✓✓	starts at £3.75.
EASE ✓✓✓✓	

www.cyclesource.co.uk/link.cfm

CYCLE INDUSTRY TRADE ASSOCIATION

ORIGIN UK	How to buy the right bike, find a dealer or browse
SPEED ✓✓✓✓	the many links covering the subject – a good-looking
INFO ✓✓✓✓	site that's fast and easy to use.
EASE ✓✓✓✓	

www.tandem-club.org.uk

CAN YOU RIDE TANDEM?

ORIGIN UK	A pretty basic site devoted to the world of the
SPEED ✓✓✓	tandem with discussion groups, classifieds, buying
INFO ✓✓✓	advice, events and a newsletter.
EASE ✓✓✓	

www.a-nelson.dircon.co.uk/cyclingprelycra

BEFORE THE AGE OF LYCRA

ORIGIN UK	A look at cycling as it used to be before the Lycra
SPEED ✓✓✓✓	clad hordes took to the roads, nicely done and with
INFO ✓✓✓✓	a great nostalgic feel.
EASE ✓✓✓	

Dating

The Net is fast becoming an accepted means to meet people, but be careful about how you go about meeting up; many people aren't exactly honest about their details. If in doubt, err on the side of caution.

www.wildxangel.com

THE LOW DOWN

ORIGIN UK	An American site that tells it like it is and gives
SPEED ✓✓✓✓	advice about using chat and dating sites, it also gives
INFO ✓✓✓✓	awards for the best ones and there are links too.
EASE ✓✓✓	

www.uksingles.co.uk

FOR ALL **UK** SINGLES

ORIGIN UK	Not just about dating, this site is devoted to helping
SPEED ✓✓✓✓	you get the most out of life. There are several
INFO ✓✓✓✓✓	sections: accommodation, sport and activities, holi-
EASE ✓✓✓	days, help for single parents, and listings for match-

making and dating services. All the companies that advertise in the directories are vetted too.

Here are some additional sites, there's not much to choose between them, it's all a matter of taste. All are secure and allow you to browse and participate in relative safety.

www.dateline.co.uk – 30 years experience at the dating game gives Dateline lots of credibility and it's a good site too, easy to use and reassuring.

www.datingdirect.com – claims to be the UK's largest agency with over 200,000 members, the site is not as sophisticated as some, though they seem to have lots of success stories.

www.dinnerdates.com – one of the longest established and most respected dining and social events
clubs for unattached single people in the UK; find
out how you can get involved here.

www.ivorytowers.net – where unattached alumni
and undergraduates from the 'leading' universities
get together.

www.love-exchange.co.uk – upmarket profiles for
busy professionals, you can chat without reveal-
ing your proper e-mail address.

www.match.com – leading site in the US, get your
profile matched to someone or join in the chat,
there's an excellent magazine too.

www.singles121.com – good site, easy to use with,
on the whole, good quality photos.

www.singlesearchuk.com – introduction service -
discrete and you only get introduced if your
profile matches to 60%, whatever that means.

www.tiggle.com – seven days free registration and a
nice site, but you have to register to gain access.

www.udate.com – US site for over 25s only, an
attractive site with a good search facility.

Do-It-Yourself

*The web doesn't seem a natural home for do-it-yourself, but
there are some really useful sites, some great offers on tools and
equipment and plenty of sensible advice. The good news is that
in the past year there has been a great improvement in the quality
of sites in this area.*

Superstores

www.diy.com

THE DIY SUPERSTORE

ORIGIN UK
SPEED ✓✓✓
INFO ✓✓✓✓
VALUE ✓✓✓✓
EASE ✓✓✓✓

B&Q has a bright and busy site with lots of advice, inspiration, tips and information on projects for the home and garden. It also has an excellent searchable product database. There are also plenty of offers and the store has a good selection of products covering all the major DIY areas. Delivery costs vary according to how much you buy and how fast you want it. Returns can be made to the stores. You need to be able to accept cookies before the site can operate effectively or you want to place an order.

www.homebase.co.uk

CREATE YOUR IDEAL HOME, FROM HOME

ORIGIN UK
SPEED ✓✓✓
INFO ✓✓✓✓✓
VALUE ✓✓✓✓
EASE ✓✓✓✓

A good looking and logically laid out site, with a fairly large selection of products to buy, you can also get help with projects, plenty of inspirational ideas and decorating tips for each room of the house, as well as offers and competitions. Delivery times and charges vary, although the minimum is £2.95. You can return unwanted or faulty goods to your nearest store.

www.wickes.co.uk

DIY SPECIALISTS

ORIGIN UK
SPEED ✓✓✓
INFO ✓✓✓✓
EASE ✓✓✓✓

Good ideas, inspiration and help are the key themes for this site, it's easy to use and genuinely helpful with well laid out project details. You can visit their showrooms for product information and even take a 3-D tour of a conservatory. There's a handy calculator section where you can work out how many tiles or rolls of wallpaper you may need. The site does suffer from lots of graphic errors though.

www.focusdoitall.co.uk

FOCUS DO-IT-ALL

ORIGIN UK
SPEED ✓✓✓
INFO ✓✓✓✓✓
VALUE ✓✓✓✓
EASE ✓✓✓

A functional site, which attempts to put over lots of ideas and inspiration, it also carries a wide range of products at good prices. Delivery is £4.99 minimum and you can return unwanted goods to your nearest store.

Other DIY stores worth checking out are:

www.jewson.co.uk – Jewson's site is more corporate than anything but it does have a small section on each part of the house and how they can help.

www.decoratingdirect.co.uk – functional and easy-to-use site that concentrates on home décor products at excellent prices.

Buying tools and equipment

www.screwfix.com

PRODUCTS FOR ALL DIY NEEDS

ORIGIN UK
SPEED ✓✓✓✓
INFO ✓✓✓✓✓
VALUE ✓✓✓✓✓
EASE ✓✓✓✓

Rightly considered to be one of the best online stores, Screwfix offer excellent value for money with free delivery and wholesale prices on a massive range of DIY products. You need cookies enabled for it to work effectively.

www.cooksons.com

TOOLS A-PLENTY

ORIGIN UK
SPEED ✓✓✓
INFO ✓✓✓✓
VALUE ✓✓✓✓
EASE ✓✓✓✓

An award-winning site from this Stockport firm, it has a huge number of tools and related products available, with free delivery on orders over £38.29 ex VAT. There are plenty of special offers and a loyalty scheme for regulars.

www.draper.co.uk
QUALITY SINCE 1919

ORIGIN UK
SPEED ✓✓✓
INFO ✓✓✓✓
VALUE ✓✓✓
EASE ✓✓✓

An attractive but slow site from Draper tools with advice sections and an online shop which seems to have a life of its own.

www.diytools.co.uk
MORE TOOLS

ORIGIN UK
SPEED ✓✓✓✓
INFO ✓✓✓✓
VALUE ✓✓✓✓
EASE ✓✓✓✓

Another well-designed and extensive tool store with a huge range of products, there's also free delivery for orders over £50. Also check out the nicely designed **www.toolfast.co.uk** and **www.blackand-decker.co.uk** who have lots of advice on how to use power tools correctly.

DIY help and advice

www.fmb.org.uk/consumers
THE FEDERATION OF MASTER BUILDERS

ORIGIN UK
SPEED ✓✓✓
INFO ✓✓✓✓✓
EASE ✓✓✓✓

Get help to avoid cowboys and advice on getting the best out of a builder. There's information and articles on most aspects of home maintenance, plus hints on finding reputable help. See also **www.quali-tymark.org.uk** which covers the government's scheme to ensure the reliability of tradesmen.

www.homepro.com
THE HOME IMPROVEMENT SPECIALISTS

ORIGIN UK
SPEED ✓✓✓✓
INFO ✓✓✓✓✓
EASE ✓✓✓✓✓

An excellent and very helpful site split into four major sections, a 24-hour emergency call out service for your area, a 'Find a Professional' service for any household job, a help and advice section and lastly a superb inspirational section where you can go for ideas for your home. You can access via WAP or call the helplines too. See also the similarly helpful **www.tradanet.co.uk**

www.improveline.com
FIND A CONTRACTOR AND IDEAS

ORIGIN UK
SPEED ✓✓✓✓
INFO ✓✓✓✓✓
EASE ✓✓✓✓

Well-designed site offering information and inspiration for home improvements, there's also a service that puts you in touch with someone to do small jobs on the house within the hour, they have some 150,000 people registered. Inspiration comes in the form of thousands of categorised pictures which are easily pulled up via a good search facility. You can also ask an expert and get advice on financing your project.

www.buildadvice.com
EXPERT ADVICE FOR YOUR HOME

ORIGIN UK
SPEED ✓✓✓✓
INFO ✓✓✓✓
EASE ✓✓✓✓

An award winning advice site from a family firm with sections on each major DIY job, there are clear instructions on how go about them. They choose to cover some unusual areas such as disabled access, disaster recovery and asbestos.

www.hometips.com

EXPERT ADVICE FOR YOUR HOME

ORIGIN US
SPEED ✓✓✓
INFO ✓✓✓✓
EASE ✓✓✓

American the advice may be, but there is plenty here for every homeowner. The site is less fun than it was but it's well laid out and the advice good. Good alternatives are **www.naturalhandyman.com** which is fun or there is the well-designed forum site **http://homedoctor.net/main.html** where you can discuss your DIY problems; or the extensive **www.doityourself.com** which is very detailed.

www.howtocleananything.com

STAIN REMOVAL PAR EXCELLENCE

ORIGIN CANADA
SPEED ✓✓✓✓
INFO ✓✓✓✓✓
EASE ✓✓✓✓

A group of cleaners have got together to produce a site that contains over 1,000 cleaning tips for outside or inside the house, the car – you name it basically.

www.diyfixit.co.uk

ONLINE DIY ENCYCLOPAEDIA

ORIGIN UK
SPEED ✓✓✓
INFO ✓✓✓✓
EASE ✓✓✓

Get help with most DIY jobs using the search engine or browse by room or job type. The information is good but some guidance and more illustrations would help.

www.architect-net.co.uk

ARCHITECTS AND BUILDING CONTRACTORS DIRECTORY

ORIGIN UK
SPEED ✓✓✓
INFO ✓✓✓
EASE ✓✓✓

Find an architect to design your next home using the regional directory. Not a great site, but useful for good links to related sites.

www.ebuild.co.uk

BUILD YOUR OWN HOUSE

ORIGIN	UK
SPEED	✓✓✓
INFO	✓✓✓✓✓
EASE	✓✓✓

All the information and contacts you need if you're thinking of buying that plot of land and getting stuck in. There's also a continually updated list of what plots of land are available and where.

The following sites will also prove useful if you're out to build your own:
www.homebuilder.co.uk – good design and services, with a Scottish bias.
www.selfbuildit.co.uk – help for first timers.
www.selfbuildcentre.com – pretty annoying design but lots of links and advice make it worth a visit.

Specialists

www.bathroomexpress.co.uk

BETTER BATHROOMS

ORIGIN	UK
SPEED	✓✓✓
INFO	✓✓✓✓
VALUE	✓✓✓✓
EASE	✓✓✓✓

A wide range of bathrooms and accessories are available at decent prices, with some interesting luxury items such as après-shower driers and some unique toilet seats. Delivery is based on how much you spend.

www.plumbworld.co.uk

AN ONLINE PLUMBING SHOP

ORIGIN	UK
SPEED	✓✓✓
INFO	✓✓✓
EASE	✓✓✓

Good selection of plumbing tools at competitive prices. Not exactly the most informative site as you have to assume much, for example, there's very little information about shipping which, incidentally, is free to most of the UK when you spend £50 or more. If you need to find a plumber try the directory of plumbers at www.plumbers.uk.com or for information on how to do work yourself try www.plumbnet.com or www.guidetoplumbing.com

www.handlesdirect.co.uk

HANDLES GALORE

ORIGIN UK	A functional site where you can buy, well, handles.
SPEED ✓✓✓✓	It's also got a selection of locks, switches and sock-
INFO ✓✓✓✓	ets that match certain handles. The emphasis is on
VALUE ✓✓✓	contemporary style, and there's a good advice
EASE ✓✓✓	section which shows you how to fit them.

See also **www.knobsandknockers.co.uk** who offer a wide range including security products.

www.doorsdirect.co.uk

DOORS AND HANDLES

ORIGIN UK	Features replacement doors for kitchens and
SPEED ✓✓✓✓	bathrooms, you can order made-to-measure or
INFO ✓✓✓✓	standard and there's a selection of fittings as well.
VALUE ✓✓✓	
EASE ✓✓✓✓	

www.salvo.co.uk

SALVAGE AND RECLAMATION

ORIGIN UK	Salvo provides information on where to get salvaged
SPEED ✓✓✓	and reclaimed architectural and garden antiques.
INFO ✓✓✓✓✓	The site is comprehensive and easy-to-use with
VALUE ✓✓✓	interesting information such as what buildings are
EASE ✓✓✓✓	due to be demolished and when, so you can be ready

and waiting.

www.conservatoriesonline.co.uk

ALL YOU NEED TO KNOW ABOUT CONSERVATORIES

ORIGIN UK	A good portal site which offers links and advice
SPEED ✓✓✓	on conservatories, sunrooms, garden rooms and
INFO ✓✓✓✓✓	solariums. There's a buyer's guide plus information
EASE ✓✓✓✓	on materials, styles, even on pools and orangeries.

Paint and wallpaper

www.dulux.co.uk

DULUX

ORIGIN UK
SPEED ✓✓✓
INFO ✓✓✓✓✓
EASE ✓✓✓✓

A good looking and interesting site from Dulux, with a 'mouse painter' that you can use to redecorate a number of pre-selected rooms, there's also product information, a kids' zone and top tips on painting techniques. You can't buy from the site although there is a list of stockists. Crown has a similar but less interactive site that can be found at **www.crownpaint.co.uk**

www.farrow-ball.co.uk

TRADITIONAL PAINT AND PAPER

ORIGIN UK
SPEED ✓✓✓
INFO ✓✓✓✓
VALUE ✓✓✓
EASE ✓✓✓✓

Excellently designed web site featuring details on how their paint and paper is manufactured – something they obviously take pride in. You can also order from the site or request samples. For that traditional Mediterranean look try **www.casa.co.uk** who have a good selection and a nice site.

www.sanderson-online.co.uk

WILLIAM MORRIS AMONGST OTHER WALLPAPER

ORIGIN UK
SPEED ✓✓✓
INFO ✓✓✓✓
VALUE ✓✓✓
EASE ✓✓✓

Find out about the company, its heritage and what designs they have - new and old. You can also order a brochure and visit the Morris & Co pages where they have all the favourite designs. For more information on William Morris try visiting **www.morrissociety.org**

www.thedesignstudio.co.uk
GET THE RIGHT DESIGN

ORIGIN UK
SPEED ✓✓
INFO ✓✓✓✓
EASE ✓✓✓

This is an excellent database of wallpaper and fabric samples, which is easy-to-use and good fun. Once you've selected your swatch you can then find the nearest supplier. You need some patience, as it can be quite slow.

Inspiration, design and interiors

www.bhglive.com
BETTER HOMES AND GARDENS

ORIGIN US
SPEED ✓✓✓
INFO ✓✓✓✓✓
EASE ✓✓✓

There's more to this than DIY, but superb graphics and videos give this site the edge. It's American, so some information isn't applicable to the UK. The 'How-to Encyclopaedia' is excellent.

www.bluedeco.com
DESIGN ONLINE

ORIGIN UK/LUXEMBOURG
SPEED ✓✓✓
INFO ✓✓✓✓
VALUE ✓
EASE ✓✓✓

This site offers a good selection of designer products for the home, from furniture to ceramics, with free delivery to the UK. Unfortunately, returns have to go to Luxembourg.

www.design-gap.co.uk
DESIGNER DIRECTORY

ORIGIN UK
SPEED ✓✓✓
INFO ✓✓✓✓✓
EASE ✓✓✓

A directory of UK-based designers and manufacturers with some 300 pages to browse through. They are arranged alphabetically by first name or company name as well as by category. The illustrations are excellent.

www.design-online.co.uk

NEED A DESIGNER?

ORIGIN UK
SPEED ✓✓✓
INFO ✓✓✓✓
EASE ✓✓✓

Design Online's mission is to put buyers and suppliers in touch with each other and to use the Internet to promote the use of well-designed products and services. You just search for the service you want and a list of suitable suppliers with contact details quickly appears. Could do with some illustrations and examples of the work that they are trying to promote.

www.geomancy.net

FENG SHUI

ORIGIN UK
SPEED ✓✓✓
INFO ✓✓✓✓
EASE ✓✓

What a mess of a site! Considering that it's supposed to promote the principles of light and harmony, it isn't very well designed. However, there's an excellent set of links and you can learn all you need to know about Feng Shui.

www.habitat.co.uk

HABITAT STORES

ORIGIN UK
SPEED ✓✓✓✓
INFO ✓✓✓✓
EASE ✓✓✓✓

An information only site with lots of details about their product range all wrapped up in a funky design.

www.ikea.com

IKEA STYLE

ORIGIN SWEDEN
SPEED ✓✓✓
INFO ✓✓✓✓
EASE ✓✓✓✓

You can't buy from the site but you can check whether a store has the item you want to buy in stock before you go, it would be great if more stores did this. Otherwise the site is more the usual store fare with plenty of ideas, articles and product lists.

www.maelstrom.co.uk

CONTEMPORARY SELECTION

ORIGIN UK	A wide selection of contemporary gifts, accessories,
SPEED ✓✓✓	gadgets and furniture in a good-looking site.
INFO ✓✓✓✓	Delivery is 10% of the value of order with a flat
VALUE ✓✓✓	charge of £10 if you spend more than £100.
EASE ✓✓✓	

www.alarisavenue.co.uk

KITCHENS AND CANE

ORIGIN UK	A beautifully designed store that offers much in the
SPEED ✓✓✓	way of inspiration and quality products for the
INFO ✓✓✓✓	kitchen.
VALUE ✓✓✓✓	
EASE ✓✓✓✓	

www.next.co.uk

NEXT HOME WARE

ORIGIN UK	A good selection of Next homeware with an
SPEED ✓✓✓	excellent next day delivery service that costs £2.95
INFO ✓✓✓✓	whatever you buy.
VALUE ✓✓✓	
EASE ✓✓✓	

E-Mail

We've had several requests to include a selection of the best free e-mail providers, there are hundreds to chose from, but hopefully these sites should help you find the one that's right for you, whether you're after efficiency or a trendy@moniker.

www.fepg.net
FREE E-MAIL PROVIDERS GUIDE

ORIGIN US
SPEED ✓✓✓✓
INFO ✓✓✓✓
EASE ✓✓✓

Here's the place to start, it lists over 1,400 providers in 85 countries, including over 40 from the UK, so it's pretty comprehensive. It tends to just list them with a few details but there are recommended sites too. There's also a news section and a FEPG best of the best selection.

www.sneakemail.com
SNEAK E-MAIL

ORIGIN US
SPEED ✓✓✓✓
INFO ✓✓✓✓
EASE ✓✓✓✓

Sneak e-mail provides an e-mail protection service whereby you can maintain a level of anonymity, stop spam or unsuitable e-mails getting to you, avoid unwanted soliciting or prevent others from selling your e-mail address to marketing companies, for example.

www.twigger.co.uk
ANYWHERE IN THE WORLD

ORIGIN UK
SPEED ✓✓✓✓
INFO ✓✓✓✓
EASE ✓✓✓✓

An excellent service that enables you to use your chosen e-mail address wherever you may be. One advantage is that you can see attachments before you download them onto your PC. The service is subscription based.

www.emailaddresses.com
E-MAIL ADDRESS DIRECTORY

ORIGIN US
SPEED ✓✓✓✓
INFO ✓✓✓✓
EASE ✓✓✓✓

A useful directory of e-mail services and programs to help you manage your e-mail and mail to your site if you own one, there are also tips on how to find an e-mail address and a directory of address directories.

Education

Using the Internet for homework or study has become one of its primary uses; these sites will help enormously, especially alongside the reference and encyclopaedia sites listed on page 320. There is also a section aimed at students on page 396.

Homework help

www.a-levels.co.uk

A LEVELS – A DODDLE?

ORIGIN UK
SPEED ✓✓✓✓
INFO ✓✓✓
EASE ✓✓✓

Great links providing masses of information on key topics. Most of the popular A level subjects are now completed – worth checking out.

www.bbc.co.uk/education

GET EQUIPPED FOR LIFE

ORIGIN UK
SPEED ✓✓✓✓
INFO ✓✓✓✓
EASE ✓✓✓✓

Good looking site covering learning at school, college and adult education, each section tends to be tied to a particular programme rather than subject, but there is masses here and the quality of content is particularly good. The revision sections are excellent.

www.bigchalk.com

HOMEWORK CENTRAL

ORIGIN US
SPEED ✓✓✓✓
INFO ✓✓✓✓
EASE ✓✓✓

Much improved visually, just go to the appropriate area and you get put through to the chalkboard, which has well categorised links to lots of excellent information, web sites and subjects. There's help and information for parents and a teacher's section full of good resources in spite of the US bias. Access to the library costs $5 per month.

www.cln.org/int_expert.html

ASK AN EXPERT

ORIGIN CANADA	This site lists almost a hundred sites by subject,
SPEED ✓✓✓✓	where you can ask an expert your homework ques-
INFO ✓✓✓	tion – what a doddle! North American bias though.
EASE ✓✓✓	

www.educate.org.uk

EDUCATE YOURSELF

ORIGIN UK	For parents there is loads of advice on how to get
SPEED ✓✓✓✓	the best out of the system to help your children
INFO ✓✓✓	achieve, and with over 2,000 primary lesson plans,
EASE ✓✓✓	the site is great for teachers. The web search is

comprehensive for homework help (Key Stage 1 through GCSE), there's educational news, a schools guide and listings for child-friendly days out. However, it can be a bit slow and, with the exception of web search, is aimed at primary.

www.discoveryschool.com

ANSWERS TO HOMEWORK, FREE

ORIGIN US	This huge database is one of the biggest online
SPEED ✓✓✓✓	homework sites, with some 700 links to a variety of
INFO ✓✓✓✓	reference sites and the provision to ask questions
EASE ✓✓✓✓	too. Layout has been improved and you can more

easily access the information, it also has an excellent clip art gallery.

www.homeworkelephant.co.uk

LET THE ELEPHANT HELP

ORIGIN UK	Rightly considered one of the top educational sites
SPEED ✓✓✓✓	with some 5,000 resources and straightforward
INFO ✓✓✓✓✓	layout, all aimed at helping children achieve great
EASE ✓✓✓✓✓	results, there's help with specific subjects, hints and

tips, help for parents and teachers. The agony elephant is great if you get really stuck. It's constantly being updated, so worth checking regularly.

www.homeworkhigh.co.uk

LEARN WITH CHANNEL 4

ORIGIN UK
SPEED ✓✓✓✓
INFO ✓✓✓✓✓
EASE ✓✓✓✓

Split into six learning sections: history, geography, science, maths, English and languages. There's also news and a chat room plus a personal help section that covers topics like bullying. They even provide teachers online for live sessions to help you out. You can ask questions, track down lots of information and chat with fellow homework sufferers. All in all, this is one of the better-looking homework sites. Excellent.

www.learn.co.uk

LEARN WITH THE GUARDIAN

ORIGIN UK
SPEED ✓✓✓✓
INFO ✓✓✓✓✓
EASE ✓✓✓✓✓

A curriculum based site that has much to offer in terms of content. They work closely with schools and it shows, that and access to the *Guardian* content means this is one of the best sites from which to learn. The down side is that it's all a bit clinical and not much fun.

www.learn.com

SMARTEST PLACE ON THE WEB

ORIGIN UK
SPEED ✓✓✓✓
INFO ✓✓✓✓✓
VALUE ✓✓
EASE ✓✓✓

Once you've registered (very easy) you're entitled to free access to some online courses, which range from how to bake spicy fries to how to convert centigrade into Fahrenheit. It's not easy to find specific facts, but if you have a project to do there's bound to be something here to help you out. Be warned that many of the courses they offer do cost.

www.learningalive.co.uk

FOR PRIMARY AND SECONDARY

ORIGIN UK
SPEED ✓✓✓
INFO ✓✓✓✓
EASE ✓✓✓

The 'Living Library' is a useful resource for home-work help for both primary and secondary students while 'Pathways' provides over 5,000 links to a variety of reference sites. There are loads of resources for teachers too.

www.pupilline.net

FOR US BY US

ORIGIN UK
SPEED ✓✓✓✓
INFO ✓✓✓✓✓
EASE ✓✓✓✓

A massive, comprehensive site by pupils for pupils, it doesn't stop at education either, it covers social issues as well, in fact everything any pupil would want to know. As it's put together by them it speaks in their language – a wicked site then.

www.samlearning.com

EXAM REVISION

ORIGIN UK
SPEED ✓✓✓✓
INFO ✓✓✓✓✓
VALUE ✓✓✓
EASE ✓✓✓

SAM stands for self-assessment and marking, on this brilliant site you can do just that, it has mock exams covering every major subject and key stage plus GCSE and A level. There are top tips on taking exams and the chance to win some great prizes when you register. There is a 14-day free trial then you need to pay from £4.99 per month as a home user.

www.schoolsnet.com

THE EDUCATION SUPERSITE

ORIGIN UK
SPEED ✓✓✓✓
INFO ✓✓✓✓✓
EASE ✓✓✓✓

An incredibly impressive site that covers all aspects of education; there are school and site guides, jobs pages, book and computer shops, chat rooms, information on revision and exams, the latest news and, of course, plenty of chat.

www.schoolzone.co.uk

UK'S TOP EDUCATIONAL SEARCH ENGINE

ORIGIN UK
SPEED ✓✓✓✓
INFO ✓✓✓✓✓
EASE ✓✓✓

With over 30,000 sites and bits of resource all checked by teachers, Schoolzone has masses of information. It is clearly designed and easy to use with all the sites and information rated according to how useful they are. There is free software to download, plus homework help, career advice, teacher support (they do need it apparently) and much more. Don't be put off by the confusing layout; it's worth sticking with.

www.startribune.com/homework

HOMEWORK ON THE BRAIN

ORIGIN US
SPEED ✓✓✓
INFO ✓✓✓✓
EASE ✓✓✓

Just click on the right bit of the cartoon brain and you get put through to the subject you're after. There are lots of links to other learning web sites as well as bags of tips and information; you can even e-mail a question. They try to reply within 24 hours.

Pre-school and infant education

www.enchantedlearning.com

FROM APES TO WHALES

ORIGIN US
SPEED ✓✓✓✓
INFO ✓✓✓
EASE ✓✓

It's messy, uncool and largely aimed at young children, but there's loads of good information and activities hidden away, especially on nature. Use the search engine to find what you need.

www.underfives.co.uk

WEB RESOURCE FOR PRE-SCHOOL

ORIGIN UK
SPEED ✓✓✓
INFO ✓✓✓✓✓
EASE ✓✓✓✓

Loads of things to do and see here, from games and activities to download to help and advice for parents. Like the best educational sites its educational bias is not obvious or overwhelming, the tone is just right, it's also simple to use and fast.

National Curriculum

www.dfee.gov.uk/nc or www.nc.uk.net

NATIONAL CURRICULUM REVEALED

ORIGIN UK
SPEED ✓✓✓✓
INFO ✓✓✓✓
EASE ✓✓✓✓

Very detailed explanation of the National Curriculum and prescribed standards. For more information on the national curriculum see www.qca.org.uk. For information on the Scottish education system see www.sqa.org.uk

Post 16 and adult education

www.ngfl.gov.uk

THE NATIONAL GRID FOR LEARNING

ORIGIN UK
SPEED ✓✓✓✓
INFO ✓✓✓✓
EASE ✓✓✓

The official government education site with sections on every aspect of learning. There's something for everyone, whatever your needs. It is particularly good for info on further and adult education. There are also details on school web sites, a features section that covers current news and events, plus advice on Internet safety.

www.learndirect.co.uk

ADULT LEARNING

ORIGIN UK
SPEED ✓✓✓
INFO ✓✓✓✓
EASE ✓✓✓✓

A government backed site which aims to bring education to everyone whatever their needs. The site explains the background to the initiative plus details of courses and how you can find one that meets your requirements. There's also help for businesses and a jobs advice section.

Electrical Goods, Gadgets and Appliances

This section covers stores that sell the usual electrical goods but also offer a bit more in terms of range, offers or service. There's also the odd spy camera and gadget shop.

www.comet.co.uk

ALWAYS LOW PRICES, GUARANTEED

ORIGIN UK	Lots of products, split into:
SPEED ✓✓✓	1 Kitchen and home, for washing machines, microwaves and cookers.
INFO ✓✓✓✓✓	
VALUE ✓✓✓✓	2 Household with vacuums, irons, ionisers and air purifiers.
EASE ✓✓✓✓	

1 Kitchen and home, for washing machines, microwaves and cookers.

2 Household with vacuums, irons, ionisers and air purifiers.

3 Entertainment featuring TV, music, games and keyboards.

4 Computing and communication offering PCs and mobiles, phones and faxes.

5 Finance deals and offers abound and there's information on the products. Delivery costs vary.

www.dixons.co.uk

OFFERS GALORE

ORIGIN UK	The Dixons site has plenty of offers and reflects what you'd find in their stores very well. It has a similar but slightly wider product range to Comet, with an additional photographic section. Delivery costs vary.
SPEED ✓✓✓	
INFO ✓✓✓✓	
VALUE ✓✓✓✓	
EASE ✓✓✓✓	

www.maplin.co.uk

ELECTRONICS CATALOGUE

ORIGIN UK
SPEED ✓✓✓✓
INFO ✓✓✓✓✓
VALUE ✓✓✓
EASE ✓✓✓

Maplin is well established and it's a bit of an event when the new catalogue is published. Now you can always have access to the latest innovations and basic equipment at this well put together site. It features the expected massive range with online ordering, delivery over £30 is free.

www.hed.co.uk

HOME ELECTRICAL DIRECT

ORIGIN UK
SPEED ✓✓
INFO ✓✓✓
VALUE ✓✓✓✓✓
EASE ✓✓✓✓

Their motto is 'the lowest prices guaranteed all year round, and that's a promise'. They have a very large range of goods covering all the key product categories minus cameras. Delivery is free on orders over £100. See also the simple but slowish www.bestbuyappliances.co.uk and www.24-7electrical.co.uk, which is well designed with the addition of a helpful buyer's guide. The well named www.we-sell-it.co.uk is also worth a visit for good prices on kitchen and other domestic appliances.

www.richersounds.com

PROMISES TO BEAT EVERY OTHER WEB SITE BY £50

ORIGIN UK
SPEED ✓✓✓✓
INFO ✓✓✓
VALUE ✓✓✓✓
EASE ✓✓✓✓

Bargain hunters will want to include this site on their list, similar to the other electrical goods retailers but with a leaning towards music and TVs, with plenty of offers and advice. There is a search facility and the products are obviously good value, however, they are vague about delivery charges, although products are delivered within 5 working days.

www.appliancespares.co.uk

FIX IT YOURSELF

ORIGIN UK	Ezee-Fix has thousands of spare parts for a massive
SPEED ✓✓✓✓	range of products, nearly all illustrated, including
INFO ✓✓✓	fridges, cookers, microwaves, vacuum cleaners, etc.
VALUE ✓✓✓	All it needs is online fitting instructions, and more
EASE ✓✓✓	details on the products and it would be perfect.

www.flyingtoolbox.com

IF YOU CAN'T FIX IT YOURSELF

ORIGIN UK	With Flying Toolbox you can find someone to repair
SPEED ✓✓✓✓	your faulty item. Type in your location and details
INFO ✓✓✓✓	of the repair and they will provide a list of repairers
VALUE ✓✓✓	in your area with information on charges and a
EASE ✓✓✓✓	rating from previous customers. Good though it is,

could it be just a way of selling insurance policies?

www.bull-electrical.com

FOR THE SPECIALIST

ORIGIN UK	Fascinating to visit, this mess of a site offers every
SPEED ✓✓✓✓	sort of electronic device, from divining rods to radio
INFO ✓✓✓✓	kits to spy cameras. There are four basic sections:
VALUE ✓✓✓✓	
EASE ✓✓✓	

1 Surplus electronic – scientific and optical goods, even steam engines.
2 Links to specialist shops – such as spy equipment and hydroponics.
3 Free services.
4 Web services – shopping cart technology, for example.

www.innovations.co.uk

NEW TECHNOLOGY

ORIGIN	UK
SPEED	✓✓✓
INFO	✓✓✓✓
VALUE	✓✓✓
EASE	✓✓✓

Some 600 innovative, unusual or just plain daft items for sale, all on a neat web site, the best bit is probably the gift selector, which helps you find the perfect gift when you're stuck for something to buy. Other places for technology geeks to get their kicks are **www.thegadgetshop.co.uk** who have free delivery on orders over £10 and a free returns policy, **www.firebox.com** for a really wide range of gadgets amongst other boy's toys and lastly, the macho **www.big-boys-toys.net**

www.jungle.com

JUNGLE MANIA!

ORIGIN	UK
SPEED	✓✓✓✓
INFO	✓✓✓✓
VALUE	✓✓✓✓
EASE	✓✓✓✓

Jungle has turned itself into a technology store. You still get all the latest in music and a massive back catalogue and there's good information even on obscure albums, but they have moved to major on DVDs and videos, phones, electrical goods and games for PCs and other formats, plus a wide selection of computers, software, hardware and consumables (discs, ink cartridges etc). It offers a wide range, some good prices and additional services such as evening delivery.

Fashion and Accessories

The big brands have never been cheaper. Selling fashion and designer gear is another Net success, as customers flock to the great discounts that are on offer. Many people still prefer to try clothes on before buying but the good sites all offer a convenient returns policy.

Fashion

www.fuk.co.uk
FASHION UK

ORIGIN UK
SPEED ✓✓✓✓
INFO ✓✓✓✓✓
EASE ✓✓✓

All you ever need to know about the latest in UK and world fashion, updated daily. There's also a section on beauty, a good links library, competitions, chat and, of course, shopping. It's all packaged into a really attractive site, which initially looks cluttered but is OK once you get used to it.

www.vogue.co.uk
THE LATEST NEWS FROM BRITISH VOGUE

ORIGIN UK
SPEED ✓✓✓✓
INFO ✓✓✓✓
EASE ✓✓✓✓

An absolute must for the serious follower of fashion. There's the latest catwalk news and views, and a handy who's who of fashion. There's also a section on jobs, and you can order a subscription too. For a similar experience try **www.elle.com** or the slightly less fashion-oriented but more fun **www.cosmomag.com** For access to the top designers' most recent collections and a glimpse at what could be available in the shops the following season try **www.firstview.com**

www.ftv.com

FASHION TV

ORIGIN FRANCE
SPEED ✓✓✓✓
INFO ✓✓✓✓
EASE ✓✓✓✓

The 24 hour fashion station, so popular in gyms and bars, has a good site offering the latest from around the world. Features include video clips, radio interviews with designers plus links, gossip and horoscopes.

www.net-a-porter.com

PRET A PORTER

ORIGIN UK
SPEED ✓✓✓✓
INFO ✓✓✓✓
VALUE ✓✓✓
EASE ✓✓✓✓

A new site that incorporates the old Intofashion one, it looks great and is easy to use with information on the latest fashions in the 'What's New' section. There's also competitions and shopping where you can browse by designer or product type. Delivery costs vary according to what you buy. For an alternative try www.theclothesstore.com who also have a good selection of clothes and accessories.

www.fnmare.com

FASHION NIGHTMARE

ORIGIN UK
SPEED ✓✓✓
INFO ✓✓✓✓✓
EASE ✓✓✓✓

Outstanding graphics and creative look make this site stand out, but that's not all, the Fashion Nightmare team will keep you up-to-date with all the latest trends and fashion no-nos too.

www.fashionmall.com

FASHION STORE DIRECTORY

ORIGIN US
SPEED ✓✓✓✓
INFO ✓✓✓✓
VALUE ✓✓✓✓
EASE ✓✓✓✓

A huge number of stores listed by category, packed with offers and the latest new designs. Most stores are American and their ability to deliver outside the US and delivery charges vary considerably. The site is well-designed and easy to browse.

www.yoox.com

TOP DESIGNERS

ORIGIN UK	Great looking site with top offers from the top
SPEED ✓✓✓✓	designers, it's well laid out and easy to navigate with
INFO ✓✓✓✓	a good returns policy. You can search by designer or
VALUE ✓✓✓✓	category and the quality of the photos is good. Offers
EASE ✓✓✓✓	range from a few pounds to massive discounts.

www.zercon.com

CUT-PRICE DESIGNER CLOTHES FOR MEN AND WOMEN

ORIGIN UK	Not a big range of clothes but excellent prices.
SPEED ✓✓✓✓	Clear, no-nonsense design makes the site easy to use.
INFO ✓✓✓✓	
VALUE ✓✓✓✓	
EASE ✓✓✓✓	

www.apc.fr

FRENCH CHIC FROM A.P.C.

ORIGIN FRANCE	Unusual in style and for something a little different
SPEED ✓✓✓	A.P.C.'s site is worth a visit. Delivery is expensive in
INFO ✓✓✓	line with the clothes, which are beautifully designed
VALUE ✓✓	and well presented. For more of the French look go
EASE ✓✓✓✓	to www.redoute.co.uk

www.gap.com

FOR US RESIDENTS ONLY

ORIGIN US	A clear, uncluttered design makes shopping here
SPEED ✓✓✓	easy if you live in the United States! For UK
INFO ✓✓✓✓	residents it's window-shopping only.
EASE ✓✓✓✓	

www.next.co.uk

THE NEXT DIRECTORY

ORIGIN UK	The online version of the Next catalogue is available
SPEED ✓✓✓	including clothes for men, women and children as
INFO ✓✓✓✓	well as products for the home. Prices are the same as
VALUE ✓✓✓	the directory, next day delivery is £2.50 and return
EASE ✓✓✓✓	of unwanted goods is free. You can order the full
	catalogue for £3.

www.extremepie.com

EXTREME FASHION FROM EXTREME SPORTS

ORIGIN UK
SPEED ✓✓✓✓
INFO ✓✓✓✓
EASE ✓✓✓✓

A brand led selection of clothes from the world of BMX, surf, skate and other so called sports. The site is excellent with clear visuals and delivery costs start at £2.95.

www.arcadia.co.uk

THE ARCADIA GROUP – THE UK'S LEADING FASHION RETAILER

ORIGIN UK
SPEED ✓✓✓
INFO ✓✓✓✓
VALUE ✓✓✓✓
EASE ✓✓✓✓

The Arcadia Group has over 1,200 stores in the UK and the web sites are accessible, easy to use and offer good value for money. Each site has its own personality that reflects the high street store. Delivery charges vary.

www.evans.ltd.uk – women's clothes
www.racinggreen.co.uk – fashion
www.dorothyperkins.co.uk – women's clothes
www.tops.co.uk – Topshop
www.topman.co.uk – men's clothes
www.burtonmenswear.co.uk – men's clothes
www.hawkshead.com – outdoor clothes
www.principles.co.uk – for both men and women
www.zoom.co.uk – fashion

www.fashionbot.com

THE FASHION SEARCH ENGINE

ORIGIN UK
SPEED ✓✓✓✓
INFO ✓✓✓✓
VALUE ✓✓✓✓
EASE ✓✓✓✓

Quickly searches the major online stores (mainly those from the Arcadia Group) and compares prices. Just click on the item you want to check. If you can't find what you want here try **www.fashion.net** an American site that also offers news, jobs and a good set of links to other fashion sites.

Where the top designers hang out:
www.alexandermcqueen.net – Alexander McQueen
www.armaniexchange.com – cheap Armani
www.bensherman.co.uk – Ben Sherman
www.chanel.com – Chanel
www.christian-lacroix.fr – Christian Lacroix
www.georgioarmani.com – pukka Armani
www.gucci.com – Gucci
www.hugo.com – Hugo Boss
www.jpgaultier.fr – Jean Paul Gaultier
www.kenzo.com – Kenzo
www.paulsmith.co.uk – Paul Smith
www.tedbaker.co.uk – Ted Baker
www.tommy.com – Tommy Hilfiger

General clothes stores

www.kaysnet.com

KAYS CATALOGUE

ORIGIN UK	Massive range combined with value for money is the
SPEED ✓✓✓✓	formula for success with Kays. While they lead with
INFO ✓✓✓✓	clothes there are plenty of other sections outside of
VALUE ✓✓✓✓	that: jewellery, home entertainment, toys, etc.
EASE ✓✓✓✓	Delivery charge depends on how much you spend.

www.freemans.co.uk

FREE DELIVERY IN THE UK AND GOOD PRICES

ORIGIN UK	A similar site to Kays, not the full catalogue but
SPEED ✓✓✓	there's a wide range to choose from including top
INFO ✓✓✓✓	brands. Split into five major sections; women, men,
VALUE ✓✓✓✓	children, home and sports, they offer free delivery
EASE ✓✓✓✓	for UK customers. There are also prizes to be won, a

special feature on the latest trends and fashions and
information on how to get the full catalogue. See
also **www.grattan.co.uk** for Grattan's catalogue.

The excellent Shoppers Universe has closed but they recommend **www.aboundonline.com**, which is a similar catalogue site with a very good choice and offers a style guide and outfit finder service.

Specialist clothes stores

www.asseenonscreen.com.

BUY WHAT YOU SEE ON FILM OR TV

ORIGIN UK	Now you can buy that bit of jewellery or cool gear
SPEED ✓✓✓✓	that you've seen your favourite TV or film star wear-
INFO ✓✓✓✓	ing, As Seen on Screen specialises in supplying just
VALUE ✓✓✓	that. You can search by star or programme, it isn't
EASE ✓✓✓✓	cheap but you'll get noticed. They also have a handy
	gift ideas section if you're looking for inspiration.

www.noveltytogs.com

FOR CHARACTER MERCHANDISE

ORIGIN UK	Merchandise for Pokemon, The Simpsons, South
SPEED ✓✓✓	Park, Garfield and Peanuts, there are the usual T-
INFO ✓✓✓✓	shirts plus boxer shorts, socks and nightshirts.
VALUE ✓✓✓	Delivery is £1.95 for the UK and there are links to
EASE ✓✓✓	other character web sites.

www.bloomingmarvellous.co.uk

MATERNITY WEAR

ORIGIN UK	The UK's leading store in maternity and babywear
SPEED ✓✓✓✓	has an attractive site that features a good selection
INFO ✓✓✓✓	of clothes and nursery products. There are no
VALUE ✓✓✓✓	discounts on the clothes, but they do have regular
EASE ✓✓✓✓	sales with some good bargains. Delivery in the UK is
	£3.95 per order.

www.tienet.co.uk

THE INTERNET TIE STORE

ORIGIN UK
SPEED ✓✓✓✓
INFO ✓✓✓✓
VALUE ✓✓✓✓
EASE ✓✓✓✓

Hundreds of ties in seemingly every colour and design, there are sections on fashion ties, bow ties, tartan and character ties. Selection and payment is simple and delivery charge depends on size of order though it starts at 99p.

www.shoe-shop.com

EUROPE'S BIGGEST SHOE SHOP

ORIGIN UK
SPEED ✓✓✓✓
INFO ✓✓✓✓
VALUE ✓✓✓✓
EASE ✓✓✓✓

A massive selection of shoes and brands to chose from, the site is nicely designed with good pictures of the shoes, some of which can be seen in 3-D, a facility they are expanding. Delivery is included in the price and there's a good returns policy.
For an alternative try the straightforward **www.shoesdirect.co.uk** who have a similar offer.

Underwear and lingerie

www.smartbras.com

BRAS, BASQUES AND BRIEFS

ORIGIN UK
SPEED ✓✓✓✓
INFO ✓✓✓✓
VALUE ✓✓✓
EASE ✓✓✓✓

The easy, embarrassment-free way to buy under-wear. Choose from a selection of around 200 lingerie products including brand names at high street prices. Delivery is £2.50 for the UK.

See also:
www.rigbyandpeller.com – for up-market lingerie.
www.victoriassecret.com – for designer style.
www.kiniki.com – for men's underwear.
www.figleaves.com – for wide range and value for money.
www.mylingerie.net – the Simone Perele range.

Accessories and jewellery

www.jewellers.net

THE BIGGEST RANGE ON THE NET

ORIGIN UK
SPEED ✓✓✓✓
INFO ✓✓✓✓
VALUE ✓✓✓
EASE ✓✓✓✓

Excellent range of products, fashion jewellery, gifts, gold and silver, the watch section is particularly strong. There is also information on the history of gems, the manufacturers and brands available. Delivery to the UK is free for orders over £50, and there is a 30-day no quibble returns policy.

Also check out:
www.jewellerycatalogue.co.uk – guarantee low prices.
http://argenteus.co.uk – odd site but good for designer jewellery.
www.tateossian.com – great contemporary jewellery and accessories.

www.topbrands.net

WATCH HEAVEN

ORIGIN UK
SPEED ✓✓✓✓
INFO ✓✓✓✓
VALUE ✓✓✓✓
EASE ✓✓✓✓

A large range of watches including Swatch, Casio, G Shock, Baby G and Seiko are available here. The site is fast and easy-to-use, but a better search facility would save time. Delivery is free for the UK, but prices appear to be similar to the high street.

Finance, Banking and Shares

The Internet is proving to be a real winner when it comes to personal finance, product comparison and home share dealing, with these sites you will get the latest advice and may even make some money.

General finance information sites, directories and mortgages

www.fsa.gov.uk

FINANCIAL SERVICES AUTHORITY

ORIGIN UK
SPEED ✓✓✓✓
INFO ✓✓✓✓✓
EASE ✓✓✓✓

The regulating body that you can go to if you need help with your rights or if you want to find out about financial products; it will also help you to verify that the financial institution you're dealing with is legitimate. See also **www.oft.gov.uk** for the Office of Fair Trading and its informative site.

www.financial-ombudsman.org.uk

FINANCIAL OMBUDSMAN SERVICES

ORIGIN UK
SPEED ✓✓✓✓
INFO ✓✓✓✓✓
EASE ✓✓✓✓

When you have a complaint about a financial service this is a good point of call for sensible advice and help on how to go about getting a fair hearing.

www.checkmyfile.com

IS YOUR CREDIT GOOD?

ORIGIN UK
SPEED ✓✓✓✓
INFO ✓✓✓✓
VALUE ✓✓✓✓
EASE ✓✓✓✓

For £9.40 you can get a basic credit rating on your-self, or if you pay £19.99 they'll send you a more detailed report. Very useful and informative, they even keep updating your file for a yearly sum. You can also work out your likely credit score using their online calculator for free. Data protection is guaranteed too.

www.find.co.uk

INTERNET DIRECTORY FOR FINANCIAL SERVICES

ORIGIN UK
SPEED ✓✓✓✓
INFO ✓✓✓✓✓
EASE ✓✓✓✓

Access to over 6,000 financial sites; split into nine sections: life and pensions, investment, insurance, information, advice and share dealing, banking and saving, mortgages and loans, information services and a centre for Independent Financial Advisers. Superb.

www.ft.com
www.ftyourmoney.com

FINANCIAL TIMES

ORIGIN UK
SPEED ✓✓✓
INFO ✓✓✓✓
EASE ✓✓✓✓

FT.com offers up to date news and information. The 'Your Money' section is biased towards personal finance. Although it looks daunting, it is easy-to-use and provides sound, independent advice for everyone.

www.moneyextra.com

THE UK'S PERSONAL FINANCE GUIDE

ORIGIN UK
SPEED ✓✓✓
INFO ✓✓✓✓✓
EASE ✓✓✓✓

A very comprehensive personal finance guide; there are comparison tables for mortgages, loans and other financial services, advice for investors, an excellent financial glossary, tax and mortgage calculators. There's also an online mortgage broker with support from several leading lenders. In fact, it seems to cover everything financial.

www.fool.co.uk

THE MOTLEY FOOL

ORIGIN US
SPEED ✓✓✓
INFO ✓✓✓✓
EASE ✓✓✓✓

Finance with a sense of fun, The Fool is exciting and a real education in shrewdness. It not only takes the mystery out of share dealing but gives great advice on investment and personal finance. You need to register to get the best out of it, unfortunately, it has got very advert laden.

www.thisismoney.com
MONEY NEWS AND ADVICE

ORIGIN UK
SPEED ✓✓✓✓
INFO ✓✓✓✓✓
EASE ✓✓✓✓

Easy-to-use, reliable, 24-hour financial advice from the *Daily Mail* group. It has loads of information on all aspects of personal finance and is particularly good for comparison tools, especially mortgages, and there's a good 'Ask the Experts' section.

www.iii.co.uk
INTERACTIVE INVESTOR INTERNATIONAL

ORIGIN UK
SPEED ✓✓✓✓
INFO ✓✓✓✓✓
VALUE ✓✓✓✓
EASE ✓✓✓✓

Now known as Ample, the emphasis is on investment and share dealing with some personal finance thrown in. It retains the interactivity of the original site but with some additional investment information. Also can be reached through **www.ample.com**

www.blays.co.uk
BLAYS GUIDES

ORIGIN UK
SPEED ✓✓✓✓
INFO ✓✓✓✓✓
EASE ✓✓✓✓

Excellent design and impartial advice make the Blays guide a must visit site for personal finance. It has all the usual suspects: mortgages, savings etc, plus very good sections for students. There's also a comparative section for phone services and utilities.

www.moneynet.co.uk
IMPARTIAL AND COMPREHENSIVE

ORIGIN UK
SPEED ✓✓✓
INFO ✓✓✓✓
EASE ✓✓✓✓

Rated as one of the best independent personal finance sites, it covers over 100 mortgage lenders, has a user-friendly search facility plus help with conveyancing and financial calculators. It now also covers medical and life insurance well too.

For other similar sites go to:

www.marketplace.co.uk – 'independent' advisers from Bradford and Bingley help you make the right financial choices from mortgages to investments and pensions.

www.moneybrain.co.uk – a slick site offering a wide range of financial products and independent advice.

www.moneyfacts.co.uk – a no-nonsense information site which shows the cheapest and best value financial products with lots of authority, it's also a comparatively fast site and less tricky than some. It also covers annuities and offshore banking.

www.moneysupermarket.com – a very good all-rounder with help in most of the important areas of personal finance; good site layout and lots of practical advice add to the package.

www.sexymoney.co.uk – a good attempt at making money fun, in reality it offers solid advice on most aspects of finance.

www.unbiased.co.uk

FIND AN INDEPENDENT FINANCIAL ADVISER

ORIGIN UK
SPEED ✓✓✓✓
INFO ✓✓✓✓
EASE ✓✓✓✓

A good independent financial adviser is hard to come by, if you need one, then here's a good place to start. Just type in your postcode and the services you need and up pops a list of specialists in your area. See also **www.financialplanning.org.uk** for the Institute of Financial Planning and **www.sofa.org** for the Society of Financial Planners, both sites give information on how to get a financial adviser and plan your finances.

Mortgage specialists

www.charcoalonline.co.uk

JOHN CHARCOAL

ORIGIN	UK
SPEED	✓✓✓
INFO	✓✓✓✓
EASE	✓✓✓✓

This established mortgage adviser owned by Bradford & Bingley offers over 500 mortgages from over 45 lenders. There are also sections on pensions, investments and insurance.

It's worth shopping around so check out these sites too:

www.mortgages-online.co.uk – good independent source of information.

www.yourmortgage.co.uk – *Your Mortgage* magazine.

www.mortgagepoint.co.uk – geared towards first time buyers and those with a less than perfect credit history.

www.mortgageman.co.uk – aimed at the self-employed or those having difficulty getting a mortgage from the usual lenders, or with CCJs.

www.mortgagecode.org.uk

MORTGAGE CODE COMPLIANCE BOARD

ORIGIN	UK
SPEED	✓✓✓✓
INFO	✓✓✓✓✓
EASE	✓✓✓✓

The role of the mortgage board is to ensure that consumers are protected. They have a code of conduct that the lenders sign up to and they back that up by continually monitoring them. The site is packed with sensible information and help.

Insurance

www.insurancewide.com

HOME OF INSURANCE ON THE WEB

ORIGIN UK
SPEED ✓✓✓
INFO ✓✓✓✓✓
EASE ✓✓✓✓

Claiming to be the fastest way to get insurance cover, they offer a wide range of insurance policies covering life, travel, transport, home and business.

www.easycover.com

UK'S BIGGEST INDEPENDENT INSURANCE WEB SITE

ORIGIN UK
SPEED ✓✓✓
INFO ✓✓✓✓✓
EASE ✓✓✓✓✓

Here you can get a wide range of quotes just by filling in one form. The emphasis is on convenience and speed.

Other sites worth checking out:
www.theaa.com/services/insuranceandfinance/ –
   AA Insurance covers travel, cars and home.
www.screentrade.co.uk – the right deal on your
   motor, home and travel insurance.
www.quotelinedirect.co.uk – quotes on a wide range
   of insurance areas.
www.inspop.com – choose the specially selected
   policy and buy online.
www.insurancewide.com – cover from the top
   names in insurance.
www.morethan.com – hyped with the 'Where's
   Lucky' ads, this site is from Royal Sun Alliance
   and it's good for quotes in most areas including
   pets.

For advice on insurance or problems with insurance:
www.gisc.co.uk – General Insurance Standards
   Council, where to go if you have a problem,
   it is responsible for a code of conduct amongst
   insurers.

www.abi.org.uk – Association of British Insurers,
lots of advice on all aspects of insurance plus
industry information.

Investing and share dealing

www.schwab-worldwide.com

CHARLES SCHWAB EUROPE

ORIGIN US
SPEED ✓✓✓
INFO ✓✓✓✓✓
EASE ✓✓✓✓

Although you'll need to register and put up a deposit,
this is the biggest and probably the most reliable
Internet share dealer for the UK. You can trade online
from various different accounts depending on how
much you trade and your level of expertise.

*Any of the following are worth checking out, they
are all good sites, each with a slightly different
focus, so find the one that suits you.*

www.barclays-stockbrokers.co.uk – good value for
smaller share deals and possibly the best for
beginners. Can be slow.

www.tdwaterhouse.co.uk – slightly more expensive
than Barclays, but still quite good value, well
designed with good information to back it all up.

www.sharepeople.com – owned by American
Express, it has a nice design, is easy to use with
lots of explanation on how it all works. Costs
vary depending on the size of trade.

www.sharexpress.co.uk – the Halifax share dealing
service that is a good beginner's site and charges
competitively.

www.freeserve.advfn.com – incorporating
www.ukinvest.com – part of the Freeserve
network, its strengths are in news and company
information.

www.itsonline.co.uk – a well-designed site that
concentrates on explaining and campaigning for
investment trusts.

> **www.freequotes.co.uk** – an all singing and dancing site with the latest share information, tips and links to related and important sites.
>
> **http://uk.csfbdirect.com** – allows you to open an account to trade on the London stock exchange or to trade on the U.S. market. It's straightforward and offers a reliable service with good customer backup.
>
> **www.investorschronicle.co.uk** – this established magazine offers a useful site for share information and dealing, especially good for data on medium-sized and large companies.

Pensions

www.pensionsorter.com
FIND A PENSION

ORIGIN UK	Excellent site if you need help around the pensions
SPEED ✓✓✓✓	minefield, with lots of jargon-free and independent
INFO ✓✓✓✓✓	information. It tells you how to buy one, how much
EASE ✓✓✓✓✓	you should be paying and advice on what you
	should be saving if you want a golden retirement.

www.pensionguide.gov.uk
KNOW YOUR OPTIONS

ORIGIN UK	An impartial guide to pensions from the
SPEED ✓✓✓✓	government, which aims to help you choose the
INFO ✓✓✓✓✓	right option, there's also information for employers
EASE ✓✓✓✓✓	and current pension holders.

www.PensionsNetwork.com
STAKEHOLDER PENSIONS

ORIGIN UK	A good site dedicated to bringing you the best value
SPEED ✓✓✓✓	stakeholder pensions. It's easy to use and comes
INFO ✓✓✓✓	with a good pensions calculator.
EASE ✓✓✓✓	

For more information on pensions see:

www.opra.gov.uk – the Occupational Pensions Regulatory Authority ensures pension schemes are run properly.

www.dwp.gov.uk – the Department for Work and Pensions represents the government line on pensions and gives good advice and the latest news.

www.opas.org.uk – the Office of the Pensions Advisory Service helps when things go wrong.

Banks

www.bankfacts.org.uk

BRITISH BANKERS ASSOCIATION

ORIGIN UK
SPEED ✓✓✓
INFO ✓✓✓✓✓
EASE ✓✓✓✓

Answers to the most common questions about banking, advice about Internet banks, the banking code and general information. There's also a facility that helps you resurrect dormant accounts. See also **www.bankingcode.org.uk** where you can find details of the standards of service that all the banks have signed up to.

Here are the high street and Internet banks, building societies and the online facilities they currently offer:

www.abbeynational.co.uk – full service up and running including a very competitive Internet-only savings account. Following the trend for high street banks to set up Internet-only banks with wacky names, Abbey National have set up Cahoot at **www.cahoot.com** and they also offer a competitive service wrapped up in a neat web site.

www.alliance-leicester.co.uk – a comprehensive service offering mortgages, insurance and banking.

www.bankofscotland.co.uk – good all-rounder with business banking included on the site, along with services for students and young people.

www.barclays.co.uk – one of the original innovators in Internet banking, they offer an exhaustive service covering all aspects of personal and small business banking.

www.bradford-bingley.co.uk – defaults to **www.marketplace.co.uk** – see page 125.

www.citibank.co.uk – very impressive site with a complete Internet personal banking service with competitive rates. Citibank have few branches and this is their attempt at a bigger foothold in the UK.

www.co-operativebank.co.uk – acknowledged as the most comprehensive of the banking sites and it's easy to use. Excellent, but they have also launched the trendier and more competitive Smile banking site **www.smile.co.uk** which is aimed at a younger audience.

www.egg.co.uk – low rates combined with an attempt at individuality make Egg a bank with a difference. Caters for the young by offering WAP banking plus all the usual facilities.

www.halifax.co.uk – comprehensive range of services via an easy-to-use and well-designed site and you'll find a great deal of advice and infor-mation all clearly explained. Their Internet-only banking offshoot is called Intelligent Finance, which is excellent and can be found at the memorable **www.if.com**

www.banking.hsbc.co.uk – straightforward and easy-to-use site offering online banking alongside the usual services from HSBC, like most other big banks they've also launched a trendier Internet bank called **www.firstdirect.co.uk** which offers all the expected features plus WAP banking from an impressive site.

www.lloydstsb.co.uk – combined with Scottish Widows, The Post Office (Consignia) and Cheltenham and Gloucester, Lloyds offer a more rounded and comprehensive financial service than most. The online banking is well established and efficient. They provide help for small businesses too.

www.nationwide.co.uk – don't be put off by the dated appearance of the Nationwide site which looks rather like a tabloid newspaper, they offer a complete online banking service as well as loans and mortgages.

www.natwest.com – NatWest offer both online and WAP banking and share dealing, with good sections for students and small businesses. It's got a nice design, it's straightforward and there is a non-animated version as well.

www.newcastlenet.co.uk – a nice-looking and easy-to-use site from one of the smaller banking/building societies, offering all the usual services including online mortgage applications.

www.woolwich.co.uk – online banking and a WAP mobile phone banking service plus all the other usual personal financial services make the Woolwich site a little different.

www.virgin-direct.co.uk – access to Virgin's comprehensive financial services site featuring a share dealing service, pension advice, banking, mortgages and general financial advice.

www.standardchartered.com – good looking and user-friendly site from this small bank.

www.ybs.co.uk – a good all-rounder from the Yorkshire Building Society.

www.switchwithwhich.co.uk

SWITCH BANK ACCOUNTS EASILY

ORIGIN UK
SPEED ✓✓✓✓
INFO ✓✓✓✓
EASE ✓✓✓✓

Which? Magazine's site devoted to a campaign to encouraging people to switch to less costly bank accounts. There is advice on the best account for you and how to move your account to the recommended account one painlessly.

Tax

www.inlandrevenue.gov.uk

TALK TO THE TAXMAN

ORIGIN UK
SPEED ✓✓✓✓
INFO ✓✓✓✓✓
EASE ✓✓✓

The Inland Revenue has a very informative site where you can get help on all aspects of tax. You can even submit your tax return over the Internet and there's a good set of links to other government departments.

www.tax.org.uk

CHARTERED INSTITUTE OF TAXATION

ORIGIN UK
SPEED ✓✓✓
INFO ✓✓✓✓✓
EASE ✓✓✓

A great resource, they don't provide information on individual questions but they can put you in touch with a qualified adviser. It's a good place to start if you have a problem with your tax. For the latest tax news go to **http://e-tax.org.uk**, which is comprehensive and has an excellent set of links. For a list of sites all relating to tax go to **www.taxsites.com**

http://listen.to/taxman

THE TAX CALCULATOR

ORIGIN UK
SPEED ✓✓✓
INFO ✓✓✓✓
EASE ✓✓✓✓✓

Amazingly fast, just input your gross earnings and your tax and actual earnings are calculated.

Business

www.economist.com

THE ECONOMIST MAGAZINE

ORIGIN UK
SPEED ✓✓✓✓✓
INFO ✓✓✓✓✓
EASE ✓✓✓✓

The airports' best-selling magazine goes online with a wide-ranging site that covers business and politics worldwide. You can get access to the archive and also their excellent country surveys. If you're in business you need this in your favourites box.

www.asiannet.com

BUSINESS INFORMATION ON ASIA

ORIGIN US
SPEED ✓✓✓
INFO ✓✓✓✓
EASE ✓✓✓

Market information, news, services and links all geared to the main Asian markets each of which has a feature site. There are company profiles as well as an online shop where you can contact companies to get product samples.

www.islamiq.com

ISLAMIC FINANCE AND BUSINESS

ORIGIN UK
SPEED ✓✓✓✓
INFO ✓✓✓✓✓
EASE ✓✓✓✓

Excellent British site aimed at being in their words 'a finance and investment portal synchronised with Islamic principles'. There is a great deal of information about personal finance, share dealing and investing as well as news and shopping. Can be slow.

www.uk.sage.com

BUSINESS SOFTWARE

ORIGIN UK
SPEED ✓✓✓
INFO ✓✓✓✓
VALUE ✓✓✓
EASE ✓✓✓✓

If you need accounting software to solve virtually any sort of problem or provide a new service, you should find it here. Sage has a good reputation for helping small businesses.

Debt management

www.nacab.org.uk
CITIZENS ADVICE BUREAU

ORIGIN UK
SPEED ✓✓✓
INFO ✓✓✓✓✓
EASE ✓✓✓✓

Often the first port of call for people with debt issues, the site offers useful information and the latest campaigns. There's a search facility to find your nearest office and a link to www.adviceguide.org.uk which contains basic advice and information on your rights.

See also:
www.debtcounsellors.co.uk – specialists in advising people on what to do if they get into financial difficulty and dealing with creditors.
www.debtadvicecentre.co.uk – lots of useful advice and information on what to do if you find yourself in debt; excellent for links.

Miscellaneous

www.young-money.co.uk
ONLINE MONEY GAME SHOW

ORIGIN UK
SPEED ✓✓✓
INFO ✓✓✓✓
EASE ✓✓✓✓

Combines general knowledge and financial games aimed at turning the little ones into financial whiz-kids of the future. There's a lot that most adults can learn from the site as well as it's a fun way of learning about the world of finance. You need Shockwave for it to work.

www.ifs.org.uk
INSTITUTE OF FISCAL STUDIES

ORIGIN UK
SPEED ✓✓✓✓
INFO ✓✓✓✓
EASE ✓✓✓✓

Independent analysis of all things financial especially the tax system, surprisingly interesting but a pretty dull site.

www.paypal.com

SEND AND RECEIVE MONEY ONLINE

ORIGIN UK
SPEED ✓✓✓✓
INFO ✓✓✓✓
EASE ✓✓✓✓

A genuinely useful service, especially for small businesses and online auction junkies, it's very easy and straightforward to use. There's a directory of over 25,000 web sites that use paypal and details of how your site can get involved.

Finding Someone

Following the success of Friends Reunited, there's been a massive explosion of sites dedicated to finding old friends and colleagues. Here we've listed all the best sites, and also the place to go to find a phone number, contacts for business and the home.

Directory sites

www.yell.co.uk

THE YELLOW PAGES ONLINE – JUST YELL!

ORIGIN UK
SPEED ✓✓✓
INFO ✓✓✓✓✓
EASE ✓✓✓✓✓

There are basically three sections:
1 Its primary service is the search engine – this enables you to search for the business or service you want by region, type or name. It is very quick, and you get plenty of details on each entry.
2 Offers a number of guides which provide links on films, health, motoring, shopping, property, weather and weddings.
3 Business – provides sections on international trading, UK business, recruitment and financial information.

There is an equivalent service in the USA with the intriguing title of **www.bigfoot.com** It is very similar to Yell, except there is a feature that enables you to search for personal e-mail addresses, as well as business ones. They also offer an e-mail and a mobile messaging service. If you're still stuck then try **www.bigyellow.com**

www.scoot.co.uk

THE SIMPLE WAY TO FIND A BUSINESS

ORIGIN UK
SPEED ✓✓✓
INFO ✓✓✓✓✓
EASE ✓✓✓✓✓

Register, type in the person's name or profession then hit the scoot button and the answer comes back in seconds. Oriented towards finding businesses but useful nonetheless. There's also a cinema finder.

www.thomweb.co.uk

THE ANSWER COMES OUT OF THE BLUE

ORIGIN UK
SPEED ✓✓✓✓
INFO ✓✓✓✓✓
EASE ✓✓✓✓

Thomson's offer an impressive site and provide local directories online. It's divided up into five major categories:

1 A business finder – search using a combination of name, type of business or region.
2 People finder – track down phone numbers and home or e-mail addresses.
3 Comprehensive local information – available on the major cities and regions.
4 News.
5 Net search and directory.

www.phonenumbers.net

VIRTUALLY EVERYONE WHO'S LISTED

ORIGIN EUROPE
SPEED ✓✓✓✓
INFO ✓✓✓✓
EASE ✓✓✓✓

Start by clicking on the country or area you need, then you can easily find the phone, fax or e-mail address of anyone who is in the book. It also has a section with a number of links to other search engines such as Yell.

www.bt.com

BRITISH TELECOM SERVICES

ORIGIN UK
SPEED ✓✓
INFO ✓✓✓✓
EASE ✓✓

BT offers a site that gives a very thorough overview of its services. To get the best out of it you need to register; have your account number handy and you can view your telephone bill. It's pretty slow and access to the main services isn't exactly obvious.

See also:

www.ukphonebook.com – simple to use, quick with a no-nonsense design, also has mapping, a business finder and lots of adverts.

www.anywho.com – straightforward American-oriented search site.

www.infospace.com – another good search engine with yellow (business) and white (people) pages sections.

www.royalmail.co.uk – The mail may have a silly name nowadays but this site offers a useful address finder and you can track your recorded deliveries too.

www.emailaddresses.com – a free e-mail directory plus other information relating to e-mails.

www.192.com

THE UK'S LARGEST DIRECTORY SERVICE

ORIGIN UK
SPEED ✓✓✓✓
INFO ✓✓✓✓
VALUE ✓✓✓
EASE ✓✓✓✓

192 has changed, there's now more available for non-fee payers such as people and business finders, directories and route planning. There are also various subscription options, providing access to other databases such as the electoral role, company reports and the UK-info CD.

Finding old friends

www.friendsreunited.co.uk

THE ONE STOP SITE TO REUNITE

ORIGIN UK
SPEED ✓✓✓
INFO ✓✓✓✓
EASE ✓✓✓✓✓

Possibly the UK's most visited web site nowadays. It's a phenomenal success story and millions of people have made contact with old friends using the site. To get the best out of it you have to register which costs £5. For that you get access to the schools and workplace data base and the ability to contact people through the site. It's very easy to use and you'll quickly lose yourself.

See also:
www.school-friends.co.uk – similar to Friends Reunited but with a very good search facility.
www.gradfinder.com – good site covering much of the world's schools and universities.
www.arielbruce.com – Ariel Bruce is an ex-social worker with a good track record of finding missing people.
www.missing-you.net – free message posting designed to help find lost friends thought to be in the UK.
www.peopletracer.co.uk – people traced for a fee – from £15.

Three very similar sites dedicated to re-uniting old service colleagues:
www.armedforcesfriends.co.uk
www.servicepals.com
www.the-ex-forces-network.org.uk

www.andys-penpals.com

FIND A PENPAL

ORIGIN UK
SPEED ✓✓✓✓
INFO ✓✓✓✓
EASE ✓✓✓✓

A site devoted to penpals around the world, covering 95 countries. It's easy to use and free; there are also links to similar sites and a chat room.

Flowers

www.interflora.co.uk

TURNING THOUGHTS INTO FLOWERS

ORIGIN UK
SPEED ✓✓✓✓
INFO ✓✓✓✓
VALUE ✓✓✓
EASE ✓✓✓✓

Interflora can send flowers to over 140 countries, many on the same day as the order. They'll have a selection to send for virtually every occasion and they offer a reminder service. The service is excellent, although they are not very up front on delivery costs, which can be high. If you can't get what you need here then try www.teleflorist.co.uk who offer a similar service.

www.flyingflowers.com

EUROPE'S LEADING FLOWERS BY POST COMPANY

ORIGIN UK
SPEED ✓✓✓✓
INFO ✓✓✓✓
VALUE ✓✓✓
EASE ✓✓✓✓

Freshly picked flowers flown from Jersey to the UK from £8.99. All prices include delivery and you save at least £1 on all bouquets against their standard advertised off-line prices. They'll also arrange next day delivery in the UK. The site is simple and there's a reminder service just to make sure you don't forget anyone.

www.clareflorist.co.uk

STYLISH BOUQUETS AND PRETTY PICTURES

ORIGIN UK
SPEED ✓✓✓✓
INFO ✓✓✓✓
VALUE ✓✓✓✓
EASE ✓✓✓✓

You know what you're sending as all the bouquets are photographed. Cost reflects the sophistication of the flowers. Easy to use with good customer services and free delivery to UK with surcharge for same day delivery.

www.daisys2roses.com
MAKE YOUR OWN BOUQUET

ORIGIN UK	A simple, step-by-step approach to making up a
SPEED ✓✓	bouquet of your choice. You can select from a large
INFO ✓✓✓✓	range of flowers and there's help to get you started,
VALUE ✓✓✓	you can even search by flower type. Delivery is
EASE ✓✓✓✓	free in the UK. Unfortunately, the process is a bit
	laborious, but persistence pays.

Food and Drink

Whether you want to order from the comfort of your own home, indulge yourself, find the latest food news or get a recipe, this collection of sites will fulfil your foodie desires. It features super-markets, online magazines and information sites, specialist food retailers, vegetarian and organic stockists, drinks information and suppliers, where to go for kitchen equipment and help in finding the best places when eating out.

Supermarkets and general food stores

www.icelandfreeshop.com
FROZEN FOOD SPECIALIST DELIVERS

ORIGIN UK	Iceland's online service is considered one of the best
SPEED ✓✓	with nearly all of the UK covered. Easy to navigate,
INFO ✓✓✓✓	but can be ponderous to use. Your order is saved
VALUE ✓✓✓	each time, which then acts as the basis for your next
EASE ✓✓✓✓	order. Information on the products is good, and
	there's a wide range available; orders must be £40
	or more.

www.waitrose.com

IF YOU ARE REALLY INTO FOOD

ORIGIN	UK
SPEED	✓✓✓
INFO	✓✓✓✓✓
VALUE	✓✓✓
EASE	✓✓✓✓

Waitrose is offering a very good comprehensive and well designed site that oozes quality, so it's a pleasure to do your grocery shopping online. You can buy wine, gifts, organics and some John Lewis products. In addition it also has all the features you'd expect from an Internet Service Provider, including the fab Waitrose *Illustrated Food* Magazine, *Hardens Restaurant* Guide, gardening and travel sections along with news and even a section on food education.

www.tesco.co.uk

THE LIFESTYLE SUPERSTORE

ORIGIN	UK
SPEED	✓✓✓
INFO	✓✓✓✓
VALUE	✓✓✓✓
EASE	✓✓✓✓

This functional site has a comprehensive offering and they've improved it visually. Food aside, there's a wide range of goods on offer though, including electrical goods, clothes and books. There's also a section on personal finance, other shops, parenting advice and healthy living.

www.sainsburys.co.uk

NOT JUST GOOD TASTE

ORIGIN	UK
SPEED	✓✓✓✓
INFO	✓✓✓✓✓
VALUE	✓✓✓
EASE	✓✓✓✓

Sainsbury's site is similar, (but jollier) in content to Tesco, it's more fun to use, and faster too, with the emphasis being on good food, cooking, recommendation and taste. The facility to place an advance order at their Calais store, which you can then pick up, and pay for in France, will appeal to those who wish to save time on their booze run.

www.somerfield.co.uk

MEGADEALS

ORIGIN	UK
SPEED	✓✓✓✓
INFO	✓✓✓
VALUE	✓✓✓
EASE	✓✓✓✓

The emphasis is firmly on offers with a rolling feature, which changes every few seconds, but there's also a recipe finder, wine guide and essential food facts. Delivery covers most of the UK and it's free if you spend more than £25, provided you live near enough to the store.

www.asda.co.uk

VALUE MAD

ORIGIN	UK
SPEED	✓✓
INFO	✓✓✓✓
VALUE	✓✓✓✓✓
EASE	✓✓✓

A comparatively dull site. There's lots of information about the company and what it stands for plus links to its online shop. There are also sections on insurance, gardening, health and parenting information plus the clothing brand George. Delivery is £3.50, but free if you spend more than £99.

www.safeway.co.uk

FOR THE FAMILY WITH YOUNG CHILDREN

ORIGIN	UK
SPEED	✓✓✓
INFO	✓✓✓✓
EASE	✓✓✓✓

A much better offering from Safeway than the last time we reviewed it. It provides much in the way of information on lifestyle subjects including cookery advice, recipes, a drinks guide and advice on healthy eating. There's no online shopping though.

www.heinz-direct.co.uk

DELIVERING MORE THAN 57 VARIETIES OF FOOD

ORIGIN	UK
SPEED	✓✓
INFO	✓✓✓
VALUE	✓✓✓✓
EASE	✓✓✓✓

To get the best value for money it's best to order in bulk, as delivery charges can be high. It can be very slow to use and is split into product feature sections: Weightwatchers, canned grocery, Heinz and Farley's baby food, hampers, and sauces and pickles.

www.homefarmfoods.com

DELICIOUS FROZEN FOOD DELIVERED FREE

ORIGIN UK	Good selection of frozen foods and huge range of
SPEED ✓✓✓	ready meals with a good use of symbols indicating
INFO ✓✓✓	whether the product is low fat, microwavable,
VALUE ✓✓✓✓✓	vegetarian etc. With free delivery, it's especially
EASE ✓✓✓✓	good value, and there is no minimum order.

See also **www.foodhall.co.uk** who have a good selection of specialist stores to choose from.

www.farmersmarkets.net

NATIONAL ASSOCIATION OF FARMERS' MARKETS

ORIGIN UK	A farmers' market sells locally produced goods,
SPEED ✓✓✓✓	locate your nearest market or get advice on how to
INFO ✓✓✓✓	set one up.
EASE ✓✓✓✓	

www.fresh-fish-online.co.uk

FRESH FISH DELIVERED

ORIGIN UK	A Devon company who own their own trawlers will
SPEED ✓✓✓✓	deliver overnight so that your fish is very fresh. They
INFO ✓✓✓✓	also deliver frozen, shell fish and smoked fish.
VALUE ✓✓✓	Delivery costs vary but it's free if you spend over £60.
EASE ✓✓✓✓	

Asian and Indian cookery

www.curryhouse.co.uk

EVERYTHING YOU NEED TO KNOW ABOUT CURRY

ORIGIN UK	Curryholics can get their fill of recipes, recommen-
SPEED ✓✓✓	dations, taste tests, interviews with famous chefs
INFO ✓✓✓✓✓	and a restaurant guide. Spices and curry mixes can
VALUE ✓✓✓	be bought from Chilli Willies online shop, orders
EASE ✓✓✓✓✓	charged from £2.99 p&p.

See also:
www.thecurryguide.co.uk – messy site with a guide
   to Indian restaurants.
www.curryworld.com – the home of National Curry
   Day.
www.currysauce.com – get all the sauces delivered
   and even win a year's supply.
www.currybox.com – spices for curry delivered to
   your door postage paid, some recipes too.

www.chopstix.com

CHINESE AND ASIAN COOKERY NEWSLETTER

ORIGIN UK
SPEED ✓✓✓✓
INFO ✓✓✓
EASE ✓✓✓✓

An e-mailed newsletter with contributors such as
Ken Hom. It also offers advice guides on food
preparation and how to use the utensils.

www.orientalfood.com

ASIAN COOKING COVERED

ORIGIN US
SPEED ✓✓✓✓
INFO ✓✓✓✓
EASE ✓✓✓✓

Masses of information on all forms of Asian cuisine
including a Chinese recipe archive, nutritional information and articles on food culture. There's also a
links section with a good range of oriental food
stores to visit.

www.straitscafe.com

RECIPES FROM SINGAPORE

ORIGIN SINGAPORE
SPEED ✓✓✓✓
INFO ✓✓✓✓
EASE ✓✓✓✓

A straightforward site with lots of recipes not only
from Singapore, but also Japan and China, there's
also a good set of links and a gallery. For Indonesian
cooking go to the enjoyable Henks Hot Kitchen
which can be found at **www.indochef.com**

www.japanweb.co.uk

JAPANESE CUISINE

ORIGIN JAPAN
SPEED ✓✓✓✓
INFO ✓✓✓✓
VALUE ✓✓✓
EASE ✓✓✓✓

An interesting and growing site covering the basics of Japanese cooking along with recipes and a UK restaurant guide. It also has a glossary and tips on etiquette. 'Itadakimasu' as they say. See also www.yosushi.com who offer a hi-tech site which feature their restaurants and a sushi ordering service.

www.thaifood2.com

DIRECTORY AND RECIPES

ORIGIN US
SPEED ✓✓✓✓
INFO ✓✓✓
EASE ✓✓✓✓

A directory of Thai food around the world with links to related sites. See also www.thaicuisine.com which is a more rounded site with recipes and ingredient information, and www.tat.or.th/food/ which has a good overview.

See also:
www.asiarecipe.com – a messy site with a range of recipes and ingredients covering the whole of Asia.

www.chinatown-online.co.uk – what's on in London's China Town; it has an excellent food section.

www.chinesefood.org – our old favourite is being revamped but if the old site is anything to go by, then it'll be worth a visit.

www.chinavista.com/culture/cuisine/recipes.html – a listing of over 100 Chinese recipes.

www.spiceadvice.com – useful spice encyclopedia from this American spice retailer who doesn't ship outside the US.

Barbecues

www.barbecuen.com
BARBECUES

ORIGIN	US	In the unlikely event that our weather will be good
SPEED	✓✓✓	enough to have a barbecue, then here's a site with
INFO	✓✓✓✓✓	all you need to know on the subject. See also
EASE	✓✓✓✓	www.britishbarbecue.co.uk

British and Irish cookery

www.hwatson.force9.co.uk
BEST OF BRITISH

ORIGIN	UK	Helen Watson is a champion of British cuisine and
SPEED	✓✓	here you'll find her online cookbook, there's also a
INFO	✓✓✓✓	magazine and a guide to regional cooking. The site
EASE	✓✓✓✓	is slow but the content is very good. Check out
		www.greatbritishkitchen.co.uk too, and also
		www.recipes4us.co.uk who have over 2,000 recipes
		although some are international.

www.btinternet.com/~scottishcookery/
CLASSIC SCOTTISH COOKERY

ORIGIN	UK	You need patience with this site but again the
SPEED	✓✓✓	recipes are well worth the wait, and they are well
INFO	✓✓✓	illustrated.
EASE	✓✓✓✓	

www.tasteofireland.com
A TASTE OF IRELAND

ORIGIN	UK	Recipes, a restaurant guide and a shop all in one, it's
SPEED	✓✓✓	not that comprehensive but well worth a visit
INFO	✓✓✓	nonetheless.
EASE	✓✓✓✓	

www.red4.co.uk/recipes.htm

WELSH RECIPES

ORIGIN UK
SPEED ✓✓✓
INFO ✓✓✓
EASE ✓✓✓✓

Here are over 120 traditional recipes including lava bread, wines, cawl and Welshcakes.

www.baxters.co.uk

TRADITIONAL FARE

ORIGIN UK
SPEED ✓✓✓
INFO ✓✓✓✓
VALUE ✓✓✓
EASE ✓✓✓✓

An old Scottish firm offering their range of soups, jams, sauces, hampers and gift foods online through a well-designed and easy-to-use site; there are also recipes from top chef Nick Nairn. Shipping charges vary according to destination.

Celebrity chefs

www.delia.co.uk

DELIA SMITH

ORIGIN UK
SPEED ✓✓✓✓
INFO ✓✓✓✓
EASE ✓✓✓✓

The queen of British cookery has a clean, well-designed site with lots of recipes, which can be accessed by the good search facility. If you join you get added features such as daily tips, competitions and the chance to chat to Delia. There's also a section on what Delia is up to and you can ask questions and get advice at the cookery school. In the past year a shop has been added to the site, it has a wide range of products which are supplied via other online retailers.

www.jamieoliver.net
WHAT HE'S ABOUT

ORIGIN UK
SPEED ✓✓✓
INFO ✓✓✓
EASE ✓✓✓

A rather strange looking opening page but here is a site offering all you need to know about Jamie, it has some good features such as the kids' club which is designed to get kids cooking, recipies and also a game called the Pukkatron. There's also a few pictures to download, Jamie's diary to read and you can buy the books too.

www.bbc.co.uk/food/garyrhodes
GARY RHODES

ORIGIN UK
SPEED ✓✓✓
INFO ✓✓✓✓
EASE ✓✓✓✓

A page from the BBC web site, tied to his TV program, it offers seasonal recipes and links to related sites.

www.rickstein.co.uk
PADSTOW, STEIN AND SEAFOOD

ORIGIN UK
SPEED ✓✓✓
INFO ✓✓✓✓
VALUE ✓✓✓
EASE ✓✓✓✓

Information on Rick, his restaurants and cookery school all wrapped up in a tidy web site. You can also book a table or a room as well as order products from the online deli.

www.rosemary-conley.co.uk
CONLEY'S DIET AND FITNESS CLUBS

ORIGIN UK
SPEED ✓✓✓
INFO ✓✓✓✓
EASE ✓✓✓✓

Get information on how to stay fit and keep healthy as well as recipes and details of her books.

www.kenhom.com
KEN HOM

ORIGIN UK
SPEED ✓✓✓✓
INFO ✓✓✓
EASE ✓✓✓✓

A web site that rhymes! Ken's site is nicely designed and has a small selection of recipes and products, which you can buy.

Cheese

www.cheese.com
IT'S ALL ABOUT CHEESE!

ORIGIN US
SPEED ✓✓✓✓
INFO ✓✓✓✓✓
EASE ✓✓✓✓

Not a shop, but a huge resource site about 652 types of cheese. There's advice about the best way to eat cheese, a vegetarian section, a cheese bookshop and links to other cheese-related sites and online stores. You can even find a suitable cheese searching by texture, country or type of milk. For more cheese information try the attractive Cheesenet site at **http://cheesenet.wgx.com**, it has an excellent search facility, or the American Dairy Association's **www.ilovecheese.com** which also offers a cheese guide and lots of recipes.

www.cheesemongers.co.uk
OPULENT SITE FROM UK'S OLDEST CHEESEMONGERS

ORIGIN UK
SPEED ✓✓✓✓
INFO ✓✓✓✓
VALUE ✓✓
EASE ✓✓✓✓

Paxton and Whitfield, the royal cheesemongers, provide a very clear and easy-to-use online shop but charge £7.50 to ship goods. A superb selection of cheese and luxury produce, with hampers, cheese kitchen, accessories and wine. A pleasure to browse and it's tempting to buy; you can also join the Cheese Society.

www.teddingtoncheese.co.uk
BRITISH AND CONTINENTAL CHEESEMONGERS

ORIGIN UK
SPEED ✓✓✓
INFO ✓✓✓✓
VALUE ✓✓✓
EASE ✓✓✓✓

Much-acclaimed site offering over 130 types of cheese at competitive prices. The sections are split by country and there's a good system for showing whether the cheese is suitable for vegetarians, pregnant women, etc. There is also a small selection of wine and other produce; you can even design your own hamper. When buying you can stipulate how much cheese you want in grams (150 minimum), shipping from £5.95 for the UK.

www.fromages.com

TRADITIONAL FRENCH CHEESE

ORIGIN FRANCE
SPEED ✓✓✓✓
INFO ✓✓✓✓
VALUE ✓✓
EASE ✓✓✓✓

French cheese available to order and delivered within 24 hours along with wine recommendations and express shipping from France. Delivery is included in the price but if you're worried about cost you probably shouldn't be shopping here.

Confectionery, cake and chocolate

www.chocexpress.com

DEDICATED TO GOOD CHOCOLATE

ORIGIN UK
SPEED ✓✓✓✓
INFO ✓✓✓✓
VALUE ✓✓✓✓
EASE ✓✓✓✓

An excellent and well-illustrated site from an experienced retailer, they also offer lots of choice and a wide range of chocolate-related gifts and you can even buy in bulk! There's a really good selection facility and the chocolate tasting club. Delivery starts at £3.50 and they will guarantee that it's delivered by a specified date.

www.thorntons.co.uk

WELCOME TO CHOCOLATE HEAVEN

ORIGIN UK
SPEED ✓✓✓✓
INFO ✓✓✓
VALUE ✓✓✓
EASE ✓✓✓✓

Thorntons offer a comprehensive and easy-to-use site, with an emphasis on gifts. The range is extensive and they supply worldwide – at a cost. Orders costs start at £2.99 for the UK. There are product sections for continental, premier, gifts and hampers plus flowers and wine.

www.cakeandcookie.co.uk

FOR ALL SPECIAL OCCASIONS

ORIGIN UK
SPEED ✓✓✓✓
INFO ✓✓
VALUE ✓✓
EASE ✓✓✓✓

Order a selection of cakes and cookies, personalise them and send them to any one of 86 countries. Delivery charges vary and there's also a corporate service.

www.pastrywiz.com

PASTRY HEAVEN

ORIGIN US

SPEED ✓✓✓✓

INFO ✓✓✓✓

EASE ✓✓✓✓

A general food site with the emphasis on pastry in all its forms, there are plenty of recipes and links to keep all cake fans happy.

Diet and nutrition

www.3fatchicks.com

THE SOURCE FOR DIET SUPPORT

ORIGIN US

SPEED ✓✓✓✓

INFO ✓✓✓✓✓

EASE ✓✓✓✓✓

The awesome Three Fat Chicks have produced one of the best food web sites. It's entertaining and informative about dieting or trying to stay healthy. There are food reviews, how to live on fast food, recipes, links to other low fat sites, a section for chocoholics, diet tips and 'tool box' which has calorie tables and calculators; also getting started, on losing weight and how to get free samples.

www.cookinglight.com

THE BEST FROM COOKING LIGHT MAGAZINE

ORIGIN US

SPEED ✓✓

INFO ✓✓✓✓

EASE ✓✓✓✓

One of the world's best-selling food magazines, their slow site offers a huge selection of healthy recipes and step-by-step guides to cooking. There are also articles on healthy living.

www.weightwatchers.co.uk

WELCOME TO WEIGHTWATCHERS UK

ORIGIN UK

SPEED ✓✓✓✓

INFO ✓✓✓

VALUE ✓✓✓

EASE ✓✓✓✓

A much improved site with more information on how to lose weight, keep motivated, keep fit, chat and, of course, where to find your local group. There's also a shop where you can buy specially selected foods and related diet products – delivery starts at £2.

http://atkinscenter.com

DR ATKINS

ORIGIN	UK
SPEED	✓✓✓✓
INFO	✓✓✓
VALUE	✓✓✓
EASE	✓✓✓✓

The world's best selling dietician offers a site that gives the background to his low carbohydrate diet and how you can lose weight and get healthy on it. For a more straightforward approach try www.low-carb.com who have a good online shop.

www.mynutrition.co.uk

ONLINE GUIDE TO HEALTHY EATING

ORIGIN	UK
SPEED	✓✓✓✓
INFO	✓✓✓✓
VALUE	✓✓
EASE	✓✓✓✓

Find out what you really should be eating from this cool British site, which has been put together by a professional nutritionist. It features:

Myconditions – an alphabetical listing of diseases and ailments with a short description of what effect they have on the diet, and advice on dietary needs and supplements.

Mynews – a newsletter with all the latest information on nutrition.

Mylibrary – with articles and book excerpts by the sites author.

Myconsultation – fill in a questionnaire about your health and get the dietary advice on eating and supplements.

Mystuff – records how you get on after the consultation so that when you revisit you can check on progress.

In Myshopping – buy those vitamins and supplements that have been recommended.

For all its beauty and efficiency, you can't help thinking that this is just a very good vehicle for selling vitamins and supplements. Delivery is £1.50 for the UK.

See also:

www.caloriecontrol.org – low fat information from the Calorie Control Council

www.eatwellcard.co.uk – personal dietary advice

www.fatfreekitchen.com – Indian vegetarian and
low fat recipes

http://lowfatcooking.about.com/ – a well presented
and informative section from the About website

www.fatfree.com – some 5,000 recipes all fat free or
very low fat

www.cyberdiet.com – a good all rounder with a
wide range of advice, including specialist diets.

SPECIAL DIETARY NEEDS

www.diabeticgourmet.com

DELICIOUS FOR DIABETICS

ORIGIN UK	Lots of recipes and ideas to make food palatable
SPEED ✓✓✓✓	without endangering your blood sugar levels from
INFO ✓✓✓✓	*Diabetic Gourmet* magazine, see also
EASE ✓✓✓✓	www.diabetic.com/cookbook/ where there's a great
	archive of recipes.

www.gfcfdiet.com/

GLUTEN FREE

ORIGIN UK	Not a great site but it has very good information on
SPEED ✓✓✓	gluten free products and food. See also
INFO ✓✓✓✓	www.celiac.com who have some good recipes and
EASE ✓✓✓	www.glutenfreemall.com whose temperamental site
	has lots of information on products, although they
	don't deliver to the UK at time of writing.

Also refer to the section on health, page 209.

French food

www.gourmet2000.co.uk

LE GOURMET FRANÇAIS

ORIGIN	UK	High quality French ingredients and recipes, combined
SPEED	✓✓✓✓	with a nicely designed site and convenient shopping.
INFO	✓✓✓✓	Delivery is very pricey at £7.99 for the minimum £20
VALUE	✓✓	order, but once you spend £100 it's free.
EASE	✓✓✓✓	

http://frenchfood.about.com

FRENCH CUISINE

ORIGIN	US	About.com have created a superb resource at this
SPEED	✓✓✓✓	site with a huge amount of data, articles and recipes.
INFO	✓✓✓✓✓	Every aspect of French cooking seems to be covered
EASE	✓✓✓✓	from the ingredients to the shops and presentation.

See also:

www.afrenchkiss.com – make your own gourmet
   meals with this fun French recipe creation
   program.

www.manoir.com – world class recipes from
   Raymond Blanc as well as details of his hotels
   and restaurants.

Hygiene and food safety

www.foodsafety.gov/~fsg/fsgadvic.html

FOOD SAFETY

ORIGIN	UK	A government site with basic advice on handling
SPEED	✓✓✓	foods in all sorts of situations from product-specific
INFO	✓✓✓✓	advice to helping those with special needs; there's
EASE	✓✓✓✓	also good links to related topics. See also

www.foodstandards.gov.uk home of the Food
Standards Association who have lots of information
on what is safe to eat.

Italian food

www.mangiarebene.net

EAT WELL

ORIGIN US	An award-winning site that covers everything to do
SPEED ✓✓✓✓	with Italian cookery. Its aim is to give a grand tour
INFO ✓✓✓✓✓	of Italian cuisine – and it succeeds, including some
EASE ✓✓✓✓	600 recipes in the English language section, but over

1,600 overall. See also **http://italy1.com/cuisine** which has good regional cooking and food information as well as lots of recipes.

www.ilovepasta.org

US NATIONAL PASTA ASSOCIATION

ORIGIN US	250 recipes, tips, fast meals and healthy options all
SPEED ✓✓✓✓	wrapped up in a clear and easy-to-use site. There's
INFO ✓✓✓✓✓	also information on the different types of pasta and
EASE ✓✓✓✓	advice on the right sauces to go with them.

www.getoily.com

OLIVE OIL

ORIGIN UK	All you need to know about olive oil, cooking with
SPEED ✓✓✓✓	it, health benefits and history, oh and you can buy it
INFO ✓✓✓✓	too, along with a good selection of other
VALUE ✓✓✓	Mediterranean products.
EASE ✓✓✓✓	

www.dominos.co.uk

PIZZA DELIVERY

ORIGIN UK	Order your pizza online and get it delivered to your
SPEED ✓✓✓	home providing you live near enough to one of their
INFO ✓✓✓	outlets that is. It's a nicely designed site, which also
VALUE ✓✓✓	has a few games if you get bored waiting.
EASE ✓✓✓✓	

Kitchen equipment

www.lakelandlimited.co.uk
EXCELLENT CUSTOMER SERVICE

ORIGIN UK	Lakeland pride themselves on service and it shows,
SPEED ✓✓✓✓	they aim to get all orders dispatched in 24 hours
INFO ✓✓✓✓	and delivery on orders over £38 is free. The
VALUE ✓✓✓	product listing for both kitchen and homeware
EASE ✓✓✓✓	is comprehensive too.

See also:

www.kitchenware.co.uk who also have a good
range, with postage for the UK being £2.95
per order.

www.divertimenti.co.uk – Divertimenti are also
worth a look, they go for quality and they are
good for gifts.

www.pots-and-pans.co.uk – Scottish company
offering kitchen equipment through a good online
store; it's good value but delivery charges may
vary.

www.alessi.com – a tour round the kitchen design
powerhouse that is Alessi, sadly you can't
buy from the site, for that go to
www.rainbow-keswick.co.uk who carry a
large range.

Kosher cookery

www.koshercooking.com
JEWISH CUISINE

ORIGIN UK	Lots of recipes and links covering all forms of
SPEED ✓✓✓✓	kosher cookery and occasions. See also
INFO ✓✓✓✓	www.jewishcuisine.com
EASE ✓✓✓✓	

Luxury food, deli and gift sites

www.stgeorgessquare.com

A VIRTUAL VILLAGE MARKET SQUARE

ORIGIN UK
SPEED ✓✓✓✓
INFO ✓✓✓✓
VALUE ✓✓✓
EASE ✓✓✓✓

St Georges Square features an expanding range of gifts, incentives and prizes for delivery in the UK and overseas. You can send flowers, chocolates, fruit, wine, and a range of themed hampers, Edinburgh crystal, or simply send a gift voucher. It's fast and easy to use, with some good offers too. Delivery depends on type of order placed.

www.allpresent.com

GIFTS FOR THE DISCERNING

ORIGIN UK
SPEED ✓✓✓✓
INFO ✓✓✓✓
VALUE ✓✓
EASE ✓✓✓✓

An Amazon-style shop offering gifts in the form of chocolates, drinks and bakery items such as cakes and biscuits all beautifully boxed. They also sell flowers and cards; delivery costs vary according to what you buy.

www.fortnumandmason.co.uk

EXQUISITE GIFTS

ORIGIN UK
SPEED ✓✓✓
INFO ✓✓✓✓
VALUE ✓✓
EASE ✓✓✓✓

A wide range of gift chocolates, hampers and more from one of the leading luxury stores, UK residents have a wider choice including condiments, teas and wines. Carriage is £7 for UK residents unless you're a F&M account holder then it's free when you spend £50.

www.realmeatco.sageweb.co.uk

WELFARE WITHOUT COMPROMISE

ORIGIN UK
SPEED ✓✓✓✓
INFO ✓✓✓✓
VALUE ✓✓✓
EASE ✓✓✓✓

Produces meat in a caring and compassionate way, they are against things like livestock markets for example. You can buy online or visit one of the approved list of butchers. The shop is split into several areas featuring different meat products, its easy to use but the minimum order is £35.

www.traditionalbutcher.co.uk

A TRADITIONAL BUTCHER

ORIGIN UK
SPEED ✓✓✓✓
INFO ✓✓✓✓
VALUE ✓✓✓
EASE ✓✓✓✓

John Miles is based in Herefordshire and knows a thing or two about meat, you can buy meats and deli products online, there's a good range and delivery is charged at cost. They seem to take a great deal of care on quality.

See also:
www.hampers.uk.com – a wide range of hampers large and small.
www.champershampers.co.uk – family run hamper business.
www.hamper.com – good design and a wide range of products.
www.fifthsense.com – odd design but a wide range and good value.

Middle Eastern cookery

www.al-bab.com/arab/food.htm

MIDDLE EAST CUISINE

ORIGIN UK
SPEED ✓✓✓✓
INFO ✓✓✓✓✓
EASE ✓✓✓✓

An excellent overview of Arab cuisine from Arab Gateway with links to key sites covering all the major styles. See also the enjoyable Nadia's Middle Eastern Cookery site at http://twdg.com/cooking/home.html

www.arabicslice.com

STEP BY STEP ARABIC CUISINE

ORIGIN UK
SPEED ✓✓✓✓
INFO ✓✓✓✓
EASE ✓✓✓✓

A well designed and well written cookery site featuring the best of Arabic food with simple step-by-step recipes, lots of explanation and illustrations.

Miscellaneous food sites

www.leapingsalmon.co.uk

STRESS IS FOR OTHER FISH

ORIGIN UK
SPEED ✓✓✓✓
INFO ✓✓✓✓✓
VALUE ✓✓✓
EASE ✓✓✓✓

This well publicised site is about providing creative and inspirational products to make gourmet cooking fun and achievable in the home. Each meal kit is created for two people by a top chef with step-by-step instructions, order your meal the day before and it gets delivered overnight so that the food is as fresh as possible. They deliver anywhere in the UK for £4.50. Same day delivery is available in London. It really works.

www.reluctantgourmet.com

GOURMET COOKING FOR BEGINNERS

ORIGIN US
SPEED ✓✓✓✓
INFO ✓✓✓✓✓
EASE ✓✓✓✓

Basically a beginner's cookery book, it's well designed and easy to follow with a glossary, guide to techniques, equipment, tips and recipes.

www.cheftalk.com

THE FOOD LOVER'S LINK TO PROFESSIONAL CHEFS

ORIGIN UK
SPEED ✓✓✓✓
INFO ✓✓✓✓✓
EASE ✓✓✓✓

Excellent site devoted to articles and discussion about food with tips and advice from the top chefs. There's a good links section, recipes and a recommended restaurant guide.

www.foodtv.com

FOOD NETWORK

ORIGIN US
SPEED ✓✓✓✓
INFO ✓✓✓✓
EASE ✓✓✓

A rather strange but quite appealing site devoted to TV cooks. It has some video footage and a search engine that covers 20,000 recipes, plus some good articles.

Recipes, general food sites and magazines

www.kitchenlink.com
YOUR GUIDE TO WHAT'S COOKING ON THE NET

ORIGIN US
SPEED ✓✓✓
INFO ✓✓✓✓✓
EASE ✓✓✓

A bit clunky to use, but it has so many links to other key foodie sites and food-related sections that it has to be the place to start your online food and drink experience. The design can make it irritating to use and it's got a little slow, but persevere and you'll be rewarded with a resource that is difficult to beat.

Other American sites worth checking out are these, all have loads of recipes and it's just a matter of finding one you like.

www.cyber-kitchen.com – excellent for links and specialised subjects.

www.chef2chef.net – outstanding cookery portal site with masses of links.

www.foodstop.com – excellent articles about food.

www.goodcooking.com - another excellent food site, with some good food writing.

www.ichef.com – good search facility, nice design.

www.meals.com – good for meal planning and recipes.

www.netcooks.com – hundreds of recipes submitted by the public.

www.recipezaar.com – the world's smartest cook-book.

www.ucook.com – the ultimate cookery shop with recipes added.

www.yumyum.com – good fun.

www.tudocs.com

THE ULTIMATE DIRECTORY OF COOKING SITES

ORIGIN US
SPEED ✓✓✓✓
INFO ✓✓✓✓✓
EASE ✓✓✓✓

The main difference with Tudocs is that it grades each cookery site on its site listing. The listing is divided up into 19 sections, such as meat, beverages, low fat and ethnic. British cookery is in the ethnic section. See also **www.cookingindex.com**

http://epicurious.com

FOR PEOPLE WHO EAT

ORIGIN US
SPEED ✓✓✓✓
INFO ✓✓✓✓✓
EASE ✓✓✓✓

Owned by Condé Nast, this massive site combines articles from their magazines with information generated by the Epicurious team, the site has been tidied up but there's still plenty of advice on topics such as recipes, cooking tips, TV, restaurant reviews, live-chat, forums, wine and kitchen equipment. It's fast, easy to navigate and international in feel.

www.foodlines.com

FOR THOSE WITH A PASSION FOR FOOD

ORIGIN CANADA
SPEED ✓✓✓✓
INFO ✓✓✓✓
EASE ✓✓✓✓

It's easy to find the right recipe at this comprehensive site with a modern touch. There are some good recipes, as well as food quizzes and food jokes.

www.allrecipes.com

THE HOME OF GREAT RECIPES

ORIGIN US
SPEED ✓✓✓✓
INFO ✓✓✓✓✓
EASE ✓✓✓✓

This site gets its own review because it's not overly cluttered, it's just got loads of recipes which can be found easily and each is rated by people who have cooked them.

Vegetarian and organic

www.organicfood.co.uk

A WORLD OF ORGANIC INFORMATION

ORIGIN UK
SPEED ✓✓✓
INFO ✓✓✓✓✓
EASE ✓✓✓✓

A very informative site which gives the latest news on organic food. There are sections on why you should shop organic, recommendations on retailers, lifestyle tips, shopping and chat. There's also links to key related sites.

www.organicsdirect.co.uk

ORGANIC FOOD DELIVERED NATIONWIDE

ORIGIN UK
SPEED ✓✓✓✓
INFO ✓✓✓✓
VALUE ✓✓✓✓
EASE ✓✓✓✓

An award-winning site, this company offers a wide variety of organic food and other related products. The whole thing is well put together with the emphasis on ethical living and it's much better value than supermarkets, delivery (UK) is £5.95 up to 20kg, with a further 25p a kilo after that.

www.theorganicshop.co.uk

GOOD VALUE ORGANIC FOOD

ORIGIN UK
SPEED ✓✓✓✓
INFO ✓✓✓✓
VALUE ✓✓✓✓✓
EASE ✓✓✓✓

Excellent organic store with some great introductory offers, charity donations and free delivery if you spend up to a certain amount on food and wine.

See also:

www.crueltyfreeshop.com the animal-friendly superstore who sell a wide range of products but a limited amount of foodstuffs.

www.organicdelivery.co.uk – a good organic food retailer with some good offers.

www.simplyorganic.net – the organic supermarket, a range of around 2,500 products.

www.freshfood.co.uk

THE FRESH FOOD COMPANY

ORIGIN UK
SPEED ✓✓✓
INFO ✓✓✓✓
VALUE ✓✓✓✓
EASE ✓✓

Another combined supermarket and information site with a wide range of produce to choose from, this one has a recipe section too. They have a subscription system, which delivers your chosen goods on a regular basis. Delivery charges are included in the prices quoted for the mainland UK, if you live offshore then you pay a surcharge.

www.vegsoc.org

THE VEGETARIAN SOCIETY

ORIGIN UK
SPEED ✓✓✓✓
INFO ✓✓✓✓✓
VALUE ✓✓✓
EASE ✓✓✓✓

This is the official site of the UK branch with sections on: news, new veggies, environment, business opportunities, recipes and the Cordon Vert school, youth with virtual schoolroom, health, membership info and online bookstore. Each section is packed with information, written in plain English, and there is a search engine for information on any veggie topic.

www.vegweb.com

VEGGIES UNITE!

ORIGIN US
SPEED ✓✓✓
INFO ✓✓✓✓✓
EASE ✓✓

If you're a vegetarian this is a great place, though not a great design. There are hundreds of recipes, plus features, chat and ideas in the VegWeb newsletter.

www.vegansociety.com

AVOIDING THE USE OF ANIMAL PRODUCTS

ORIGIN UK
SPEED ✓✓✓✓
INFO ✓✓✓✓
VALUE ✓✓✓
EASE ✓✓✓✓

The official site of the Vegan Society, promotes veganism by providing information, links to other related sites and books. You can't shop from the site but it does recommend suitable retailers. For shopping go to www.veganstore.co.uk who offer over 500 suitable products.

Drink: non-alcoholic

www.thebevnet.com

FOR NON-ALCOHOLICS ONLY

ORIGIN US	Short for the Beverage Network, the idea is to test
SPEED ✓✓✓	non-alcoholic soft drinks and to provide a written
INFO ✓✓✓✓	critique of each. There are over 700 listed, sadly you
EASE ✓✓✓✓	can't order them from the UK. The fun of the site is
	spoilt by too much advertising.

www.whittard.com

SPECIALITY TEAS DELIVERED WORLDWIDE

ORIGIN UK	An excellent site dedicated to their selection of teas
SPEED ✓✓✓✓	and coffee's, it's easy to use and they will ship
INFO ✓✓✓✓	throughout the world. Delivery is £3.50 for the
VALUE ✓✓✓✓	UK - free if you spend £50 or more.
EASE ✓✓✓✓	

Also see:
www.koffekorner.com – a slightly bizarre but
    enthusiastic site dedicated to coffee.
www.coffeeselect.co.uk – fine coffee and tea delivered
    to your home.
www.tea.co.uk – great looking site from the Tea
    Council with lots of facts and reasons given why
    we should drink more of the stuff.
www.redmonkeycoffee.com – modern online coffee
    retailer with free UK delivery.

Drink: beer

www.camra.org.uk

THE CAMPAIGN FOR REAL ALE STARTS HERE

ORIGIN UK	A comprehensive site that has all the news and views
SPEED ✓✓✓	on the campaign for real ale. Sadly, it only advertises
INFO ✓✓✓	its *Good Beer Guide* and local versions, with only a
EASE ✓✓✓✓	small section on the best beers. Includes sections on
	beer in Europe, cider and festivals.

www.realbeer.com

THE BEER PORTAL

ORIGIN US	Over 150,000 pages dedicated to beer, with articles,
SPEED ✓✓✓	reviews, links and shopping all wrapped up in a well
INFO ✓✓✓	designed site.
EASE ✓✓✓✓	

Drink: wine and spirits

There are many web sites selling wine and spirits, these are the best so far.

www.berry-bros.co.uk or www.bbr.co.uk

THE INTERNET WINE SHOP

ORIGIN UK	This attractive and award-winning site offers over
SPEED ✓✓✓	1,000 different wines and spirits at prices from £4 to
INFO ✓✓✓✓	over £4,000. There is a great deal of information
VALUE ✓✓✓	about each wine and advice on the different
EASE ✓✓✓✓	varieties. You can also buy related products such

as cigars. Delivery for orders over £120 is free; otherwise it's £9 for the UK. They will deliver abroad and even store the wine for you.

www.winecellar.co.uk

NOT JUST WINE AND GOOD VALUE

ORIGIN UK	They also sell spirits as well as wine and, while the
SPEED ✓✓✓✓	choice isn't as good as some online wine retailers,
INFO ✓✓✓✓	Wine Cellar are good value. Use the search facility
VALUE ✓✓✓✓	to find the whole range which isn't obvious from the
EASE ✓✓✓	home page. Delivery is free for orders of 12 bottles

or more; otherwise it's £4.99.

www.chateauonline.co.uk

THE WINE SPECIALIST ON THE INTERNET

ORIGIN FRANCE
SPEED ✓✓✓
INFO ✓✓✓✓✓
VALUE ✓✓✓
EASE ✓✓✓✓✓

This much advertised retailer offers some 3,000 wines, and if you know a bit about wine, then this is a good site with lots of expert advice and recommendation. They claim to be up to 30% cheaper than other wine retailers, but you really have to order 12 bottles. Delivery is £7.99 for the UK. There is also a section with good links to other wine-related sites.

www.wine-lovers-page.com

ONE OF THE BEST PLACES TO LEARN ABOUT WINE

ORIGIN US
SPEED ✓✓✓✓
INFO ✓✓✓✓✓
VALUE ✓✓✓
EASE ✓✓✓✓

Highly informative for novices and experts alike, this site has it all. There are categories on learning about wine, reading and buying books and tasting notes for some 50,000 wines. Also within the 28 sections there's a glossary, a label decoder, a list of Internet wine shops, wine writers archive, wine search engine and much more.

www.winespectator.com

THE MOST COMPREHENSIVE WINE WEB SITE

ORIGIN UK
SPEED ✓✓✓
INFO ✓✓✓✓✓
EASE ✓✓✓

From *Wine Spectator* magazine you get a site packed with information. There are eleven comprehensive sections, including news, features, a wine search facility, forums, weekly features, a library, the best wineries, wine auctions and travel. The dining section has a world restaurant guide, tips on eating out, wine matching and a set of links to gourmet food. You can subscribe to the whole site, which includes access to their archive material for $49.95 a year.

www.wine-pages.com

A GREAT BRITISH NON-COMMERCIAL WINE SITE

ORIGIN UK
SPEED ✓✓✓
INFO ✓✓✓✓✓
EASE ✓✓✓

Most independently written wine sites are poor, however wine expert Tom Cannavan has put together a strong offering, which is updated daily. It's well written, informative and links to other good wine sites and online wine merchants.

www.wineanorak.com

THE WINE ANORAK

ORIGIN UK
SPEED ✓✓✓✓
INFO ✓✓✓✓✓
EASE ✓✓✓✓

For another good British independent wine site, try the Wine Anorak, it's just a great wine magazine, with lots of advice, articles, issues of the day and general information on wines and regions.

www.jancisrobinson.com

TV WINE EXPERT

ORIGIN UK
SPEED ✓✓✓
INFO ✓✓✓
EASE ✓✓✓

Jancis Robinson has a bright site with wine news, tips, and features on the latest wines and information on her books and videos.

www.ozclarke.com

OZ ON OZ

ORIGIN UK
SPEED ✓✓✓
INFO ✓✓✓✓
EASE ✓✓✓

Lots about Oz and what he's up to plus information on how to get his books and CD-ROM. There's also his wine magazine to browse, which includes tips on tasting, producer profiles, wine basics and the latest news.

www.superplonk.com

MALCOLM GLUCK

ORIGIN UK
SPEED ✓✓✓✓
INFO ✓✓✓✓✓
EASE ✓✓✓✓

Excellent site from Malcolm Gluck, the author of the Superplonk books, there are offers and tips on where to buy good value high quality wines.

Other wine sites worth checking out are:

www.cyberbacchus.com – wine portal with hundreds of links.

www.cephas.co.uk – superb images of wines and vineyards around the world.

www.englishwineproducers.co.uk – info on English wine-making.

www.wineontheweb.com – good wine magazine with audio features.

www.wine-searcher.com – a wine search engine, type in the wine you want and up pops a selection from various retailers from around the world and UK, all suppliers are vetted for quality and service.

www.vintageroots.co.uk – excellent for organic wines, spirits and beers.

www.drinkboy.com

ADVENTURES IN COCKTAILS

ORIGIN US
SPEED ✓✓✓✓
INFO ✓✓✓✓
EASE ✓✓✓✓✓

You can't shop from this site, but it contains virtually everything you need to know about cocktails including instructions for around 100. There is also a section in the making on party games. See also **www.idrink.com** who enable you to create cocktails from over 160 ingredients.

www.barmeister.com

THE ONLINE GUIDE TO DRINKING

ORIGIN US
SPEED ✓✓✓
INFO ✓✓✓✓
EASE ✓✓✓✓

Packed with information on everything to do with drink, there are over 2,500 drink recipes available and over 500 drinking games. If you have another, then send it to be featured in the site. See also **www.idrink.com**

Eating out

www.goodguides.com

HOME OF THE GOOD PUB GUIDE

ORIGIN UK
SPEED ✓✓✓✓
INFO ✓✓✓✓
EASE ✓✓✓✓

Once you've registered it has an easy-to-use regional guide to the best pubs, which are rated on food, beer, value, good places to stay and good range of wine. You can also get a listing by award winner. It also houses the *Good Guide to Britain*, which is a good resource for what's on where.

www.dine-online.co.uk

UK-BASED WINING, DINING AND TRAVEL REVIEW

ORIGIN UK
SPEED ✓✓✓✓
INFO ✓✓✓✓
EASE ✓✓✓✓

A slightly pretentious, but a sincere attempt at an independent eating out review web site. It has a good and expanding selection of recommended restaurants, covers wine and has some well-written feature articles. It relies heavily on reader recommendation, so there's a good deal of variation in coverage and review quality.

www.theaa.co.uk

NOT JUST MOTORING AND TRAVEL ADVICE

ORIGIN UK
SPEED ✓✓✓✓
INFO ✓✓✓✓✓
EASE ✓✓✓✓✓

The superb AA site has a little known gem in its hotels section – an excellent regional restaurant guide to the UK. Each hotel and restaurant is graded and there are comments on quality of food, ambience, an idea of the price and, of course, how to get there.

www.viamichelin.co.uk

MICHELIN

ORIGIN UK
SPEED ✓✓✓✓
INFO ✓✓✓✓
EASE ✓✓✓✓

A revamped site from Michelin with improved route finding and a good restaurant and hotel guide.

www.gofortea.com

TEA TIME

ORIGIN	UK
SPEED	✓✓✓✓
INFO	✓✓✓✓
EASE	✓✓✓✓

A site devoted to finding the best spots for the traditional British afternoon tea, though it does concentrate on hotels rather than tea shops.

Other restaurant review sites worth looking at before you go out are:

www.restaurantreview.co.uk – good design, but London only.

www.ukrestaurantguide.com – good for links and finding a restaurant but slow and not comprehensive.

www.cuisinenet.co.uk – book online at selected restaurants, nice design.

www.local-restaurant.com – good restaurant finder.

www.toptable.co.uk – co-ordinates free booking at over 1000 restaurants, nice design too.

www.conran.com/eat – a guide to Terence Conran's restaurants with online booking and some special offers, nice design too.

Free Stuff

Free stuff is exactly what the term suggests, and these are sites whose owners have trawled the Net or been offered free services, software, trial products and so on. It's amazing what you can find but as most sites are American some offers won't apply.

www.allforfree.co.uk

DELIVERED DAILY IN YOUR E-MAIL

ORIGIN	UK
SPEED	✓✓✓
INFO	✓✓✓✓✓
VALUE	✓✓✓✓✓
EASE	✓✓✓✓

All for free will let you know all the latest 'free' news with their e-mail service. There's a lot here, the highlights being how to ensure that you are getting the most out of government services, free Internet access, free magazines and where to go for the best competitions. Members get even more tips and information.

www.free.com

GET SOMETHING FOR NOTHING

ORIGIN US	One of the best and largest sites of its type, there are
SPEED ✓✓✓	literally hundreds of pages of free goodies waiting to
INFO ✓✓✓✓✓	be snapped up. Very wide-ranging and very much
VALUE ✓✓✓✓✓	geared towards the US, but with over 9,000 links
EASE ✓✓✓✓✓	you should find something.

www.2001freebies.co.uk

ONE STOP SHOP FOR FREE STUFF

ORIGIN UK	Nothing but UK freebies here, so it's all available
SPEED ✓✓✓✓	from computer accessories, games, masses of
INFO ✓✓✓✓	samples and software to books and magazines.
VALUE ✓✓✓✓	The site is well designed and simple to use.
EASE ✓✓✓✓	

Other sites worth looking into are these listed below, but most are American so some offers may not apply for the UK.

www.1freestuff.com – one of oldest and probably best categorised.

www.freeandfun.com – they'll e-mail offers tailored to your interests.

www.totallyfreestuff.com – massive selection.

www.thefreesite.com – more of the same, nice layout.

www.thefreezone.co.uk – an excellent collection of link pages.

www.freeinuk.co.uk – better than most featuring charities and competitions.

www.freebielist.com – a well categorised listing – easy to use and good links.

Furniture

Believe it or not it's becoming quite common to order items of furniture for the home over the Net, or at least to browse online catalogues before venturing out into the stores.

www.mfi.co.uk
MFI HOMEWORKS

ORIGIN UK
SPEED ✓✓✓
INFO ✓✓✓✓
VALUE ✓✓✓
EASE ✓✓✓✓

MFI offer a nicely designed site with all the best aspects of online shopping and a wide range of surprisingly good furniture for home and office available for order online or via a hotline. Delivery is included in the price.

www.habitat.net
DESIGN OVER CONTENT

ORIGIN UK
SPEED ✓✓✓
INFO ✓✓✓
EASE ✓✓✓

A clever, beautiful if slightly irritating web site giving an overview of what Habitat are about and what they stock, you can't order online though you can check store availability.

www.mccord.uk.com
MCCORDS CATALOGUE

ORIGIN UK
SPEED ✓✓✓
INFO ✓✓✓✓✓
EASE ✓✓✓

McCords offer a huge range of furniture, gift ideas and accessories for the home via their online catalogue. It's very quick, easy to use, good value and delivery is £2.95 per order. Straightforward returns policy.

www.furniture123.co.uk
SMART PLACE TO BUY FURNITURE

ORIGIN UK
SPEED ✓✓✓
INFO ✓✓✓✓
VALUE ✓✓✓✓
EASE ✓✓✓✓

This company has a well laid out web site offering a good range of furniture, many offers, tips and free delivery. There's also a magazine with the latest in trends and ideas for the home.

www.heals.co.uk

STYLISH CONTEMPORARY DESIGN

ORIGIN UK
SPEED ✓✓✓✓
INFO ✓✓✓✓
VALUE ✓✓✓
EASE ✓✓✓✓

Heals has a beautifully designed web site which gives information about the store and inspiration for the home. There's an online store which stocks primarily gifts and home accessories, but there's a special services section where you can get information on furniture and interior design.

www.conran.com

TERENCE CONRAN STYLE

ORIGIN UK
SPEED ✓✓✓
INFO ✓✓✓
VALUE ✓✓✓
EASE ✓✓✓✓

As well as information on all his restaurants, this site has an online shopping facility that allows you to buy Conran-designed accessories as well as stuff for the home including a good range of furniture and kitchen products.

www.ancestralcollections.co.uk

REPRODUCTIONS FROM THE BEST HOMES

ORIGIN UK
SPEED ✓✓✓✓
INFO ✓✓✓✓
VALUE ✓✓✓
EASE ✓✓✓✓

If you've ever fancied a Regency stool or any decent piece of antique furniture but couldn't run to the expense, then this company will supply you with a reproduction. They have a wide range of products not just furniture and are great for unusual gifts too.

www.amazingemporium.com

REPRODUCTIONS FROM THE BEST HOMES

ORIGIN UK
SPEED ✓✓✓✓
INFO ✓✓✓✓
VALUE ✓✓✓✓
EASE ✓✓✓✓

A web site that has developed well with a wide range of high quality beds and furniture on an attractive site with good pictures and descriptions of the products. They've expanded into gifts too and offer good value for money.

Other furniture retailers that may be worth a virtual visit are:

www.cjfurniture.com – contemporary furniture.

www.davidlinley.com – posh contemporary classics.

www.mufti.co.uk – more posh beautifully designed furniture.

www.new-heights.co.uk – simple, stylish solid wood.

www.bedbathandhome.co.uk – excellent for soft furnishings with delivery from £2.99.

www.sofaworkshopdirect.co.uk – well designed with quality photos of the sofas and what looks like a good online service.

Gambling and Betting Sites

Gambling sites abound on the Internet and they often use some of the most sophisticated marketing techniques to keep you hooked, new screens pop up as you click on the close button tempting you with the chance to win millions. All the gaming sites are monitored by gaming commissions but above all be sensible, it's easy to get carried away.

www.national-lottery.co.uk

IT COULD BE YOU

ORIGIN UK	Find out about Camelot, good causes, the National
SPEED ✓✓✓	Lottery and whether you've won. Also, find out
INFO ✓✓✓✓	whether your premium bonds are worth anything
EASE ✓✓✓✓	at www.nationalsavings.co.uk, you need your
	bondholder number handy.

www.jamba.co.uk

WHERE THE WEB IS FUN

ORIGIN	UK
SPEED	✓✓✓
INFO	✓✓✓✓
VALUE	✓✓✓✓
EASE	✓✓✓✓

Owned by Carlton TV, this is probably the most complete set of games and trivia; in the gaming section you can place serious or fun bets and go shopping as well. You have to register to take part in the prize-winning games.

www.gamblehouse.com

YOUR ONLINE GAMBLING GUIDE

ORIGIN	US
SPEED	✓✓✓
INFO	✓✓✓✓✓
EASE	✓✓✓✓

A very good place to start, they review online casinos and rank them according to whether they are licensed, make payments quickly, offer good odds, variety and quality of games and lastly customer service.

These are the casinos we liked:
www.24ktgoldcasino.com – good graphics and fast response times make this great fun, but you need a decent PC to download the software. There are 40 or so games and you can either play for fun or for money.
www.intercasino.com – easy to use and they've got 35 games to choose from.
www.entercasino.com – the Gamble House number 1 casino, need we say more.

www.oddschecker.co.uk

COMPARE THE ODDS

ORIGIN	UK
SPEED	✓✓✓✓
INFO	✓✓✓✓✓
EASE	✓✓✓✓

A great way to ensure you get the best deal from the online bookmakers, you just choose the sport and the event, then you get a read out of the latest odds and from a selection of bookies – you can click on the bookmaker to visit and place your bet. It's continually being updated; we'd say the site was a must for the committed gambler.

www.ukbetting.com
LIVE INTERACTIVE BETTING

ORIGIN UK	Concentrating on sports betting, this is a clear, easy-to-use site; take a guest tour before applying to join.
SPEED ✓✓✓✓	
INFO ✓✓✓✓	You need to open an account to take part, using
EASE ✓✓✓✓	your credit or debit card, bets are £1 minimum. See

also **www.inter-bet.com** which is straightforward with loads of options and is probably better value than most sites. The heavily advertised, and popular **www.bluesq.com** also offers a similar service, but with a football bias and special bets on things like soap operas and political elections. Also worth a visit is **www.bet365.co.uk** who cover a wide variety of areas and offer some good deals.

www.mybetting.co.uk
FREE BETTING

ORIGIN UK	My betting works as a collation site for free bets and
SPEED ✓✓✓✓	offers from bookmakers around the Internet. It
INFO ✓✓✓✓✓	takes a minute or so to get used to the design but
VALUE ✓✓✓✓✓	once you're on board it's easy to get yourself a few
EASE ✓✓✓	free bets, albeit at the price of a registration or two.

www.racingpost.co.uk
THE RACING POST

ORIGIN UK	A combination of news, racing and betting on a
SPEED ✓✓✓✓	clearly laid out and well-designed site. Also features
INFO ✓✓✓✓	greyhounds and information on bloodstock.
EASE ✓✓✓✓	

www.ladbrokes.co.uk
UK'S NUMBER 1 BOOKMAKER

ORIGIN UK	Ladbrokes offer a combination of news, information
SPEED ✓✓✓✓	and betting, which is geared to sport with excellent
INFO ✓✓✓✓	features on racing, golf and the other major sporting
EASE ✓✓✓✓	events. There's even a casino, lotteries, a fantasy

league and a sort of bingo game called balls!

www.willhill.com

THE MOST RESPECTED NAME IN BOOKMAKING

ORIGIN UK
SPEED ✓✓✓✓
INFO ✓✓✓✓
EASE ✓✓✓✓✓

The best online betting site in terms of speed, layout and design, it has the best event finder, results service and betting calculator. The bet finder service is also very good and quick. All the major sports are featured and there is a specials section for those out of the ordinary flutters. Betting is live as it happens.

See also:

www.paddypower.com – a strong site from Irelands' biggest bookmaker with betting on horses, football and other top sports – even politics.

www.sportingindex.com – excellent and wide ranging spread betting site with offers and competitions.

www.tote.co.uk

BET ON THE HORSES, LIVE

ORIGIN UK
SPEED ✓✓✓✓
INFO ✓✓✓✓
EASE ✓✓✓✓

Devoted to horse racing, the Tote fairly successfully attempts to bring you the excitement and feel of live betting online. It explains what the bets mean and has a very good set of links relating to horses and racing.

www.thedogs.co.uk

GONE TO THE DOGS

ORIGIN UK
SPEED ✓✓✓
INFO ✓✓✓✓✓
EASE ✓✓✓✓

Everything you need to know about greyhounds and greyhound racing. You can adopt or get advice on buying a dog, find the nearest track, get the latest results and learn how to place bets. You can't gamble from the site but they provide links.

www.betasyouclick.com

THE ONLINE GAMBLER'S DIRECTORY

ORIGIN US
SPEED ✓✓✓✓
INFO ✓✓✓
EASE ✓✓✓✓

A betting and gambling directory with links to web sites from around the world, which offer sportsbooks, casinos, financial spread betting, lotteries and competitions.

Games

There's a massive selection of games on the Internet, here's just some of the very best ones; from board games to quizzes to your everyday 'shoot 'em up' type. There are more games for Macs listed on page 22.

It's worth remembering that before downloading a game from a site it's wise to check for viruses. If you've not got anti-virus software on your PC then check out our section on Virus management on page 8.

Finding games

http://gamespotter.com

GAMES SEARCH ENGINE

ORIGIN	US	A really handy site where you can get links to virtually
SPEED	✓✓✓✓	every type of game whether it be a puzzle or action.
INFO	✓✓✓✓	Alternatively, you can use the search facility to find
EASE	✓✓✓✓	something. Each game on the list is reviewed as well.

Games magazines

www.avault.com

THE ADRENALINE VAULT

ORIGIN	US	A comprehensive games magazine with demos, reviews
SPEED	✓✓✓✓	and features on software and hardware – good looking
INFO	✓✓✓✓	too. There's also a good cheats and hints section.
EASE	✓✓✓✓	

www.gamespy.com

GAMINGS HOMEPAGE

ORIGIN	US	Lots here, apart from the usual reviews and features.
SPEED	✓✓✓	There are chat and help sections and links to the
INFO	✓✓✓✓	arcade section with some 300 demos plus free games
EASE	✓✓✓✓	to play. See also **www.gamespot.co.uk** which offers
		lots of info as well.

www.gamers.com

A MOMENT ENJOYED IS NOT WASTED

ORIGIN US
SPEED ✓✓✓✓
INFO ✓✓✓✓
EASE ✓✓✓✓

A great-looking site with all the features you'd expect from a games magazine but it has more in the way of downloads and games to play. There is also a chat section and competitions.

www.gamesdomain.co.uk

THE GAMES DOMAIN

ORIGIN US
SPEED ✓✓✓✓
INFO ✓✓✓✓
EASE ✓✓✓✓

A strong combination of freebies, competitions, good links, news and reviews make this site a great place to start online gaming. It's clear, fast and easy to use.

www.happypuppy.com

GAMES REVIEWED

ORIGIN US
SPEED ✓✓✓✓
INFO ✓✓✓✓✓
EASE ✓✓✓✓

Happy Puppy has been around a while now reviewing games in all the major formats. Each is given a thorough test, then it's rated and given a review. There are also links to related games sites. It's all packaged on a really good web site which is quick and user-friendly.

www.gamehelp.com

ALL ON ONE SITE

ORIGIN US
SPEED ✓✓✓✓
INFO ✓✓✓✓✓
EASE ✓✓✓✓

The aim is to get as much information about games and gaming as possible all on one site and all in a simple package; and it largely succeeds. The design is great, the information current and the links work. There's more than enough information including reviews, cheats and demos of the latest games. Formally www.pcgame.com See also www.gamefaqs.com which is also very informative.

Games to play

www.barrysworld.com
GAMES ONLINE

ORIGIN UK
SPEED ✓✓✓✓
INFO ✓✓✓✓✓
EASE ✓✓✓

Barrysworld specialise in providing online servers for players to play their games and you can take part in several from this site. There's also more information and links than you'll ever need, which makes it a little daunting at first, but it's also helpful and very well written.

www.boxerjam.com
ONLINE GAMESHOW

ORIGIN UK
SPEED ✓✓✓✓
INFO ✓✓✓✓✓
VALUE ✓✓✓✓
EASE ✓✓✓✓

Excellent site devoted to giving the user access to original and traditional games played online, for cash and prizes.

www.classicgaming.com
GAMING THE WAY YOU REMEMBER IT

ORIGIN US
SPEED ✓✓✓✓
INFO ✓✓✓
EASE ✓✓✓✓

Probably one for older gamers but there's some good stuff on here so it's at least worth a look and it's amazing how new some of the games are.

www.gamehippo.com
OVER 1000 FREE GAMES

ORIGIN US
SPEED ✓✓✓✓
INFO ✓✓✓✓✓
EASE ✓✓✓✓

Enough to keep you occupied for hours with games of every type from board to action to puzzles and sports. There's also a really good set of links to other sites. It's worth checking out www.freeloader.com which has a more modern selection available, but you have to register and jump through a few hoops to get them.

www.gamearchive.com

PINBALL MACHINES

ORIGIN UK
SPEED ✓✓✓✓
INFO ✓✓✓
EASE ✓✓✓✓

A site devoted to pinball machines and similar games put together by real fans. There's also a selection of video games and links to similar sites, however, there are no console games. See also **www.videogames.org**

www.gamebrew.com

JAVA GAMING

ORIGIN US
SPEED ✓✓✓
INFO ✓✓✓✓
EASE ✓✓✓✓

Gamebrew specialise in Java games and there are some brilliant ones to download and play here. The Java program gives gaming an extra edge with brilliant graphics in particular. Send them to your friends. The site has some really annoying pop-up ads.

http://games.yahoo.com

YAHOO!

ORIGIN US
SPEED ✓✓✓
INFO ✓✓✓✓
EASE ✓✓✓✓

This popular search engine has its own games section. Here you can play against others or yourself online. The emphasis is on board games, puzzles and quizzes although there are other games available plus links to games sites.

www.ogl.org

ONLINE GAMING LEAGUE

ORIGIN US
SPEED ✓✓✓
INFO ✓✓✓✓
EASE ✓✓✓✓

Join a community of gamers who play in leagues for fun. You can play all the major online games and compete in the leagues and ladders if you like. To quote them: 'What matters is that people are meeting and interacting with other people on the Internet via our services and their game.'

www.pokemon.co.uk
POKEMON GAMES FANS GO HERE

ORIGIN UK	If you're into Pokemon there are games to play,
SPEED ✓✓✓✓	download and buy, links, news, latest updates,
INFO ✓✓✓✓	cartoons and comics.
VALUE ✓✓	
EASE ✓✓✓	

www.planetquake.com
THE EPICENTRE OF QUAKE

ORIGIN US	Quake is the most popular game played on the
SPEED ✓✓	Internet, and this slightly slow site gives you all the
INFO ✓✓✓✓	background and details on the game. It's got loads
EASE ✓✓✓✓	of links and features as well as reviews and chat.

www.shockwave.com
SHOCKWAVE GRAPHICS

ORIGIN US	Shockwave's fantastic site offers much more than
SPEED ✓✓✓✓	games, there are cartoons, greeting cards and music
INFO ✓✓✓✓✓	too. Click on 'games' and you get access to five
EASE ✓✓✓✓	sections: action, adventure, sports, jigsaws and
	board games plus two sections of arcade games.
	The graphics are superb.

www.lysator.liu.se/tolkien-games
LORD OF THE RINGS

ORIGIN SWEDEN	Get immersed in Tolkien's Middle Earth with some
SPEED ✓✓✓✓	100 games. It's got action games, quizzes and puzzles,
INFO ✓✓✓✓✓	strategy games and, of course, role playing games.
EASE ✓✓✓	

www.wireplay.com
THE GAMES NETWORK

ORIGIN US	A new look site that was being rebuilt when we
SPEED ✓✓✓✓	visited, it still had all the old features but improve-
INFO ✓✓✓✓✓	ments where being made. Worth keeping an eye on
VALUE ✓✓✓✓	because quality will be high when it's back.
EASE ✓✓✓✓	

www.zone.com

MICROSOFT GAMES ZONE

ORIGIN US	With over 100 games to choose from you shouldn't
SPEED ✓✓✓	be disappointed. They range from board and card
INFO ✓✓✓✓	games to multi-player strategy and simulation
EASE ✓✓✓✓	games, there's a good kids' section too.

Game manufacturers and console games

www.dreamcast.com

DREAMCAST FROM SEGA

ORIGIN US	Get the latest information on what's coming, try
SPEED ✓✓✓✓	it out or play online; you can also get the latest
INFO ✓✓✓✓	technology.
EASE ✓✓✓✓	

www.gbstation.com

GAME BOY NEWS

ORIGIN UK	Here you can get all the latest information on Game
SPEED ✓✓✓✓	Boy, plus reviews and features such as chat forums
INFO ✓✓✓✓✓	and cheats. You can also buy from the site.
VALUE ✓✓✓	
EASE ✓✓✓✓	

www.gamecube.com

THE GAME CUBE

ORIGIN UK	The ever developing game consul from Nintendo has
SPEED ✓✓✓✓	a typically original site where you can learn all
INFO ✓✓✓✓✓	about it and the games that go with it. See also
EASE ✓✓✓✓	http://cube.ign.com

www.hasbrointeractive.com

HASBRO GAMES

ORIGIN US	No games to download, but there are details of all
SPEED ✓✓✓✓	the games they sell and you can get patches on the
INFO ✓✓✓✓	site. The most useful bit is the links to sites that
EASE ✓✓✓✓	either sell games or allow you to play online.

www.nintendo.com

OFFICIAL NINTENDO

ORIGIN US
SPEED ✓✓✓✓
INFO ✓✓✓✓✓
EASE ✓✓✓✓

Get the latest news from Nintendo and its spin-offs – N64, Game Boy and Game Cube. There's also information on the hardware and details of the games new and old. For a site with wider Nintendo info go to the **excellent www.nintendojo.com**

http://uk.playstation.com

OFFICIAL PLAYSTATION SITE

ORIGIN US
SPEED ✓✓✓✓
INFO ✓✓✓✓
EASE ✓✓✓✓

Looks good with games information, information on the hardware, previews, new release details and a special features section featuring reviews by well-known gamers. There's also a chat section and a shop.

Also check out:
www.psxextreme.com
www.absolute-playstation.com
www.playstation.com

www.pocketgamer.org

GAMES FOR POCKET PCS

ORIGIN UK
SPEED ✓✓✓✓
INFO ✓✓✓✓
VALUE ✓✓✓
EASE ✓✓✓✓

OK so you've bought your handheld PC, you've impressed the boss, now, what do you really use it for? Oh yes, play games! There's a lot here for most different types of operating systems, if not, then there are links to related sites. If you still can't find what you're looking for, try **www.handango.com**

www.planetxbox.com

XBOX

ORIGIN US
SPEED ✓✓✓✓
INFO ✓✓✓✓
EASE ✓✓✓✓

Part of the Gamespy network, this site gives background on Microsoft's toy, with the latest game news, reviews, demos and previews too. See also **www.xbox.com, www.xboxweb.com** and **www.play-more.com** who offer some exclusive previews.

www.station.sony.com

SONY ONLINE GAMES

ORIGIN	US
SPEED	✓✓✓
INFO	✓✓✓✓✓
VALUE	✓✓✓✓
EASE	✓✓✓✓✓

Sony have put together an exceptional site for online gaming, and with over 6 million members, it's one of the most popular. It's well designed and easy to use. There are lots of games to choose from. Providing you can put up with the adverts, it's a real treat to use.

www.segaweb.com

SEGA AND DREAMCAST

ORIGIN	US
SPEED	✓✓✓✓
INFO	✓✓✓✓
EASE	✓✓✓✓

News, reviews, cheats and much more including chat and a letters section. For the official site with links and information on the products go to www.sega-europe.com

Fantasy league and strategy games

www.dreamleague.com

PLAY FANTASY SPORT

ORIGIN	US
SPEED	✓✓✓✓
INFO	✓✓✓✓
EASE	✓✓✓✓

Dream League offer fantasy games in several sports including football, formula 1 and cricket. Even with the sports you can play foreign leagues. It's easy to register and join in – and it's free.

www.fantasyleague.com

FANTASY FOOTIE

ORIGIN	UK
SPEED	✓✓✓✓
INFO	✓✓✓✓✓
VALUE	✓✓
EASE	✓✓✓

Be a football manager, play for yourself, in a league, or even organise a game for your workplace or school. Get the latest team news on your chosen players and how they're doing against the rest. It's also worth checking out http://uk-fantasyfootball.20m.com

www.primagames.com

PRIMA

ORIGIN US	The largest fantasy game publisher offers a site
SPEED ✓✓✓✓	packed with reviews, demos and articles. You can
INFO ✓✓✓✓	also buy a book on virtually every strategy game.
EASE ✓✓✓✓	See also **www.strategy-gaming.com** which is pretty
	comprehensive.

Cheats, hints and tips

www.computerandvideogames.com

THE CHEAT STATION

ORIGIN US	Select the console or game type that you want a
SPEED ✓✓✓✓	cheat on, then drill down the menus until you get
INFO ✓✓✓✓✓	the specific game or cheat that you want. There are
EASE ✓✓✓✓	cheats for almost 9,000 games so you should find
	what you're looking for. If you can't, check out
	www.xcheater.com who have a smaller selection,
	but you never know your luck.

Games shops

*If you know which game you want, then it's probably better to use a price checker such as Kelkoo (**http://uk.kelkoo.com**) to find the best price on the game. They will put you through to the store offering the best all round deal. If you want to browse, then these are considered the best online stores for a wide range of games:*

> **www.chipsworld.co.uk** – good for Sega and
> Nintendo. (UK)
> **www.eb.uk.com** – Electronic Boutique is easy to use
> with a good loyalty scheme. (UK)
> **www.gameplay.com** – Gameplay is one of the most
> visited games sites. Once a magazine site, it's now
> transformed into a well designed store, browsable
> by platform and good value. (UK)

> **www.game-retail.co.uk** – the high street store
> offering an easy-to-use site, good range of prod-
> ucts and a loyalty scheme. (UK)
>
> **www.gamesstreet.co.uk** – part of the Streets Online
> group one of the top shops on the Internet – good
> kids' section. Delivery costs start at £1. (UK)
>
> **www.telegames.co.uk** – around 5,000 types of game
> in stock, covering all makes. Also has a bargain
> section. (UK)
>
> **www.ukgames.com** – excellent range and good
> prices. (UK)

www.gameswapshop.com

DON'T BUY NEW GAMES, SWAP THEM

ORIGIN	UK	A user-friendly site with a secure swapping system,
SPEED	✓✓✓✓	you can swap games with anyone in the UK who is
INFO	✓✓✓✓	also registered.
EASE	✓✓✓	

www.wargames.co.uk

WAR GAMES FORUM

ORIGIN	UK	All you need to know about war-gaming on one site,
SPEED	✓✓	albeit a slow one. There are links to specialist
INFO	✓✓✓	traders and to every aspect of the game from
EASE	✓✓✓	figurines to books to software.

Miscellaneous

www.etch-a-sketch.com

REMEMBER ETCH-A-SKETCH?

ORIGIN	UK	For those of you who don't remember back that far,
SPEED	✓✓✓	Etch-a-Sketch is a rather annoying drawing game. It's
INFO	✓✓✓	been faithfully recreated here and it's still just as diffi-
EASE	✓✓✓	cult to do curves. There are also a few other simple
		games and some links to children's games sites.

Board and card games

www.chess.co.uk
ULTIMATE CHESS

ORIGIN UK	Massive chess site that's got information on the
SPEED ✓✓✓✓	game, news and views, reviews and shopping. There
INFO ✓✓✓✓	are lots of links to other chess sites and downloads.
EASE ✓✓✓	Check out the similar **www.bcf.ndirect.co.uk** for the
	British Chess Federation and the Internet Chess club
	at **www.chessclub.com**

www.gammon.com
BACKGAMMON

ORIGIN US	If you like backgammon, here's the place to start.
SPEED ✓✓✓✓	There are links to live game playing and masses of
INFO ✓✓✓✓	related information. Also check out **www.bkgm.com**
EASE ✓✓✓	

www.msoworld.com
BOARD GAMES, PUZZLES AND QUIZZES

ORIGIN US	The ultimate site of its type, there are over 100
SPEED ✓✓✓✓	board games and masses of quizzes and tests; on top
INFO ✓✓✓✓	of that, there are over 1,000 links to games sites.
VALUE ✓✓✓✓	
EASE ✓✓✓✓	

www.scrabble.com
SCRABBLE

ORIGIN US	Scrabble addicts start here, unfortunately you can't
SPEED ✓✓✓✓	play the game online, but there are some good word
INFO ✓✓	games on the site. You can also get loads of tips and
EASE ✓✓✓✓	word lists, which will help you, get to grips with the
	real game.

www.monopoly.com

MONOPOLY

ORIGIN US	A pretty boring site along similar lines to the
SPEED ✓✓✓✓	Scrabble one. It offers a history plus information on
INFO ✓✓	where you can buy, along with tips on how to play
EASE ✓✓✓✓	and how you can get involved in tournaments.

www.thehouseofcards.com

LOADS OF CARD GAMES

ORIGIN US	Huge number of card games to play and download
SPEED ✓✓✓✓	with sections on card tricks, history, links and word
INFO ✓✓✓✓	games – there's not much missing here. See also
EASE ✓✓✓✓	**www.pagat.com** for an alternative.

www.playsite.com

EASY TO PLAY

ORIGIN US	A collection of straightforward multi-player online
SPEED ✓✓✓	games, specialising in cards and board games.
INFO ✓✓✓✓	
EASE ✓✓✓✓	

www.solitairegames.com

SOLITAIRE

ORIGIN US	Play online or download a game onto your PC, there
SPEED ✓✓✓✓	are plenty to choose from and it's quick. There's also
INFO ✓✓✓✓	a good set of links to other online card games.
EASE ✓✓✓✓	

Crosswords, puzzles and word games

www.cluemaster.com

CROSSWORDS AND WORD PUZZLES

ORIGIN	UK	1,000 pages of puzzles, word games and crosswords,
SPEED	✓✓✓✓	all free. The site is pretty straightforward, although
INFO	✓✓✓✓	you have to register to get the best out of it. See also
EASE	✓✓✓✓	**www.kidscrosswords.com** which is great for children.

www.crosswordsite.com

ALL CROSSWORDS

ORIGIN	UK	Hundreds to chose from, with the option either to
SPEED	✓✓✓✓	print off or fill in online. There are four levels of
INFO	✓✓✓	difficulty with the hardest being quite tough.
EASE	✓✓✓✓	

www.fun-with-words.com

THE WORDPLAY WEBSITE

ORIGIN	US	Dedicated to amusing English, the Fun with Words
SPEED	✓✓✓✓	site offers games, puzzles and an insight into the
INFO	✓✓✓✓	sorts of tricks you can play with the language.
EASE	✓✓✓✓	

Quizzes and general knowledge

www.thinks.com

FUN AND GAMES FOR PLAYFUL BRAINS

ORIGIN	UK	Massive collection of games, puzzles and quizzes
SPEED	✓✓✓	with something for everyone, it's easy to navigate
INFO	✓✓✓✓✓	and free.
EASE	✓✓✓✓	

www.mensa.org.uk

THE HIGH IQ SOCIETY

ORIGIN UK
SPEED ✓✓✓
INFO ✓✓✓✓
EASE ✓✓✓

Mensa only admit people who pass their high IQ test – see if you've got what it takes. The site which has been upgraded, has a few free tests and, if eligible, you can join the club.

www.queendom.com

SERIOUSLY ENTERTAINING

ORIGIN US
SPEED ✓✓✓✓
INFO ✓✓✓✓
EASE ✓✓✓✓

Excellent site for all sorts of brain tingling tests, the major difference is that it also offers personality profiles and psychometric tests so that they may be useful in getting on in your career or just keeping your brain healthy see also **www.emode.com**

www.uselessknowledge.com

MASSIVE TRIVIA

ORIGIN US
SPEED ✓✓✓✓
INFO ✓✓✓✓✓
EASE ✓✓✓✓

Useless information and trivia by the ton plus quizzes and tests just to see how good you really are.

Check out these sites:

www.coolquiz.com – several different types of quiz from sports to movies and quotes. Nice wacky design. (USA)

www.quiz.co.uk – a couple of hundred questions in several unusual categories including kids, nature, food and sport. (UK)

www.test.com – mainly serious tests, but you can find out your IQ and find out how creative you are. Visit the family section to take tests on entertainment and sports amongst others. You have to pay for some of the tests. (USA)

Gardening

There are several high quality British gardening sites, but many of the best sites are still based in America, so bear this in mind for tenderness, soil and climate advice. Those recommended give good general information and good links to specialist sites. Due to regulations on importing of seeds and plants, these can't be imported from outside the UK.

www.gardenworld.co.uk

THE UK'S BEST

ORIGIN UK
SPEED ✓✓✓✓
INFO ✓✓✓✓✓
VALUE ✓✓✓
EASE ✓✓✓✓

Described as the UK's best garden centre and horticultural site. It includes a list of over 1,000 garden centres, with addresses, contact numbers and e-mail addresses. Outstanding list of links to other sites on most aspects of gardening. Truly comprehensive with sections on wildlife, books, holidays, advice, societies and specialists, it now also has the addition of a link to the RHS plant finder service – excellent.

www.greenfingers.com

COMPREHENSIVE GARDENING

ORIGIN UK
SPEED ✓✓✓✓
INFO ✓✓✓✓✓
EASE ✓✓✓✓

There's so much here it takes a while to find your way around. It features sections on gardens to visit, finding a gardener, tips, chat, what's on, weather reports, a plant selector and articles written by celebrities and well known gardeners. It's also got an excellent selection of online shops and links to related sites.

www.expertgardener.com

GARDENING COMMUNITY

ORIGIN UK
SPEED ✓✓✓✓
INFO ✓✓✓✓✓
EASE ✓✓✓✓

Advice and articles from experts such as Alan Titchmarsh and other award-winning gardeners combined with good design makes this site stand out. There are links to a good selection of online shops, a magazine and access to chat rooms and communities on various subjects from urban gardening to plantaholics corner.

www.gardenweb.com

GARDEN QUESTIONS ANSWERED

ORIGIN UK
SPEED ✓✓✓✓
INFO ✓✓✓✓✓
EASE ✓✓✓✓

Probably the best site for lively gardening debate; it's enjoyable, international, comprehensive and has a nice tone. There are several discussion forums on various gardening topics, garden advice, plant dictionary and competitions. Using the forums is easy and fun, and you're sure to find the answer to almost any gardening question.

www.kew.org.uk

ROYAL BOTANIC GARDENS

ORIGIN UK
SPEED ✓✓✓✓
INFO ✓✓✓✓
VALUE ✓✓✓✓
EASE ✓✓✓✓

Kew's mission is to increase knowledge about plants and conserve them for future generations. This site gives plenty of information about their work, the collections, features and events. There are also details of the facilities at the gardens, conservation, educational material and lots of links to related sites.

www.rhs.org.uk
ROYAL HORTICULTURAL SOCIETY

ORIGIN UK
SPEED ✓✓✓✓
INFO ✓✓✓✓
VALUE ✓✓✓✓
EASE ✓✓✓✓

An excellent site from the RHS which features a plant finder service covering some 70,000 plant types, a garden finder and an event finder. There's also advice and information about the RHS and what they do, as well as a good online shop, which can also be visited, at www.grogro.com.

Other gardening advice sites well worth trying are:

www.plants-magazine.com – very good garden magazine, broad in scope but particularly strong on new plants.

www.garden-uk.org.uk – a gardener's web-ring and chat room which is great for links to other related and specialist sites. It's quite slow though and the site needs a re-design.

www.gardenlinks.ndo.co.uk – links to gardening sites in 32 categories, a good place to start searching for something specific.

www.gonegardening.com – nice design, wide ranging magazine and shop.

www.gardenguides.com – a useful American resource site with loads of information on every aspect of gardening. It has lots of tips, handy guides, and a free online newsletter.

Gardening stores

www.dig-it.co.uk
GARDENING IN STYLE

ORIGIN	UK
SPEED	✓✓✓✓
INFO	✓✓✓✓
VALUE	✓✓✓
EASE	✓✓✓✓

This is a beautifully designed garden shop and magazine, although sometimes the graphics overlap. The magazine section offers features, tips and well-written articles, while in the consultancy bit you can get online advice or e-mail a gardening expert. The shop offers a wide range of plants and gardening equipment and related products, delivery to mainland UK is £3.95 or £10.95 if you live on the islands or in Northern Ireland.

www.crocus.co.uk
GARDENERS BY NATURE

ORIGIN	UK
SPEED	✓✓✓✓
INFO	✓✓✓✓
VALUE	✓✓✓✓
EASE	✓✓✓✓

A good-looking site full of ideas enhanced by excellent photographs, there are some good articles and features, but it's basically a gorgeous shop with thousands of plants and products to choose from and some good offers. Delivery costs depend on where you live, those living in the South get their plants delivered by trained gardeners but for the rest of the UK they have a mandate to get plants to you in the best possible state.

www.blooms-online.com
ONE-STOP GARDENER'S RESOURCE

A beautiful site that will supply all your garden needs and desires. In addition to ordering your seeds and buying your garden furniture, there's a great plant search where you can find plants of specific size and colour for that difficult hole in the border. There are DIY projects and a design service too, a gardener's club and advice. Delivery cost depends on your order or you can pick up at their nearest store.

Other gardening shops worth checking out are:

www.glut.co.uk – the Gluttonous Gardener provides unusual presents for every gardener.

www.chilternseeds.co.uk – a bit slow, this superb site offers a massive selection of seeds (over 5,000 types) and growing information.

www.earth-to-earth.com – supplies natural and environmentally friendly products.

www.e-garden.co.uk – nice looking site with a magazine and shop, a little slow, but with some good offers.

Garden design

www.dreamgardens.co.uk

TURNING DREAMS INTO REALITY

ORIGIN UK	Complete Anne and Suze's questionnaire from
SPEED ✓✓✓	which you'll get a suggested ideal garden, it's
INFO ✓✓✓✓	easy to use and full of good ideas, but the real
VALUE ✓✓✓	design costs from £75. For more ideas try
EASE ✓✓✓	**www.creativegardener.com** which is devoted to

providing inspiration for your garden.

Organic gardening

www.hdra.org.uk

HENRY DOUBLEDAY RESEARCH ASSOCIATION

ORIGIN UK	The leading authority on organic gardening, this
SPEED ✓✓✓	site offers a superb resource if you're into gardening
INFO ✓✓✓✓✓	the natural way. It's particularly good if you're grow-
EASE ✓✓✓	ing vegetables with fact sheets and details on why

you should garden organically. See also **www.soilas-sociation.org** for advice on growing organic food plus the latest news on their campaigns.

For information, compost lovers should go to
www.oldgrowth.org/compost and for shopping go
to the excellent **www.greengardener.co.uk**

British wildflowers and plants

www.nhm.ac.uk/science/projects/fff
FLORA AND FAUNA

ORIGIN UK	Using the postcode search, find out the plants that
SPEED ✓✓✓	are native to your area, where to get seeds and then
INFO ✓✓✓✓✓	how to look after them once they're in your garden.
EASE ✓✓✓	Sponsored by the Natural History Museum.

www.british-trees.com
FORESTRY AND CONSERVATION

ORIGIN UK	Information on British trees which, while compre-
SPEED ✓✓✓	hensive, could really do with more illustrations. It
INFO ✓✓✓✓	has also got a good set of links and a list of books
EASE ✓✓✓✓	and magazines.

www.wildflowers.co.uk
BRITISH WILDFLOWERS

ORIGIN UK	An online store specialising in British wildflowers
SPEED ✓✓✓	with advice on how to grow them, there's also a
INFO ✓✓✓	search engine where you can find the plants you
EASE ✓✓✓	need using common or Latin names.

Specific plants and specialists

www.herbnet.com
GROWING, COOKING HERBS, GOOD LINKS

ORIGIN US	An American network specialising in herbs, with links
SPEED ✓✓✓	to specialists, trade and information sites. It can be
INFO ✓✓✓✓	hard work to negotiate, but there's no doubting the
EASE ✓✓✓	quality of the content. See also the excellent Breckland
	nursery site at **http://herbs.get-the-web.com**

www.discoveringannuals.com

ANNUALS GALORE

ORIGIN UK
SPEED ✓✓✓
INFO ✓✓✓✓
EASE ✓✓✓✓

Based on the successful book, this site offers information on hardy annuals, half-hardy annuals, biennials and seed-raised bedding plants of all kinds. There's an A–Z listing on the plants and it tells you where you can buy them.

www.windowbox.com

CONTAINER GARDENING

ORIGIN US
SPEED ✓✓✓✓
INFO ✓✓✓✓✓
EASE ✓✓✓✓

A really good American site which is well worth a look if you're into container gardening in any form, it's well laid out and very well written with great ideas for unusual plant combinations. Worth a long browse.

www.rareplants.co.uk

RARE PLANT NURSERY

ORIGIN UK
SPEED ✓✓✓
INFO ✓✓✓✓
EASE ✓✓✓✓

A site developed by a specialist nursery, which is well illustrated, and pretty comprehensive, it offers information on the plants and can supply plants worldwide. Delivery costs vary.

www.rosarian.com

ROSES

ORIGIN UK
SPEED ✓✓✓✓
INFO ✓✓✓✓✓
EASE ✓✓✓✓

As this is a generalist guide we wouldn't normally review such a specialist site, but it's so well-designed in terms of how an online magazine should look for its audience, that we couldn't resist including it. If you love roses or just need information on them, drop in here for a good, long browse. See also **www.davidaustinroses.com** the outstanding rose specialist.

Gardening peripherals

www.lawnmowersdirect.co.uk

BUY A LAWNMOWER ONLINE

ORIGIN UK   A retailer specialising in mowers and other power
SPEED ✓✓✓✓   tools, you can browse by make and it's quick and
INFO ✓✓✓✓✓   easy to use, if a little basic. Delivery within the UK is
VALUE ✓✓✓✓   free, if you spend more than £50.
EASE ✓✓✓✓

www.lightingforgardens.co.uk

LIGHT UP YOUR GARDEN

ORIGIN UK   A specialist that offers advice, ideas and a wide
SPEED ✓✓✓✓   range of products to light up your garden, all on a
INFO ✓✓✓✓   nicely designed site.
VALUE ✓✓✓
EASE ✓✓✓✓

www.agriframes.co.uk

GARDEN STRUCTURES

ORIGIN UK   A wide range of non-plant garden products from
SPEED ✓✓✓   pergolas to watering cans from probably the UK's
INFO ✓✓✓✓   leading supplier; it could be a much more user-
VALUE ✓✓✓   friendly site.
EASE ✓✓✓

TV tie-ins and celebrities

www.bbc.co.uk/gardening

GARDENING AT THE BEEB

ORIGIN UK   A set of web pages from the BBC site which offer a
SPEED ✓✓✓✓   great gardening magazine, with celebrities mixed
INFO ✓✓✓✓   with helpful advice and features such as plant
EASE ✓✓✓✓   profiles, ask the expert and what to expect in the
month ahead.

www.barnsdalegardens.co.uk
GEOFF HAMILTON'S GARDEN

ORIGIN UK	To many people the real home of Gardener's World,
SPEED ✓✓✓	this site tells you all about Barnsdale and has
INFO ✓✓✓✓	features about the garden, Geoff and his work.
VALUE ✓✓✓	There's also an online store selling a limited range of
EASE ✓✓✓✓	products and a good set of gardening site links.

www.alantitchmarsh.com
ALAN TITCHMARSH

ORIGIN UK	Part of the Expert Gardener site with competitions,
SPEED ✓✓✓	biographical details, sponsored events and some
INFO ✓✓	gardening details.
EASE ✓✓✓✓	

Other important gardeners:
www.gertrudejeckll.co.uk – a biography of the
   great woman with useful links.
www.capability-brown.org – an overview of his work.

Visiting gardens

www.gardenvisit.com
GARDENS TO VISIT AND ENJOY

ORIGIN UK	With over 1,000 gardens listed worldwide, this site
SPEED ✓✓✓	offers information on all of them and each is rated for
INFO ✓✓✓✓	design, planting and scenic interest with Sissinghurst
EASE ✓✓✓✓	scoring top marks. There's also information on the

history of gardening, tours and hotels with good
gardens.
   See also **www.nationaltrust.org.uk** which offers
information on their gardens and places of interest.
For the grandest garden scheme of them all go to
www.edenproject.com who also have a top site covering all the progress they're making along with visiting
times and details.

www.ngs.org.uk

NATIONAL GARDEN SCHEME

ORIGIN UK
SPEED ✓✓✓✓
INFO ✓✓✓
EASE ✓✓✓✓

This is basically the famous yellow book converted into a web site with details on over 2,000 gardens to visit for charity and the work they undertake with the money they earn from your support.

Gardeners with special needs

www.thrive.org.uk

NATIONAL HORTICULTURAL CHARITY

ORIGIN UK
SPEED ✓✓✓
INFO ✓✓✓✓
EASE ✓✓✓✓

This charity exists to provide expert advice on gardening for people with disabilities and older people who want to continue gardening with restricted mobility. The site gives information on how the charity works and links to related sites. See also **www.gardenforever.com** who offer lots in the way of horticultural therapy.

Gay and Lesbian

www.rainbownetwork.com

LESBIAN & GAY LIFESTYLE

ORIGIN UK
SPEED ✓✓✓
INFO ✓✓✓✓✓
EASE ✓✓✓✓

A very well thought out magazine-style web site catering for all aspects of gay and lesbian life. It primarily covers news, fashion, entertainment and health, but there's a travel agency as well. There are also forums and chat sections, classified ads as well as profiles on well-known personalities.

For other good gay/lesbian sites try:

www.uk.gay.com – British page from the big American magazine site.

www.glinn.com – the gay gateway to the web.

www.gaypride.co.uk – gay Britain network - strong on links and great design.

www.gaybritain.co.uk – excellent graphics, a gay portal site.

www.blackberricafe.com – sisterhood chat site.

www.kenric.co.uk – the long running lesbian support and social site.

www.gay365.co.uk – chat and dating.

www.gaytravel.co.uk – gay travel guide, UK oriented but with some good worldwide information.

www.channel4.com/entertainment/tv/showcards/S/s o_graham_norton.html – Channel 4's site for Graham Norton – So excellent!

Genealogy

www.sog.org.uk

THE SOCIETY OF GENEALOGISTS

ORIGIN UK
SPEED ✓✓✓✓
INFO ✓✓✓✓
EASE ✓✓✓✓

This is the first place to go when you're thinking about researching your family tree. It won't win awards for web design, but it contains basic information and there is an excellent set of links you can use to start you off.

See also the excellent **www.cyndislist.com** where you'll find almost 100,000 links in 150 categories to help with your family research.

www.pro.gov.uk

PUBLIC RECORD OFFICE

ORIGIN UK
SPEED ✓✓✓
INFO ✓✓✓✓✓
EASE ✓✓✓✓

To quote the introduction 'The Public Record Office is the national archive of England, Wales and the United Kingdom. It brings together and preserves the records of central government and the courts of law, and makes them available to all who wish to consult them. The records span an unbroken period from the 11th century to the present day.' The site is easy to use, the information is concisely presented and easy to access. It also has information on how you can access the 1901 census.

See also **www.familyrecords.gov.uk** which can help enormously with tracing your family tree, the links selection is excellent.

www.accessgenealogy.com

GENEALOGY WEB PORTAL

ORIGIN US
SPEED ✓✓✓✓
INFO ✓✓✓✓
EASE ✓✓✓✓

A massive number of links and access to different countries' web rings give this site 'must check out' status. It is biased to an American audience but it's very useful none-the-less. See also another portal site **www.genealogyportal.com** which is less cluttered.

www.everton.com

GENEALOGICAL HELPER

ORIGIN US
SPEED ✓✓✓✓
INFO ✓✓✓
EASE ✓✓✓✓

No we haven't gone mad and put a football team in the wrong section, Everton is the name of one of the best magazines devoted to genealogy. It's an attractive site which has articles and features on the subject along with tips on how to conduct your search.

www.origins.net

DEFINITIVE DATABASES

ORIGIN UK
SPEED ✓✓✓✓
INFO ✓✓✓✓
EASE ✓✓✓✓

This site has information provided from the Society of Genealogists' records, from Scotland going back to 1553 and from England going back to 1568, and unlike many other sites in this area, it's also well designed and easy to use. There are also search tips, access to discussion groups and a new section devoted to Ireland.

www.brit-a-r.demon.co.uk

THE OFFICIAL BRITISH ANCESTRAL RESEARCH SITE

ORIGIN UK
SPEED ✓✓✓✓
INFO ✓✓✓
VALUE ✓✓
EASE ✓✓✓✓

For £375 they will research one surname or line, for £675 two or a minimum of 6 hours work for £140. They guarantee results to four generations. Not as much fun as doing it yourself though.

www.genuki.org.uk

VIRTUAL LIBRARY OF GENEALOGICAL INFORMATION

ORIGIN UK
SPEED ✓✓✓✓
INFO ✓✓✓
EASE ✓✓✓✓

An excellent British-oriented site with a huge range of links to help you find your ancestors. There is help for those starting out, news, bulletin boards, FAQs on genealogy and a regional search map of the UK and Ireland.

www.ancestry.com

NO 1 SOURCE FOR FAMILY HISTORY

ORIGIN US
SPEED ✓✓✓✓
INFO ✓✓✓
VALUE ✓✓
EASE ✓✓✓✓

Find out about your ancestors for a subscription beginning at $24.95 per year. This US-oriented site has 1 billion names and access to 3,000 databases. It offers some information for free, but for real detail you have to join. It's especially good if you're searching for someone in the US or Canada. Linked to this is the chat site **www.familyhistory.com** where you can visit surname discussion groups.

www.surnameweb.org
ORIGINS OF SURNAMES

ORIGIN US
SPEED ✓✓✓✓
INFO ✓✓✓✓✓
EASE ✓✓

A great place to start your search for your family origins. On top of the information about your name, there are thousands of links and they claim 2 billion searchable records.

Other useful sites that may help in your family research:
www.gendoor.com – genealogy search engine.
www.rootsweb.com – free genealogy site supported
    by Ancestry.com with interactive guides and
    research tools.
www.gengateway.com – claims to have the
    number 1 family tree making software.
www.familysearch.org – The church of Jesus Christ
    and the latter day Saint's excellent research site
    with good step-by-step information.

Government

www.ukonline.gov.uk (formally www.open.gov.uk)
THE ENTRY POINT FOR GOVERNMENT INFORMATION

ORIGIN UK
SPEED ✓✓✓✓
INFO ✓✓✓✓✓
EASE ✓✓✓✓

A massive web site devoted to the workings of our government, it is a superb resource if you want to know anything official both at a national and a local level. Use the index or the search facility to navigate, as it's easy to get sidetracked. There are several major sections – in 'Citizenspace' you can have your say and take part in decision making, there's life stage support and advice in 'Yourlife', in 'Do It Online' there's information on achieving things online from booking a driving test to help with debt recovery. There's also a newsroom and a quick search facility.

Other key links
www.clicktso.com – the Stationery Office bookstore.
www.conservatives.com – Conservative party.
www.europarl.eu.int – how the European
  Parliament works.
www.labour.org.uk – Labour party.
www.libdems.org.uk – Liberal Democrats.
www.parliament.uk/commons/hsecom.htm – what's
  on in the House of Commons.
www.royal.gov.uk – for the monarchy.
www.ukmeps.info – Information on Members Of
  European Parliament.
www.ukmps.info – A definitive non-political portal
  for United Kingdom Members of Parliament.
www.un.org – United Nations.

Greetings Cards

www.intercarte.com
SEND A REAL CARD

ORIGIN UK	Expensive at £4.99 but they print your message and
SPEED ✓✓✓	delivery on orders placed before 5pm will be posted
INFO ✓✓✓	via Royal Mail that day. The site only features the
EASE ✓✓✓	up-market Woodmansterne cards.

www.bluemountain.com
E-CARDS

ORIGIN US	Blue Mountain has thousands of cards for every
SPEED ✓✓✓	occasion; it's easy to use but you now have to
INFO ✓✓✓✓	subscribe to get the best designs. There are all sorts
VALUE ✓✓	of extras you can build in like music, cartoons and
EASE ✓✓✓✓	even voice messages. If you can't find what you
	want here then check out **www.egreetings.com**

which is similar but has a different selection, it's slushy and very American. Both sites were offering free trials when we visited. Although **www.greeting-cards.com** remains free, it probably breaks the record for the number of adverts and pop-ups that hit you as it downloads. Nice selection if you can bear the ads. The best of the bunch is probably **www.regards.com** which is a little slow but free and not cluttered.

www.nextcard.co.uk
3D CARDS

ORIGIN UK
SPEED ✓✓✓
INFO ✓✓✓
EASE ✓✓✓

Send three-dimensional cards using this site, there are great pictures of animals, sunsets and mountain scenery to choose from.

www.charitycards.co.uk
CONTRIBUTIONS TO CHARITY

ORIGIN UK
SPEED ✓✓✓✓
INFO ✓✓✓✓
VALUE ✓✓✓✓✓
EASE ✓✓✓✓

Buy your cards here and give money to charity, this is traditionally a Christmas thing but Charitycards have turned it into an all year round possibility. There are also discounts available and free postage if you buy in quantity and they also sell stamps.

Health Advice

Here are some of the key sites for getting good health advice, featuring online doctors, fitness centres, nutrition and sites that try to combine all three. As with all health sites, there is no substitute for the real thing and if you are ill, your main port of call must be your doctor. Dietary advice sites are listed on page 152, specialist sites aimed at men, on page 243 and for women, on page 486. The advice for parents, page 290 and teens, page 399 may also be useful.

General health

www.nhsdirect.nhs.uk

NHS ADVICE ONLINE

ORIGIN UK
SPEED ✓✓✓✓✓
INFO ✓✓✓✓✓
EASE ✓✓✓✓

NHS Direct is a telephone advice service and this is the Internet spin-off, it comprises of an excellent guide to common ailments with the emphasis on treating them at home, a health magazine with monthly features, audio clips on a wide range of health topics and a superb selection of NHS-approved links covering specific illnesses or parts of the body. There's also health information and an A–Z guide to the NHS.

www.bupa.co.uk

BUPA HOMEPAGE

ORIGIN UK
SPEED ✓✓✓✓
INFO ✓✓✓✓✓
EASE ✓✓✓

Health fact-sheets, special offers on health cover, health tips and competitions are all on offer at this well-designed site. You can also find your nearest BUPA hospital and instructions on referral. See also **www.ppphealthcare.co.uk** who have over 150 fact-sheets available on a wide range of health conditions.

www.healthfinder.com

A GREAT PLACE TO START FOR HEALTH ADVICE

ORIGIN US
SPEED ✓✓✓
INFO ✓✓✓✓✓
EASE ✓✓✓

Run by the US Department of Health, this provides a link to more or less every health organisation, medical and fitness site you can think of. In several sections you can learn about hot medical topics, catch the medical news, make smart health choices, discover what's best for you and your lifestyle and use the medical dictionary in the research section. The site is well designed, fast once it's fully down-loaded and very easy to use.

www.patient.co.uk

FINDING INFORMATION FROM UK SOURCES

ORIGIN UK
SPEED ✓✓✓
INFO ✓✓✓✓✓
EASE ✓✓✓✓✓

This excellent site has been put together by two GPs. It's essentially a collection of links to other health sites, but from here you can find a web site on health-related topics with a UK bias. You can search alphabetically or browse within the site. All the recommended sites are reviewed by a GP for suitability and quality before being placed on the list.

For a second opinion you could visit **www.surgery-door.co.uk** which is more magazine-like in style with up to the minute news stories. It's comprehensive and has an online shop. Also try the well-designed **www.netdoctor.co.uk** who describe themselves as the 'UK's independent health web site' and offer a similar service.

www.embarrassingproblems.co.uk

FIRST STEP

ORIGIN UK
SPEED ✓✓✓✓
INFO ✓✓✓✓✓
EASE ✓✓✓✓✓

An award-winning and much-recommended site that works well; it's what the Internet should be about really. The site helps you deal with health problems that are difficult to discuss with anyone; it's easy to use and comprehensive. Younger people and teenagers should also check out www.coolnurse.com, which is an excellent American site with similar attributes.

www.drkoop.com

THE BEST PRESCRIPTION IS KNOWLEDGE

ORIGIN US
SPEED ✓✓✓✓
INFO ✓✓✓✓✓
EASE ✓✓✓✓

Don't let the silly name put you off, Dr C. Everett Koop is a former US Surgeon General and is acknowledged as one of the best online doctors. The goal is to empower you to take care of your own health through better knowledge. The site is very comprehensive covering every major health topic and is aimed at all, including both young and old.

www.mayohealth.org

RELIABLE INFORMATION FOR A HEALTHY LIFE

ORIGIN US
SPEED ✓✓✓✓
INFO ✓✓✓✓✓
EASE ✓✓✓✓

Mayo has a similar ethic to Dr Koop but is less fussy and very easy to use. However, the amount of information can be overwhelming, as they claim the combined knowledge of some 2,000 doctors in the 11 'centers'. Essentially it's a massive collection of articles that combine to give you a large amount of data on specific medical topics. There are also guides on how to live a healthy life, first aid and a newsletter, plus information on specific medical conditions and diseases.

www.quackwatch.com

HEALTH FRAUD, QUACKERY AND INTELLIGENT DECISIONS

ORIGIN US
SPEED ✓✓✓✓
INFO ✓✓✓✓
EASE ✓✓✓

Exposes fraudulent cures and old wives tales, then provides information on where to get the right treatment. It makes fascinating reading and includes exposés on everything from acupuncture to weight loss. Use the search engine or just browse through it; many of the articles leave you amazed at the fraudulent nature of some medical claims.

www.allcures.com

UK'S FIRST ONLINE PHARMACY

ORIGIN UK
SPEED ✓✓✓
INFO ✓✓✓✓
VALUE ✓✓✓
EASE ✓✓✓

After a fairly lengthy but secure registration process you can shop from this site which has all the big brands and a wide range of products. There are also sections on toiletries, beauty, alternative medicine and a photo-shop. You can arrange to have your prescriptions made up and sent to you with no delivery charge. See also www.academyhealth.com who deliver free in the UK.

www.medicalanswer.com

THE MEDICAL SEARCH ENGINE

ORIGIN US
SPEED ✓✓✓
INFO ✓✓✓✓
EASE ✓✓✓✓

A search engine that looks rather like yahoo, with some 800 medical and health sites listed and rated. See also www.medisearch.co.uk which is more UK-orientated.

www.tummybutton.com

COMPREHENSIVE GUIDE TO HEALTH RESOURCES

ORIGIN US
SPEED ✓✓✓
INFO ✓✓✓✓
EASE ✓✓✓✓

Once a fitness site this is now a very good directory site covering health resources by topic and type.

The following sites also offer good health information:
www.bbc.co.uk/health - good all rounder covering
lots of topics, good links.
http://medlineplus.gov/ - a health information centre
from the U.S. National Library of Medicine.
www.studenthealth.co.uk - written by doctors, sensible and funny with some good competitions.
www.mypharmacy.co.uk - good basic health site
from a real pharmacist.

Fitness and exercise

www.netfit.co.uk
DEFINITIVE GUIDE TO HEALTH AND FITNESS

ORIGIN UK ✓✓✓
SPEED ✓✓✓
INFO ✓✓✓✓✓
EASE ✓✓✓✓

Devoted to promoting the benefits of regular exercise with a dedicated team who put a great deal of
effort into the site. You can gauge your fitness,
there's information on some 200 exercises, tips on
eating and dieting, nutrition and links to useful
(mainly sport) sites.

www.hfonline.co.uk
HEALTH & FITNESS MAGAZINE

ORIGIN UK ✓✓✓
SPEED ✓✓✓
INFO ✓✓✓✓
EASE ✓✓✓

A spin-off site from the magazine, which offers the
latest health news and advice, it's attractive and it's
quite comprehensive.

www.fitnessonline.com
PROVIDING PERSONAL SUPPORT

ORIGIN US ✓✓✓✓
SPEED ✓✓✓✓
INFO ✓✓✓✓✓
EASE ✓✓✓

This good-looking site is from an American magazine group. It takes a holistic view of health offering
advice on exercise, nutrition and health products. In
reality what you get is a succession of articles from
their magazines, all are very informative but getting
the right information can be time-consuming.

The following sites also offer good advice and fitness information:

www.exercisegroup.com – natural body building.

www.workout.com – over 500 exercises, lots of information too.

www.getfitta.co.uk – with the Territorial Army.

www.exercise.co.uk – information on exercise and the right equipment to use and buy.

www.fitnesspeak.co.uk – the best prices for gym equipment.

Alternative medicine and therapies

www.alt-med.co.uk

DIRECTORY OF ALTERNATIVE MEDICINE

ORIGIN UK
SPEED ✓✓✓
INFO ✓✓✓✓
EASE ✓✓✓✓

This directory is aimed at people looking for complementary and alternative health therapies in their area. There are links to other relevant web sites and descriptions and information on the benefits of each of the major therapies. For more information on alternative medicines and therapies also check out www.therapy-world.co.uk a magazine site with lots of articles on the subject.

www.altmedicine.com

ALTERNATIVE HEALTH NEWS

ORIGIN US
SPEED ✓✓✓✓
INFO ✓✓✓✓
EASE ✓✓✓✓

Keep up-to-date with the latest therapies and trends with articles and features from some of the key figures in the world of alternative medicine. The site is supplemented by an excellent medical search engine, an overview of the major philosophies and associated healing techniques plus a good set of related links.

www.medical-acupuncture.co.uk

ACUPUNCTURE

ORIGIN UK	A good looking site with information from the
SPEED ✓✓✓✓	British Medical Acupuncture Society on the nature
INFO ✓✓✓✓	of acupuncture and where to find a practitioner
EASE ✓✓✓✓	in your area. There are also good links and
	information on courses.

www.drlockie.com

HOMEOPATHY MADE EASY

ORIGIN US	An interesting, clear and simple site that offers sensi-
SPEED ✓✓✓	ble advice at all levels. Click on any of the medicine
INFO ✓✓✓✓	jars to get what you need:
EASE ✓✓✓✓✓	

1 Information on homeopathy.
2 Homeopathic news.
3 Treatments for a range of diseases and ailments.
4 Review and add to the list of 'Most Frequently Asked Questions' on homeopathy.
5 Buy Dr Lockie's books via the Amazon bookstore.
6 Links to other Homeopathic sites.
7 Search the site.

www.homeopath.co.uk

ONLINE HOMEOPATHIC SERVICES

ORIGIN UK	An excellent and attractive site that offers a direc-
SPEED ✓✓✓✓	tory of practising homeopaths in the UK plus infor-
INFO ✓✓✓✓	mation on college courses and a bookshop. In
EASE ✓✓✓✓	addition there is access to an online pharmacy via
	ThinkNatural where you can buy homeopathic
	medicines.

See also:
www.homeopathyhome.com – slightly confusing but comprehensive.
www.trusthomeopathy.org – home of the British Homeopathic Association.

www.homeopathy-soh.org – home of the Society of Homeopaths.

www.drweil.com – the vitamin guru has a site that offers much in advice and his own brand of balanced living.

www.ukselfhelp.info – a listing of almost 800 self-help groups and nearly 700 links to self-help sites.

www.pilates.co.uk

PURELY PILATES

ORIGIN UK	Keep up with the latest information on pilates; find
SPEED ✓✓✓	out what it can do for you and where to find a qual-
INFO ✓✓✓✓	ified instructor. There's also a newsletter and an
EASE ✓✓✓	events listing.

www.thinknatural.com

THINK NATURALLY

ORIGIN UK	A nicely designed site with a mass of information on
SPEED ✓✓✓✓	every aspect of natural health including a compre-
INFO ✓✓✓	hensive shop with loads of special offers and a very
VALUE ✓✓✓✓	wide range of products.
EASE ✓✓✓✓	

www.yogauk.com

YOGA

ORIGIN UK	Welcome to the yoga village where you can get
SPEED ✓✓✓	information on yoga in the UK, subscribe to their
INFO ✓✓✓✓	magazine, or browse the links section, which has a
EASE ✓✓✓	comprehensive list of stores. See also
	www.yogaplus.co.uk who offer courses and work-
	shops, and also www.yogatherapy.org

Sites catering for a specific condition or disease

Here is a list of the key sites relating to specific diseases, addictions and ailments, we have not attempted to review them, but if you know of a site we've missed and would like it included in the next edition of this book please e-mail us at goodwebsiteguide@hotmail.com

Alcohol and drug abuse
   www.drugnet.co.uk
   www.alcoholics-anonymous.org
   www.al-anon-alateen.org
Allergies
   www.allergy-info.com (sponsored by Zyrtec)
   www.allergy.co.uk
Alzheimers and dementia
   www.alzheimers.org.uk
   www.dementia.ion.ucl.ac.uk
Aids and HIV
   www.tht.org.uk
   www.lovelife.hea.org.uk
   www.avert.org
   www.hiv-development.org
Anxiety
   www.healthanxiety.com
Arthritis
   www.arc.org.uk
   www.aboutarthritis.com
Asthma
   www.asthma.org.uk
Blindness
   www.rnib.org.uk
   www.sense.org.uk
Brain disease
   www.bbsf.org.uk

Breast Cancer Campaign
www.bcc-uk.org
Bullying
www.bullying.co.uk
Cancer
www.cancerresearchuk.org
www.cancerbacup.org
www.bowelcancer.org
Cerebral palsy
www.scope.org.uk
Chiropody
www.feetforlife.org
Deafness
www.britishdeafassociation.org.uk
Dental
www.gdc-uk.org
www.priory.co.uk
www.bda-dentistry.org.uk
Depression
http://www.depressionalliance.org/
Dermatology
www.skinhealth.co.uk
Diabetics
www.diabetic.org.uk
Digestion
www.digestivedisorders.org
www.digestivecare.co.uk
Disabled
www.disability.gov.uk
www.radar.org.uk
Drugs
www.release.org.uk
www.acde.org
www.urban75.com/drugs/

Epilepsy
  www.epilepsy.org.uk
  www.epilepsynse.org.uk
Eczema
  www.eczema.org
Fertility
  www.ifconline.org
Fibromyalgia
  www.ukfibromyalgia.com
Gambling
  www.gamblersanonymous.org.uk
Heart and stroke
  www.bhf.org.uk
  www.stroke.org.uk
  www.familyheart.org
High blood pressure
  www.hbpf.org.uk
Kidney problems
  www.kidney.org.uk
Liver problems
  www.britishlivertrust.org.uk
Meningitis
  www.meningitis-trust.org
Mental health
  www.mentalhealth.com
  www.mind.org.uk
  www.youngminds.org.uk
  www.uzone.org.uk
Migraine
  www.migraine.org.uk
  www.migrainetrust.org
Multiple sclerosis
  www.mssociety.org.uk
Older people
  www.elderabuse.org.uk

Repetitive Strain Injury
www.rsi.org.uk

Smoking
www.ash.org.uk

Solvent abuse
www.canban.com

Spina bifida
www.asbah.org

Stress
www.stressrelease.com
www.isma.org.uk

History and Biography

The Internet is proving to be a great storehouse, not only for the latest news but also for cataloguing historical events in an entertaining and informative way, here are some of the best sites.

www.thehistorychannel.com

THE BEST SEARCH IN HISTORY

ORIGIN	US	Excellent for history buffs, revision or just a good
SPEED	✓✓✓✓	read, the History Channel provides a site that is
INFO	✓✓✓✓✓	packed with information. Search by key word or
EASE	✓✓✓	timeline, by date and by subject, get biographical

information or speeches. It's fast and easy to get carried away once you start your search.

www.historytoday.com

WORLD'S LEADING HISTORY MAGAZINE

ORIGIN	UK	Contains some excellent articles from the magazine,
SPEED	✓✓✓✓	but probably the most useful bit is the related links
INFO	✓✓✓✓	section, which offers many links to other history sites.
EASE	✓✓✓✓	

www.newsplayer.com

RELIVE THE LAST CENTURY

ORIGIN UK
SPEED ✓✓✓
INFO ✓✓✓✓✓
VALUE ✓✓
EASE ✓✓✓✓

Relive the events of the past hundred years, witness them at first hand as they happened. A truly superb site with real newsreel footage worth the £25 annual subscription fee.

www.ukans.edu/history/VL

HISTORY LINKS

ORIGIN US
SPEED ✓✓✓✓
INFO ✓✓✓✓✓
EASE ✓✓✓

The folks at the University of Kansas love their history and have put together a huge library, organised by country and historical period. It's got an easy to use search engine too. For modern history go to **www.fordham.edu/halsall/mod/modsbook.html**, while for hundreds of links in over 50 categories go to Horus' History links at **http://horus.ucr.edu/horuslinks.html**

http://history.about.com

HISTORY AT ABOUT.COM

ORIGIN US
SPEED ✓✓✓✓
INFO ✓✓✓✓✓
EASE ✓✓✓

A massive archive including bringing history to life by using the eyewitness accounts of people who were actually there. This site is excellent for most periods of history. You could also try **www.history-place.com** which is biased towards the US but has some great historic photos. There's also **www.ibis-com.com** who have a large catalogue of historical recollections both ancient and modern, and take the 'history through the eyes of those who lived it' approach.

Good sites covering history for specific periods:

www.roman-empire.net – excellent site covering all aspects of the Roman Empire with a good kids section.

www.tudorhistory.org – a who's who of Tudor times with background on what it was like to live then.

www.pastforward.co.uk/vikings – a directory of all things Viking.

www.regia.org – Anglo-Saxons, Vikings and Normans.

Other types of history sites

www.biography.com

FIND OUT ABOUT ANYONE WHO WAS ANYONE

ORIGIN US
SPEED ✓✓✓✓
INFO ✓✓✓✓✓
EASE ✓✓✓

Over 25,000 biographical references and some 4,000 videos make this site a great option if you need to find out about someone in a hurry. There are special features such as a book club and a magazine. There is a shop but at time of going to press they don't ship to the UK.

www.francisfrith.co.uk

HISTORY IN PHOTOGRAPHS

ORIGIN UK
SPEED ✓✓✓✓
INFO ✓✓✓✓
VALUE ✓✓✓✓
EASE ✓✓✓✓

This remarkable archive was started in 1860 and there are over 365,000 photographs featuring some 7,000 cities, towns and villages. The site is very well designed with a good search facility. You can buy from a growing selection of shots, different sizes are available and it's good value too.

www.old-maps.co.uk

FREE OLD MAPS

ORIGIN UK
SPEED ✓✓
INFO ✓✓✓✓
EASE ✓✓✓✓

Access to mapping as it was between 1846 and 1899, just type in your town and you get a view of what it looked like in those times. The quality is variable but it's fun to try and spot the changes.

www.museumofcostume.co.uk

COSTUME THROUGH THE AGES

ORIGIN UK
SPEED ✓✓✓
INFO ✓✓✓✓
EASE ✓✓✓

Excellent site showing how the design of costume has changed through the ages. There's a virtual tour and links to other museums based in Bath.

www.yesterdayland.com

YOUR CHILDHOOD REVISITED

ORIGIN US
SPEED ✓✓✓✓
INFO ✓✓✓✓✓
EASE ✓✓✓✓

A modern history site devoted to those things that made up our childhood, mainly aimed at those of us who are in our thirties and forties. It provides a great nostalgia trip covering areas such as toys, TV programs, arcade games, fashion and music.

www.blackhistorymap.com

BLACK AND ASIAN HISTORY ACROSS THE BRITISH ISLES

ORIGIN UK
SPEED ✓✓✓
INFO ✓✓✓✓✓
EASE ✓✓✓✓

A beautifully designed and important site, which graphically describes how Black people and Asians, have contributed to British history. Search by region, use the timeline or category headings. It's well written and very informative with a wide range of contributions, there's also a selection of videos.

www.findagrave.com

FIND A GRAVE!

ORIGIN US
SPEED ✓✓✓
INFO ✓✓✓✓✓
EASE ✓✓✓✓

Find graves of the rich and famous or a long lost relative, either way there's a database of over 3 million to search. It really only covers the USA.

www.the-reenactor.co.uk

TAKE PART IN A BATTLE

ORIGIN UK
SPEED ✓✓✓
INFO ✓✓✓✓
EASE ✓✓✓

OK so you feel the urge to play at being a Viking for the day, well here's where to start where there are some 100 societies to join and play a part in. The site is divided into sections according to time period and you can find out where events are being held plus the latest news.

Hobbies

www.yahoo.co.uk/recreation/hobbies

IF YOU CAN'T FIND YOUR HOBBY THEN LOOK HERE

ORIGIN UK
SPEED ✓✓✓✓
INFO ✓✓✓
VALUE ✓✓
EASE ✓✓✓

Hundreds of links for almost every conceivable pastime from amateur radio to urban exploration, it's part of the Yahoo service (see page 335); also try www.about.com/hobbies who have a similarly large list but with an American bias.

See also:
www.hobbywebguide.com – a modest list with some good hobby sites.
www.ehobbies.com who don't ship outside the USA, but are worth a visit anyway for information and links.
www.hobbyseek.net/cgi-search/Great_Britain/ – a German site with good links to modelling sites.

www.cass-arts.co.uk

ONE STOP SHOP FOR ART MATERIALS

ORIGIN UK
SPEED ✓✓✓✓
INFO ✓✓✓
VALUE ✓✓✓✓
EASE ✓✓✓✓

A huge range of art and craft products available to buy online, also hints and tips and step-by-step guides for the novice. There is an online gallery and a section of art trivia and games. The shop has a decent search engine which copes with over 20,000 items, delivery is charged according to what you spend.

www.sewandso.co.uk

SHOP AT THE SPECIALISTS

ORIGIN UK
SPEED ✓✓✓
INFO ✓✓✓✓
VALUE ✓✓✓✓
EASE ✓✓✓✓

This site offers a huge range of kits and patterns for cross-stitch, needlepoint and embroidery. In addition, there's an equally large range of needles and threads, some 10,000 products in all. There are some good offers and delivery starts at £1 for the UK, but the cost is calculated by weight.

www.horology.com

THE INDEX

ORIGIN US
SPEED ✓✓✓✓
INFO ✓✓✓
EASE ✓✓✓

The complete exploration of time, this is essentially a set of links for the committed horologist. It's pretty comprehensive, so if your hobby is tinkering about with clocks and watches, then this is a must.

www.royalmint.com

THE VALUE OF MONEY

ORIGIN UK
SPEED ✓✓✓✓
INFO ✓✓✓✓✓
VALUE ✓✓✓
EASE ✓✓✓✓

The Royal Mint's web site is informative, providing a history of the Mint, the coins themselves, plus details on the coins they've issued. You can buy from the site and delivery is free.

See also:
www.tokenpublishing.com – owners of *Coin News*.
http://coins.to – US coins and much more from the
    Austin Coin Collecting Society.
www.tclayton.demon.co.uk/coins.html – Tony
    Clayton's informative home page on coins.
www.coinclub.com – good for information and
    links.

www.stanleygibbons.com

STAMPS ETC.

ORIGIN UK	The best prices and a user-friendly site for philate-
SPEED ✓✓✓	lists, you can buy a whole collection or sell them
INFO ✓✓✓	your own. Their catalogue is available online and
EASE ✓✓✓✓	you can take part in auctions.

See also:
www.corbitts.com – auctioneers for stamps, coins,
    notes and medals.
www.robinhood-stamp.co.uk – for good prices and
    range.
www.duncannon.co.uk – for accessories and
    albums.
www.ukphilately.org.uk/abps – information on
    exhibitions and events at the Association of
    British Philatelic Societies.

www.towerhobbies.com

EXCITING WORLD OF RADIO CONTROLLED MODELLING

ORIGIN US	An excellent, clearly laid out site offering a vast
SPEED ✓✓✓✓	range of radio-controlled models along with thou-
INFO ✓✓✓	sands of accessories and parts. The delivery charge
VALUE ✓✓✓	depends on the size of the order.
EASE ✓✓✓✓	

www.brmodelling.com

BRITISH RAILWAY MODELLING

ORIGIN UK
SPEED ✓✓✓✓
INFO ✓✓✓✓
EASE ✓✓✓✓

A high quality magazine site devoted to model railways, it includes a virtual model set for you to play with and articles on specific types of trains and railways. There's also a forum where you to can chat to fellow enthusiasts. For more links and information see www.ukmodelshops.co.uk. While for model cars go to www.motormodels.co.uk and for model boats check out www.modelboats.co.uk

www.ontracks.co.uk

MODEL AND HOBBY SUPERSTORE

ORIGIN UK
SPEED ✓✓✓
INFO ✓✓✓
VALUE ✓✓✓✓
EASE ✓✓✓

They sell over 35,000 models and hobby items, but it's tricky to find what you want as the site is a bit messy with lots of annoying graphics. Having said that there are some good special offers and delivery prices are reasonable.

Humour

Jokes, links and directories

www.comedy-zone.net

COMPLETE COMEDY GUIDE

ORIGIN UK
SPEED ✓✓✓
INFO ✓✓✓✓✓
EASE ✓✓✓

Excellent and wide-ranging comedy site with lots of links and competitions, alongside quotes, jokes and chat.

For other comedy portals and loads of jokes go to:

www.funny.co.uk – what was a good portal site but being re-built at time of writing.

www.funs.co.uk – lots here from jokes to games.

www.jokepost.com – hundreds, all well categorised.

www.jokecenter.com – hundreds of jokes, vote for your favourites.

www.jokes2000.com – e-mail you the latest jokes.

www.funnybone.com – huge database with lots of rude jokes.

www.kidsjokes.co.uk – 12,000+ jokes, great for the family.

www.humorlinks.com – massive portal for all things funny.

www.humournet.co.uk – categorised jokes, links and funny pictures.

www.funnymail.com – lots of jokes well categorised with good features such as tests, top 10 jokes of all time, newest jokes and so on.

www.bored.com – a great directory of humour sites.

www.olleysplace.com

VERY NAUGHTY MULTI-MEDIA

ORIGIN US
SPEED ✓✓✓
INFO ✓✓✓✓
EASE ✓✓✓✓

Olleysplace is justifiably popular for visual and multimedia humour. Its sections include bizarre film clips, voyeur and crazy clips; you should be aware that some of the content is unsuitable for children, and some people may find this site more disturbing than funny. Much of it is geared to selling the accompanying CD-ROM and there's lots of advertising. See also the very entertaining **www.videoparodies.com** who offer loads of parodies on the pop video theme and more; and there's also **www.cyberparodies.com** with the classic 'Oops I've farted again' by Britney.

www.pickthehottie.com

PICK THE HOTTIE!

ORIGIN US
SPEED ✓✓✓
INFO ✓✓✓✓
EASE ✓✓✓✓✓

Probably the best of many sites where people post photos of themselves and their friends (or enemies) the idea being that you vote for the hottest-looking people and the ugliest too.

www.uebersetzung.at/twister

TONGUE TWISTERS

ORIGIN AUSTRIA
SPEED ✓✓✓✓
INFO ✓✓✓✓
EASE ✓✓✓✓

An international collection of tongue twisters, over 2,000 in 87 languages when we last visited, nearly 400 in English - 'Can you can a can as a canner can can a can?' as they say.

British humour

www.britcoms.com

BRITISH COMEDY LINKS

ORIGIN UK
SPEED ✓✓✓✓
INFO ✓✓✓✓
EASE ✓✓✓✓

If you want to find a link to a British comedy show or comedian, then start here. The sites are selected for quality and there's also a broader selection of links for you to browse. You can also sign up for their newsletter. For traditional humour check out www.britishcomedy.org.uk and www.britishsitcoms.com

www.comedybutchers.com

SURREAL BRITISH COMEDY

ORIGIN UK
SPEED ✓✓✓
INFO ✓✓✓✓✓
EASE ✓✓✓✓

A really good attempt at creating a web site that shows off surreal adult comedy in the traditional British style, you click on various rooms within a floating town to get clips and sketches.

Stand-up comedy

www.chortle.co.uk
GUIDE TO LIVE COMEDY IN THE UK

ORIGIN UK
SPEED ✓✓✓✓
INFO ✓✓✓✓
VALUE ✓✓✓✓
EASE ✓✓✓✓

Chortle provides a complete service, listing who's on, where and when – also whether they're any good or not. There's also a comic's A–Z so that you can find your favourites and get reviews on how they're performing, or not, as the case may be.

www.comedyonline.co.uk
STAND UP COMEDY IN YOUR AREA

ORIGIN UK
SPEED ✓✓✓✓
INFO ✓✓✓✓
EASE ✓✓✓✓

News, links, interviews, clubs and listings; its all here at this comprehensive and well put together site, so if you're looking to check out a new comedian or just want to see an old favourite, start here. See also **www.jongleurs.co.uk** whose entertaining site has audio clips and details of what's on and when at their clubs.

www.thespark.com
TAKE THE SPARK TESTS

ORIGIN UK
SPEED ✓✓✓✓
INFO ✓✓✓✓
EASE ✓✓✓✓

The Spark consists of a humorous news magazine and a few other jokey bits and bobs plus lots of annoying adverts, but its main feature, and the reason why millions visit, is for the tests. From the popular personality test, through bitch and bastard tests to the wealth test, all are good for a laugh and of course very accurate. Dare you take the 'Death test' or the new 'Cut-throat' test though?

TV comedy

www.comedycentral.com

THE HOME OF SOUTH PARK AND MORE

ORIGIN US
SPEED ✓✓✓✓
INFO ✓✓✓✓
EASE ✓✓✓✓

Great for South Park and selected American TV shows, but also with clips and background information and stand up comedy too.

www.thesimpsons.com

HOME OF THE SIMPSONS

ORIGIN US
SPEED ✓✓✓✓
INFO ✓✓✓✓
VALUE ✓✓
EASE ✓✓✓✓

A much-improved official site with biographies, background, quizzes and more, plus the ever-present merchandise store. If you are a real fan then go to the Simpsons archive at **www.snpp.com**

Miscellaneous

www.theonion.com

AMERICA'S FINEST NEWS SOURCE

ORIGIN US
SPEED ✓✓✓✓
INFO ✓✓✓✓✓
EASE ✓✓✓✓

A great send-up of American tabloid newspapers, this is one of the most visited sites on the Internet and easily one of the funniest. See also **www.slipup.com** who chronicle the errors and typos of the American media.

www.losers.org

THE WEB'S LOSERS

ORIGIN US
SPEED ✓✓✓
INFO ✓✓✓✓
EASE ✓✓✓✓

A site that catalogues and rates the saddest sites and sights on the web, note that some of the content is strictly adults only. Still, it's one of the most fascinating giggles available, all web site designers should see this.

www.strangereports.com

PRANKS ONLINE

ORIGIN US
SPEED ✓✓✓✓
INFO ✓✓✓✓
EASE ✓✓✓✓

Play pranks on your friends using the service available here, with trick web sites and fake news reports it's almost irresistible but beware their revenge...

www.darwinawards.com

FATAL MISADVENTURES

ORIGIN US
SPEED ✓✓✓✓
INFO ✓✓✓✓
EASE ✓✓✓✓

The Darwin awards have been going several years now and their site is packed with stories, urban legends and personal accounts of those who have 'improved our gene pool by removing themselves from it in really stupid ways'.

www.freakydreams.com

DREAM INTERPRETED

ORIGIN US
SPEED ✓✓✓✓
INFO ✓✓✓✓
EASE ✓✓✓✓

You just type in the description of your dream and an 'accurate' interpretation pops up in seconds.

www.joecartoon.com

FREAKY CARTOONS

ORIGIN US
SPEED ✓✓✓
INFO ✓✓✓✓
EASE ✓✓✓✓

Follow the gruesome, messy adventures of Joe, download the cartoons and send them to your friends and buy the T-shirt - he's a legend after all. Superb animation and very funny, but you need patience for the downloads.

www.user-error.co.uk
EXCUSE GENERATOR

ORIGIN UK
SPEED ✓✓✓✓
INFO ✓✓✓
VALUE ✓✓✓
EASE ✓✓✓

Apart from the excellent excuse generator which is very handy, there's also a virtual makeover section, articles on the unusual universe we live in and, if you're in a disagreement with someone over some fact or other, they'll help you settle your bet.

www.createafart.com
FARTS

ORIGIN US
SPEED ✓✓✓✓
INFO ✓✓✓✓
EASE ✓✓✓✓✓

Create your fart based on duration, smelliness, type and density – well no one said we had to make this book a sophisticated one...

www.justatip.com
ANONYMOUS TIPS

ORIGIN US
SPEED ✓✓✓✓
INFO ✓✓✓✓
EASE ✓✓✓✓

So your friend has an annoying habit, let them know anonymously.

www.museumofhoaxes.com
HOAXES

ORIGIN US
SPEED ✓✓✓✓
INFO ✓✓✓✓
EASE ✓✓✓

The world's greatest hoaxes and April Fools are catalogued here, makes entertaining browsing and is sometimes unbelievable.

www.smalltime.com/dictator
GUESS THE DICTATOR

ORIGIN UK
SPEED ✓✓✓
INFO ✓✓✓✓
EASE ✓✓✓✓

You think of dictator or TV sit-com character, answer the questions put to you and the site will guess who you are thinking of...it's spookily accurate.

Internet Service Provision

There are so many Internet Service Providers (ISPs) that it would be impossible to review them all and it's moving so fast that any information soon becomes outdated. However, help is at hand and here are some sites that will help you chose the right one for you.

www.net4nowt.com

THE PLACE TO START LOOKING FOR THE BEST ISP

ORIGIN UK
SPEED ✓✓✓✓✓
INFO ✓✓✓✓✓
EASE ✓✓✓✓✓

This is a directory of Internet service providers offering news and advice on the best ones. There is an up-to-date critique on each ISP with comments on costs and reliability. There is also a good summary table featuring all the ISPs, which proves useful for comparisons.

www.ispreview.co.uk

INTERNET NEWS

ORIGIN UK
SPEED ✓✓✓✓
INFO ✓✓✓✓✓
EASE ✓✓✓✓✓

Find out what's really going on at this impressive site - they are especially good at exposing the worst performers. There's plenty in the way of news, offers and a top 10 ISP list. Also check out www.thelist.com which is international.

Jobs and Careers

There are over 200 sites offering jobs or career advice but it's largely a matter of luck if you come across a job you like. Still, it enables you to cover plenty of ground in a short space of time without trawling the newspapers. These sites offer the most options and best advice.

Career guidance

www.careerguide.net

ONLINE CAREER ADVICE RESOURCE

ORIGIN UK
SPEED ✓✓✓✓
INFO ✓✓✓✓✓
EASE ✓✓✓

This is a comprehensive service with many sections on job hunting, vacancies, CVs, careers advice and professional institutions that can help.

www.careers-gateway.co.uk

THE CAREER GATEWAY

ORIGIN UK
SPEED ✓✓✓✓
INFO ✓✓✓✓✓
EASE ✓✓✓✓

Great advice and lots of information. For example, how to launch a proper career, evaluate your options and read articles to help you decide what you can do with your life. There's a virtual career show, quizzes designed to help and advice for HR professionals too.

www.reachforthesky.co.uk

CAREER ADVICE FROM SKY TV

ORIGIN UK
SPEED ✓✓✓✓
INFO ✓✓✓✓
EASE ✓✓✓✓

Sky has put together a great web site that doesn't just look good. However, it's developed into more of a teen magazine, but there is a good deal of advice here plus some fun too.

www.careersolutions.co.uk

HELP TO GO FORWARD

ORIGIN UK
SPEED ✓✓✓
INFO ✓✓✓✓✓
EASE ✓✓✓✓

A good place to start if you're not sure what you want to do next with your career, don't know where to start or you've been made redundant. Using the site enables you to narrow your options and clarify things. The list of links is logically laid out and very helpful.

www.careerstorm.com

WHERE DO YOU GO FROM HERE?

ORIGIN HOLLAND
SPEED ✓✓✓
INFO ✓✓✓✓
EASE ✓✓✓✓

A site that will help you make decisions about your next career steps by a series of quizzes and question-naires designed to find out what you're really good at. It's interesting anyway, and it costs nothing.

www.icg-uk.org

INSTITUTE OF CAREER GUIDANCE

ORIGIN UK
SPEED ✓✓✓✓
INFO ✓✓✓✓
EASE ✓✓✓✓

A useful place to go for basic advice and resource information on what to do wherever you are in your career, it has a good links section too.

www.jobability.com

LEADING JOB SITE FOR DISABLED PEOPLE

ORIGIN UK
SPEED ✓✓✓✓
INFO ✓✓✓✓
EASE ✓✓✓✓

A straightforward site designed to help disabled people find employment; it covers the UK by region plus Europe. There's also advice on careers and how to find a job. See also **www.yourable.com** who have a good jobs section.

Job finders

www.transdata-inter.co.uk/jobs-agencies

DIRECTORY OF JOB SITES

ORIGIN UK
SPEED ✓✓✓
INFO ✓✓✓✓✓
EASE ✓✓✓✓✓

Don't let the long URL put you off, this is an excellent place to start on your search. The Directory lists all the major online employment agencies and ranks them by the average number of vacancies, the regions they cover, whether they help create and store CVs and what industries they represent. Clicking on the name takes you right to the site you need.

www.gisajob.co.uk

SEARCH FOR YOUR NEXT JOB HERE

ORIGIN UK
SPEED ✓✓✓✓
INFO ✓✓✓✓
EASE ✓✓✓✓✓

The largest of the UK online job sites with over 80,000 vacancies. You can search by description or sector or get advice on your career. It's good for non-senior executive types.

www.workthing.com

IT'S A WORK THING

ORIGIN UK
SPEED ✓✓✓✓
INFO ✓✓✓✓✓
EASE ✓✓✓✓

One of the best-looking job sites with a reputation to match, this site must be one of the first to visit when job hunting across a wide range of industries. Registered users can set up an e-mail alert when a job matching their search criteria appears. They also work with businesses to develop their people skills and recruitment; you can also get advice on training and personal development too.

www.monster.co.uk

GLOBAL JOBS

ORIGIN UK
SPEED ✓✓✓✓
INFO ✓✓✓✓✓
EASE ✓✓✓✓✓

With over 1 million jobs available worldwide there are plenty to chose from. The site is well-designed and easy to use with the usual help features. At time of writing there were over 22,000 UK jobs listed in over 20 categories.

www.stepstone.co.uk

EUROPEAN INTERNET RECRUITMENT

ORIGIN UK
SPEED ✓✓✓✓
INFO ✓✓✓✓
EASE ✓✓✓✓

Regarded as one of the best, Stepstone has a huge number of European and international vacancies. It's quick, easy to use and offers lots of timesaving cross-referencing features. You can also register your CV. For other overseas jobs see www.overseasjobs.com

Other job finder sites worth checking out:
www.jobpilot.co.uk – good for European jobs, over 60,000 listed.
www.totaljobs.co.uk – 28,000 jobs listed in a wide range of sectors.
www.fish4jobs.co.uk – in excess of 27,000 listed, nice design.
www.doctorjob.com – graduates only need apply.
www.reed.co.uk – some 80,000 vacancies from a wide range of categories.

Other careers and related sites

www.i-resign.com/uk

THE INS AND OUTS OF RESIGNATION

ORIGIN UK

SPEED ✓✓✓

INFO ✓✓✓✓✓

EASE ✓✓✓

Pay a visit before you send the letter, it offers a great deal of advice both legal and sensible. The best section contains the funniest selection of resignation letters anywhere. There are also jobs on offer, links to job finder sites and a career guide service.

www.freelancecentre.com

SELF EMPLOYED

ORIGIN UK

SPEED ✓✓✓

INFO ✓✓✓✓

EASE ✓✓✓✓

Great for anyone thinking of going it alone, or are looking for help if you're already working for yourself. There's plenty of advice here – good deal of it is absolutely free.

www.homeworking.com

WORKING FROM HOME

ORIGIN UK

SPEED ✓✓✓✓

INFO ✓✓✓✓✓

EASE ✓✓✓✓

A site full of advice and information for anyone considering or actually working from home. There are links, directories and classified ads, as well as forum pages where you can share experiences with other home workers.

Legal Advice and the Law

We all need help with certain key events in life: marriages, moving house, making a will or getting a divorce. Maybe you need advice on lesser issues like boundary disputes or problems with services or property? Here are several good sites that could really make a difference.

www.compactlaw.co.uk
LEGAL INFORMATION FOR ENGLAND AND WALES

ORIGIN	UK	An extremely informative and useful site that covers
SPEED	✓✓✓✓	many aspects of the law in a clear and concise style,
INFO	✓✓✓✓✓	there are usable documents – you can download
VALUE	✓✓✓✓	some free, others to buy, case histories, news, tips
EASE	✓✓✓✓	and plenty of fact-sheets. Formally
		www.lawrights.co.uk

www.uklegal.com
LEGAL RESOURCES AT YOUR FINGERTIPS

ORIGIN	UK	This site offers a superb selection of links to
SPEED	✓✓✓✓	everything from private investigators to barristers
INFO	✓✓✓✓✓	to legal equipment suppliers.
EASE	✓✓✓✓	

www.family-solicitors.co.uk
FAMILY LAW REFERENCE

ORIGIN	UK	Excellent resource for everyday legal issues covering
SPEED	✓✓✓✓	everything from wills to neighbourhood disputes.
INFO	✓✓✓✓✓	Great for links too with an excellent search facility
EASE	✓✓✓✓	for finding a family law solicitor near you.

www.desktoplawyer.net

THE UK'S FIRST ONLINE LAWYER

ORIGIN UK
SPEED ✓✓✓✓
INFO ✓✓✓✓✓
VALUE ✓✓✓
EASE ✓✓✓✓

This site is quite straightforward if you know what you need and have read through the instructions carefully. First you register, then download the software (Rapidocs) enabling you to compile the document you need. The legal documents you create will cost from £2.99 upwards depending on complexity. The range of documents available is huge and there are more being added.

www.legalservices.gov.uk

GOVERNMENT ADVICE

ORIGIN UK
SPEED ✓✓✓✓
INFO ✓✓✓✓✓
EASE ✓✓✓

The replacement for legal aid, this is the official line on legal matters with guidance on how to access legal assistance, where to get information and news on latest changes to the Community Legal Service and Criminal Defence Service. It could be a lot more user-friendly. For Scottish legal aid go to **www.slab.org.uk**

See also:
www.divorce-online.co.uk – fast track divorces and good advice.
www.emplaw.co.uk – the low down on British employment law.
www.legaladvicefree.co.uk – excellent all rounder that provides the answer to many legal questions.
www.legalpulse.com – well designed site along the lines of Desktop Lawyer although not as comprehensive.
www.lawassure.co.uk – subscribe to excellent personal legal advice and related services.

www.dumblaws.com
THE DAFTEST, STUPIDEST LAWS

ORIGIN US	Did you realise that in England placing a postage
SPEED ✓✓✓✓	stamp that bears the Queen's head upside down is
INFO ✓✓✓✓	considered treasonable, or that in Kentucky it's
EASE ✓✓✓✓	illegal to fish with a bow and arrow? These are just

a couple of the many dumb laws that you can find on this very entertaining site. It's now been expanded to include dumbest criminals, dumbest warnings and placenames.

Magazines

Where to buy and subscribe to your favourite magazines.

http://www.magsuk.com
UK MAGAZINES TO YOUR DOOR

ORIGIN UK	A strong selection of magazines covering
SPEED ✓✓	13 categories, but it's a slow site. Delivery costs
INFO ✓✓✓	appear to be built into the price.
VALUE ✓✓✓✓	
EASE ✓✓✓✓	

See also:
www.whsmith.co.uk – some good offers but you
   have to pay for delivery, they sell subscriptions
   too.
www.worldofmagazines.co.uk – 3,000 mags
   featured but they provide information only;
   however, they will point you in the direction of
   the nearest stockist.
www.actualidad.com – newspapers of the world and
   links to their sites.

Men

Maybe not what you think, these are just a few sites especially for blokes, lads and real men.

Magazines

www.fhm.co.uk
FHM MAGAZINE

ORIGIN UK
SPEED ✓✓✓✓
INFO ✓✓✓✓
EASE ✓✓✓✓

A good reflection of the real thing, with sections on everything from serious news to the lighter side, with the usual blokey features, it suffers from lots of advertising though.

www.gqmagazine.co.uk
GENTLEMEN'S QUARTERLY

ORIGIN UK
SPEED ✓✓✓✓
INFO ✓✓✓
EASE ✓✓✓✓

A stylish site, which gives a flavour of the real magazine, it contains a few stories, competitions, fashion tips and the odd feature.

www.sharpman.com
SHARP!

ORIGIN UK
SPEED ✓✓✓✓
INFO ✓✓✓✓
EASE ✓✓✓✓

While a little odd, it's good fun and there's some useful advice. Split into six key sections:
Dating – with tips on conversation and repartee.
Health – how to keep in tip-top condition.
Work – getting the best out of the Internet.
Travel – staying sharp abroad.
Grooming – looking the part.
Toys – the best advice on windsurfing.

www.fathersdirect.com

A MAGAZINE FOR FATHERS

ORIGIN UK
SPEED ✓✓✓✓
INFO ✓✓✓✓
VALUE ✓✓✓
EASE ✓✓✓✓

Written by fathers for fathers, this entertaining e-zine has all the advice and support you need if you're a new dad or you're trying to fit in both work and kids. There are competitions, a rant section where you can let off steam and a games room. Rather twee graphics let it down somewhat. See also **www.dadah.co.uk** who support stay-at-home fathers.

See also:

www.askmen.com – a very good American men's magazine covering almost every topic you're likely to need.

www.modernman.com – nicely designed men's magazine site from the US with loads of interesting articles and features.

www.dullmen.com – the dullest website from the National Council for Dull Men, very funny too.

Health

www.menshealth.co.uk

MEN'S HEALTH MAGAZINE

ORIGIN UK
SPEED ✓✓✓✓
INFO ✓✓✓✓✓
EASE ✓✓✓✓

Lots of advice on keeping fit, healthy and fashionable too. There's also an excellent section on the number one topic – sex, plus others on wealth, health, sport and a shop that sells subscriptions and recommends the latest gear.

www.menshealthforum.org.uk
STOP MOANING!

ORIGIN UK	An excellent all-rounder revealing the truth behind
SPEED ✓✓✓✓	the state of men's health and lots of discussion about
INFO ✓✓✓✓✓	specific and general health issues facing men today –
EASE ✓✓✓✓	good for links too.

Other men's health sites:

www.malehealth.co.uk – comprehensive site where
you can check the state of your health and your
health knowledge; excellent links and advice
make up the picture.

www.orchid-cancer.org.uk – promotes the awareness of testicular and prostate cancer.

www.vasectomy-clinic.co.uk – no scalpel vasectomy
– honest!

www.impotence.org.uk – the Impotence
Association.

Shopping

www.firebox.com
WHERE MEN BUY STUFF

ORIGIN UK	An online shop aimed totally at boy's toys, with it's
SPEED ✓✓✓✓	own bachelor pad containing all you need for the
INFO ✓✓✓✓	lifestyle. There's masses of games, videos, toys and,
VALUE ✓✓✓	of course, the latest gadgets. Delivery costs vary.
EASE ✓✓✓✓	See also **www.big-boys-toys.net** and

www.boysstuff.co.uk both are worth a visit if you
can't find what you want at Firebox.

www.condomsdirect.co.uk

CONDOMS UK

ORIGIN UK
SPEED ✓✓✓✓
INFO ✓✓✓✓
VALUE ✓✓✓✓
EASE ✓✓✓✓

Many different types of condoms are available to buy, and you get free delivery if you spend more than £10 – there's even a price promise and the assurance of a fast and discreet service. It's also worth checking out **www.condomania.com**

www.giftsforbirds.co.uk

SO YOU DON'T KNOW WHAT TO BUY...

ORIGIN UK
SPEED ✓✓✓✓
INFO ✓✓✓✓
VALUE ✓✓✓✓
EASE ✓✓✓✓

Full of ideas for clueless men, and it comes with a reminder service built in for those important dates. You can even type in a price and it'll suggest appropriate presents. Delivery costs are built in, along with enough wrapping paper to cover the gift. For a similar service try **www.emmajulia.co.uk** who promise answers to your present-giving prayers and also offer free delivery within the UK.

Motorcycles

www.bmf.co.uk

BRITISH MOTORCYCLISTS FEDERATION

ORIGIN UK
SPEED ✓✓✓
INFO ✓✓✓✓
EASE ✓✓✓✓

At this site you can join the BMF, get involved with their activities or just use the site for information or for their magazine *Rider*. You can also get club information and e-mail them on any issues. For the international governing body go to **www.fim.ch/en**

www.motorcycle.co.uk

THE UK'S MOTORCYCLE DIRECTORY

ORIGIN UK
SPEED ✓✓✓
INFO ✓✓✓
EASE ✓✓✓✓

Essentially a list of links by brand, dealer, importer, classics, gear, books and auctions. For more information on motorcycle clubs go to **www.motor-cycle.org.uk**

www.moto-directory.com

THE WORLD MOTORCYCLE DIRECTORY

ORIGIN US
SPEED ✓✓✓✓
INFO ✓✓✓✓
VALUE ✓✓✓
EASE ✓✓✓✓

US-oriented, but links to over 800 sites ensure that you'll know what's going on in motorcycling and find the information you need.

www.motorworld.com

ALL YOU NEED TO KNOW ABOUT MOTORCYCLES

ORIGIN US
SPEED ✓✓✓
INFO ✓✓✓✓
EASE ✓✓✓

Good coverage of both machines and events with multimedia features. Although the site is American there's a good British section.

www.bikenet.com

MOTORCYCLING AT YOUR FINGERTIPS

ORIGIN UK
SPEED ✓✓✓
INFO ✓✓✓✓
EASE ✓✓✓✓

Lots of features, articles, news and links on a well designed site that also offers a shop. It can be a little slow and the photos don't always download but otherwise it's still worth a visit.

www.motorcycle-search.co.uk

FREE CLASSIFIED ADS

ORIGIN UK
SPEED ✓✓✓✓
INFO ✓✓✓✓
EASE ✓✓✓✓

A good, fast site with a good selection of used bikes, luggage, clothing, parts and accessories. See also Bike Exchange at **www.biketrader.co.uk** who also offer other services such as insurance and finance.

Movies

All you need to know about films and film stars including where to go to get the best deals on DVDs and videos. For information on film stars also check out the celebrities section on page 64.

http://uk.imdb.com

INTERNET MOVIE DATABASE

ORIGIN US
SPEED ✓✓✓✓
INFO ✓✓✓✓✓
VALUE ✓✓✓✓
EASE ✓✓✓✓

The best and most organised movie database on the Internet. It's very easy to use and every film buff's dream with lots of features and recommendations, plus games, quizzes, chat and movie news. Another good database site is **www.allmovie.com** which has a really good search engine.

www.aintitcoolnews.com

AIN'T IT JUST COOL

ORIGIN US
SPEED ✓✓✓✓
INFO ✓✓✓✓✓
EASE ✓✓✓

A renowned review site that can make or break a movie in the US, it's very entertaining and likeable, albeit a bit messy. Harry Knowles' movie reviews are by far the best bit of the site, although they can go on a bit. You can search the archive for a particular review or contribute a bit of juicy gossip by e-mailing Harry direct.

www.corona.bc.ca/films

COMING ATTRACTIONS

ORIGIN US
SPEED ✓✓✓
INFO ✓✓✓✓
EASE ✓✓✓✓

An excellent site that previews upcoming movie releases, giving background information on how films were made (or are progressing), gossip and links. You can join in with your own film ratings or just read the articles, which are generally well written. It's not perfect but it's very entertaining.

www.insidefilm.com

FILM FESTIVAL DIRECTORY

ORIGIN US	Comprehensive news on the film festival with a
SPEED ✓✓✓	calendar and features on awards.
INFO ✓✓✓✓	
EASE ✓✓✓✓	

www.eonline.com

E IS FOR ENTERTAINMENT

ORIGIN US	This is one of the most visited entertainment news sites
SPEED ✓✓✓✓	and it has a reputation for being first with the latest
INFO ✓✓✓✓	gossip and movie news. It's vibrant, well designed and
EASE ✓✓✓✓	has a tongue in cheek style, which is endearing; sadly
	some of the reporters prattle on though.

www.variety.com

VARIETY MAGAZINE

ORIGIN US	The online version of the show business stalwart
SPEED ✓✓✓	magazine has an excellent and entertaining site with all
INFO ✓✓✓✓✓	the hot topics, news and background information you'd
EASE ✓✓✓✓	expect plus biographies and international film news.

For more gossip see:

www.hollywood.com – over one million pages of
gossip, news and trailers.

www.hollywoodreporter.com – all the latest gossip
and you can subscribe to the magazine.

www.ew.com – *Entertainments Weekly* has a really
attractive site with lots of features.

www.bollywood.com

LINKING BOLLYWOOD FANS WORLDWIDE

ORIGIN INDIA	All the latest gossip, supposition and intrigue, plus
SPEED ✓✓✓✓	chat, poetry, ratings and reviews at this sweeping
INFO ✓✓✓✓✓	site. There are also fashion tips, a movie club, a
EASE ✓✓✓✓	Hollywood section and sport – massive in fact.

www.oscars.com

THE ACADEMY AWARDS

ORIGIN US
SPEED ✓✓✓✓
INFO ✓✓✓✓
EASE ✓✓✓✓

Stylish and as glitzy as you'd imagine it should be, this is the official tie-in site for the Oscars. There's an archive and even some games to play. For the Golden Globes go to **www.goldenglobes.org**

www.bafta.org

BRITISH ACADEMY OF FILM & TELEVISION ARTS

ORIGIN UK
SPEED ✓✓✓
INFO ✓✓✓✓
EASE ✓✓✓✓

A site giving all the information you need on the Baftas, their history and how it all works.

www.bfi.org.uk

BRITISH FILM INSTITUTE

ORIGIN UK
SPEED ✓✓✓✓
INFO ✓✓✓✓✓
EASE ✓✓✓✓

A top site from the BFI packed with information on how the film industry works with archive material, links and how to make movies. Refreshing that there's not much mention of Hollywood!

www.britmovie.co.uk

DEDICATED TO BRITISH CINEMA

ORIGIN UK
SPEED ✓✓✓✓
INFO ✓✓✓✓✓
EASE ✓✓✓✓

A site devoted to the history of British cinema and its wider contribution to film-making in general. There's a great deal of information, links and background and it's all well cross-referenced, although it could do with a search facility.

Cinemas

www.virgin.net/cinema

VIRGIN CINEMA

ORIGIN UK
SPEED ✓✓✓✓
INFO ✓✓✓✓
VALUE ✓✓✓
EASE ✓✓✓✓

Excellent magazine-style film site with links to their shop and a what's on guide. There are sections on gossip, news and what's coming soon, as well as competitions and a chat room.

Other cinema company sites:
www.cineworld.co.uk – straightforward and easy-to-use guide.
www.odeon.co.uk – book online at this attractive site.
www.showcasecinemas.co.uk – lots here to see and do, but a little slow to download.
www.uci-cinemas.co.uk – good looking site with all the usual information and previews.
www.warnervillage.co.uk – excellent site with online booking.

Movie humour

www.moviesounds.com

LISTEN TO YOUR FAVOURITE MOVIES

ORIGIN US
SPEED ✓✓✓✓
INFO ✓✓✓✓
EASE ✓✓✓✓

Download extracts from over 50 movies, it's a little confusing at first but once you've got the technology sorted out it's good fun.

http://rinkworks.com/movieaminute

DON'T HAVE TIME TO WATCH IT ALL?

ORIGIN US
SPEED ✓✓✓✓
INFO ✓✓✓✓
EASE ✓✓✓✓

Summaries of the top movies for those who either can't be bothered to watch them or just want to pretend they did, either way it's really funny.

www.moviecliches.com

THE MOVIE CLICHÉ LIST

ORIGIN US	Clichés listed by topic from aeroplanes to wood,
SPEED ✓✓✓✓	there's something for everyone here...
INFO ✓✓✓	
EASE ✓✓✓✓	

www.moviebloopers.com

BLOOPERS GALORE

ORIGIN US	A catalogue of mistakes and continuity errors from
SPEED ✓✓✓✓	many of the world's greatest films – rather than be
INFO ✓✓✓✓	funny though, it just makes you wonder how long
VALUE ✓✓✓	some people study films to spot such small errors!
EASE ✓✓✓✓	There are also reviews and quizzes.

Film companies

Some of the best web sites are those that promote a particular film. Here is a list of the major film producers and their web sites, all of which are good and have links to the latest releases. Most have clips, downloads, screensavers and lots of advertising.

www.disney.com
www.mca.com
www.miramax.com
www.paramount.com
www.spe.sony.com
www.foxmovies.com
www.uip.com
www.universalpictures.com
www.warnerbros.com

Buying movies

*It's probably best to start with visiting a price checker site first
such as* **www.kelkoo.com** *(see page 312) or* **www.dvdupdate.com**
but these are the best of the movie online stores.

www.blackstar.co.uk

THE UK'S BIGGEST VIDEO STORE

ORIGIN UK
SPEED ✓✓✓✓
INFO ✓✓✓✓
VALUE ✓✓✓✓
EASE ✓✓✓✓

The biggest online video and DVD retailer, it claims
to be able to get around 50,000 titles. Blackstar is
very good value, boasts cheap delivery prices and
has a reputation for excellent customer service. If
you want to shop around try **www.blockbuster.com**
who have a less packed site and offers on a wide
variety of films.

www.dvdstreet.infront.co.uk

FOR DVD ONLY

ORIGIN UK
SPEED ✓✓✓✓
INFO ✓✓✓✓
VALUE ✓✓✓✓
EASE ✓✓✓✓

Part of the Streets Online group, this is a great value
and easy-to-use site that only sells DVD. There are
lots of other movie-related features too, such as the
latest news and gossip or reviews. Delivery is £1 for
the UK. See also the good looking
www.musicbox.cd who have good offers and
delivery is £1 whatever the order.

www.movietrak.com

RENT A DVD MOVIE

ORIGIN UK
SPEED ✓✓✓✓
INFO ✓✓✓✓
VALUE ✓✓✓
EASE ✓✓✓✓

The latest films are available to rent for £2.99 (plus
50p p&p) for seven days. Pick the title of your
choice and it's dispatched the same day, you then
return it seven days later in the pre-paid envelope.
The range offered is excellent covering eleven major
categories plus the latest releases, coming soon and a
good search facility too.

www.in-movies.co.uk

IT'S IN THE MOVIES

ORIGIN UK
SPEED ✓✓✓✓
INFO ✓✓✓✓
VALUE ✓✓✓
EASE ✓✓✓✓

The latest trailers, short films, competitions and DVD rental are just some of the things you can see and do here at this good-looking site. DVD rental is £15 a month but you can take out as many as you like, you can also buy DVDs from their shop.

www.reel.com

OVER 100,000 MOVIES

ORIGIN US
SPEED ✓✓✓✓
INFO ✓✓✓✓
VALUE ✓✓✓
EASE ✓✓✓✓

Here is a mixture of news, gossip, interviews, event listings and US-style outright selling. The content is good and you can get carried away browsing. The search facility is very efficient but shipping to the UK costs a minimum of $6. The shop sells DVD and CDs.

See also:
www.play.com – nice design with some good offers, sells games and CDs too.
www.dvdreview.com – great for reviews, but the shop doesn't supply the UK.
www.discshop.com – a wide-ranging DVD shop that sells hardware too.

Memorabilia

www.vinmag.com

POSTERS, CARDS AND T-SHIRTS

ORIGIN UK
SPEED ✓✓✓✓
INFO ✓✓✓✓
VALUE ✓✓✓
EASE ✓✓✓✓

Vintage magazines, stand-up cutouts, posters, T-shirts and magazine covers complete the picture from this established dealer. Shipping to the UK starts at around $2, but it depends on how much you spend.

www.asseenonscreen.com

AS SEEN ON SCREEN

ORIGIN UK	At this site you can buy what you see on the screen,
SPEED ✓✓✓✓	your favourite star's shirt or dress can be replicated
INFO ✓✓✓✓✓	just for you. You can also search by star, film and
VALUE ✓✓✓	TV show.
EASE ✓✓✓✓	

www.propstore.co.uk

PROPS FOR SALE

ORIGIN UK	An extensive selection of props and replicas await
SPEED ✓✓✓✓	you here with everything from snow globes to cloth-
INFO ✓✓✓✓	ing. Each piece is unique and has been bought from
VALUE ✓✓	the relevant film company and a provenance is
EASE ✓✓✓✓	provided.

See also:
www.memomine.com – for Hollywood memorabilia.
www.efilmposters.com – who sell posters from a good site.
www.ricksmovie.com – some 14,000 posters and related items for sale.

Music

Before spending your hard earned cash on CDs it's worth investigating MP3. MP3 technology allows the compression of a music track into a file, which can be stored and played back.

An MP3 player can be downloaded free onto your PC from several sites, the best being the original at **www.mp3.com** *or the popular* **www.real.com** *and its RealPlayer. It takes minutes to download the player and if you play CDs on your PC it will also record them.*

You'll then be able to listen to samples available on music stores. Once you've joined the MP3 revolution, there's an amazing amount of free music available, start at either web site where there are excellent search facilities. Other good MP3 players can be found at:

> **www.winamp.com** – the Winamp play is versatile and easy to use.
>
> **http://sonique.lycos.com/** - the Sonique Player is good looking with lots of options.
>
> **www.liquidaudio.com** – the Liquid player is great and works well with Windows XP.
>
> **www.listen.com** – the Rhapsody player is adequate but there's probably more music choice on the site.

Other sites with lots of MP3 downloads that are worth checking out are listed below. Also have a look at **www.100topmp3sites.com** *who list all the good MP3 sites including specialist ones.*

> **www.artistdirect.com** – great design, with the latest music news and tunes from over 100,000 artists.
>
> **www.audiofind.com** – brilliant search engine, many free downloads.
>
> **www.eclassical.com** – many free classical greats and many more to buy.
>
> **www.eatsleepmusic.com** – free karaoke! You need RealPlayer to play.
>
> **www.emusic.com** – over 6,700 artists, great but you have to pay.
>
> **www.icrunch.co.uk** – offers exclusive DJ mixes, live performances and prides itself on quality alternative music.
>
> **www.listen.com** – good for previewing a wide variety of music.

www.mp3.com – the original and still one of the best.

www.mp3example.com – well categorised, great for links and free tunes.

www.mp3-mac.com – MP3 for Mac users.

www.musicnet.com – the combined might of AOL, Bertlesmann, EMI and Real providing top name downloads from three of the five major labels.

www.napster.com – the original free music site now in the process of re-inventing itself.

www.real.com – quality and range but you have to subscribe.

www.soundresource.net – great for sound effects – some rude!

www.taxi.com

FOR UNSIGNED BANDS

ORIGIN US
SPEED ✓✓✓✓
INFO ✓✓✓✓
EASE ✓✓✓✓

Looking to get a music contract for your band? You should start here, there's loads of information, contacts and links that will help you on the rocky road to success and stardom – well that's the theory anyway!

For more places to find something new see also:

www.burbs.co.uk – British Underground Rock Bands, home of the UK's real music scene.

www.getoutthere.bt.com – tomorrows' new young talent.

www.iuma.com – massive selection of unsigned groups all well categorised.

www.2bdiscovered.com – good use of video footage as well as sound, but you have to register to use it.

www.joescafe.com/bands

BAND NAMES

ORIGIN	UK
SPEED	✓✓✓✓
INFO	✓✓✓✓
VALUE	✓✓✓✓
EASE	✓✓✓

So you can't think of a name for your band? Here is the 'Band-o-matic' which will offer all sorts of never before used band names in seconds. This time we got Snurge and the Clown Hammers.

Downloading free music

Much has been written about the effect on the music industry that downloading free music has had at the expense of copyright, with some suggesting that it's damaging to the industry by taking away musicians' livelihood, while others say it stimulates sales by enabling potential customers to sample music they wouldn't have heard otherwise.

The following sites are basically different file-sharing programs that allow users to exchange files easily whether it is music or not. It's best to read up on the subject before downloading any of the programs, but once you're up to speed it couldn't be easier. Be aware that some may contain adult material and most carry some sort of spyware so that they can adapt to your tastes and advertise accordingly.

http://opennap.sourceforge.net - *a variant of the original Napster program this is freeware and you can select some of the many specialist and general servers which hold music, (see* **www.napigator.com** *for a server list) then use the program to search them for the music you like.*

www.espra.net – a new version of espra is now available to download, it offers anonymity because it doesn't work from a central point like the other sharing software, so, in theory, you can download to your heart's content. It also attempts to create a way of remunerating the artist for what you download.

www.gnutella.co.uk – sounds like something you spread on toast, but is basically a mini search engine and file sharing system on one site. It consists of a network of thousands of computer users, all of whom use Gnutella software 'clones' which link them directly to other users to find music, movies and other files. At **www.gnutelli-ums.com** you'll find more similar programs that do the same thing, but may be easier to use or just more efficient, and there are good tutorials too. Also check out the advert free **http://gnucleus.sourceforge.net**

www.imesh.com – iMesh is really a Napster clone; you type in an artist and song, and then a list of available matches from a centralised server appears. Since it's an Israeli site, it's likely to be immune from U.S. copyright lawsuits, so it'll probably be around for a while yet.

www.madster.com – This used to be Aimster, it combines AOL's instant message service with the ability to search for files and trade them with other users of the network, of Gnutella or even of Napster. It includes encryption software, so nobody can monitor your files while they're in transit and will even tell you which other AOL messenger buddies use it.

www.musiccity.com – uses the FastTrack file sharing system, their version is called Morpheus, it's quite secure, but lots of ads.

www.rootnode.org – this file-sharing network gets around legal shenanigans by concentrating on live recordings that are made available with the permission of the original artists. It's a good music magazine too.

www.winmx.com – a very flexible file-sharing program that does not contain spyware.

Buying music

It's as well to start by checking prices of CDs through price comparison sites such as those listed on page 312. These will take you to the store offering the best combination of price and postage. All the stores listed below offer good value plus a bit extra.

www.hmv.co.uk

HIS MASTERS VOICE ONLINE

ORIGIN US	Excellent features and offers on the latest CDs and
SPEED ✓✓✓✓	videos. There are sections on most aspects of music
INFO ✓✓✓✓✓	as well as video, DVD and games with a good
VALUE ✓✓✓	search facility. You can listen to selections from
EASE ✓✓✓✓	albums before buying if you have RealPlayer.
	Spoken word or books on tape are available as well.

www.cd-wow.com

OUTSTANDING VALUE

ORIGIN UK	A very easy site to use with some great offers on
SPEED ✓✓✓✓	CDs and there's free delivery too. Probably the best
INFO ✓✓✓✓	site for value at time of writing, lets hope they can
VALUE ✓✓✓✓✓	keep it going.
EASE ✓✓✓✓	

www.cdnow.com

NOT JUST CDS

ORIGIN US	One of the original music sites and one of the easiest
SPEED ✓✓✓✓	to use, it has lots of features: downloads which
INFO ✓✓✓✓✓	enable you to sample albums for 30 days, a video
VALUE ✓✓✓	section and a recommendation service. Shipping can
EASE ✓✓✓✓	be expensive compared to UK stores.

www.cduniverse.com

FOR THE WIDEST RANGE AND GREAT OFFERS

ORIGIN	US
SPEED	✓✓✓
INFO	✓✓✓✓
VALUE	✓✓✓✓
EASE	✓✓✓✓

There is a massive range to choose from and some good discounts; delivery normally takes only five days. You can also buy games, DVDs and videos. Excellent, but can be quite slow, and delivery is very expensive.

www.secondsounds.com

THE USED CD STORE

ORIGIN	UK
SPEED	✓✓✓
INFO	✓✓✓✓
VALUE	✓✓✓✓✓
EASE	✓✓✓

With a huge range to choose from and prices from as low as £1.99 you can't really go wrong, they guarantee mint condition or your money back. You can browse by artist or through the bargain bins, delivery starts at a £1 and of course they are interested in buying from you too.

www.minidisco.com

HOME OF THE MINIDISC

ORIGIN	US
SPEED	✓✓✓✓
INFO	✓✓✓✓
EASE	✓✓✓✓

The minidisc is alive and well here with some good offers on the players and information on the latest developments. Delivery to Europe takes about a week, costs vary. See also **www.minidisc.org** which is a messy site but contains everything you need to know about minidiscs.

For more great offers on CDs try these sites:
www.101cd.com – renowned for offering good value, choose from 1.6 million titles.
www.recordstore.co.uk – choose from thousands of vinyl records, CDs, T-shirts, record bags and assorted DJ gear.
www.musicbox.cd – CDs, videos and DVD and postage is only £1 whatever the size of order. Nice design too.

www.towerrecords.co.uk – wide variety and some
good offers – better service than you get from the
real store.

www.amazon.co.uk – as good as you'd expect from
Amazon.

www.virgin.net/music – average music store with
reviews.

www.audiostreet.co.uk – some good prices, free
delivery in UK.

www.htfr.co.uk

HARD TO FIND RECORDS

ORIGIN UK	Although they specialise in new and deleted house,
SPEED ✓✓✓	garage, techno, electro, disco, funk, soul and
INFO ✓✓✓✓	hip-hop vinyl, they will try and find any record
VALUE ✓✓✓	previously released. They also offer a complete
EASE ✓✓✓	service to all budding and serious DJs. See also

www.popetc.com who offer a wide range of
memorabilia, vinyl and rare CD singles.

Bands, groups and stars

www.sonicnet.com/news/musicnewswire/

MUSIC STOP-PRESS

ORIGIN US	All the latest music headlines plus background
SPEED ✓✓✓✓	articles and links to hundreds of music sites. They
INFO ✓✓✓✓✓	also provide information on thousands of bands
EASE ✓✓✓✓	and artists with links all cross-referenced by genre

and category too.

http://ubl.artistdirect.com/

THE ULTIMATE BAND LIST

ORIGIN US	It is the place for mountains of information on
SPEED ✓✓✓✓	groups or singers. It has a totally brilliant search
INFO ✓✓✓✓✓	facility, and you can buy and download from the
VALUE ✓✓✓✓	site as well, although the prices are not as good as
EASE ✓✓✓✓	elsewhere. For a similar, but better organised site try

www.allmusic.com where you can also get excellent
information and videos.

www.eartothesound.fsnet.co.uk

REVIEWS AND RATINGS

ORIGIN US	They call themselves the ultimate review site and it's
SPEED ✓✓✓✓	great, except that they concentrate almost entirely
INFO ✓✓✓✓	on rock music, so if that's your poison, then it's
EASE ✓✓✓✓	perfect.

Music TV and magazine sites

www.bbc.co.uk/totp/
www.totp.beeb.com

TOP OF THE POPS

ORIGIN UK	The Top of the Pops sites are different, the site at
SPEED ✓✓✓✓	bbc.co.uk is more of a magazine, the one at
INFO ✓✓✓✓✓	beeb.com basically a shop and both are aimed at
VALUE ✓✓✓	teenagers. That said, there are loads of good features
EASE ✓✓✓	and articles as well as competitions, trivia and lots

of information in both of them, so maybe it doesn't
matter which one you visit.

www.cdukweb.com

UK'S NUMBER ONE MUSIC SHOW

ORIGIN UK
SPEED ✓✓✓✓
INFO ✓✓
EASE ✓✓✓✓

Considering their boast, the web site is a bit of a disappointment with not much in the way of information or interaction. There are some quizzes, competitions and you can download a few things but it has none of the buzz of the show.

www.mtv.co.uk

MUSIC TELEVISION

ORIGIN UK
SPEED ✓✓✓✓
INFO ✓✓✓✓
EASE ✓✓✓

MTV offers loads of info on events, shows and the artists as well as background on the presenters and creative bits like movie and music video clips. Great design.

www.music-mag.com

NEWS AND REVIEWS

ORIGIN UK
SPEED ✓✓✓✓
INFO ✓✓✓✓
EASE ✓✓✓✓

A good, cool-looking all rounder covering all aspects of modern music in a straightforward style, it has a really good section on clubbing and the latest dance news. There's also a good links section and hundreds of ringtones and logos to download.

www.nme.com

NEW MUSICAL EXPRESS

ORIGIN UK
SPEED ✓✓✓
INFO ✓✓✓✓✓
EASE ✓✓✓✓

If you're a rock fan then this is where it's at. There's all the usual information, it's well laid out and easy to access. The archived articles are its greatest asset, featuring 150,000 artists and every article, feature and review they've ever published plus full UK discographies, pictures, e-cards, ringtones and links to the best web sites.

www.q4music.com

Q MAGAZINE

ORIGIN UK
SPEED ✓✓✓
INFO ✓✓✓✓✓
EASE ✓✓✓✓

A music magazine site that reflects its parent magazine extremely well. It has 20,000 reviews, plus features and articles that cover most aspects of music, it doesn't miss much.

www.popworld.com

WHERE POP COMES FIRST

ORIGIN UK
SPEED ✓✓✓✓
INFO ✓✓✓✓
EASE ✓✓✓

Brilliant site that concentrates on pop, it's fun and has great graphics. You have to register to join but once you're in you get access to competitions, features on your favourite bands, clips from Popworld TV, fashion tips and much more. You need the latest Flash download from Macromedia to get the best out of it.

www.thebox.co.uk

SMASH HITS YOU CONTROL

ORIGIN UK
SPEED ✓✓✓✓
INFO ✓✓✓✓
EASE ✓✓✓✓

Similar to Q but with added features such as the ability for you to select a tune to be played on their TV channel and you can influence their overall selection by voting for your favourite songs.

Sites for specific types of music

BLUES

www.darkerthanblue.com

HOME OF BLACK MUSIC

ORIGIN UK
SPEED ✓✓✓✓
INFO ✓✓✓✓✓
EASE ✓✓✓✓

Very well-designed site dedicated to black-influenced music and musicians, it has all the latest news, gig guides, artist features and downloads as well as sections on reggae, garage, soul and hip-hop.

www.bluesworld.com

HOMAGE TO THE BLUES

ORIGIN US
SPEED ✓✓✓
INFO ✓✓✓✓
EASE ✓✓✓✓

If you're into the blues then this is your kind of site. There are interviews, memorabilia, 78 auctions, bibliographies, discographies and lists of links to other blues sites. You can order CDs via affiliated retailers and if the mood takes you, order a guitar too.

CLASSICAL AND OPERA

www.classicalmusic.co.uk

CLASSICAL MUSIC REVEALED

ORIGIN UK
SPEED ✓✓✓✓
INFO ✓✓✓✓✓
EASE ✓✓✓

Excellent for lovers of classical music, with articles, guides, reviews and concert listings, you can play in a fantasy concert or just browse the excellent links section.

www.operabase.com/en

OPERA BASE

ORIGIN US
SPEED ✓✓✓✓
INFO ✓✓✓✓
EASE ✓✓✓

This site offers opera listings, information on festivals and provides background to the history of opera. For the *Opera* magazine site go to www.opera.co.uk, which offers articles and links.

Other key classical music sites:
www.classical.net – great for information and links.
www.eclassical.com – download MP3s, many
   are free.
www.mdcmusic.co.uk – good offers on CDs.
www.orchestranet.co.uk – excellent selection
   of links.

COUNTRY

www.thatscountry.com

COUNTRY MUSIC SCENE

ORIGIN CANADA   A good overview of country music with offers and
SPEED ✓✓✓✓   links as well as information on the artists and bands.
INFO ✓✓✓✓
EASE ✓✓✓✓

> *See also:*
> **www.countrymusic.org.uk** – a very naff site that
> covers the UK scene.
> **www.cmdn.net** – country music dance.
> **www.countrystars.com** – good all rounder with a
> messy design but the shop does supply the UK.

DANCE AND BEAT

www.anthems.com

DANCE, HOUSE AND GARAGE

ORIGIN UK   Great design combined with brilliant content, there's
SPEED ✓✓✓✓   everything here for dance fans, news, information
INFO ✓✓✓✓✓   and samples of the latest mixes or if you're feeling
VALUE ✓✓✓   rich you can buy them too, although you'll probably
EASE ✓✓✓   find cheaper elsewhere. For alternative views of the
dance scene try **www.fly.co.uk** who have a real
urban look to their site, while for links to over 500
dance-related sites and a complete listing of new
releases go to **www.juno.co.uk**

www.burnitblue.com

LIVING AND BREATHING DANCE MUSIC

ORIGIN UK   Concentrating on dance and club culture this coolly
SPEED ✓✓✓✓   designed site offers up all the information you need
INFO ✓✓✓✓✓   to keep up with the scene; it's been critically
EASE ✓✓✓✓   acclaimed as one of the best sites of its type.

See also:

www.crasher.co.uk – details on over 600 clubs listed.

www.garagemusic.co.uk – reviews and samples plus the latest on the UK scene, annoying adverts though.

www.hitthedecks.co.uk – a great e-zine covering the dance scene.

FOLK

www.folkmusic.net
FOLK ON THE WEB

ORIGIN	UK
SPEED	✓✓✓✓
INFO	✓✓✓✓
EASE	✓✓✓✓

A straightforward site from *Living Traditions* magazine, a collection of articles, features, reviews and news, but see also **www.folking.com** which offers more in the way of shopping.

HIP HOP AND RAP

www.thedsc.com
HIP-HOP AND RAP

ORIGIN	UK
SPEED	✓✓✓✓
INFO	✓✓✓✓
EASE	✓✓✓✓

Da saga continues… news, reviews and features on hip-hop, there's a good selection of links to other related sites and if you're a real fan you can voice your opinions by becoming a writer for them. See also **www.britishhiphop.co.uk** for information on the UK scene.

INDIE

www.playlouder.com

INDIE MUSIC

ORIGIN US
SPEED ✓✓✓
INFO ✓✓✓✓
EASE ✓✓✓✓

Great graphics and excellent design make Playlouder stand out from the crowd, it covers the Indie music scene in depth with all the usual features, but with a bit more style. Another really well designed web site covering Indie music in great depth is Channel Fly www.channelfly.com – take your pick!

JAZZ

www.jazzonln.com

JAZZ ONLINE

ORIGIN US
SPEED ✓✓✓✓
INFO ✓✓✓✓✓
EASE ✓✓✓✓

Whether you need help in working your way through the minefield that is jazz music, or you know what you want, Jazz Online can provide it. Its easy format covers all styles and it has a brilliant search facility. There is a good chat section and you can ask 'Jazz Messenger' just about anything. You can't buy from the site but there are links to Amazon's music section. Try also www.jazze.com and the beautifully designed www.jazzcorner.com

KARAOKE

www.streamkaraoke.com

SING A LONG

ORIGIN US
SPEED ✓✓✓✓
INFO ✓✓✓✓
VALUE ✓✓
EASE ✓✓✓✓

Over 1,000 tunes to download but you have to subscribe which is from $19 a month depending on which package you take.

Music information

www.clickmusic.co.uk

EVERYTHING YOU NEED TO KNOW ABOUT MUSIC

ORIGIN UK
SPEED ✓✓✓✓
INFO ✓✓✓✓✓
EASE ✓✓✓✓

This is great for all music fans. It has quick access to details on any particular band, tickets, and downloads, gigs or gossip. Shopping is straightforward using their 'Best 10' listings, just click on the store or use the search engine to find something specific. The search engine needs improving though. See also www.musites.com where you can find a rather variable but improving music search engine.

www.dotmusic.com

ALL THE MUSIC NEWS

ORIGIN UK
SPEED ✓✓✓✓
INFO ✓✓✓✓✓
VALUE ✓✓✓
EASE ✓✓✓✓

Get the latest 'insider' views from the music industry, with reviews, charts, chat and a good value online shop where you buy tickets and books too. These combined with great design make this an excellent site. There are sections on each major music genre and a broadband section where you can watch the latest pop videos.

www.musicsearch.com

THE INTERNET'S MUSIC SEARCH ENGINE

ORIGIN US
SPEED ✓✓✓✓
INFO ✓✓✓✓
EASE ✓✓

Musicsearch is a directory site with over 20,000 links to reviewed music sites, the search facility has improved and you can offer up sites to be included. See also http://musiccrawl.com

Learning music

Long-winded though the site URL is, it's worth visiting www.si.umich.edu/chico/mhn/enclpdia.html *where you can find a music encyclopaedia in which you can sample the sound of many instruments.*

www.happynote.com/music/learn.html
LEARN MUSIC WITH A GAME

ORIGIN US	You download the game, which helps you learn the
SPEED ✓✓✓✓	basics, but the more you learn and the better you get
INFO ✓✓✓✓	the higher the score. See also
EASE ✓✓✓✓	www.abachamusic.com.au, www.musicnotes.net
	and www.talentz.com/MusicEducation/index.mv
	who also offer fun ways to learn music.

Sites for specific instruments

General
www.harmony-central.com – all sorts of instruments reviewed and rated.

Strings
www.guitar.com – good all rounder, all you need to know.
www.guitarsite.com – masses of information.
www.aic.se/basslob – playing the bass.
www.sitar.co.uk – comprehensive plus good links.
www.violin-world.com – complete resource for all string instruments.

Percussion
www.drummersweb.com – drummer's delight.
www.drumnetwork.com – online shop includes a virtual drum kit and the latest hot licks!

Wind

www.brassworld.co.uk – guide for all types of brass player.

www.wfg.sneezy.org – woodwind.

http://kristin.newdream.net/flute – the flute resource.

www.saxophone.org – great for info and links.

Electronic

http://nmc.uoregon.edu/emi – great introduction to electronic music and instruments.

www.synthzone.com – excellent source for articles, links and reviews for all things to do with electronic music making.

Keyboard

www.pianonanny.com – complete piano course.

www.pianoshop.co.uk – masses of links, pianos for sale and information on learning.

Sheet music

www.sunhawk.com

DOWNLOAD SHEET MUSIC

ORIGIN US	Well-designed site where you can download music
SPEED ✓✓✓	from a wide variety of styles including pop,
INFO ✓✓✓✓	Christian, country, Broadway, jazz and classical, you
VALUE ✓✓✓	have to pay but there are some freebies. See also the
EASE ✓✓✓✓	wide range at **www.sheetmusicplus.com**

Lyrics

www.lyrics.com

THE WORDS TO HUNDREDS OF SONGS

ORIGIN US
SPEED ✓✓✓✓
INFO ✓✓✓✓
EASE ✓✓✓✓

There are songs from hundreds of bands and artists including Oasis, Madonna, Britney Spears and Queen, you'll have to ignore the directory section that makes up most of the page, there's an A–Z listing at the bottom. Hopefully they'll redesign soon.

Other good lyric sites:
www.execpc.com/~suden – songs from the 50s, 60s and 70s.
http://home.iae.nl/users/kdv/en/ring.htm – the Lyric's Web Ring.
www.letssingit.com – big archive plus karaoke!

www.kissthisguy.com

MISHEARD LYRICS

ORIGIN US
SPEED ✓✓✓✓
INFO ✓✓✓✓
EASE ✓✓✓✓

Mr Misheard lists all those lyrics that you thought were being sung but in reality you were just not quite listening properly. This time we liked 'Mamma mia, here I go again' misheard as 'Diarrhoea, here I go again' but there are hundreds more.

Concerts and tickets

www.liveconcerts.com

WELCOME TO THE CYBERCAST

ORIGIN US
SPEED ✓✓✓✓
INFO ✓✓✓✓
VALUE ✓✓✓
EASE ✓✓✓✓

Watch live concerts online! A great idea but let down by 'Net congestion'. You'd think it was designed just to sell RealPlayer though, which you'll need to see the concerts and listen to the interviews and recordings. It's actually very good for sampling different types of music and you can buy CDs as well.

See also:
www.live-online.com – the digital jukebox.
www.pollstar.com – the concert hotwire!

www.bigmouth.co.uk

UK'S MOST COMPREHENSIVE GIG GUIDE

ORIGIN UK
SPEED ✓✓✓✓
INFO ✓✓✓✓
EASE ✓✓✓✓

UK-based, with lots of links to band sites, news, events listing and information on what's up and coming. Great search facilities and the ability to buy tickets make this a really useful site for gig lovers everywhere. It's geared to rock and pop though.

www.ticketmaster.co.uk

TICKETS FOR EVERYTHING

ORIGIN UK
SPEED ✓✓✓✓
INFO ✓✓✓✓✓
VALUE ✓✓✓✓
EASE ✓✓✓✓

Book tickets for just about anything and you can run searches by venue, city or date. The site is split into five key sections:
Theatre – theatre, drama and musical
Performing arts – comedy, classical and opera
Music – gigs, jazz, clubs, rock and pop.
Family – shows, anything from Disney on Ice to air shows.
Sports – tickets for virtually every sporting occasion.

www.concertphoto.co.uk

PHOTOS OF YOUR FAVOURITE BANDS

ORIGIN UK
SPEED ✓✓✓✓
INFO ✓✓✓✓
VALUE ✓✓✓
EASE ✓✓✓✓

OK so you've been to the gig and you didn't take a camera, well the chances are that Pete Still has a photo available for you to buy from this great web site. There are hundreds of bands to choose from both old and new and he's covered the major festivals too. Costs vary according to size and quantity.

Nature and the Environment

The Internet offers charities and organisations a chance to highlight their work in a way that is much more creative than ever before, it also offers the chance for us to get in-depth information on those species and issues that interest us.

www.panda.org

THE WORLD WIDE FUND FOR NATURE

ORIGIN UK
SPEED ✓✓✓
INFO ✓✓✓✓
EASE ✓✓✓✓

Called the WWF Global Network, this is the official site for the WWF. Information on projects designed to save the world's endangered species by protecting their environment. You can find out how to support their work or how to get involved; there is also a good kids' section, the latest news and information on the key projects.

An American organisation called the National Wildlife Fund has a similar excellent site at **www.nwf.org**

www.nhm.ac.uk

THE NATURAL HISTORY MUSEUM

ORIGIN UK
SPEED ✓✓✓
INFO ✓✓✓✓✓
EASE ✓✓✓✓

A superb user-friendly web site that covers everything from ants to eclipses. You can get the latest news, check out exhibitions, take a tour, browse the Dinosaur database or explore the wildlife garden. There are details on the collections, galleries, educational resources and contacts for answers to specific questions. See also the Smithsonian National Museum of Natural History who also has a great site at **www.mnh.si.edu**

www.bbc.co.uk/nature

WILDLIFE EXPOSED

ORIGIN UK
SPEED ✓✓✓
INFO ✓✓✓✓
VALUE ✓✓
EASE ✓✓✓✓

A brilliant nature offering from the BBC with sections on key wildlife programmes and animal groups. The information is good and enhanced by video clips. Also visit **www.bbcwild.com** the commercial side of the BBC wildlife unit with over 100,000 wildlife images available to buy. It's aimed at commercial organisations but plans to offer pictures for personal use at £15 each. It is a great place to browse just for the remarkable images in the premium selection alone.

www.naturenet.net

COUNTRYSIDE, NATURE AND CONSERVATION

ORIGIN UK
SPEED ✓✓✓
INFO ✓✓✓✓✓
EASE ✓✓✓✓

Ignore the rather twee graphics and you'll find a great deal of information about nature in the UK. Their interests include: countryside law, upkeep of nature reserves, voluntary work, education and environmental news. You can also search the site for specifics and there is a good set of links to related sites. See also **www.wildlifetrust.org.uk** who care for over 2,000 of Britain's nature reserves. For details on all our nature reserves go to **www.englishnature.org.uk** who supply maps, photos and information on why reserves are so important - all on an excellent site.

www.foe.co.uk

FRIENDS OF THE EARTH

ORIGIN UK
SPEED ✓✓✓✓
INFO ✓✓✓✓
EASE ✓✓✓✓

Not as worthy as you might imagine, this site offers a stack of information on food, pollution, green power, protecting wildlife in your area and the latest campaign news.

www.envirolink.org

THE ONLINE ENVIRONMENTAL COMMUNITY

ORIGIN US
SPEED ✓✓✓✓
INFO ✓✓✓✓✓
EASE ✓✓✓✓

A huge site focused on personal involvement in environment issues. There are seven key sections: organisations, educational resources, jobs, governmental resources, actions you can take to help, environment links and information on the contributors. There is also a good search facility on environment-related topics.

For more real campaigning go to the Greenpeace site **www.greenpeace.org** where you can find out about their latest activities and how to get involved. For more campaign work check out the International Fund for Animal Welfare who do a great deal of work protecting animals and their environment. Find out how you can help by going to **www.ifaw.org**

www.planetdiary.com

WHAT'S REALLY HAPPENING ON THE PLANET

ORIGIN US
SPEED ✓✓✓
INFO ✓✓✓✓✓
EASE ✓✓✓✓

Every week Planetdiary monitors and records world events in geological, astronomical, meteorological, biological and environmental terms and relays them back via this web site. It's done by showing an icon on a map of the world, which you then click on to find out more. Although very informative, a visit can leave you a little depressed.

http://library.thinkquest.org/C003603

FORCES OF NATURE

ORIGIN US
SPEED ✓✓✓✓
INFO ✓✓✓✓✓
EASE ✓✓✓✓

An amazing site that covers all the known natural disasters, giving background information, simulations and multimedia explanations with experiments for you to try at home.

See also:
www.naturalhazards.org – interesting site with basic information on natural phenomena and links.
www.fema.gov/kids – great for young kids.
www.earthquake.com – check out the most recent seismic activity.

www.coralcay.org

HOW YOU CAN JOIN IN

ORIGIN UK
SPEED ✓✓
INFO ✓✓✓✓
EASE ✓✓✓✓

In Coral Cay's words its aim is 'providing resources to help sustain livelihoods and alleviate poverty through the protection, restoration and management of coral reefs and tropical forests'. Sign up for an expedition or a science project in Honduras or the Philippines.

See also:
www.ecovolunteer.com – if you want to give your services to a specific animal benefit project.
www.ecotourism.org/ecotourist – American site with useful links.

Animals

www.arkive.org.uk

RAISING AWARENESS OF ENDANGERED SPECIES

ORIGIN UK
SPEED ✓✓✓
INFO ✓✓✓✓✓
EASE ✓✓✓✓

Sponsored by the Wildscreen Trust this site will eventually catalogue and picture all the world's endangered species. Each animal and plant has a page devoted to it giving details on how and where it lives, including pictures and movie clips. You can help by donating pictures and film.

www.wdcs.org

WHALE AND DOLPHIN SOCIETY

ORIGIN UK
SPEED ✓✓✓✓
INFO ✓✓✓✓
EASE ✓✓✓✓

All the latest news and developments in the fight to save whales and dolphins. There's also information on them, how and where they live, a sightings and strandings section and details of how to book a whale-watching holiday.

See also:

www.cetacea.org – an excellent site where you can get background info on every species of dolphin, whale and porpoise.

www.flmnh.ufl.edu/fish – the University of Florida's department of ichthyology has a good site where you can find an overview of all things fishy plus links and a good selection of photographs.

www.seawatchfoundation.org.uk – here you can learn more about cetaceans, and their sightings around the UK.

www.africam.com

ALWAYS LIVE, ALWAYS WILD

ORIGIN S. AFRICA
SPEED ✓✓✓
INFO ✓✓✓✓✓
EASE ✓✓✓✓

Web cameras have come a long way and this is one of the best uses of them. There are strategically placed cameras at water holes and parks around Africa and other of the world's wildlife areas, and you can tap in for a look at any time. You have to register to get the best out of it, but even a quick visit is rewarding.

See also:

http://elephant.elehost.com – an excellent elephant only site.

www.lioncrusher.com – all large carnivores and a good picture archive.

www.rainforestlive.org.uk

THE RAINFOREST – LIVE!

ORIGIN UK
SPEED ✓✓✓✓
INFO ✓✓✓✓
EASE ✓✓✓✓

A largely educational site about rainforests and their importance. It gives a good illustrated overview of the subject plus chat, links, competitions and colouring pages for the very young.

See also:
www.rainforest.org – home of the Tropical Rainforest Coalition with up-to-date information on rainforest destruction and how you can help.
www.rainforest-alliance.org – excellent for information and links to related sites.

www.bugbios.com

BUGS AND INSECTS

ORIGIN US
SPEED ✓✓✓✓
INFO ✓✓✓✓✓
EASE ✓✓✓✓

A beautifully designed site exposing insects as miracles of nature, with amazing macro-photography, information and links.

www.birds.com

ALL ABOUT BIRDS

ORIGIN US
SPEED ✓✓✓
INFO ✓✓✓✓✓
EASE ✓✓✓

An online directory and guide to birds covering both wild and pets, biased to America but excellent except that it's a bit too commercial.

See also:
www.rspb.org.uk – the Royal Society for the Protection of Birds have a nice site detailing what they do, and how you can help.
www.ornithology.com – a good, if serious site dedicated to wild birds.
www.birdsofbritain.co.uk – a strong monthly web magazine for British bird watchers.

www.prehistoricplanet.com

PREHISTORIC PLANET

ORIGIN	US
SPEED	✓✓✓✓
INFO	✓✓✓✓✓
EASE	✓✓✓✓

A great site put together by some dinosaur enthusiasts. It's got information on what the planet looked like in prehistoric times, you can ask a palaeontologist a question or just browse the many articles.

See also:
www.dinosaur.org – a messy site, but packed with dino facts and links.
www.bbc.co.uk/dinosaurs – excellent Walking with Dinosaurs site with lots of features.
www.dinodata.net – easy to use and information packed.

Zoos and safari parks

www.safaripark.co.uk

SAFARI ONLINE

ORIGIN	UK
SPEED	✓✓✓
INFO	✓✓✓✓
EASE	✓✓✓

A detailed site on the UK's safari parks including opening times, animal information and facts on endangered species. At **www.zoo-keeper.co.uk** you get information on the most common zoo animals and some background about what it's like to work with them.

www.sandiegozoo.org

SAN DIEGO ZOO

ORIGIN	US
SPEED	✓✓✓✓
INFO	✓✓✓✓
EASE	✓✓✓✓

Probably the best zoo site. You can get conservation information, check out the latest arrivals and browse their excellent photo gallery. The highlight is definitely the Panda Cam.

Other good zoo sites:
www.bristolzoo.co.uk – good looking and fun for kids.
www.dublinzoo.ie – slow but good content.
www.marwell.org.uk – masses to see and do.
www.londonzoo.co.uk – excellent and comprehensive zoo site, also covers Whipsnade Wildlife Park.
www.seaworld.com – information on holidays and the attractions at their three zoos.

www.bornfree.co.uk

ZOO CHECK

ORIGIN	UK
SPEED	✓✓✓
INFO	✓✓✓✓
EASE	✓✓✓✓

Zoo Check is a charity whose mission is to promote Born Free's core belief that wildlife belongs in the wild. They expose the suffering of captive wild animals and investigate neglect and cruelty. They want tighter legislation and the phasing out of all traditional zoos. If you want to know more then this is where to go.

News and the Media

The standard of web sites in this sector is usually very high making it difficult to pick out one or two winners, just find one which appeals to you and you won't go far wrong.

www.sky.co.uk/news

WITNESS THE EVENT

ORIGIN	UK
SPEED	✓✓✓
INFO	✓✓✓✓✓
EASE	✓✓✓✓

Sky News has fast developed a reputation for excellence and that is reflected in their web site. It has a well rounded news service with good coverage across the world as well as the UK. You can view news clips, listen to news items or just browse the site. There are special sections on sport, business, technology and even a few games.

www.bbc.co.uk/news

FROM THE BBC

ORIGIN UK
SPEED ✓✓✓
INFO ✓✓✓✓✓
EASE ✓✓✓✓

As you'd expect the BBC site is excellent - similar to Sky but without the adverts. You can also get the news in several languages and tune into the World Service or any of their radio stations.

www.itn.co.uk

INDEPENDENT TELEVISION NEWS

ORIGIN UK
SPEED ✓✓✓✓
INFO ✓✓✓
EASE ✓✓✓✓

A corporate site where you get information on what they do plus links to their news sites, which are clear and to the point.

www.teletext.com

TELETEXT NEWS

ORIGIN UK
SPEED ✓✓✓✓
INFO ✓✓✓✓
EASE ✓✓✓✓✓

Excellent and clear layout makes Teletext's site stand out, it has lots of added features and links too.

www.cnn.com

THE AMERICAN VIEW

ORIGIN US
SPEED ✓✓✓
INFO ✓✓✓✓✓
EASE ✓✓✓✓

CNN is superb on detail and breaking news with masses of background information on each story. It has plenty of feature pieces too. However, it is biased towards the American audience, for a similar service try www.abcnews.com

www.telegraph.co.uk

NEWSPAPERS ONLINE

ORIGIN UK
SPEED ✓✓✓
INFO ✓✓✓✓
EASE ✓✓✓✓

The Telegraph has the best site for news and layout with all its sections mirrored very effectively on the site.

Other major newspapers with sites worth a visit include:

www.dailymail.co.uk – not so much the paper as a portal for Associated Newspapers, which is disappointing, but there are some good articles and features.

www.guardian.co.uk – clean site with lots of added features and guides.

www.thesun.co.uk – very good representation of the paper with all you'd expect.

www.fish4news.co.uk

LOCAL NEWS MADE EASY

ORIGIN UK	An outstanding web site, just type in your postcode
SPEED ✓✓✓✓	and back will come a collated local 'newspaper'
INFO ✓✓✓✓✓	with regional news headlines, sport and links to the
EASE ✓✓✓✓	source papers sites and small ads.

www.whatthepaperssay.co.uk

WHEN YOU'VE NOT GOT TIME

ORIGIN UK	Can't be bothered to sift through the papers? At this
SPEED ✓✓✓	site you can quickly take in the key stories and be
INFO ✓✓✓✓✓	linked through to the relevant newspaper site too.
EASE ✓✓✓✓	You can also sign up to its daily e-mail bulletin so
	you need never buy a paper again.

http//:ask.elibrary.com

RESEARCH WITHOUT THE LEGWORK

ORIGIN US	A subscription only site which has access to over
SPEED ✓✓✓	600 newspapers on a searchable database. It can be
INFO ✓✓✓✓	tailored to your needs and includes books, maps and
VALUE ✓✓	photos too. The subscription cost is $79.95 per
EASE ✓✓✓✓	annum.

www.newsnow.co.uk

NEWS NOW!

ORIGIN	UK
SPEED	✓✓✓
INFO	✓✓✓✓✓
EASE	✓✓✓

A superb news gathering and information service that you can tailor to your needs and interests. The layout is confusing at first but it allows you to flick between latest headlines from 3,000 leading news sources without visiting each site separately, you can then read their choice of stories in full on the publishers' web sites. It's updated every 5 minutes!

www.moreover.com

DYNAMIC CONTENT

ORIGIN	US
SPEED	✓✓✓
INFO	✓✓✓✓✓
EASE	✓✓✓✓

With real time news and rumour reporting, Moreover has become the news site of choice for many business people and journalists as it enables them to target the type of news and information they are looking for, saving time and effort all round.

www.drudgereport.com

NOW FOR THE REAL NEWS

ORIGIN	US
SPEED	✓✓✓
INFO	✓✓✓✓✓
EASE	✓✓

One of the most visited sites on the web. It's a pain to use, but the gossip and tips about upcoming features in the papers make it worthwhile. One of its best features is its superb set of links to other news sources.

www.foreignreport.com

PREDICT THE FUTURE

ORIGIN	UK
SPEED	✓✓✓
INFO	✓✓✓✓
EASE	✓✓✓

The Foreign Report team attempt to pick out trends and happenings that might lead to bigger international news events. Browsing through their track record shows they're pretty good at it too.

www.wwevents.com
WORLD EVENTS

ORIGIN UK
SPEED ✓✓✓✓
INFO ✓✓✓✓
EASE ✓✓✓✓

Details of events that are happening in the world today, tomorrow and this weekend all available at the touch of a button, it really is that simple. You can search by country or even region and county.

Organiser and Diary

www.organizer.com
ORGANISE YOURSELF

ORIGIN US
SPEED ✓✓
INFO ✓✓✓✓
EASE ✓✓✓✓

An American site that is just what it says it is, an organiser that allows you to list all your commitments and it will send e-mail reminders in good time.

www.opendiary.com
THE ONLINE DIARY FOR THE WORLD

ORIGIN US
SPEED ✓✓✓
INFO ✓✓✓✓
EASE ✓✓✓

Your own personal organiser and diary, easy to use, genuinely helpful and totally anonymous. Simply register and away you go but follow the rules faithfully or you get deleted. Use it as you would any diary, go public or just browse other entries.

See also:
www.yourorganiser.com.au – good looking site, easy to use with a group organiser facility.
www.webdiary.net – flexible diary for business users.

Over 50s

If you're over 50 then you're part of the fastest growing group of Internet users, and some sites have cottoned on to the fact with specific content just for you.

www.idf50.co.uk
I DON'T FEEL FIFTY

ORIGIN UK	Graham Andrews is retired and this is his irreverent
SPEED ✓✓✓✓	and opinionated magazine site. It's very positive
INFO ✓✓✓✓✓	about the power of being over 50 and it has a great
EASE ✓✓✓	deal of motivational advice on how to get the best

out of life combined with a superb set of links to useful sites.

See also:
www.theoldie.co.uk – *The Oldie* magazine, which is great fun.
www.togs.org – where devoted fans of Terry Wogan meet.

www.vavo.com
REDEFINING THE INTERNET GENERATION

ORIGIN UK	This well laid out site is aimed at over 45s, but it
SPEED ✓✓✓✓	offers a great deal if you register, in terms of special
INFO ✓✓✓✓	deals on travel, health info, financial advice,
EASE ✓✓✓	consumer tips, education and features on history

and politics. There's an online shop with some very good offers and also a great section on making retirement work for you. You can also reminisce and take part in the chat rooms and forums.

www.50connect.co.uk

LIVE LIFE TO THE FULL

ORIGIN UK
SPEED ✓✓✓✓
INFO ✓✓✓✓✓
EASE ✓✓✓✓

A very strong portal site with masses of information and links covering a wide range of topics. It's incredibly useful, however, there are plenty of annoying adverts to go with it.

See also:
www.age-net.co.uk – another portal site but one that takes a magazine-style approach.
www.maturetymes.co.uk – lots of links and good for offers on a wide range of products.
www.lifes4living.co.uk – an upbeat site dedicated to chat and links, some good offers too.

www.silversurfers.net

LINKS GALORE

ORIGIN UK
SPEED ✓✓✓✓
INFO ✓✓✓✓✓
EASE ✓✓✓

Not the easiest site to get to grips with but it has a huge number of links in over 50 categories.

See also:
http://ourworld.compuserve.com/homepages/Smiln e6/silv.htm – A long-winded URL, but you are rewarded with a good set of links to sites for senior citizens.

www.ageconcern.co.uk

WORKING FOR ALL OLDER PEOPLE

ORIGIN UK
SPEED ✓✓✓✓
INFO ✓✓✓✓✓
EASE ✓✓✓✓

Learn how to get involved with helping older people, get information and practical advice on all aspects of getting old. You can also make a donation. There are also over 100 links to related and special interest sites.

www.arp.org.uk

ASSOCIATION OF RETIRED PERSONS

ORIGIN UK
SPEED ✓✓✓✓
INFO ✓✓✓✓✓
EASE ✓✓✓✓

ARP's mission is to change the attitude of society and individuals towards age in order to enhance the quality of life for people over 50 – and this site goes a long way to achieving that. It has great design and plenty of features aimed at helping you get the most out of life. It's excellent for a place to chat if nothing else.

www.helptheaged.org.uk

HELP THE AGED

ORIGIN UK
SPEED ✓✓✓✓
INFO ✓✓✓✓✓
VALUE ✓✓✓
EASE ✓✓✓✓

Find out how you can get involved in their work, what they do plus the latest news. You can also go to 'home shopping' and buy all sorts of useful gadgets to make life easier.

www.hairnet.org

TECHNOLOGY EXPLAINED

ORIGIN UK
SPEED ✓✓✓✓
INFO ✓✓✓✓
EASE ✓✓✓✓

So you've bought the PC and now you need to know how to work it properly? Hairnet explains all through a series of forums and specific courses designed to help you get the most from technology. See also **www.seniornet.org**

www.age-exchange.org.uk

MAKE YOUR MEMORIES MATTER

ORIGIN UK
SPEED ✓✓✓✓
INFO ✓✓✓✓
EASE ✓✓✓✓

Share your experiences and pass them on, Age Exchange aims to 'improve the quality of life for older people by emphasising the value of their memories to old and young, through pioneering artistic, educational, and welfare activities', they are also active in improving care for older people. This site gives details of how you can join in.

www.saga.co.uk/travel
HOLIDAYS FOR THE OVER 50S

ORIGIN UK
SPEED ✓✓✓✓
INFO ✓✓✓✓
VALUE ✓✓✓
EASE ✓✓✓✓

A superbly illustrated and rich site from Saga who've been specialising in holidays for older people for many years. Here you'll find everything from top quality cruises to weekend breaks.

See also:
www.travel55.co.uk – a great database of travel sites specialising in travel for older people.
www.takeaholiday.co.uk – Direct Reader holidays specialise in the over 50s.

Parenting

As a source of advice the Internet has proved its worth and especially so for parents. As well as information, there are great shops and useful sites that filter out the worst of the web and give advice on specific problems. Some of the education web sites, page 104, also have useful resources for parents as do the health sites, page 209. In addition, there is loads of useful stuff for parents about taking children on holiday and activities to do with the children in the UK in the travel section, page 461.

Advice and information

www.babyworld.co.uk
BE PART OF IT

ORIGIN UK
SPEED ✓✓✓
INFO ✓✓✓✓✓
EASE ✓✓✓✓

Babyworld is an online magazine that covers all aspects of parenthood, there's excellent advice on how to choose the right products for your baby and for the pregnancy itself. The layout is much improved and it's easier to find information.

www.babycentre.co.uk

A HANDS-ON GUIDE

ORIGIN UK
SPEED ✓✓✓
INFO ✓✓✓✓✓
EASE ✓✓✓✓

A superb site with a massive amount of information and links to all aspects of pregnancy, childbirth and early parenthood. The content is provided by experts and you can tailor-make your profile so that you get the right information for you. There's also a series of buying guides to help you make the right decision on baby shopping.

www.babyzone.com

PARENTAL ADVICE

ORIGIN US
SPEED ✓✓✓✓
INFO ✓✓✓✓✓
EASE ✓✓✓

This massive, comprehensive, American site on parenting gives a week-by-week account of pregnancy, information on birth and early childhood. The shop is not open to UK residents, but they have a good set of links to UK stores and community activities. See also the similarly well-put-together **www.parentsoup.com**

www.ukparents.co.uk

YOUR PARENTING LIFELINE

ORIGIN UK
SPEED ✓✓✓✓
INFO ✓✓✓✓
VALUE ✓✓✓
EASE ✓✓✓✓

Chat, experiences, stories and straightforward advice make this site worth a visit – there are competitions, links and a good online shop.

www.tigerchild.com

A BALANCED SOURCE OF INFORMATION

ORIGIN UK
SPEED ✓✓✓✓
INFO ✓✓✓✓
VALUE ✓✓✓
EASE ✓✓✓✓

Covering health, leisure, education, childcare and parenting, this attractive and well laid out site offers unbiased and straightforward information with over 1,000 links throughout. The shop is actually a directory with a review for each retailer.

www.all4kidsuk.com

IF YOU'RE LOOKING FOR SOMETHING TO DO

ORIGIN UK
SPEED ✓✓✓
INFO ✓✓✓✓✓
EASE ✓✓✓✓

This aims to be a comprehensive directory covering all your parental needs from activities to schools. It's got an easy-to-use search engine, where you can search by county if you need to.

www.miriamstoppard.com

MIRIAM STOPPARD LIFETIME

ORIGIN UK
SPEED ✓✓✓✓
INFO ✓✓✓✓
EASE ✓✓✓✓

An excellent web site from the best selling author with lots of advice on being a parent, how to cope with pregnancy and keeping you and your family healthy. New information is continually being added, so it's very up-to-date and will become a great resource for parents.

www.babydirectory.com

A–Z OF BEING A PARENT

ORIGIN UK
SPEED ✓✓✓
INFO ✓✓✓
EASE ✓✓✓✓

The Baby Directory catalogue is relevant to most parts of the UK. It lists local facilities plus amenities that care for and occupy your child. The quality of information varies by area though.

www.babyweb.co.uk

BABY PICTURES

ORIGIN UK
SPEED ✓✓✓
INFO ✓✓✓
VALUE ✓✓✓
EASE ✓✓✓

If you want to have a picture of your new arrival and a personalised web page with all the birth details highlighted for all to coo over, here's where to go!

www.gingerbread.org.uk

SUPPORT FOR LONE PARENT FAMILIES

ORIGIN UK
SPEED ✓✓✓
INFO ✓✓✓
EASE ✓✓✓

Gingerbread is an established charity run by lone parents with the aim of providing support to lone parents. The site is fun to use and well designed, the best aspect being that it's available in several languages.

Other useful sites:
www.oneparentfamilies.org.uk – advice for single parents.
www.fnf.org.uk – support for fathers at Families Need Fathers.

Childcare

www.bestbear.co.uk

MARY POPPINS ONLINE

ORIGIN UK
SPEED ✓✓✓✓
INFO ✓✓✓✓
EASE ✓✓✓✓

Select your postcode and they will provide you with a list of reputable childcare agencies or nurseries in your area. There are also homepages for parents, childcarers and agencies all with information and ideas. There is also a parents' forum. See also www.sitters.co.uk

www.daycaretrust.org.uk

CHILDCARE ADVICE

ORIGIN UK
SPEED ✓✓✓
INFO ✓✓✓
EASE ✓✓✓

Daycare Trust is a national childcare charity which works to promote high quality, affordable childcare for all. This site is designed to give you all the information you need on arranging care for your child, there are sections on finance, news and you can become a member.

Shopping

www.bloomingmarvellous.co.uk

MATERNITY, NURSERY AND BABY WEAR

ORIGIN UK
SPEED ✓✓✓✓
INFO ✓✓✓✓
VALUE ✓✓✓✓
EASE ✓✓✓✓

Excellent online store with a selection of maternity, baby and nurseryware available to buy, or you can order their catalogue. Delivery in the UK is £3.95.

www.mothercare.com

MOTHERCARE

ORIGIN UK
SPEED ✓✓✓✓
INFO ✓✓✓✓
VALUE ✓✓✓✓
EASE ✓✓✓✓

An attractive site with a good selection of baby and toddler products, also clothing, entertainment and equipment. It's good value and there are some excellent offers, delivery is £3 for the UK. It's not all about shopping though, there are advice sections on baby care, finance, tips on how to keep kids occupied and chat rooms where you can share your experiences.

www.go-help.co.uk

SHOP AND GIVE

ORIGIN UK
SPEED ✓✓✓
INFO ✓✓✓✓
VALUE ✓✓✓✓
EASE ✓✓✓✓

Go-help allows you to raise money for a good cause from your Internet shopping. It's basically a store list set in the usual shopping categories, with each store pledging a certain percentage of the amount you spend with them to your chosen beneficiary be it a school, charity or club.

www.ethosbaby.com

FOR GREEN BABIES

ORIGIN UK
SPEED ✓✓✓✓
INFO ✓✓✓✓
VALUE ✓✓✓
EASE ✓✓✓

A good store where all products are environmentally friendly, there's not a huge selection but you can order a catalogue. Delivery charges vary according to spend.

Dealing with areas of concern

BULLYING

www.bullying.co.uk
HOW TO COPE WITH BULLYING

ORIGIN UK   Advice for everyone on how to deal with a bully;
SPEED ✓✓✓✓   there are sections on tips for dealing with them,
INFO ✓✓✓✓   school projects, problem pages and links to related
EASE ✓✓✓✓   sites.

COMPUTERS AND THE INTERNET

www.cyberpatrol.com
INTERNET FILTERING SOFTWARE

ORIGIN US   The best for filtering out unwanted web sites,
SPEED ✓✓✓   images and words. As with all similar programs, it
INFO ✓✓✓✓   quickly becomes outdated but will continue to weed
VALUE ✓✓✓✓   out the worst. You can download a free trial from
EASE ✓✓✓✓   the site. See also **www.netnanny.com** whose site
offers more advice and seems to be updated more
regularly.

www.pin-parents.com
PARENTS' INFORMATION NETWORK

ORIGIN US   Provides good advice for parents worried about chil-
SPEED ✓✓✓✓   dren using computers. It has links to support sites,
INFO ✓✓✓✓✓   guidance on how to surf the Net, evaluations of
VALUE ✓✓✓   software and buyer's guides to PCs.
EASE ✓✓✓✓

DRUGS

www.theantidrug.com

TRUTH. THE ANTIDRUG

ORIGIN US
SPEED ✓✓✓
INFO ✓✓✓✓✓
EASE ✓✓✓✓

An outstanding site devoted to the fight against drugs with help for parents and children alike. There's plenty of advice, articles and general information and it's all written in an accessible style, and in several languages.

www.trashed.co.uk

DON'T GET TRASHED

ORIGIN UK
SPEED ✓✓✓✓
INFO ✓✓✓✓✓
EASE ✓✓✓✓

The NHS's drug site has non-judgemental, factual information on all the major recreational drugs with useful information on what to do in an emergency. For the government's line on drugs and good no-nonsense information go to www.ndh.org.uk – The National Drugs Helpline 0800 776600.

DYSLEXIA

www.bda-dyslexia.org.uk

BRITISH DYSLEXIA ASSOCIATION

ORIGIN UK
SPEED ✓✓✓✓
INFO ✓✓✓✓
EASE ✓✓✓✓

A good starting point for anyone who thinks that their child might be dyslexic. There is masses of information on dyslexia, choosing a school, a list of local Dyslexia Associations where you can get assessment and teaching, articles on the latest research and educational materials for sale. There is also information on adult dyslexia. For similar material visit www.dyslexia-inst.org.uk who also offer testing and teaching through their centres.

EATING DISORDERS

www.edauk.com
EATING DISORDERS ASSOCIATION

ORIGIN UK
SPEED ✓✓✓
INFO ✓✓✓✓
EASE ✓✓✓✓

If you think you have a problem with eating then at this site you can get advice and information. It doesn't replace going to the doctor but it's a place to start. There are help lines - youth is 01603 765 050, others 01603 621 414.

HEALTH

www.iemily.com
GIRL'S HEALTH

ORIGIN US
SPEED ✓✓✓
INFO ✓✓✓✓
EASE ✓✓✓✓

A massive A–Z listing of all the issues and problems you might face, it's easy to use and the information is straight to the point and often accompanied by articles relating to the subject. If you can't find what you need here try **www.prematuree.com** which is especially useful for older teenage girls. See also section on Health Advice page 209.

MISSING CHILDREN

www.missingkids.co.uk
UK'S MISSING CHILDREN

ORIGIN UK
SPEED ✓✓✓
INFO ✓✓✓✓✓
EASE ✓✓✓✓

This site is dedicated to reuniting children with their families, the details of those missing are based on police and home office data. You can search by town or date and there's also a section on those who've got back together.

Also try:

www.salvationarmy.org.uk for their family tracing service.

www.missingpersons.org – the missing persons helpline – 0500 700 700.

RACISM

www.britkid.org

DEALING WITH RACISM

ORIGIN	UK
SPEED	✓✓✓
INFO	✓✓✓✓✓
EASE	✓✓✓✓

A game that shows how different ethnic groups live in the Britain of today, full of interesting facts and information. There's a serious side, which has background information on dealing with racism, information on different races and their religious beliefs.

SAFETY

www.childalert.co.uk

CHILD SAFETY

ORIGIN	UK
SPEED	✓✓✓
INFO	✓✓✓✓✓
VALUE	✓✓✓
EASE	✓✓✓✓✓

This is about bringing up children in a safe environment; there are tips, product reviews and a shop, stories, links and masses of advice and information. Except for the shop, the site is well-designed and it's easy to find things.

SEX

www.lovelife.uk.com

HERE TO ANSWER YOUR QUESTIONS

ORIGIN UK
SPEED ✓✓✓✓
INFO ✓✓✓✓✓
EASE ✓✓✓✓

Great site that has lots of information on sex as well as games and links to related sites. The emphasis is on safe sex and AIDS prevention. See also the Terence Higgins Trust at **www.tht.org.uk** this is the leading AIDS charity. The section on Health, page 209, Men page 244 and Women, page 483 may also provide relevant information.

www.likeitis.org.uk

TELLING IT LIKE IT IS

ORIGIN UK
SPEED ✓✓✓✓
INFO ✓✓✓✓✓
EASE ✓✓✓✓

An outstanding site from the Marie Stopes Institute giving good, straight information on all the major issues around sex and puberty that face teenagers today.

www.fpa.org.uk

FAMILY PLANNING ASSOCIATION

ORIGIN UK
SPEED ✓✓✓
INFO ✓✓✓✓
EASE ✓✓✓✓

Straightforward and informative, you can find out where to get help and there's a good list of web links too. See also the British Pregnancy Advisory service at **www.bpas.org**

SPEECH

www.speechteach.co.uk

SPEECH THERAPY

ORIGIN UK
SPEED ✓✓✓
INFO ✓✓✓✓
EASE ✓✓✓✓

Information, help and advice on what to do if your child has speech problems or communication difficulties. The site aims to provide a learning resource for parents and teachers alike. It also needs funding.

STRESS AND MENTAL HEALTH

www.at-ease.nsf.org.uk

YOUR MENTAL HEALTH

ORIGIN UK
SPEED ✓✓✓
INFO ✓✓✓✓
EASE ✓✓✓✓

At-ease offers loads of good advice on how to deal with stress and is aimed specifically at young people. Go to the A–Z section which covers a large range of subjects from dealing with aggression to exam stress to how to become a volunteer to help others.

www.isma.org.uk/exams.htm

EXAM STRESS

ORIGIN UK
SPEED ✓✓✓
INFO ✓✓✓✓
EASE ✓✓✓✓

Top tips on coping with exams from the International Stress Management Association.

Pets

Here's a selection of web sites devoted to pets, shop and information sites and specialists too.

www.pets-pyjamas.co.uk

THE COMPLETE PETS WEB SITE

ORIGIN UK
SPEED ✓✓✓
INFO ✓✓✓✓
VALUE ✓✓✓
EASE ✓✓✓✓

An excellent site split into four sections:
1 **Entertainment** – quizzes and chat.
2 **Services** – vet finder, insurance and a funeral service.
3 **News and information** – topics such as health.
4 **Shopping** – via their own shop plus www.animail.co.uk a more general value-led pet shop and a specialist bookstore.

There are also subsections on dogs, cats and small animals.

For other good online pet information and stores visit:

www.mypetstop.com – superb for information and health advice.

www.petplanet.co.uk – good for the shop and up-to-the-minute news.

www.ukpets.co.uk – a directory of pet shops and suppliers, plus advice and a magazine devoted to pets.

www.bluepet.co.uk – specialists in organic food for pets.

www.pethealthcare.co.uk

PET INSURANCE

ORIGIN UK
SPEED ✓✓✓
INFO ✓✓✓✓
VALUE ✓✓✓
EASE ✓✓✓✓

This is a good place to start looking for insurance to cover your vet's bill. It also has lots of good advice on how to look after pets and what to do when you first get a pet.

www.naturallypaws.com

COMPLEMENTARY MEDICINE FOR PETS

ORIGIN UK
SPEED ✓✓✓✓
INFO ✓✓✓✓
EASE ✓✓✓✓

An informative site giving details of how you can look after your pets using natural foods and complementary medicines.

www.pets-on-holiday.com

UK HOLIDAYS WITH PETS

ORIGIN UK
SPEED ✓✓✓
INFO ✓✓✓✓
EASE ✓✓✓✓

This site is devoted to finding holiday accommodation where your pets are always welcome simply arranged by region, easy. There's also a bookshop and a good set of links.

See also:
www.petswelcome.co.uk – pet friendly hotels
throughout the UK.
www.preferredplaces.co.uk – a holiday specialist
with a good pets welcome section.
www.defra.gov.uk/animalh/quarantine/index.htm –
animal quarantine and advice on overseas travel.

Animal charities

www.rspca.org

THE RSPCA

ORIGIN UK
SPEED ✓✓✓
INFO ✓✓✓✓
EASE ✓✓✓

News (some of which can be quite disturbing) and
information on the work of the charity plus animal
facts and details on how you can help. There's also a
good kids' section. It's a good site but a bit tightly
packed.

Other charity sites:
www.aht.org.uk – applying clinical and research
techniques to help animals.
www.animalrescuers.co.uk – a directory of centres
and people who will help distressed animals.
www.animalrescue.org.uk – fight animal pain and
suffering.
www.bluecross.org.uk – excellent site with information, help and advice.
www.pdsa.org.uk – Peoples Dispensary for Sick
Animals has a good looking site with details on
how to look after pets and how you can help.
www.petrescue.com – home of the pet action league.
www.animalsanctuaries.co.uk – index of charities
and animal rescue centres.

www.giveusahome.co.uk
RE-HOMING A PET

ORIGIN UK
SPEED ✓✓✓
INFO ✓✓✓✓✓
EASE ✓✓✓

A nice idea, a web site devoted to helping you save animals that need to be re-homed, it's got a large amount of information by region on shelters, vets and the animals themselves as well as entertainment for kids.

TV-related

www.channel4.com/petrescue
PET RESCUE

ORIGIN UK
SPEED ✓✓✓✓
INFO ✓✓✓✓
EASE ✓✓✓✓

Details of the program plus information and links on animal charities and sites, there are also stories, games and chat. See also the excellent BBC web pages on pets which can be found at www.bbc.co.uk/nature/animals/pets

Sites for different species

BIRDS

www.avianweb.com
FOR BIRD ENTHUSIASTS

ORIGIN US
SPEED ✓✓✓✓
INFO ✓✓✓✓✓
EASE ✓✓✓✓

A massive site devoted to birds, it's especially good for information on parrots. There are sections on species, health and equipment as well as advice on looking after birds. See also www.rspb.org.uk

www.bird-shop.co.uk

BIRDS AND EXOTIC PETS

ORIGIN	UK
SPEED	✓✓✓✓
INFO	✓✓✓
VALUE	✓✓✓
EASE	✓✓✓✓

Online pet shop devoted mainly to birds but also covers more exotic animals too, there's advice on food and a breeder's directory. It could do with more information and unless you really like bird-calls, turn the sound off. www.birdcare.co.uk is another commercial site with useful information.

CATS

www.cats.org.uk

HOME OF CAT PROTECTION

ORIGIN	UK
SPEED	✓✓✓✓
INFO	✓✓✓✓
VALUE	✓✓✓
EASE	✓✓✓✓

A well-designed and informative site, with advice on caring, re-homing, news and general advice, an archive of cat photos and competitions for the best. The online shop offers delivery in the UK but charges vary.

See also:
www.moggies.co.uk – home of the Online Cat Guide, not an easy site to use, but has exceptional links to pet sites.
www.fabcats.org – a charity devoted to cat care.
www.crazyforkitties.com – nice site devoted to all things cat and kitty.
www.freddie-street.com – fantastic and funny the story of the Freddie Street cats, there's some good information in there too.
www.i-love-cats.com – a directory of cat sites.

DOGS

www.dogsonline.co.uk

DOGS, DOGS AND MORE DOGS

ORIGIN UK
SPEED ✓✓✓
INFO ✓✓✓✓✓
VALUE ✓✓
EASE ✓✓✓✓

All you'd ever want from a web site about dogs. There's information on breeding, where to get dogs, events, directories, how to find hotels that accept dogs, classified ads and insurance.

See also:
www.canismajor.com/dog – an American magazine site.
www.canineworld.com – an average site with some good links.
www.the-kennel-club.org.uk – for the official line on dogs and breeding with information on Crufts and links to related web sites.
www.dogs-and-diets.com – comprehensive nutritional information for dogs.
www.i-love-dogs.com – a directory of web sites devoted to dogs.
www.howtoloveyourdog.com – a children's guide to caring for dogs.

www.ncdl.org.uk

NATIONAL CANINE DEFENCE LEAGUE

ORIGIN UK
SPEED ✓✓✓
INFO ✓✓✓✓✓
VALUE ✓✓✓
EASE ✓✓✓✓

Excellent web site featuring the charitable works of the NCDL the largest charity of its type. Get advice on how to adopt a dog, tips on looking after one and download a doggie screensaver. For Battersea Dogs Home go to **www.dogshome.org** who have a well-designed site.

FISH

www.ornamentalfish.org

ORNAMENTAL AQUATIC TRADE ASSOCIATION

ORIGIN UK
SPEED ✓✓✓
INFO ✓✓✓✓
EASE ✓✓✓✓

An excellent site beautifully designed and well executed. Although much of it is aimed at the trade and commercial side, there is a great deal of information for the hobbyist about looking after and buying fish.

See also:
www.fishlinkcentral.com – a good directory site for information on fish.
www.aquariacentral.com – a huge site with masses of information on every aspect of looking after fish.

HORSES

www.equiworld.net

GLOBAL EQUINE INFORMATION

ORIGIN UK
SPEED ✓✓✓
INFO ✓✓✓✓✓
EASE ✓✓✓✓

A directory, magazine and advice centre in one with incredible detail plus some fun stuff too including video and audio interviews and footage, holidays and the latest news. The shop consists of links to specialist traders.

See also:
www.horseadvice.com – a health-oriented site that supplies a huge amount of information.
www.equine-world.co.uk – lots here too including classified ads, shopping and links.

RABBITS AND RODENTS

http://www.rabbit.org
HOUSE RABBIT SOCIETY

ORIGIN US
SPEED ✓✓✓✓
INFO ✓✓✓✓✓
EASE ✓✓✓✓

It's all here, from feeding, breeding, behaviour, health advice and even info on house-training your rabbit. Has a nice kids' section and plenty of cute pictures.

See also:
www.rabbitworld.com – a personal tribute to rabbits, which also has information on caring for your fluffy friend.
www.rabbitwelfare.co.uk – lots of chat, advice and links frown the Rabbit Welfare Association.
www.rodentfancy.com – good all round site about the small creatures.
www.gerbils.co.uk – home of the National Gerbil Society.

OTHER PETS

www.ukreptiles.com – an OK directory site for reptile enthusiasts, good for links.
www.petreptiles.com – comprehensive pet reptile information.
www.insectpets.co.uk – a guide to keeping insects as pets and there's a shop too.

Photography

www.photographyworld.co.uk

COMMUNITY OF PHOTOGRAPHERS

ORIGIN UK
SPEED ✓✓✓
INFO ✓✓✓✓
EASE ✓✓✓

A very good portal site with links to all aspects of photography, there's information on everything from models to lessons.

www.rps.org

THE ROYAL PHOTOGRAPHIC SOCIETY

ORIGIN UK
SPEED ✓✓✓
INFO ✓✓
VALUE ✓✓✓
EASE ✓✓✓

A worthy, dull site dedicated to the works of the RPS; you can get details of the latest exhibitions and the collection, become a member, get the latest news about the world of photography. Good for links to other related sites. Sadly there aren't many pictures, which is an opportunity missed.

www.nmpft.org.uk

NATIONAL MUSEUM OF PHOTOGRAPHY, FILM AND TELEVISION

ORIGIN UK
SPEED ✓✓✓
INFO ✓✓✓✓
EASE ✓✓✓✓

Details of this Bradford museum via a high tech web site, opening times and directions, what's on, education resources and a very good museum guide.

www.eastman.org

THE INTERNATIONAL MUSEUM OF PHOTOGRAPHY

ORIGIN US
SPEED ✓✓✓
INFO ✓✓✓✓
EASE ✓✓✓✓

George Eastman founded Kodak and this New York-based museum too. This site is comprehensive and amongst other things you can learn about the history of photography, visit the photographic and film galleries, or obtain technical information. Become a member and you're entitled to benefits such as free admission and copies of their *Image* magazine.

www.nationalgeographic.com/photography

HOME OF THE NATIONAL GEOGRAPHIC MAGAZINE

ORIGIN US
SPEED ✓✓✓✓
INFO ✓✓✓✓✓
EASE ✓✓✓✓

Synonymous with great photography, this excellent site offers much more. There are sections on travel, exhibitions, maps, news, education, and for kids. In the photography section pick up tips and techniques, follow their photographers' various locations, read superb articles and accompanying shots in the 'Visions Galleries'. Good links to other photographic sites.

www.masters-of-photography.com

ONLINE GALLERIES

ORIGIN US
SPEED ✓✓✓
INFO ✓✓✓✓✓
EASE ✓✓✓✓

A simple site with a superb array of galleries devoted to the real masters of the art of photography – you can spend hours browsing here.

www.life.com/Life

LIFE MAGAZINE

ORIGIN US
SPEED ✓✓✓
INFO ✓✓✓✓✓
EASE ✓✓✓✓✓

Life Magazine, it's wonderfully nostalgic and still going strong. There are several sections, features with great photos, excellent articles, and an option to subscribe; however they could do much more and it's a little frustrating to use.

www.corbis.com

THE PLACE FOR PICTURES ON THE INTERNET

ORIGIN US
SPEED ✓✓✓✓
INFO ✓✓✓✓✓
VALUE ✓✓✓
EASE ✓✓✓✓

Another Microsoft product, this is probably the world's largest online picture library. Use the pictures to enhance presentations, web sites, screensavers, or to make e-cards for friends. You can also buy pictures framed or unframed which are good value, but shipping to the UK can be expensive. You can also now buy high quality digital images at $4.50 a go. See also **www.freefoto.com** who offer the largest free image database and **www.webshots.com** which is great for wallpaper and screensavers.

www.getmapping.com
AERIAL PHOTOGRAPHS

ORIGIN UK	Just type in your postcode and get a picture of your
SPEED ✓✓✓✓	home taken from above on a sunny day last year.
INFO ✓✓✓✓	There are lots of cost options and you can also get a
VALUE ✓✓✓	map to go with it.
EASE ✓✓✓	

www.bjphoto.co.uk
THE BRITISH JOURNAL OF PHOTOGRAPHY

ORIGIN UK	An online magazine with loads of material on
SPEED ✓✓✓	photography. Access their archive or visit picture
INFO ✓✓✓✓	galleries that contain work from contemporary
EASE ✓✓✓✓	photographers, find out about careers in photography and where to buy the best photographic gear.

www.betterphoto.com
TAKE BETTER PICTURES

ORIGIN UK	A very well laid out and comprehensive advice site
SPEED ✓✓✓✓	for new and experienced photographers with a
INFO ✓✓✓✓✓	buyer's guide and introductions to and overviews of
EASE ✓✓✓✓	traditional and digital photography.

www.jessops.com
TAKE ADVICE TAKE GREAT PICTURES

ORIGIN UK	Jessops are the largest photographic retailer in the UK
SPEED ✓✓✓	and they offer advice on most aspects of photography
INFO ✓✓✓✓	plus courses and free software for their digital print-
VALUE ✓✓✓	ing service. They do give you an opportunity to go
EASE ✓✓✓✓	shopping for your camera and accessories, of course.

See also:

www.internetcamerasdirect.co.uk – a good value independent store with reviews and a digital dictionary.

www.camerasdirect.co.uk – well designed store, delivery from £4.99.

www.whichcamera.co.uk

FIND THE RIGHT CAMERA

ORIGIN	UK
SPEED	✓✓✓
INFO	✓✓✓✓✓
EASE	✓✓✓

Get advice on the best camera for you then use links to find your local dealer or to the manufacturer direct. The information is very good, there's a good search engine and camera finder service too. The graphics could be better though. See also www.camerareview.com

www.fotango.com

ONLINE DEVELOPERS

ORIGIN	UK
SPEED	✓✓✓✓
INFO	✓✓✓✓
VALUE	✓✓✓
EASE	✓✓✓✓

Fotango will take your film and digitise it, then place your pictures on a secure site for you to view and select for printing the ones you like. The service is quick and easy to use; costs don't seem much different from the high street although single prints can be expensive.

Other sites offering a similar service are:

www.photoscrapbook.com – an American site offering good value.

www.photobox.co.uk – nice design, best for digital photo storage.

Other good photography sites:

www.photo.net – an American site with lots of advice and reviews.

www.photobuzz.com – the place to discuss digital photography.

Price Checkers

Here's a good place to start any online shopping trip - a price comparison site. There are many price checker sites, however, the sites listed here allow you to check the prices for online stores across a much wider range of merchandise than the usual books, music and film.

www.kelkoo.com
COMPARE PRICES BEFORE YOU BUY

ORIGIN EUROPE
SPEED ✓✓✓
INFO ✓✓✓✓✓
VALUE ✓✓✓✓✓
EASE ✓✓✓✓

Kelkoo is probably the best price-checking site with 18 categories in their shop directory including books, wine, white goods, even cars and second hand goods – they have links with eBay. There are plenty of bargains to be had in fact they keep popping up on every page. In the features section you'll find reviews and news of the latest goods and consumer advice.

www.shopsmart.co.uk
SHOP SMART

ORIGIN UK
SPEED ✓✓✓✓
INFO ✓✓✓✓✓
VALUE ✓✓✓✓✓
EASE ✓✓✓✓

Now owned by Barclaycard this is a wide ranging shop review site which is fully reviewed in the shopping section, but it deserves a place here for its excellent price checking facility which covers books, DVD & video, games, computer hardware and electronics.

www.checkaprice.com
CONSTANTLY CHECKING PRICES

ORIGIN UK
SPEED ✓✓✓
INFO ✓✓✓✓
VALUE ✓✓✓✓✓
EASE ✓✓✓✓

Compare prices across nearly 60 different product types, from the usual books to cars, holidays, mortgages and electrical goods. If it can't do it for you, it patches you through to a site that can.

Other good sites:

www.buy.co.uk – excellent for the utilities - gas, water and electrical as well as credit cards and mobile phones.

www.dealtime.co.uk – easy-to-use directory and price checker covering a wide range of goods.

www.pricechecker.co.uk – straightforward site, also covers flights and telephone tariffs.

www.pricescan.com – all the usual, plus watches, jewellery, sports goods and office equipment – good store finder. ˹

www.price-guide.co.uk – a comprehensive offering including unusually wines.

www.priceoffers.co.uk – not really a checker, but has access to the best bargains, also a regular newsletter covering the latest offers.

www.pricerunner.com – a good all-rounder with a news section giving the latest information on deals and technology updates.

www.price-search.net – mainly computers and gadgets.

www.pricewatch.co.uk – good for computers and personal finance.

Property

Every estate agent worth their salt has got a web site, and in theory finding the house of your dreams has never been easier. These sites have been designed to help you through the real life minefield.

www.upmystreet.com

FIND OUT ABOUT WHERE YOU WANT TO GO

ORIGIN UK
SPEED ✓✓✓
INFO ✓✓✓✓✓
EASE ✓✓✓✓

Type in the postcode and up pops almost every statistic you need to know about the area in question. Spooky, but fascinating, it's a good guide featuring not only house prices, but also schools, the local MP, local authority information, crime and links to services. It also has a classified section and puts you in touch with the nearest items to your area.

www.conveyancing-cms.co.uk

CONVEYANCING MARKETING SERVICE

ORIGIN UK
SPEED ✓✓✓
INFO ✓✓✓✓
VALUE ✓✓✓✓
EASE ✓✓✓

Conveyancing is a bit of a minefield if you're new to it, this site aims to help with advice and competitive quotes. See also **www.easier2move.com** which is nicely designed and very informative.

www.reallymoving.com

MAKING MOVING EASIER

ORIGIN UK
SPEED ✓✓✓
INFO ✓✓✓✓✓
EASE ✓✓✓✓

A directory of sites and help for home buyers including mortgages, removal firms, surveyors, solicitors, van hire and home improvements. You can get online quotes on some services and there's good regional information. The property search is fast and has plenty to choose from.

For more properties try these sites:
www.homefreehome.co.uk – finding and selling
  property for no charge.
www.08004homes.com – good, well categorised site
  with estate agents listed by county.
www.assertahome.com – excellent site with lots of
  advice, information, houses and associated
  services.

www.easier.co.uk – free, no hassle advertising, also has a finance section.

www.bambooavenue.com – moving help, advice and service quotes, good layout and simple to use.

www.beach-huts.co.uk – great site, providing you want to buy or rent a beach hut.

www.findaproperty.com – over 30,000 properties, good for the South East.

www.flatmate.com – find a flatmate from anywhere in the world.

www.helpiammoving.com – helpful directory of removal and storage companies with information and advice.

www.heritage.co.uk – covers listed buildings for sale only plus information on their upkeep.

www.hol365.com – really good site design and a massive range of services and properties from 6,000 estate agents.

www.homelet.co.uk – claim to take the risk out of renting by offering sound advice and insurances for both tenants and landlords – good design.

www.houseweb.co.uk – highly rated with comprehensive advice and thousands of properties for sale.

www.itlhomesearch.com – independent home search and advice site that also covers Spain and Ireland – rent or buy.

www.knightfrank.com – worldwide service, easy-to-use site.

www.propertyfinder.co.uk – Britain's biggest house database.

www.propertylive.co.uk – advice and properties from the National Association of Estate Agents.

www.rightmove.com – very clear information site with a good property search engine.

www.smartnewhomes.com – search engine dedicated to new homes.

www.ukpropertyshop.com – claims to be the most comprehensive covering 3,000 towns in the UK.

Property abroad

www.french-property.com

NO. 1 FOR FRANCE

ORIGIN UK
SPEED ✓✓✓✓
INFO ✓✓✓✓
EASE ✓✓✓

If you are fed up with the UK and want to move to France this is the first port of call. They offer properties for rent or for sale in all regions and can link you with other estate agents.

www.spanish-property-online.com

MOVING TO SPAIN

ORIGIN UK
SPEED ✓✓✓✓
INFO ✓✓✓✓
EASE ✓✓✓

Avoid all the pitfalls by stopping off for a browse at this informative site that covers all you need to know about buying property in Spain.

Radio

You need a decent downloadable player such as RealPlayer or Windows Media Player before you start listening. RealPlayer in particular gives you access to loads of stations and allows you to add more. The downside is that quality is sometimes affected by 'Net congestion'.

www.mediauk.com/directory

DIRECTORY OF RADIO STATIONS

ORIGIN UK
SPEED ✓✓✓✓
INFO ✓✓✓✓✓
EASE ✓✓✓✓

Excellent site. You can search by station, presenter or by type, there's also background on the history of radio and articles on topics such as digital radio. The site also offers similar information on television and magazines.

See also:

http://windowsmedia.com – home to Microsoft's media listings, which is very comprehensive.

www.broadcast.com/radio – Yahoo's massive list of stations.

www.radio-locator.com – a huge directory of radio, US oriented.

www.radioacademy.org

UK'S GATEWAY TO RADIO

ORIGIN UK
SPEED ✓✓✓
INFO ✓✓✓✓✓
EASE ✓✓✓✓

Radio Academy is a charity that covers all things to do with radio including news, events and its advancement in education and information. It has a list of all UK stations including those that offer web casts. You get more from the site if you become a member.

www.bbc.co.uk/radio

THE BEST OF THE BBC

ORIGIN UK
SPEED ✓✓✓
INFO ✓✓✓✓✓
EASE ✓✓✓✓

Listen to the news and the latest hits while you work, just select the station you want. There's also information on each major station, as well as a comprehensive listing service. Some features such as football commentary on certain matches will be missing due to rights issues. Most of the stations have some level of interactivity, with Radio 1 being the best and most lively, you can also tap into their local stations and of course the World Service.

www.virginradio.co.uk

VIRGIN ON AIR

ORIGIN UK
SPEED ✓✓✓
INFO ✓✓✓✓✓
EASE ✓✓✓✓

Excellent, if slightly messy site, with lots of ads plus plenty of stuff about the station, its schedule and stars, there's also a good magazine with the latest music news. You can listen if you have Quicktime, Windows Media Player or RealPlayer.

Other independent radio stations online are:
www.classicfm.com – classical music and background information.
www.jazzfm.com – live broadcasts, cool site too.
www.galaxyfm.co.uk – good range of dance music.
www.capitalfm.com – Capital Radio.
www.coolfm.co.uk – Northern Ireland's number one.
www.heart1062.co.uk – London's heart.
www.lbc.co.uk – the voice of London.
www.wwfm.co.uk – international, pop all-rounder.
www.comfm.com – a French site with access to over
   4,000 stations.

www.mediamazing.com
CUSTOMISE YOUR LISTENING

ORIGIN US
SPEED ✓✓✓
INFO ✓✓✓✓
VALUE ✓✓✓✓
EASE ✓✓✓✓

At this site you can pick the types of music you like then customise your listening accordingly. You have to subscribe but at $35 per annum it's a fairly reasonable sum for advert free listening. See also www.radio.mp3.com where you can also customise your radio experience.

Railways

These are sites aimed at the railway enthusiast. For information on trains and timetables see page 469.

www.nrm.org.uk
NATIONAL RAILWAY MUSEUM

ORIGIN UK
SPEED ✓✓✓✓
INFO ✓✓✓✓
EASE ✓✓✓✓

An excellent museum site packed with information and details on their collection, you can even take a virtual tour. See also Great Western's very informative museum site at **www.steam-museum.org.uk**

http://ukrail.uel.ac.uk

HERITAGE RAILWAY ASSOCIATION

ORIGIN UK
SPEED ✓✓✓✓
INFO ✓✓✓✓✓
EASE ✓✓✓✓

This site offers an online guide to the entire heritage railway scene in the UK, including details of special events and operating days for all heritage railways with lots of links worldwide.

www.therailwaystation.co.uk

UK'S BEST RAIL RESOURCE

ORIGIN UK
SPEED ✓✓✓✓
INFO ✓✓✓✓✓
EASE ✓✓✓✓

A wide ranging site covering all aspects of railway related hobbies from spotting to model making, there's a bookstore, links and classified ads too.

www.narrow-gauge.co.uk

NARROW GAUGE

ORIGIN UK
SPEED ✓✓✓✓
INFO ✓✓✓✓✓
EASE ✓✓✓✓

Currently being updated and improved, the new site will have the latest news and a better photo gallery plus all the narrow gauge information you'll need. You can also contribute your own articles or just browse.

See also:

www.heritagerailway.co.uk – geared to selling the mag but plenty of links and some archive material.

www.trainspotters.de – a good site from a German rail fan.

www.gensheet.co.uk – keep up to date with timetable changes and diversions.

Reference and Encyclopaedia Sites

If you are stuck with your homework or want an answer to any question, then this is where the Internet really comes into its own. With these sites you are bound to find what you are looking for.

www.refdesk.com

THE BEST SINGLE SOURCE FOR FACTS

ORIGIN US
SPEED ✓✓✓
INFO ✓✓✓✓✓
EASE ✓✓✓✓

Singled out for its sheer size and scope, this site offers information and links to just about anything. Its mission is 'only about indexing quality Internet sites and assisting visitors in navigating these sites'. It's won numerous awards and it never fails to impress.

www.xrefer.co.uk

FREE REFERENCE

ORIGIN UK
SPEED ✓✓✓✓
INFO ✓✓✓✓✓
EASE ✓✓✓✓✓

The UK's answer to RefDesk with access to some 100 books and reference works, and it's pretty comprehensive. Its real strength is in the speed of its search engine and its clean user-friendly design.

www.knowuk.co.uk

ALL ABOUT BRITAIN

ORIGIN UK
SPEED ✓✓✓
INFO ✓✓✓✓✓
EASE ✓✓✓✓

A subscription service which offers a massive amount of data about the UK from the arts to the civil service, education, the Hutchinson Encyclopaedia, government, law, travel and sport. Although most of the information can be accessed through separate sites, the advantage here is that you only need the one. Prices aren't listed on the site but you can contact them for a free trial.

www.about.com

IT'S ABOUT INFORMATION

ORIGIN US
SPEED ✓✓✓
INFO ✓✓✓✓✓
EASE ✓✓✓✓✓

A superb resource, easy-to-use and great for beginners learning to search for information, experts help you to find what you need every step of the way. It offers information on a wide range of topics from the arts and sciences to shopping. Also worth a visit is **www.libraryspot.com** which is similar in scope but has a more literary emphasis. It has an entertaining trivia section for those obsessed by top tens and useless facts.

www.ipl.org

THE INTERNET PUBLIC LIBRARY

ORIGIN US
SPEED ✓✓✓
INFO ✓✓✓✓✓
EASE ✓✓✓

Another excellent resource, there are articles on a vast range of subjects concentrating on literary criticism. Almost every country and its literature is covered. If there isn't anything at the library, there is invariably a link to take you to an alternative web site. It also has sections for young people.

www.allexperts.com

ASK AN EXPERT

ORIGIN UK
SPEED ✓✓✓✓
INFO ✓✓✓✓✓
EASE ✓✓✓✓

Staffed by expert volunteers, you can ask any question in some thirty three categories from arts to TV, in fact there's an expert covering most subjects or topics no matter how inane.

www.askoxford.com

ASK OXFORD UNIVERSITY

ORIGIN UK
SPEED ✓✓✓✓
INFO ✓✓✓✓
EASE ✓✓✓✓

A pretty decent effort at making a dry subject interesting, you can ask an expert, get advice on how to improve your writing and, of course, use the famous dictionary and thesaurus.

www.homeworkelephant.co.uk

LET THE ELEPHANT HELP WITH HOMEWORK

ORIGIN UK
SPEED ✓✓✓✓
INFO ✓✓✓✓✓
EASE ✓✓✓✓

A resource with some 5,000 links and resources aimed at helping students achieve great results. There's help with specific subjects, hints and tips, help for parents and teachers. It's constantly being updated, so worth checking regularly.

See also:
www.homeworkhigh.co.uk – Channel 4's excellent homework help site.
www.kidsclick.org – more than 600 topics and subjects covered.

www.maths-help.co.uk

E-MAIL YOUR MATHS PROBLEMS

ORIGIN UK
SPEED ✓✓✓
INFO ✓✓✓✓✓
EASE ✓✓✓✓✓

Send your queries to maths-help and they'll e-mail you back the answers in a couple of days. You can also visit the knowledge bank to see past queries and answers. See also **www.mathacademy.com** for a more bizarre view of maths and also the well put together **www.easymaths.com** which is much more conventional.

www.eserver.org

THE ENGLISH SERVER

ORIGIN US
SPEED ✓✓✓
INFO ✓✓✓✓✓
EASE ✓✓✓

A much-improved humanities site, which provides a vast amount of resource data about almost every cultural topic, there are some 30,000 texts, articles and essays available on subjects from the arts, fiction through to web design.

http://classics.mit.edu
THE INTERNET CLASSICS ARCHIVE

ORIGIN US
SPEED ✓✓✓✓
INFO ✓✓✓✓✓
EASE ✓✓✓✓

An excellent site for researching into the classics, it's easy to use and fast, with more than enough information for homework whatever the level. See also the excellent **www.bibliomania.com** for a wider range of resource materials.

www.perseus.tufts.edu
PERSEUS DIGITAL LIBRARY

ORIGIN US
SPEED ✓✓✓✓
INFO ✓✓✓✓✓
EASE ✓✓✓

An excellent source of data for ancient Classics and Mythology, history and early science. It also offers most of Shakespeare and Marlowe and, although it concentrates largely on pre-1600, it's ever expanding.

www.ntu.edu.sg/library/stat/statdata.htm
STATISTICS AND MORE STATISTICS

ORIGIN SINGAPORE
SPEED ✓✓✓
INFO ✓✓✓✓✓
EASE ✓✓✓

Free information and statistics about every world economy, not that easy to use at first, but it's all there.

See also:
www.population.com – which has a huge amount of data and information.
www.statistics.gov.uk – great for statistics on the UK.
www.cia.gov/cia/publications/factbook – the CIA's famous fact book albeit a little out of date.

www.atlapedia.com
THE WORLD IN BOTH PICTURES AND NUMBERS

ORIGIN US
SPEED ✓✓
INFO ✓✓✓✓✓
EASE ✓✓✓✓

Contains full colour political and physical maps of the world with statistics and very detailed information on each country. It can be very slow, so you need patience, but the end results are worth it.

Encyclopaedias

http://encarta.msn.com
THE ENCARTA ENCYCLOPAEDIA

ORIGIN US
SPEED ✓✓✓✓
INFO ✓✓✓✓✓
EASE ✓✓✓✓

Even though the complete thing is only available to buy, there is access to thousands of articles, maps and reference notes via the concise version. It's fast and easy to use.

Other useful encyclopaedias:
http://i-cias.com/e.o/index.htm – Encyclopaedia of the Orient – for North Africa and the Middle East.
www.si.edu/resource – encyclopaedia and links to the massive resources of the Smithsonian.
http://encyclozine.com – wide range of topics covered plus good use of games, quizzes and trivia.
www.archive.org – an encyclopaedic resource in the making, the 'Wayback Machine' is fun though. Beware lots of annoying pop-up adverts, we got at least seven.
www.babloo.com – encyclopaedia aimed at kids.
www.eb.com – Encyclopaedia Britannica for $9.95 per month.
www.ehow.com – instructions on how to do just about anything.
www.elibrary.com – outstanding site with access to huge amounts of data, from newswires to books, maps and images. You have to subscribe though.

www.encyberpedia.com – some 500 links to reference sites.

www.encyclopedia.com – the most comprehensive free encyclopedia on the net, nice design too.

www.infoplease.com – the biggest collection of almanacs, plus an encyclopedia and an atlas.

www.utm.edu/research/iep – the Internet Encyclopaedia of Philosophy.

www.digitalcentury.com/encyclo – Jones Digital Century with a wide range of resources and the usual encyclopaedia – recently updated.

www.quibs.co.uk – a massive database of lists.

www.spartacus.schoolnet.co.uk – Spartacus Encyclopaedia is excellent for history homework.

http://plato.stanford.edu – Stanford Encyclopaedia of philosophy.

www.wsu.edu/DrUniverse/ – ask Dr Universe a question – any question...

Dictionaries and thesauruses

www.cup.cam.ac.uk/elt/dictionary

CAMBRIDGE UNIVERSITY

ORIGIN UK	This site has five dictionaries including English,
SPEED ✓✓✓✓	American English, Idioms, Phrasal Verbs and a
INFO ✓✓✓✓	Learner's dictionary – all free. See also
EASE ✓✓✓✓✓	**www.oed.com** where you can find the Oxford English Dictionary which is available by subscription.

www.thesaurus.com

IF YOU CAN'T FIND THE WORD

ORIGIN US	Based on Roget's Thesaurus, this site will enable you
SPEED ✓✓✓	to find alternative words, useful but not worth turn-
INFO ✓✓✓✓✓	ing your PC on for in place of the book. For the
EASE ✓✓✓✓	equivalent dictionary site, go to the useful **www.dictionary.com** where you can play word games as an added feature.

www.techweb.com

THE TECHNOLOGY DICTIONARY

ORIGIN US
SPEED ✓✓✓✓
INFO ✓✓✓✓✓
EASE ✓✓✓✓

Get the latest business and technology news plus an excellent technology encyclopedia. For a dictionary that specialises in jargon and Internet terms only go to either http://webopedia.internet.com, www.jargon.net or www.netdictionary.com for enlightenment.

www.onelook.com

DICTIONARY HEAVEN

ORIGIN US
SPEED ✓✓✓
INFO ✓✓✓✓✓
EASE ✓✓✓✓

Onelook claim to offer access to almost 750 dictionaries and over 4 million words, at a fast, user-friendly site, it also offers a price checking service for online shopping.

www.plumbdesign.com/thesaurus

THE VISUAL THESAURUS

ORIGIN US
SPEED ✓✓✓
INFO ✓✓✓✓
EASE ✓✓✓

If you get bored looking up words or looking for alternative meanings for words in the usual way, then check out the Visual Thesaurus at Plumb Design. It's fun to use if a bit weird.

http://dictionaries.travlang.com

FOREIGN LANGUAGE DICTIONARIES

ORIGIN US
SPEED ✓✓✓✓✓
INFO ✓✓✓✓✓
EASE ✓✓✓✓✓

There are 16 language dictionaries on this site, just select the dictionary you want, and then type in the word or sentence to be translated – it couldn't be simpler. Originally aimed at the traveller, but it's very useful in this context.

www.peevish.co.uk/slang

DICTIONARY OF SLANG

ORIGIN UK
SPEED ✓✓✓✓
INFO ✓✓✓✓
EASE ✓✓✓

A comprehensive dictionary of English slang as used in the UK, with good articles and search facility.

www.acronymfinder.com

WHAT DO THOSE INITIALS STAND FOR?

ORIGIN US	✓✓✓✓	If you don't know your MP from your MP3 here's
SPEED	✓✓✓✓	where to go, with over 150,000 acronyms you
INFO	✓✓✓✓	should find what you're looking for.
EASE	✓✓✓✓✓	

www.symbols.com

WHAT DOES THAT SYMBOL MEAN?

ORIGIN US		Here you can find the meaning of over 4,500
SPEED	✓✓✓✓	symbols, with articles on their history.
INFO	✓✓✓✓	
EASE	✓✓✓✓	

Religion

In this section we've attempted to list sites that are of interest and try to explain the philosophy of the religions rather than the opinions of those who preach.

www.omsakthi.org/religions.html

RELIGION WORLD-WIDE

ORIGIN US		This site provides a clear description of each world
SPEED	✓✓✓	religion including values and basic beliefs with links
INFO	✓✓✓✓✓	to books on each one. See also the World Religion
EASE	✓✓✓	Gateway at www.academicinfo.net/religindex.html

Key religious sites in alphabetical order:
http://shamash.org/trb/judaism.html – a good
   overview of Judaism plus lots of links.
www.al-islam.org – informative site with good
   information and links.
www.buddhanet.net – useful links from this non-
   profit organisation.

www.ciolek.com/wwwvl-Buddhism.html – the Buddhist studies virtual library.

www.cofe.anglican.org - home of the Church of England.

www.directoryindia.com/religion/index.shtml – a good listing of Hindu web sites.

www.islamworld.net – a good overview of Islam.

www.jewfaq.org – an encyclopaedia devoted to Judaism.

www.methodist.org.uk – the official line in Methodism.

www.newadvent.org/cathen/ – the Catholic encyclopaedia.

www.panthkhalsa.org – information on the Sikh nation.

www.pres-outlook.com/ – a magazine site covering all forms of Presbyterianism.

www.quaker.org.uk – information on what it is to be a Quaker.

www.russian-orthodox-church.org.ru/en.htm – the home site with the latest news.

www.salaam.co.uk – wide ranging site covering all aspects of Islamic culture.

www.salvationarmy.org.uk – excellent site with lots of background information.

www.scientology.org.uk – comprehensive site on Scientology and what it is.

www.singhsabha.com/sikh_links.htm – a Sikh links directory.

www.thetablet.co.uk – a well-designed Catholic news site.

www.vatican.va – the official site of the Vatican, slow but informative, with some content being in Italian only.

More general information sites about religion:
www.religioustolerance.org – an organisation
   devoted to religions co-operating with each other,
   it has good information on all major faiths.
http://about.com/religion – about has an excellent
   overview of the major religions and some minor
   ones, it also offers a newsletter and covers areas
   such as spirituality too.
http://religion.rutgers.edu/vri/index.html – Rutgers
   University has made available a library of information on the world's religions.

Science

*The Internet was originally created by a group of scientists who
wanted faster, more efficient communication and today, scientists
around the world use the Net to compare data and collaborate.
In addition, the layman has access to the wonders of science in a
way that's never been possible before, and as for homework -
well now it's a doddle.*

www.sciseek.com
ONLINE RESOURCE FOR SCIENCE AND NATURE

ORIGIN US
SPEED ✓✓✓
INFO ✓✓✓✓
EASE ✓✓✓

A good place to start, Sciseek lists over 1,000
reviewed sites on everything from agriculture to
chemistry to health to physics, each site is reviewed
and you have the opportunity to leave comments
too. See also **www.scicentral.com** a wide ranging
science search engine.

www.royalsoc.ac.uk

THE ROYAL SOCIETY

ORIGIN UK
SPEED ✓✓✓
INFO ✓✓✓
EASE ✓✓✓✓

An attractive site where you can learn all about the workings of the society, how to get grants and what events they are running. They've improved the content to include more links and more interactivity.

www.sciencemag.org

SCIENCE MAGAZINE

ORIGIN US
SPEED ✓✓✓
INFO ✓✓✓✓✓
EASE ✓✓✓

A serious overview of the current science scene with articles covering everything from global warming to how owls find their prey. The tone isn't so heavy that a layman can't follow it and there are plenty of links too. You need to register to get the best out of it.

www.sciencemuseum.org.uk

THE SCIENCE MUSEUM

ORIGIN UK
SPEED ✓✓✓
INFO ✓✓✓✓
EASE ✓✓✓✓

An excellent site detailing the major attractions at the museum with 3-D graphics and features on exhibitions and forthcoming attractions, you can also shop and browse the galleries. See also www.exploratorium.edu a similar site by an American museum.

www.madsci.org

THE LAB THAT NEVER SLEEPS

ORIGIN US
SPEED ✓✓✓
INFO ✓✓✓✓
EASE ✓✓✓

A site that successfully combines science with fun, you can ask a question of a mad scientist, browse the links list or check out the archives in the library.

www.treasure-troves.com

TREASURE TROVE OF SCIENCE

ORIGIN US
SPEED ✓✓✓✓
INFO ✓✓✓✓
EASE ✓✓✓

A really useful growing resource consisting of a number of online encyclopedias covering the major science topics, the most amazing thing about it is that most of it seems to be the work of one man.

www.howstuffworks.com
HOW STUFF REALLY WORKS

ORIGIN US
SPEED ✓✓✓✓
INFO ✓✓✓✓✓
EASE ✓✓✓✓✓

A popular site, for nerds and kids young and old; it's easy to use and fascinating, the site has been revamped but there are sections ranging from the obvious like engines and technology, through to food and the weather. The current top ten section features the latest answers to the questions of the day. It's written in a very concise, clear style with lots of cross-referencing.

www.extremescience.com
ULTIMATE SCIENCE EXPERIENCE

ORIGIN US
SPEED ✓✓✓✓
INFO ✓✓✓✓✓
EASE ✓✓✓

Not sure that it really lives up to it's billing, but it is a really entertaining site with lots of useful and useless facts to bamboozle your brain. Features include a time portal where you can learn the effects of relativity and other sections on weather, maps, technology, nature and the Earth. It uses the word 'cool' a lot.

http://freeweb.pdq.net/headstrong
BIZARRE STUFF YOU CAN MAKE IN YOUR KITCHEN

ORIGIN US
SPEED ✓✓✓✓
INFO ✓✓✓✓
EASE ✓✓✓

The entertaining Bizarre Stuff is devoted to daft experiments that most boys (and some girls) have attempted at some time in their lives; from goo to solar ovens to crystal gardens it's all here and described in loving detail. See also the more worthy but still interesting **www.doscience.com** who have lots of straightforward experiments and check out Fun Science at **www.funsci.com**

www.voltnet.com

DON'T TRY THIS AT HOME!

ORIGIN US
SPEED ✓✓✓✓
INFO ✓✓✓✓
EASE ✓✓✓✓

This is literally a high voltage site devoted to electricity and how it works. While there is a serious side, by far the best bit is where they 'stress test' all sorts of objects by sending 20,000 volts through them – a Furby was getting the treatment when this review was written.

www.innovations.co.uk

GADGETS GALORE

ORIGIN UK
SPEED ✓✓✓
INFO ✓✓✓✓
VALUE ✓✓✓
EASE ✓✓✓

Impress your friends with your knowledge of the newest gadgets, innovations or what's likely to be the next big thing. Innovations is well established and has one of the best online stores and a wide range, there's a reward scheme with delivery costs being a flat £2.95. See also www.streettech.com who specialise in the latest hardware and also www.firebox.com who have a good selection.

www.21stcentury.co.uk

YOUR PORTAL TO THE FUTURE

ORIGIN UK
SPEED ✓✓✓✓
INFO ✓✓✓✓
EASE ✓✓✓✓

A stylish site that gives an overview of the latest technology put over in an entertaining way. Whether you're using it for homework or just for a browse, it's useful and interesting, they have 12 categories from cars through to humour, people and technology, they even cover fashion.

www.nesta.org.uk

THE CREATIVE INVENTOR'S HANDBOOK

ORIGIN UK
SPEED ✓✓✓✓
INFO ✓✓✓✓
EASE ✓✓✓✓

The National Endowment for Science Technology not only helps inventors get their ideas off the ground with support and guidance, but also encourages creativity and innovation. They'll also inspire you, as a visit to this well designed site will show. See also **www.inventorlink.co.uk**

www.newscientist.com

NEW SCIENTIST MAGAZINE

ORIGIN US
SPEED ✓✓✓
INFO ✓✓✓✓✓
EASE ✓✓✓✓

Much better than the usual online magazines because of its creative use of archive material which is simultaneously fun and serious. It's easy to search the site or browse through back features – the 'Even More Bizarre' bit is particularly entertaining. For a more traditional science magazine site go to *Popular Science* at **www.popsci.com** great for information on the latest gadgets.

www.discovery.com

THE DISCOVERY CHANNEL

ORIGIN US
SPEED ✓✓✓
INFO ✓✓✓✓✓
EASE ✓✓✓✓

A superb site for science and nature lovers, it's inspiring as well as educational. Order the weekly newsletter, get information on the latest discoveries as well as features on pets, space, travel, lifestyle and school. The 'Discovery Kids' section is very good with lots going on.

www.webelements.com

THE PERIODIC TABLE

ORIGIN US
SPEED ✓✓✓✓
INFO ✓✓✓✓✓
EASE ✓✓✓✓

So you don't know your halides from your fluorides, with this interactive depiction you can find out. Just click on the element and you get basic details plus an audio description.

www.science-frontiers.com

SCIENTIFIC ANOMALIES

ORIGIN US
SPEED ✓✓✓✓
INFO ✓✓✓
EASE ✓✓✓

Science Frontiers is a bimonthly newsletter providing digests of reports that describe scientific anomalies; that's, 'those observations and facts that challenge prevailing scientific paradigms'. There's a massive archive of the weird and wonderful, it takes patience but there are some real gems.

http://whyfiles.org

SCIENCE BEHIND THE NEWS

ORIGIN US
SPEED ✓✓✓✓
INFO ✓✓✓✓
EASE ✓✓✓✓

If you've ever wondered why things happen and what's the real story behind what they tell you in the papers, then a visit here will be rewarding. With in-depth studies and brief overviews Why Files is easy to follow and you'll get the latest news too.

Search Engines

The best way to find what you want from the Internet is to use a search engine. Even the best only cover at most 60% of the available web sites; so if you can't find what you want from one, try another. These are the best and most user friendly. For children's search engines see page 82.

www.searchenginewatch.com

A GUIDE TO SEARCHING

ORIGIN US
SPEED ✓✓✓✓
INFO ✓✓✓✓✓
EASE ✓✓✓✓

This site rates and assesses all the search engines and it's a useful starting point if you're looking for a good or specific search facility. There's a newsletter and statistical analysis plus strategies on how to make the perfect search. See also **www.searchengi-neshowdown.com** who do much the same thing but it's less comprehensive.

http://uk.yahoo.com

FOR THE UK AND IRELAND

ORIGIN US
SPEED ✓✓✓
INFO ✓✓✓✓✓
EASE ✓✓✓

The UK arm of Yahoo! is the biggest and one of the most established search engines. It's now much more than just a search facility as it offers a huge array of other services: from news to finance to shopping to sport to travel to games. You can restrict your search to just UK or Irish sites. It's the place to start, but it can be a little overwhelming at first.

www.mirago.co.uk

THE UK SEARCH ENGINE

ORIGIN UK
SPEED ✓✓✓✓
INFO ✓✓✓✓✓
EASE ✓✓✓✓✓

Mirago searches the whole web but prioritises the search for UK families and businesses. It's very quick, easy to use and offers many of the services you get from Yahoo! You can tailor your search very easily to exclude stuff you won't need. For another UK-oriented site try **www.ukplus.co.uk**

www.ask.co.uk

ASK JEEVES

ORIGIN US
SPEED ✓✓✓✓
INFO ✓✓✓✓
EASE ✓✓✓✓✓

Just type in your question and the famous old butler will come back with the answer. It may be a bit gimmicky but works very well, it's great for beginners and reliable for old hands too. See also **www.ajkids.com** which is the child-oriented version.

www.mamma.com

THE MOTHER OF ALL SEARCH ENGINES

ORIGIN US
SPEED ✓✓✓✓
INFO ✓✓✓✓
EASE ✓✓✓✓

Mamma claim to have technology enabling them to search the major search engines thoroughly and get the most pertinent results to your query – it's fast too, your query comes back with the answer and the search engine it came from. You might also try **www.metacrawler.com** which uses similar technology, and **www.37.com** which is a bit of a mess but can search 37 other search engines in one go.

www.google.co.uk

BRINGING ORDER TO THE WEB

ORIGIN US
SPEED ✓✓✓✓✓
INFO ✓✓✓✓
EASE ✓✓✓✓✓

Google is all about speed and accuracy. Using a complicated set of rules they claim to be able to give the most relevant results in the quickest time, in fact they even tell you how fast they are. It's easier to use than most and a mass of information doesn't overload you. At this URL you can limit your search to the UK.

www.lii.org

THE LIBRARIANS INDEX TO THE INTERNET

ORIGIN US
SPEED ✓✓✓✓✓
INFO ✓✓✓✓
EASE ✓✓✓✓✓

This is a search engine with a difference in that all the source material has been selected and evaluated by librarians specifically for their use in public libraries. This doesn't stop you using it though, and it is very good for obscure searches and research – like putting together a web site guide, for example.

www.dmoz.org

THE OPEN DIRECTORY PROJECT

ORIGIN WORLD
WIDE
SPEED ✓✓✓✓✓
INFO ✓✓✓✓
EASE ✓✓✓✓

The goal is to produce the most comprehensive directory of the web, by relying on an army (some 36,000) of volunteer editors, and if you want to get involved it's easy to sign yourself up. If it can't help with your query it puts you through to one of the mainstream search engines.

Finding the search engine that suits you is a matter of personal requirements and taste, here are some other very good, tried and trusted ones:

> http://uk.altavista.com – limited but very efficient.
>
> http://gwu.edu/~gprice/direct.htm – specialises in information that is not readily available on traditional search engines.
>
> www.alltheweb.com – no frills, similar to Google, becoming very popular.
>
> www.bbc.co.uk – a heavily advertised and new search engine that is simple to use.
>
> www.completeplanet.com – chooses from over 100,000 searchable databases.
>
> www.dogpile.com – straightforward and no mess.
>
> www.go.com – very popular news-oriented US site.
>
> www.hotbot.com – good for shopping and entertainment.
>
> www.infoplease.com – good for homework.
>
> www.invisibleweb.com – a pretty OK directory and search engine.
>
> www.iwon.com – US site that's great for prizes and shopping.
>
> www.kidtastic.com – safe search for kids.
>
> www.looksmart.com – good business-oriented site.
>
> www.lycos.co.uk – easy to use and popular, good for highlighting offers.

www.msn.co.uk – searching is just one of the many things you can do here.

www.northernlight.com – specialist news and information search engine that has broadened out into the mainstream.

www.overture.com – straightforward, easy to use, it used to be goto.com.

www.profusion.com – an excellent and fast, advanced search tool.

www.scotland.org – small Scotland-oriented site.

Ships and Boats

Boats

www.boatlinks.co.uk

BOATING DIRECTORY

ORIGIN UK
SPEED ✓✓✓✓
INFO ✓✓✓✓✓
EASE ✓✓✓✓

A superb directory and the place to start if you're looking for any information on shipping or boating, there are 16 categories in all and several hundred links.

http://boatbuilding.com

THE BOAT BUILDING COMMUNITY

ORIGIN UK
SPEED ✓✓✓
INFO ✓✓✓✓✓
EASE ✓✓✓✓

If you want to repair or build a boat then here's where to go, with features and discussion forums to help you on your way. There's also a very good directory of links to suppliers and resource sites.

www.buyaboat.co.uk

BUY A BOAT MAGAZINE

ORIGIN UK	Primarily a vehicle to get you to subscribe to the
SPEED ✓✓✓	magazine, the site offers information on brokers and
INFO ✓✓✓✓	the details of some 11,000 boats for sale.
EASE ✓✓✓✓	

Ships and Navy

www.royal-navy.mod.uk

THE ROYAL NAVY

ORIGIN UK	An excellent site from the Royal Navy giving details
SPEED ✓✓✓	of the ships, submarines and aircraft and what it's
INFO ✓✓✓✓	like to be a part of it all. There's a video gallery
EASE ✓✓✓✓	featuring highlights from the fleet and details of all
	the Royal Navy ships. Apart from all the informa-
	tion, you can have a go on the interactive frigate.

www.red-duster.co.uk

RED DUSTER MAGAZINE

ORIGIN UK	Red Duster is a merchant navy enthusiasts' site
SPEED ✓✓✓✓	offering lots in the way of history covering sail,
INFO ✓✓✓✓	stream and shipping lines. There's also a section
EASE ✓✓✓✓	on the history of customs. To find out what the
	current merchant navy are up to go to
	www.merchantnavyofficers.com where you find
	information and links.

www.maritimematters.com

OCEAN LINERS AND CRUISE SHIPS

ORIGIN UK	An informative site with data on over 100 ships from
SPEED ✓✓✓	the earliest liners to the most modern, each has its own
INFO ✓✓✓✓	page with quality pictures and some virtual tours. It is
EASE ✓✓✓✓	also good for news and links to related sites.

Other watercraft

www.hovercraft.org.uk

HOVERCRAFT

ORIGIN UK
SPEED ✓✓✓
INFO ✓✓✓
EASE ✓✓✓✓

If you're into hovercrafts or are just interested, here's the place to look with 3 sections – Britain, Europe and the world, which just about covers it all.

www.jetski.ndirect.co.uk

JETSKI

ORIGIN UK
SPEED ✓✓✓
INFO ✓✓✓
EASE ✓✓✓✓

A comprehensive links site with sections on where to jetski, how to buy one and look after it, dealers, tips and tricks – all to the sound of Hawaii 5–0's theme tune.

www.rontini.com

SUBMARINE WORLD NETWORK

ORIGIN UK
SPEED ✓✓✓✓
INFO ✓✓✓✓
EASE ✓✓✓✓

A directory site with over 1,000 links all devoted to the world of submarines, it covers everything from navies to models.

Shopping

To many people shopping is what the Internet is all about, and it does offer an opportunity to get some tremendous bargains. Watch out for hidden costs such as delivery charges or finance deals that seem attractive until you compare them with what's available elsewhere.

For help on finding comparative prices, see the price comparison sites on page 312, in fact, starting your shopping trip at a site like **www.kelkoo.com** may prove to be a wise move.

Another good place to start is at the Which? Magazine web site,
www.which.net *who run a scheme to protect online shoppers.*
They sign up retailers to a code of practice that covers the way
they trade.
To quote Which?:
'The Which? Web Trader Scheme is designed to make sure
consumers get a fair deal and to provide them with protection if
things go wrong. Which? Web Traders agree to meet and abide
by our Code of Practice. If we receive complaints from
consumers about the service from a web trader displaying the
Which? Web Trader logo, we will investigate and may withdraw
our permission for a trader to display the logo.'

www.tradingstandards.gov.uk

TRADING STANDARDS CENTRAL

ORIGIN UK ✓✓✓
SPEED ✓✓✓
INFO ✓✓✓✓
EASE ✓✓✓✓

Find out where you stand and what to do if you think you're being ripped off or someone is not trading fairly – you can even take a quiz about it. There are advice guides to print off or download and there is help and advice to businesses and schools as well as consumers.

www.dooyoo.co.uk

MAKE YOUR OPINION COUNT

ORIGIN GERMANY
SPEED ✓✓✓
INFO ✓✓✓✓
EASE ✓✓✓✓

Media darling Doo Yoo is a site where you the consumer can give your opinion or a review on any product that's available to buy, this way you get unbiased opinions about them – in theory. The 'products' range in some 20 categories from books to TV shows and it's easy to contribute. See also **www.ciao.com** where you can actually get paid a small amount of money for your opinion.

www.recallannouncements.co.uk
CONSUMER SAFETY

ORIGIN	UK
SPEED	✓✓✓✓
INFO	✓✓✓✓
EASE	✓✓✓✓

An informative site listing all the latest product recalls covering the USA, UK and Australia, it also offers a consumer guide, an 'Ask the Experts' facility and statistics on recalls. Some of the site can only be accessed if you register.

The virtual high street

www.marks-and-spencer.co.uk
CLOTHES AND GIFTS

ORIGIN	UK
SPEED	✓✓✓✓
INFO	✓✓✓✓✓
VALUE	✓✓✓
EASE	✓✓✓✓

A much clearer, more attractive and faster site than the last time we visited, it has a good selection of products from clothes to gifts for all, as well as fashion advice and a quick order facility. There's not much emphasis on offers, more on quality. Delivery costs start at £2.95.

www.wellbeing.com
BOOTS

ORIGIN	UK
SPEED	✓✓✓✓
INFO	✓✓✓✓✓
VALUE	✓✓✓✓
EASE	✓✓✓✓

A clinical site that offers health advice as well as shopping. There's a comprehensive guide covering health, beauty and baby topics, a good hospital guide, a confidential ask the pharmacist section and a list of specialist stores in your area. The shopping bit is quite understated and is basically split into eight sections; men, fitness, mother and baby, beauty, health, nutrition, gifts and personal care – more recently there's been a move to promote the latest multi-buy offers and their loyalty card. There's also a good search facility, free delivery on some items and you can also use your Advantage card as in the store. You can't return unwanted goods to a Boots shop though; you have to send them back to Wellbeing.

www.whsmith.co.uk

W.H.SMITH

ORIGIN UK
SPEED ✓✓✓✓
INFO ✓✓✓✓
VALUE ✓✓✓
EASE ✓✓✓✓

The Smiths site has a clean, easy-to-navigate format, with the emphasis on shopping. There is a great deal here though including the usual books, music, mags, games, stationery and DVD. In addition there are details of the latest offers, author features, a section on their Amazing Adventures range, information on their ISP offer, a store finder, an excellent education zone and the Hutchinson Encyclopaedia. Delivery charges start at £1.19 and unwanted goods can be returned to your local store.

www.woolworths.co.uk

WELL WORTH IT

ORIGIN UK
SPEED ✓✓✓✓
INFO ✓✓✓✓
VALUE ✓✓✓✓
EASE ✓✓✓

A bright and breezy site from Woolworths with all you'd expect in terms of range and prices. They are particularly good on kids' stuff with strong prices on movies, chart music, clothes and games, delivery starts at £1.50 per order.

www.argos.co.uk

ARGOS CATALOGUE

ORIGIN UK
SPEED ✓✓✓✓
INFO ✓✓✓✓
VALUE ✓✓✓✓
EASE ✓✓✓✓

Argos offers an excellent range of products (some 8,000) across fourteen different categories as per their catalogue. There are some good bargains to be had. You can now reserve an item at your local store, once you've checked that they have it in stock. There's a good search facility and you can find a product via its catalogue number if you've a catalogue handy that is. Delivery is £3.95 unless you spend more than £100 in which case it's free. Returns can be made to your local store.

www.debenhams.com

AWARD WINNING FAMILY SERVICE

ORIGIN UK
SPEED ✓✓✓
INFO ✓✓✓✓
VALUE ✓✓✓✓
EASE ✓✓✓✓

Not a common sight on the high street but Debenhams have a very good site aimed at their retailing strengths: gifts, weddings and fashion. Delivery costs vary.

General retailers, directories and online department stores

www.which.net

WHICH? MAGAZINE

ORIGIN UK
SPEED ✓✓✓✓
INFO ✓✓✓✓
VALUE ✓✓✓✓✓
EASE ✓✓✓✓

By joining up you can get access to their product reviews and benefit from special arrangements with selected retailers to get good prices on their best buys. If you're a member there's an excellent selection of reports and articles on consumer subjects. Check out the alphabetical listing of several hundred stores that have met their trading criteria and show the Which? Web trader badge.

www.2020shops.com

THE SHOPPER'S FRIEND

ORIGIN UK
SPEED ✓✓✓✓✓
INFO ✓✓✓✓✓
VALUE ✓✓✓✓✓
EASE ✓✓✓✓✓

A really likeable site with a great ethic - they don't do cosy deals with other retailers for exposure so the shops they select and rate are there on merit. They are one of the few that give extra information on the shops such as delivery costs, plus some shopping advice. It's fast too. The only site in this book to get full marks.

www.goldfishguide.co.uk

GOLDFISH GUIDES

ORIGIN UK
SPEED ✓✓✓✓
INFO ✓✓✓✓✓
VALUE ✓✓✓✓
EASE ✓✓✓✓

Another good place for consumer advice and an easy approach to selecting the right store. The Goldfish guides cover a wide range of shopping categories all written by independent journalists. Essentially the idea is that you read up on it, compare prices on it then buy it – simple really. The site is well designed and easy to use.

www.shopsmart.com

ONLINE SHOPPING MADE SIMPLE

ORIGIN UK
SPEED ✓✓✓✓
INFO ✓✓✓✓
VALUE ✓✓✓✓✓
EASE ✓✓✓✓

This is probably the best of the sites that offer a directory of links to specialist online retailers. Search within the eighteen categories or the whole site for a particular item or store. Each of the 1,000 or so retail sites featured are reviewed and rated using a star system. The reviews are quite kind, and the worst sites are excluded anyway. There's a price comparison service on all the major shopping categories as well.

www.mytaxi.co.uk

SHOP AND SEARCH FOR THE BEST PRICES

ORIGIN UK
SPEED ✓✓✓
INFO ✓✓✓✓
VALUE ✓✓✓✓
EASE ✓✓✓

Personalise your online shopping experience using My Taxi to search retailers' web sites for the best prices on the goods you are interested in. Particularly strong on music and video, less so on other items. The recommended online stores are selected according to safety and service, there is no star rating system; however, they are well categorised.

www.edirectory.co.uk

IF IT'S OUT THERE, BUY IT HERE

ORIGIN UK
SPEED ✓✓✓✓
INFO ✓✓✓✓
VALUE ✓✓✓✓
EASE ✓✓✓

A nice looking directory with a wide variety of shops and goods to choose from, it has a good reputation for service as well as being topical.

www.shopspy.co.uk

THE GUIDE THAT SHOPS BEFORE IT RATES

ORIGIN UK
SPEED ✓✓✓✓
INFO ✓✓✓✓✓
VALUE ✓✓✓✓
EASE ✓✓✓

A great idea, the shop spy team actually use the shops on their listing and then report back on things like value, quality of the goods and service then rate them accordingly. The list of more than 500 stores is fairly eclectic and you can easily see the best rated ones. The site could be organised much better though and it's not always that up-to-date.

www.zoom.co.uk

MORE THAN JUST A SHOP

ORIGIN UK
SPEED ✓✓✓✓✓
INFO ✓✓✓
VALUE ✓✓✓
EASE ✓✓✓✓

This is an excellent magazine-style site, with lots of features other than shopping, such as free Internet access, e-mail and a dating service. Shopping consists of links to specialist retailers. You can earn loyalty points, enter prize draws and there are a number of exclusive offers as well. Not always the cheapest, but an entertaining shopping site.

www.virgin.net/shopping

LIFESTYLE AND SHOPPING GUIDE

ORIGIN UK
SPEED ✓✓✓
INFO ✓✓✓✓✓
VALUE ✓✓✓✓
EASE ✓✓✓✓

Virgin's shopping guide is comprehensive covering all major categories while allowing retailers to feature some of their best offers. It also attempts to be a complete service for entertainment and leisure needs with excellent sections on music, travel and cinema in particular.

www.shoppingunlimited.co.uk

INDEPENDENT RECOMMENDATION

ORIGIN	UK
SPEED	✓✓✓✓
INFO	✓✓✓✓
VALUE	✓✓✓✓
EASE	✓✓✓✓✓

Owned by the *Guardian* newspaper, this site offers hundreds of links to stores that they've reviewed. It also offers help to inexperienced shoppers and guidance on using credit cards online. There are also links to other Guardian sites such as news and sport.

www.thevirtualmall.co.uk

THE VIRTUAL SHOPPING CENTRE

ORIGIN	UK
SPEED	✓✓✓
INFO	✓✓✓✓
EASE	✓✓✓✓✓

Literally browse by floor then click on the shop you want to go into. There's no real advantage in using it other than having all the best stores represented graphically in one place, even then some links don't work, but there are some good offers to be found.

www.screenshop.co.uk

SHOP ON TV, WEB OR CATALOGUE

ORIGIN	UK
SPEED	✓✓✓✓
INFO	✓✓✓✓
VALUE	✓✓✓✓
EASE	✓✓✓✓

As a shopping channel on Sky, Screenshop was already successful; this well-put-together site shows off the breadth of their range and has some good offers. See also the wide ranging QVC shop at www.qvcuk.com which offers some 10,000 products.

www.streetsonline.co.uk

STREETS AHEAD

ORIGIN	UK
SPEED	✓✓✓✓
INFO	✓✓✓✓
VALUE	✓✓✓✓
EASE	✓✓✓✓

One of Britain's most successful online retailers, Streets Online not only offers excellent books, music and movie shops but an entertainment magazine and an exchange service where you can swap your unwanted goods. You can also download trailers, audio clips and e-books.

www.crueltyfreeshop.com

CRUELTY FREE SHOP

ORIGIN UK
SPEED ✓✓✓✓
INFO ✓✓✓✓
VALUE ✓✓✓
EASE ✓✓✓

A wide range of products on sale all of which are guaranteed not to have had any animal cruelty or exploitation in their production. The range is wide and the prices aren't bad either. It can only improve, a good idea that deserves some success. See also **www.shopethical.co.uk** who offer a directory of sites that are more aware than most of their social and environmental responsibilities.

Value for money

www.bigsave.com

SAVE, SAVE, SAVE...

ORIGIN UK
SPEED ✓✓✓
INFO ✓✓✓
VALUE ✓✓✓✓✓
EASE ✓✓✓✓

Bigsave is well designed and has four sections: electronics, clothing, sports and best buys, plus quick links for popular items. The emphasis is on value and choice. Registration is required, but you can track your purchase from order to delivery. Delivery costs vary according to product.

www.onlinediscount.com

THE VERY BEST DISCOUNTS

ORIGIN US
SPEED ✓✓✓✓
INFO ✓✓✓
VALUE ✓✓✓✓
EASE ✓✓✓✓

Online Discount specialise in monitoring Internet stores and highlighting those giving the best discounts in any one of sixteen major categories. You are quickly put through to a list of the key shops and their bargains.

www.priceoffers.co.uk

SUPERMARKETS SORTED

ORIGIN UK
SPEED ✓✓✓
INFO ✓✓✓✓
VALUE ✓✓✓✓✓
EASE ✓✓✓✓

The online guide to high street bargains, check out the site then choose which supermarket to visit for the best offers. There are several sections: the newsletter offering customised updates; an editor's choice of the best bargains; buy one get one free deals; store deals; and lastly a selection found by shoppers willing to share their bargain finds.

www.thesimplesaver.com

WHERE TO GET THE BEST DEAL

ORIGIN UK
SPEED ✓✓✓✓
INFO ✓✓✓✓
VALUE ✓✓✓✓✓
EASE ✓✓✓✓

What started off as a simple e-mail conversation about where to go for savings has snowballed into a website and newsletter that lets the whole world know where the best shopping bargains are to be had.

Gift finding

The following sites should help you find the perfect gift, but if you're shopping for the women in your life, there are more gift sites recommended in the Men's section on page 245.

www.hard2buy4.co.uk

GIFT IDEAS

ORIGIN UK
SPEED ✓✓✓
INFO ✓✓✓✓✓
VALUE ✓✓✓✓
EASE ✓✓✓✓

Excellent gift shop with a wide range of unusual products including celebrity items, activities and gifts for men, women and children in separate sections, some good offers too.

See also:
www.blissonline.com – lifestyle enhancing gifts and upmarket presents in a hurry.
www.iwantoneofthose.com – for more unusual gifts and stuff you don't need but would really like, it also has a great gift finder.

www.gotogifts.co.uk - gift ideas in profusion, a bit of mess design–wise but there's also a reminder service.

www.pressie.com who offer a free gift wrapping service amongst a wealth of good ideas.

British shopping

www.british-shopping.com

UK SHOPPING LINKS AND DIRECTORY

ORIGIN UK
SPEED ✓✓✓✓
INFO ✓✓✓✓
EASE ✓✓✓✓

An excellent comprehensive portal site specialising in British shops, it also has plenty of related links and information. See also www.shops247.com and www.ukonlineshopping.com who both have a comprehensive shop listing.

For more quintessentially British shops check out these sites:
www.brooksandbentley.com – classy British gifts.
www.harrods.com – a selection of their products available to buy from an attractive looking site.
www.classicengland.co.uk – the best British products on a fun looking and easy to use site.
www.distinctlybritish.com – a British shop directory with a wide range of food, clothing, gift and children's retailers on offer.

www.scotsmart.com

SCOTSMART

ORIGIN UK
SPEED ✓✓✓✓
INFO ✓✓✓✓✓
VALUE ✓✓✓
EASE ✓✓✓✓

A Scottish directory of sites, not just for shopping but covering most areas, you can search by theme or category and the shopping section is split into books, clothing, food, gifts and highland wear. See also www.scotch-corner.co.uk which is Scottish through and through and the broader reaching www.scotstore.com

The rest

There are hundreds, possibly thousands of online stores and shopping malls, it would be impossible to include them all, but here is a list of some of this year's best reviewed sites and what they do.

THE BEST

www.bobsshopwindow.com – Bob's Shop Window is a comprehensive directory of shops, well categorised but not rated in any way, the site descriptions are provided by the retailers.

www.eshopone.co.uk – posh products and cheap prices.

www.eshops.co.uk – great design, loads of shops listed in the directory with some excellent offers and a good search engine.

www.I-stores.com – a very good store search engine and directory.

www.mailorderexpress.co.uk – excellent for toy and kids' stuff.

www.safedoor.co.uk – from Securicor, a shopping site that guarantees safety from fraud when you shop at one of their recommended stores.

www.shopeeze.com – nice design and good prices too.

www.shoppersempire.com – nice looking and wide-ranging store with some good offers.

www.shoptour.co.uk – links to over 1,000 secure shops in 14 categories, much improved now with a price comparison tool.

www.thesimplesaver.com – a nicely designed site with access to some excellent bargains from a wide range of online retailers.

http://theukhighstreet.com – a good UK directory, with the shops rated by you the customer.

www.ukshopsearch.com – above average search engine and quality design make this stand out from the crowd, you can also vent your frustrations out on the shopping experience in the shoppers forum.

www.worthaglance.com – great looking shop with some outstanding bargains.

COULD BE USEFUL

http://orders.mkn.co.uk – Market Net simply lists retailers and gives delivery times, good for the unusual though.

www.1shop.org – mall supporting small or medium sized UK businesses. **www.oneshopforall.co.uk** - odd looking shop, good for unusual gifts though.

www.shopq.co.uk – massive set of shopping links, well categorised on a messy site.

www.shop-shop-shop.co.uk – search the databases of over 200 shops, good links.

www.shoppingtrolley.net – lots of shops and categories, boring design.

www.sortal.co.uk – very useful directory of UK shops sorted into 40 categories.

www.theukmall.co.uk – minimalist design, odd ratings and shop selection.

LOYALTY SCHEMES

www.smartcreds.co.uk

NO CREDIT CARD NEEDED

ORIGIN UK
SPEED ✓✓✓✓
INFO ✓✓✓✓
VALUE ✓✓✓✓
EASE ✓✓✓✓

You buy Smartcreds, top up your virtual wallet, then you can shop in the UKSmart shop where there are over a hundred stores including high street names who will accept Smartcreds as payment. Brilliant for children and teenagers. See also ipoints at **www.ipoints.co.uk**

Software

If you need to upgrade your software then these are the sites to go to. Shareware is where you get a program to use for a short period of time before you have to buy it, freeware is exactly what you'd think – free.

www.softwareparadise.co.uk

THE SMART WAY TO SHOP FOR SOFTWARE

ORIGIN UK
SPEED ✓✓✓✓
INFO ✓✓✓✓
VALUE ✓✓✓✓
EASE ✓✓✓

With over 250,000 products and excellent offers make this site the first stop. It's a bit messy but easy to use, there's a good search facility and plenty of products for Mac users. There are links to sister sites offering low cost software for charities and students.

www.download.com

CNET

ORIGIN US
SPEED ✓✓✓✓
INFO ✓✓✓✓✓
VALUE ✓✓✓✓
EASE ✓✓✓✓

A superb site covering all types of software and available downloads. There are masses of reviews as well as buying tips and price comparison tools; it also covers handheld PCs, Linux and Macs.

www.softseek.com

ZDNET

ORIGIN US
SPEED ✓✓✓✓
INFO ✓✓✓✓✓
VALUE ✓✓✓✓
EASE ✓✓✓✓

Another excellent site with a huge amount of resources to download, it's all a little overwhelming at first but the download directory is easy to use and there's lots of free software available.

www.tucows.com

TUCOWS

ORIGIN US
SPEED ✓✓✓✓✓
INFO ✓✓✓✓✓
VALUE ✓✓✓✓
EASE ✓✓✓✓

Probably less irritating to use than ZDNet and CNet, the software reviews are also entertaining in their own right, the best thing about it though is that it's quick.

If you feel like shopping around a bit more see also:
http://home.netscape.com/plugins – if you're a Netscape fan then you can improve its performance with 'plug-ins' from this site.
www.completelyfreesoftware.com – hundreds of free programs for you to download, from games to useful desktop accessories if it's available free, then its here.
www.davecentral.com – lots of shareware, also good for Linux fans.
www.freewarehome.com – a great selection of free programs including a specialist site aimed at software for children, **www.kidsfreeware.com**
www.freewarenet.com – a comprehensive collection of freeware.
www.handango.com – a good site specialising in downloads for handheld PCs.
www.neatnettricks.com – an archive of useful tips and downloads with regular updates, you need to subscribe though.

www.winplanet.com – specialises in improving and discussing Windows applications.

www.bugnet.com
FIX THAT BUG

ORIGIN	US
SPEED	✓✓✓
INFO	✓✓✓
VALUE	✓✓✓✓
EASE	✓✓✓

Subscribe to the Bug Net and they alert you to software bugs, keep you up-to-date with reviews, analysis and the tests they carry out. You can then be sure to buy the right fixes.

www.winzip.com
MANAGE FILES

ORIGIN	US
SPEED	✓✓✓
INFO	✓✓✓✓
EASE	✓✓✓

Winzip allows you to save space on your PC by compressing data, making it easier to e-mail files and unlock zipped files that have been sent to you. It takes a few minutes to download. For Macs go to www.aladdinsys.com

Space

www.space.com
MAKING SPACE POPULAR

ORIGIN	US
SPEED	✓✓✓
INFO	✓✓✓✓✓
VALUE	✓✓
EASE	✓✓✓

An education-oriented site dedicated to space; there's news, mission reports, technology, history, personalities, a games section and plenty of pictures. The science section explores the planets and earth. You can buy goods at the space shop with delivery cost dependent on purchase. See also Thinks Space at http://library.thinkquest.org/26220, which is great for photos and links.

www.nasa.gov

THE OFFICIAL NASA SITE

ORIGIN US
SPEED ✓✓✓
INFO ✓✓✓✓✓
EASE ✓✓✓

This huge site provides comprehensive information on the US National Aeronautical and Space Administration. There are details on each NASA site, launch timings, sections for news, kids, project updates, and links to their specialist sites such as the Hubble Space Telescope, Mars and Earth observation. For Britain's place in space go to www.bnsc.gov.uk or www.ukspace.com which is great for links.

www.spacedaily.com

YOUR PORTAL TO SPACE

ORIGIN US
SPEED ✓✓✓
INFO ✓✓✓✓✓
EASE ✓✓✓

A comprehensive newspaper-style site with a huge amount of information and news about space and related subjects. It also has links to similar sister sites covering subjects like Mars, space war and space travel.

www.astronomynow.com

THE UK'S BEST SELLING ASTRONOMY MAG

ORIGIN UK
SPEED ✓✓
INFO ✓✓✓✓
VALUE ✓✓
EASE ✓✓✓

Get the news and views from a British angle, plus reviews on the latest books. The store has widened out to include patches, T-shirts and videos as well as the magazine and posters.

www.StarTrails.com

STAR TRAILS SOCIETY

ORIGIN US
SPEED ✓✓✓
INFO ✓✓✓✓
EASE ✓✓✓✓

An entertaining magazine site that covers all aspects of popular astronomy. Features include the daily solar weather, classes on breaking science news and the latest astral headlines.

www.seds.org/billa/tnp/

THE NINE PLANETS

ORIGIN UK
SPEED ✓✓✓✓
INFO ✓✓✓✓✓
EASE ✓✓✓✓

A multimedia tour of the nine planets, stunning photography, interesting facts combined with good text. See also Bill Arnett's other interesting site on Nebulae at **http://seds.lpl.arizona.edu/billa/twn** where there are some beautiful pictures.

www.redcolony.com

MARS

ORIGIN US
SPEED ✓✓✓✓
INFO ✓✓✓✓✓
EASE ✓✓✓✓

A superb site all about the red planet. There is a synopsis of its history, plus details on past and future space missions with a focus on the colonisation of Mars. There's a great deal of information on things like terra forming and biogenesis, it's all taken very seriously too.

www.nauts.com

THE ASTRONAUT CONNECTION

ORIGIN US
SPEED ✓✓✓
INFO ✓✓✓✓✓
EASE ✓✓✓

In their words 'The Astronaut Connection has worked to create an educational and entertaining resource for space enthusiasts, young and old, to learn about astronauts and space exploration' and that just about sums up this very informative site.

www.telescope.org

BRADFORD ROBOTIC TELESCOPE PROJECT

ORIGIN UK
SPEED ✓✓
INFO ✓✓✓✓
EASE ✓✓✓

Here you can view the stars and, once you've registered, ask for the telescope to be pointed at anything in the northern sky. There are plenty of images on the site and there's good information on how the stars and our galaxy were formed.

www.heavens-above.com

IT'S ABOVE YOUR HEAD

ORIGIN US
SPEED ✓✓✓✓
INFO ✓✓✓✓✓
EASE ✓✓✓✓

Type in your location and they'll give you the exact time and precise location of the next visible pass of the International Space Station or space shuttle. They also help you to observe satellites and flares from Iridium satellites.

www.spaceadventures.com

SPACE TOURISM

ORIGIN US
SPEED ✓✓✓
INFO ✓✓✓✓
VALUE ✓
EASE ✓✓✓✓

OK so you want to be an astronaut? Well now you have a golden opportunity, so long as you have $2 million! Having said that there are actually some cheaper options including shuttle tours and a trip to the edge of space.

www.setiathome.ssl.berkeley.edu/

GET IN TOUCH WITH AN ALIEN

ORIGIN US
SPEED ✓✓✓
INFO ✓✓✓✓
EASE ✓✓✓

To borrow the official site description 'SETI@home is a scientific experiment that uses Internet-connected computers in the Search for Extraterrestrial Intelligence (SETI).' You can participate by running a free program that downloads and analyses radio telescope data. You could be the first!

Sport

One of the best uses of the Internet is to keep up-to-date with how your team is performing, or if you're a member of a team or association, keep each other updated.

General sport sites

www.sporting-life.com

THE SPORTING LIFE

ORIGIN UK
SPEED ✓✓✓✓
INFO ✓✓✓✓
EASE ✓✓✓✓

A very comprehensive sport site, with plenty of advice, tips, news and latest scores. It's considered to be one of the best, good for stories, in-depth analysis and overall coverage of the major sports.

www.sports.com

SPORTS NEWS AND BETTING

ORIGIN UK
SPEED ✓✓✓
INFO ✓✓✓✓✓
VALUE ✓✓✓
EASE ✓✓✓✓✓

With a strong international feel, this site offers much in the way of information on all key sports, particularly football, its shop has been replaced with a wide ranging betting service.

www.bbc.co.uk/sport

BBC SPORT COVERAGE

ORIGIN UK
SPEED ✓✓✓
INFO ✓✓✓✓✓
EASE ✓✓✓✓✓

They may have lost the right to broadcast many sporting events but their coverage at this level is excellent – much broader than most and it's always up-to-date.

www.skysports.com

THE BEST OF SKY SPORT

ORIGIN UK
SPEED ✓✓✓✓
INFO ✓✓✓✓
EASE ✓✓✓✓

Excellent for the Premiership and football in general, but also covers other sports very well particularly cricket and both forms of rugby. Includes a section featuring video and audio clips, and there are interviews with stars. You can vote in their polls, e-mail programmes or try sports trivia quizzes. Lots of adverts spoil it.

www.rivals.net

THE RIVALS NETWORK

ORIGIN UK
SPEED ✓✓✓✓
INFO ✓✓✓✓✓
EASE ✓✓✓✓

Independent of any news organisations, Rivals is basically a network of specialist sites covering the whole gamut of major and some minor sports, each site has its own editor who is passionate about the sport they cover. In general its promise is better than the delivery but what there is, is excellent with good quality content and pictures.

www.talksport.net

HOME OF TALK SPORT RADIO

ORIGIN UK
SPEED ✓✓✓
INFO ✓✓✓✓
VALUE ✓✓
EASE ✓✓✓✓

A pretty down-market site where you can listen to sports news and debate while you work. The information comes from *Sporting Life* but it's up-to-date. There's also an audio archive and scheduling information, view the fantastic sports babe and visit the bookstore. There's also a sister site where you can place bets.

Other good all-rounders, and sites with good links:

www.allstarsites.com – directory of several thousand sports sites, you rate the ones you like.

www.EL.com/elinks/sports – list of American-oriented sports links.

www.sportal.co.uk – good, football-oriented magazine site.

www.sportquest.com – excellent search engine and directory.

www.sportsonline.co.uk – odd looking site with lots of links and an OK search engine devoted to UK sport.

www.sportszine.co.uk – fab search engine and directory, all sites are well reviewed and well categorised.

Sites on specific sports

AMERICAN FOOTBALL

www.nfl.com

NATIONAL FOOTBALL LEAGUE

ORIGIN US
SPEED ✓✓✓
INFO ✓✓✓✓
EASE ✓✓✓✓

American football's online bible, it's a huge official site with details and statistics bursting from every page. It's got information on all the teams, players and likely draft picks; there's also information on NFL Europe and links to other key sites. All it really lacks is gossip!

See also:
http://football.espn.go.com/nfl/index – ESPN's site is authoritative and offers links to other sports.
www.nflplayers.com – for the latest news and background on all the key people in the game plus nostalgia from ex-players.

ARCHERY

www.archery.org

INTERNATIONAL ARCHERY FEDERATION

ORIGIN UK
SPEED ✓✓✓
INFO ✓✓✓✓
EASE ✓✓✓✓

Get the official news, events listings, rankings and records information from this fairly mundane site; and you can learn more about field archery at **www.fieldarcher.com** which has a great enthusiastic amateur feel. For a more entertaining and chatty site try **www.theglade.co.uk** which is basically an online magazine, devoted to all forms of archery. Lastly, check out **www.archery.net** for chat, links, equipment and advice.

ATHLETICS AND RUNNING

www.iaaf.org
INTERNATIONAL ASSOCIATION OF ATHLETICS FEDERATIONS

ORIGIN UK
SPEED ✓✓✓✓
INFO ✓✓✓✓✓
EASE ✓✓✓

The official site of the IAAF is a results-oriented affair with lots of rankings in addition to the latest news. There's also a multimedia section where you can see pictures, listen to commentary or watch video of the key events. There's a good links page and information on the organisation's activities.

www.ukathletics.net
THE GOVERNING BODY

ORIGIN UK
SPEED ✓✓✓✓
INFO ✓✓✓✓✓
EASE ✓✓✓

Many official 'governing body' sites are pretty boring affairs, not so UK Athletics which contains lots of features, is newsy and written with an obvious sense of enthusiasm. There are details on forthcoming events, reports on aspects of the sport, records, biographies of key athletes and advice on keeping fit. Somehow you get the impression the site is sponsored...

See also:

www.british-athletics.co.uk – a boring site but it has a directory of clubs and regional events. It's good for links to newsgroups though.

www.runtrackdir.com/ – details of all the UK's running tracks and their facilities.

www.nuff-respect.co.uk – see what Linford Christie is up to these days.

www.runnersworld.com
RUNNER'S WORLD MAGAZINE

ORIGIN US
SPEED ✓✓✓
INFO ✓✓✓✓
EASE ✓✓✓✓

A rather dry site with tips from getting started through to advanced level running. There's lots of information, news and records plus reviews on shoes and gear. See also the less visually exciting but comprehensive **www.runnersweb.com**

www.realrunner.com
A RUNNING COMMUNITY

ORIGIN UK
SPEED ✓✓✓✓
INFO ✓✓✓✓
EASE ✓✓✓✓

A very well put together site with lots of resources to help runners in terms of both equipment and advice. There's an online health check, details of events, marathons and profiles of the athletes. Good design ensures that the site is a pleasure to use. For equipment advice try Runnersworld **www.runnersworld.ltd.uk**

AUSTRALIAN RULES FOOTBALL

www.afl.com.au
AUSTRALIAN FOOTBALL LEAGUE

ORIGIN AUSTRALIA
SPEED ✓✓✓
INFO ✓✓✓✓✓
EASE ✓✓✓✓

A top quality site covering all aspects of the game including team news, player profiles and statistics as well as the latest gossip and speculation.

BASEBALL

www.mlb.com
MAJOR LEAGUE BASEBALL

ORIGIN US
SPEED ✓✓✓✓
INFO ✓✓✓✓
EASE ✓✓✓✓

All you need to know about the top teams and the World Series, it's not the best-designed site but there's good information and statistics on the game and the key players as well as related articles and features. If you want to find out more, a good place to try is www.baseball-links.com which is easy to use and has over 9,000 links; for the British game try www.gbbaseball.co.uk

BASKETBALL

www.nba.com
NATIONAL BASKETBALL ASSOCIATION

ORIGIN US
SPEED ✓✓✓
INFO ✓✓✓✓✓
EASE ✓✓✓✓

A comprehensive official site with features on the teams, players and games; there's also an excellent photo gallery and you can watch some of the most important points if you have the right software. For the official line on British basketball go to www.bbl.org.uk or www.britball.com which is unofficial but more fun and also covers Ireland. See also www.basketball.com who have really extensive coverage including the women's game.

BOWLS

www.bowlsengland.com

ENGLISH BOWLING ASSOCIATION

ORIGIN UK
SPEED ✓✓✓
INFO ✓✓✓✓
EASE ✓✓✓

A straightforward design making it easy to find out all you need to know about lawn bowls in England, including a good set of links to associated sites and even tips on green maintenance.

www.eiba.co.uk

ENGLAND INDOOR BOWLING ASSOCIATION

ORIGIN UK
SPEED ✓✓✓
INFO ✓✓✓✓
EASE ✓✓✓

A very basic site giving an overview of the game, links and background information on competitions and rules.

BOXING

www.boxing.com

BOXING NEWS

ORIGIN US
SPEED ✓✓✓✓
INFO ✓✓✓✓
EASE ✓✓✓✓

A comprehensive site covering world boxing in a pretty newsy way with lots of exclusives and features, there are regular columnists and it's authoritative. There's also chat, links and the latest headlines.

See also:

www.boxinginsider.com – really good looking site with lots of information on the sport plus it's good for chat and stats.

www.heavyweights.co.uk – who cover the hype around heavyweight boxing.

For the different boxing authorities:

www.wbaonline.com – the WBA has an OK looking and functional site.

www.wbcboxing.com – a straightforward site from the WBC.

www.wbu.cc - the World Boxing Union covers the sport well from an unusual site.

www.worldboxingfed.com – WBF or Fightshow.com is a really entertaining site with lots of links and info on the sport as well as training tips and where to get equipment.

www.womenboxing.com – a very comprehensive site devoted to women's boxing.

www.aiba.net – the official site from the Amateur International Boxing Association.

CLAY SHOOTING

www.clayshooting.co.uk
CLAY SHOOTING MAGAZINE

ORIGIN UK	A good introduction to the sport with a beginner's
SPEED ✓✓✓	guide to start you off and a good set of links to key
INFO ✓✓✓✓	suppliers and associated sites. There's also an online
VALUE ✓✓✓	shop where you can buy the odd essential item such
EASE ✓✓✓	as global positioning systems and dog food.

Serious shooters can go to the comprehensive **www.hotbarrels.com**

CRICKET

www.uk.cricket.org or www.cricinfo.com

THE HOME OF CRICKET ON THE NET

ORIGIN UK
SPEED ✓✓✓✓
INFO ✓✓✓✓✓
VALUE ✓✓✓
EASE ✓✓✓✓

The best all round cricket site on the Internet, with in depth analysis, match reports, player profiles, statistics, links to other more specialised sites and live written commentary. There's also a shop with lots of cricket goodies, delivery is included in the price. It also looks after the official sites of Lords and the ECB.

www.khel.com

WORLD CRICKET

ORIGIN INDIA
SPEED ✓✓✓✓
INFO ✓✓✓✓
EASE ✓✓✓✓

Khel has gone from being a labour of love to a really professional and commercial site, although cricket is it's main love you can also follow football and other sports too.

www.wisden.com

WISED CRICKET MONTHLY

ORIGIN UK
SPEED ✓✓✓✓
INFO ✓✓✓✓
EASE ✓✓✓✓

Excellent site with the best features from the magazine featuring some of the best cricket journalism you can get as well as statistics and background information on the teams. There's also links, shop directory and quizzes.

www.lords.org

THE OFFICIAL LINE ON CRICKET

ORIGIN UK
SPEED ✓✓✓
INFO ✓✓✓✓✓
EASE ✓✓✓✓

Here you'll find news with plenty of information about the game and players, even a quiz and an excellent section on women's cricket. Good links to governing bodies, associations, the MCC and ECB. If you have RealPlayer, there's access to live games on audio via the BBC.

www.webbsoc.demon.co.uk

WOMEN'S CRICKET ON THE WEB

ORIGIN	UK
SPEED	✓✓✓✓
INFO	✓✓✓✓
EASE	✓✓✓

There are not many sites about women's cricket, this is probably the best, with features, news, fixture lists, match reports and player profiles. Nothing fancy, but it works.

www.theprideside.com

CRICKET TO THE ROOTS

ORIGIN	UK
SPEED	✓✓✓
INFO	✓✓✓✓
EASE	✓✓✓✓

A good attempt at encouraging young people to take an interest in cricket with an interactive game played on a really interesting interactive site.

See also:
www.cricnet.co.uk - the Professional Cricketers Association official site.
http://sport.guardian.co.uk/cricket - good looking and up to the minute site from the *Guardian* newspaper.
www.cricketsupplies.com - a good looking online store specialising in cricket gear, delivery is £6 per order.

CYCLING

These are sites aimed at the more serious sportsman, for more leisurely cycling see page 88 and for holidays turn to page 463.

www.bcf.uk.com/

BRITISH CYCLING FEDERATION

ORIGIN	UK
SPEED	✓✓✓
INFO	✓✓✓✓
EASE	✓✓✓✓

The governing body for cycling, the site has become more comprehensive, you can get information on events, rules, clubs and rankings, as well as contact names for coaching and development, plus a news service.

www.bikemagic.com

IT'S BIKETASTIC!

ORIGIN	UK
SPEED	✓✓✓✓
INFO	✓✓✓✓
VALUE	✓✓✓
EASE	✓✓✓✓

Whether you're a beginner or an old hand, the enthusiastic and engaging tone of this site will convert you or enhance your cycling experience. There's plenty of news and features, as well as reviews on bike parts and gadgets. There's also a classified ads section and a selection of links to other biking web sites, all of which are rated. It's also worth checking out **www.bikinguk.net** who are big on mountain biking.

www.letour.fr

TOUR DE FRANCE

ORIGIN	FRANCE
SPEED	✓✓✓✓
INFO	✓✓✓✓
EASE	✓✓✓

Written in several languages this site covers the Tour in some depth with details on the teams, riders and general background information.

DARTS

www.embassydarts.com

EMBASSY WORLD DARTS

ORIGIN	UK
SPEED	✓✓✓✓
INFO	✓✓✓✓✓
EASE	✓✓✓✓

Whether you think darts qualifies as a sport or not, this well-designed site gives a great deal of information about the game, its players and the tournament. See also **www.cyberdarts.com** for more information and good links to other darts sites. For some outstanding advice on how to play the game visit the labour of love that is **www.dartbase.com**

EQUESTRIAN

www.bhs.org.uk

BRITISH HORSE SOCIETY

ORIGIN UK
SPEED ✓✓✓
INFO ✓✓✓✓✓
EASE ✓✓✓✓

A charity that looks after the welfare of horses, here you can get information on insurance, links, riding schools, competitions, events and trials.

www.horseonline.co.uk

A DEFINITIVE RESOURCE

ORIGIN UK
SPEED ✓✓✓✓
INFO ✓✓✓✓
EASE ✓✓✓✓

Another excellent horse site with lots of news, features and chat, there's also plenty of advice on buying and looking after your horse.

For more information try:
www.horseandhound.co.uk – excellent magazine site from the leading authority.
www.britisheventing.com – an attractive text based site with details on the sport and links.
www.badminton-horse.co.uk – background and information on the famous horse trials with lots of extra features and links.
http://horses.about.com/ – About.com's excellent suite of pages devoted to all things equestrian.

EXTREME SPORTS

www.extremesports.com

ACTION PACKED

ORIGIN US
SPEED ✓✓✓✓
INFO ✓✓✓✓
EASE ✓✓✓✓

A buzzy, in your face site that puts over what extreme sports is about really well using good quality photos and the latest news to give the site immediacy. See also the equally exciting **www.adrenalin-hit.com** which is probably worth a visit just for the design alone.

www.extreme.com

EXTREME SPORTS CHANNEL

ORIGIN US
SPEED ✓✓✓
INFO ✓✓✓✓
VALUE ✓✓✓✓
EASE ✓✓✓✓

The official site of the Extreme Sports Channel is hi-tech but quite slow, however once downloaded it's got lots to offer in terms of information, shopping and the latest headlines. For branded clothing for extreme sports see www.extremepie.com

FISHING

www.fishing.co.uk

HOME OF UK FISHING ON THE NET

ORIGIN UK
SPEED ✓✓✓✓
INFO ✓✓✓✓✓
VALUE ✓✓
EASE ✓✓✓✓

A huge site that offers information on where to fish, how to fish, where's the best place to stay near fish, even fishing holidays. There's also advice on equipment, a records section and links to shops and shop locations. Shop on-site for fishing books and magazines.

See also:
www.anglersnet.co.uk – good magazine site with
   lots of information and chat.
www.anglers-world.co.uk – great for fishing holidays.
www.fishandfly.co.uk – another good magazine site,
   this one devoted to fly fishing.
www.fisheries.co.uk – excellent for coarse fishing
   and links.
www.nimpopo.com – lots of bargains on fishing
   tackle.
www.specialist-tackle.co.uk – excellent store for
   equipment plus much more in the way of chat and
   information.

FOOTBALL

www.footballnews.co.uk

MORE COVERAGE AND RESULTS

ORIGIN UK
SPEED ✓✓✓✓
INFO ✓✓✓✓✓
EASE ✓✓✓✓

For depth of results coverage this site is hard to beat, but they are looking for funding at time of writing so hopefully the site will continue. It's less cluttered and easier to use than most other football sites; it's also up-to-date and doesn't miss much.

It's worth having a look at the sites listed below; just pick the one you like best.

www.e-soccer.com – hundreds of links and the latest news.

www.football365.co.uk – outspoken and fun, comprehensive too, with some good journalism.

www.guardian.co.uk/football – great writing and irreverent articles, uncluttered design.

www.onefootball.com – an excellent all-rounder with lots of features.

www.planetfootball.com – news, information and OPTA statistics and the world game.

www.soccerage.com – excellent for world soccer, in 10 languages.

www.soccerhighway.com – a strange site but good for links.

www.soccernet.com – well put together from ESPN, comprehensive but a bit boring.

www.footballtransfers.net – get the latest transfer gossip and player news.

www.teamtalk.com

CHECK OUT THE TEAMS!

ORIGIN UK
SPEED ✓✓✓✓
INFO ✓✓✓✓✓
EASE ✓✓✓✓

The place to go if you want all the latest gossip and transfer information, it's opinionated but not often wrong. They have around 90 journalists on their books and they also cover rugby and racing too.

www.icons.com

THE WORLD'S LEADING FOOTBALLERS

ORIGIN UK
SPEED ✓✓✓
INFO ✓✓✓✓✓
EASE ✓✓✓✓

Keep up-to-date with transfer news, gossip and hear the word from the players themselves. Each has a page or site devoted to them with a biography and other important details like what they think of their teammates, an interview, achievements to date and the all important gallery.

www.soccerbase.com

SOCCER STATISTICS

ORIGIN UK
SPEED ✓✓✓
INFO ✓✓✓✓✓
EASE ✓✓✓✓

The site to end all pub rows, it's described as the most comprehensive and up-to-date source of British football data on the Internet.

www.fifa.com

FIFA

ORIGIN
  SWITZERLAND
SPEED ✓✓✓✓
INFO ✓✓✓✓✓
EASE ✓✓✓✓

This is FIFA's magazine where you can get information on what they do, the World Cup and other FIFA competitions. For the UEFA go to www.uefa.com where you can see how everyone is faring in the Champions League and UEFA cup.

www.englishpremiershipfootball.com

THE PREMIER LEAGUE

ORIGIN UK
SPEED ✓✓✓✓
INFO ✓✓✓✓
EASE ✓✓✓✓

All the news and gossip plus the latest scores and fixture lists. There's also loads of links to team and betting sites. For Scottish football go to the well put together www.scottishfootball.com, while to find out the views of the managers go to www.leaguemanagers.com home of the League Managers Association.

www.footballaid.com

FOOTBALL CHARITY

ORIGIN UK
SPEED ✓✓✓✓
INFO ✓✓✓✓
EASE ✓✓✓✓

Football aid is a charity that helps good causes by running football events, you can sign on to play for the team of your choice or just send a cheque.

GOLF

www.golfix.co.uk

GOLF FIX

ORIGIN UK
SPEED ✓✓✓✓
INFO ✓✓✓✓✓
EASE ✓✓✓✓

A straightforward and informative site with masses of tips and advice on how to improve your game. Alongside this there's all the information you'd expect from a quality sports site with sections on games, fitness and news. It was up for sale when we last visited though.

www.golftoday.co.uk
THE PREMIER ONLINE GOLF MAGAZINE

ORIGIN UK
SPEED ✓✓✓
INFO ✓✓✓✓✓
EASE ✓✓✓✓

An excellent site for golf news and tournaments with features, statistics and rankings and also a course directory. It's the best all-round site covering Europe. There are also links to sister sites about the amateur game, shops and where to stay. Golf Today also hosts a comprehensive site on the amateur game; you can find it at www.amateur-golf.com

www.golfweb.com
PGA TOUR

ORIGIN US
SPEED ✓✓✓
INFO ✓✓✓✓✓
EASE ✓✓✓✓

The best site for statistics on the PGA, and keeping up with tournament scores, it also has audio and visual features with RealPlayer. For the official word on the tour go to www.pga.com, while for the European tour go to www.europeantour.com

www.golf.com
THE AMERICAN VIEW

ORIGIN US
SPEED ✓✓✓
INFO ✓✓✓✓✓
EASE ✓✓✓

Part of NBC's suite of web sites, this offers a massive amount of information and statistics on the game, the major tours and players, both men and women.

www.uk-golfguide.com
GOLF TOURISM

ORIGIN UK
SPEED ✓✓✓
INFO ✓✓✓✓
EASE ✓✓✓

A useful directory of courses and hotels with courses, with links to travel agents for the UK and abroad, you can also get information on golf equipment suppliers and insurance. See also www.whatgolf.co.uk

www.onlinegolf.co.uk

GOLF EQUIPMENT

ORIGIN UK
SPEED ✓✓✓
INFO ✓✓✓✓
VALUE ✓✓✓
EASE ✓✓✓✓

A good looking and comprehensive golf store with lots of offers and a good range, it has a ladies section, a good search facility and you can trial some clubs for 30 days. Delivery is free for standard postage in the UK. See also www.golfseller.co.uk who auction second-hand golf equipment.

See also:
www.mygolfzone.com – a good all-rounder.
www.golflinks.co.uk – a large, UK oriented site database.
www.grassrootsgolf.com – summer camps for junior golfers.
http://golfwebcenter.fol.nl – links to all things golf around the world.
www.golfingguides.net – authoritative reviews of the best golf courses.

GYMNASTICS

www.gymmedia.com

GYMNASTIC NEWS

ORIGIN GERMANY
SPEED ✓✓✓
INFO ✓✓✓✓
EASE ✓✓✓

A bi-lingual site giving all the latest news, it covers all forms of the sport and offers lots of links to related sites. For the official UK site go to www.baga.co.uk which is comprehensive.

HOCKEY

www.hockeyonline.co.uk

THE ENGLISH HOCKEY ASSOCIATION

ORIGIN UK
SPEED ✓✓✓
INFO ✓✓✓✓
EASE ✓✓✓

A slick site covering the English game with information and chat on the players, leagues and teams for both the men's and the women's games. For the Welsh game go to **www.welsh-hockey.co.uk** and for the Scottish **www.scottish-hockey.org.uk** neither are great on design but give all the relevant information. For more links to teams and chat sites check out **www.hockeyweb.co.uk**

HORSE RACING

www.racingpost.co.uk

THE RACING POST

ORIGIN UK
SPEED ✓✓✓
INFO ✓✓✓✓✓
EASE ✓✓✓✓

Superb, informative site from the authority on the sport, every event covered in-depth with tips and advice. To get the best out of it you have to register, then you have access to the database and more.

www.racenews.co.uk

RACING, COURSES AND BETTING

ORIGIN UK
SPEED ✓✓✓
INFO ✓✓✓✓
EASE ✓✓✓

A slightly different spin from Racenews, they have three main sections: their news service, a course guide and a tipsters column, there's also an excellent links section covering racing world-wide.

www.flatstats.co.uk

FLAT RACING STATISTICS

ORIGIN UK
SPEED ✓✓✓
INFO ✓✓✓✓
VALUE ✓✓✓
EASE ✓✓✓✓

This site contains masses of detailed and unique statistics - horse, trainer, jockey, sire and race statistics, favourites analysis, systems analysis and much more. The site contains three sections, one for turf, one for all-weather racing and one for general information. You have to be a member to get the best out of it.

See also:
www.bhb.co.uk – the British Horse Racing Board's excellent site.
www.jockeysroom.com – an A-Z of jockeys with biographies and pictures.
www.attheraces.co.uk – live action, tips and the latest news plus great design.

ICE HOCKEY

www.iceweb.co.uk

THE ICE HOCKEY SUPER-LEAGUE

ORIGIN UK
SPEED ✓✓✓✓
INFO ✓✓✓✓✓
EASE ✓✓✓✓

Keep up-to-date with the scores, the games and the players, even their injuries. Good for statistics as well as news.

www.nhl.com

NATIONAL HOCKEY LEAGUE

ORIGIN US
SPEED ✓✓✓✓
INFO ✓✓✓✓
EASE ✓✓✓

Catch up on the latest from the NHL including a chance to listen to and watch key moments from past and recent games.

See also:
www.britnatleague.co.uk – the British National League information and news.

www.crazykennys.com – ice hockey equipment
suppliers.
www.azhockey.com – home of the Encyclopaedia of
Ice Hockey.

ICE SKATING

www.bladesonice.com
FIGURE SKATING MAGAZINE

ORIGIN UK
SPEED ✓✓✓✓
INFO ✓✓✓✓
EASE ✓✓✓✓

From the magazine *Blades on Ice*, this site features
archive material, the latest news, details of events,
advice and of course how to subscribe.

See also:
www.iceskatingworld.com – comprehensive US site
with excellent links and the latest news.
www.iceskating.org.uk – the official site of the
National Ice Skating Association of the UK, a good
looking site covering all aspects of ice skating.

MARTIAL ARTS

www.martial-arts-network.com
PROMOTING MARTIAL ARTS

ORIGIN US
SPEED ✓✓
INFO ✓✓✓✓
EASE ✓✓✓

Possibly qualifies as the loudest introduction
sequence, but once you've cut the volume or skipped
the intro, the site offers a great deal in terms of
resources and information about the martial arts
scene, including *Black Belts* magazine. Its layout is a
little confusing and the site is quite slow.

Beginners should go to www.martialresource.com a good-looking site which explains the background to each type of martial art and gives hints and tips to those just starting out. Martial Info www.martialinfo.com is another slow but comprehensive site with an online magazine.

www.britishjudo.org.uk

JUDO

ORIGIN UK
SPEED ✓✓✓✓
INFO ✓✓✓✓
EASE ✓✓✓✓

Judo has a proud tradition in the UK, and if you want to follow that you can get all the information you need at the British Judo Association site. It gives a brief history of judo, a magazine and event information. For a broader view go to www.judoinfo.com.

www.btkf.homestead.com

BRITISH KARATE FEDERATION

ORIGIN UK
SPEED ✓✓✓✓
INFO ✓✓✓✓
EASE ✓✓✓✓

Information on all forms of the discipline as well as events listings, fun pages and an online martial arts club, which is hosted by Yahoo.

MOTOR SPORT

www.crash.net

MOTORSPORT PORTAL

ORIGIN UK
SPEED ✓✓✓✓
INFO ✓✓✓✓✓
EASE ✓✓✓

An excellent but very commercial news and directory site covering the major motor sports and most of the minor ones too. There's an online shop selling motor sport merchandise among other things and there's a good photo library.

www.ukmotorsport.com

INFORMATION OVERLOAD

ORIGIN UK	This site covers every form of motor racing; it's got
SPEED ✓✓✓✓	lots of links to appropriate sites covering all aspects
INFO ✓✓✓✓✓	of motor sport. There are also chat sections and
EASE ✓✓✓	forums plus links to product and service suppliers.

www.linksheaven.com

THE MOST COMPREHENSIVE LINKS DIRECTORY

ORIGIN US	Whatever, whoever, there's an appropriate link.
SPEED ✓✓✓	It concentrates on Formula 1, CART and Nascar
INFO ✓✓✓✓✓	though.
EASE ✓✓✓✓	

www.autosport.com

AUTOSPORT MAGAZINE

ORIGIN UK	Excellent for news and features on motor sport plus
SPEED ✓✓✓	links and an affiliated online shopping experience
INFO ✓✓✓✓✓	for related products such as team gear, books or
VALUE ✓✓✓	models.
EASE ✓✓✓	

www.itv-f1.com

F1 ON ITV

ORIGIN UK	This web site is excellent, it doesn't miss much and
SPEED ✓✓✓✓	there is plenty of action. There's all the background
INFO ✓✓✓✓✓	information you'd expect plus circuit profiles, sched-
EASE ✓✓✓✓✓	ules and a photo gallery. For more news and links to

everywhere in F1 go to www.f1-world.co.uk or the eccentric www.f1nutter.co.uk alternatively try www.f1weekly.net

www.fota.co.uk

FORMULA 3

ORIGIN UK	Formula 3 explained plus info on the teams, drivers
SPEED ✓✓✓✓	and circuits, it's the breeding ground for F1 drivers
INFO ✓✓✓✓✓	of the future which adds to the excitement reflected
EASE ✓✓✓✓✓	in the energy of this site.

www.rallysport.com

COVERING THE WORLD RALLY CHAMPIONSHIP

ORIGIN UK
SPEED ✓✓✓✓
INFO ✓✓✓✓
EASE ✓✓✓✓

Good for results and news on rallying in the UK and across the world. See also **www.rallyzone.co.uk** which is a comprehensive international e-zine. You can follow a race stage by stage at **http://rally.racing-live.com/en/** as well as get all the latest news.

www.btccpages.com

BRITISH TOURING CAR CHAMPIONSHIP

ORIGIN UK
SPEED ✓✓✓
INFO ✓✓✓✓✓
EASE ✓✓✓✓

This site offers a great deal of information and statistics on the championship, driver and team profiles, photos and links to other related sites. There are also a number of forums you can get involved with if you feel like chatting to fellow enthusiasts.

www.karting.co.uk

GO KARTING

ORIGIN UK
SPEED ✓✓✓✓
INFO ✓✓✓✓✓
EASE ✓✓✓✓

A well laid out portal site to all things karting in the UK, with links and directories covering the tracks, manufacturers, events and a photo gallery plus the latest news.

MOTORCYCLING

www.motorcyclenews.com

NEWS AND VIEWS

ORIGIN UK
SPEED ✓✓✓
INFO ✓✓✓✓✓
EASE ✓✓✓✓

A very good magazine-style site giving all the latest news, gossip and event information, there are also sections on buying a bike, where to get parts and the latest gear, off-road biking and a links directory. There's also a chat room and a good classified section.

www.acu.org.uk

AUTO-CYCLE UNION

ORIGIN UK
SPEED ✓✓✓✓
INFO ✓✓✓
EASE ✓✓✓✓

The ACU is the governing body for motorcycle sports in the UK and this site gives information on its work and the benefits of being a member. There are also links and details of their magazine.

www.motograndprix.com

TRACK AND OFF-ROAD

ORIGIN UK
SPEED ✓✓✓✓
INFO ✓✓✓✓
EASE ✓✓✓✓✓

A well laid out magazine site, which covers track grand prix and dirt biking in equal measure, even some of the more obscure areas of the sport, such as snowcross, are covered.

www.british-speedway.co.uk

SPEEDWAY

ORIGIN UK
SPEED ✓✓✓✓
INFO ✓✓✓
EASE ✓✓✓✓

A much improved site giving information on the leagues as well as the latest news, there's also an events calendar and links to related sites.

www.motocross.com

MOTOCROSS

ORIGIN US
SPEED ✓✓✓✓
INFO ✓✓✓
EASE ✓✓✓✓

An authoritative site covering the sport but it's centred on the US, although it has got some information on the European scene. See also **www.motolinks.com**

MOUNTAINEERING AND OUTDOOR SPORTS

www.mountainzone.com

FOR THE UPWARDLY MOBILE

ORIGIN US
SPEED ✓✓✓
INFO ✓✓✓✓✓
EASE ✓✓✓✓

Thoroughly covers all aspects of climbing, hiking, mountain biking, skiing and snowboarding with a very good photography section featuring galleries from major mountains and climbers.

www.rockrun.com

ALL THE RIGHT EQUIPMENT

ORIGIN UK
SPEED ✓✓✓
INFO ✓✓✓✓✓
EASE ✓✓✓

Excellent equipment shop covering climbing and walking gear, which is also pretty comprehensive on the information front too, delivery starts at £3.50 for the UK. See also www.gearzone.co.uk who have a similar offering.

Other good climbing sites:
www.cruxed.com – nice looking site with advice on techniques and training, good links.
www.climbing.co.uk – climb UK is wide-ranging from information on climbing and climbs to chat and gear suppliers.
www.thebmc.co.uk – good all-round climbing and hill-walking magazine-style site from the British Mountaineering Council with good links pages.
www.ukclimbing.com – comprehensive information on climbing in the UK.

NETBALL

www.netball.org
INTERNATIONAL FEDERATION OF NETBALL ASSOCIATIONS

ORIGIN UK
SPEED ✓✓✓✓
INFO ✓✓✓✓
EASE ✓✓✓✓

Get information on the work of the federation and the rules of the game, plus rankings and the events calendar. See also **www.netballcoaching.com** which is good for advice and links.

OLYMPICS

www.the5rings.com
INTERACTIVE INTERNET SPORT

ORIGIN UK
SPEED ✓✓✓✓
INFO ✓✓✓✓✓
EASE ✓✓✓✓

Lots of statistics on the Olympics, plus a review of the last games and details on all the events going back to the beginning of the last century. It's got excellent links to associated sites and information on future games too.

www.olympics.org
BRITISH OLYMPIC ASSOCIATION

ORIGIN UK
SPEED ✓✓✓✓
INFO ✓✓✓
EASE ✓✓✓✓

A new look site with sections on the forthcoming winter and summer games, information for collectors and also the doping policy, for a history of the games there's the Olympic museum link and links to sports federations and committees.

ROWING

www.themassive.com

ONLINE ROWING COMMUNITY

ORIGIN UK   A wide ranging and popular site offering articles and
SPEED ✓✓✓✓   features by those involved in the sport, club infor-
INFO ✓✓✓✓   mation and chat.
EASE ✓✓✓✓

www.ara-rowing.org

AMATEUR ROWING ASSOCIATION

ORIGIN UK   This site offers information on the history of the
SPEED ✓✓✓   sport, plus the latest news, coaching tips and links.
INFO ✓✓✓✓
EASE ✓✓✓✓

See also:
www.steveredgrave.com – Steve's official site offers
   biographical information, training instruction and
   tips, links and background on the sport.
www.total.rowing.org.uk – a good rowing portal site.

RUGBY

www.scrum.com

RUGBY UNION

ORIGIN UK   An excellent site about rugby union with
SPEED ✓✓✓   impressively up-to-the-minute coverage, for a
INFO ✓✓✓✓✓   similar but lighter and more fun site go to
EASE ✓✓✓✓   **www.planet-rugby.com** which has a comprehensive
round-up of world rugby with instant reports, lots
of detail and information on both union and league.

www.rfu.com

RUGBY FOOTBALL UNION

ORIGIN UK
SPEED ✓✓✓
INFO ✓✓✓✓
VALUE ✓✓✓
EASE ✓✓✓✓

Masses of features, articles and news from the official RFU site, it's got team news and information, links and a shop where you can buy gear – delivery is free for the UK for orders under £5.

www.irb.org

INTERNATIONAL RUGBY BOARD

ORIGIN UK
SPEED ✓✓✓
INFO ✓✓✓✓
EASE ✓✓✓✓

For the official line on rugby union, you will find all the rules and regulations explained, information on world tournaments, history of the game, fixtures and results.

www.rleague.com

WORLD OF RUGBY LEAGUE

ORIGIN UK
SPEED ✓✓✓
INFO ✓✓✓✓✓
EASE ✓✓✓✓

Another very comprehensive site, featuring sections on Australia, New Zealand and the UK, with plenty of chat, articles, player profiles and enough statistics to keep the most ardent fan happy. See also the magazine sites **www.rugbyleaguer.co.uk** and **www.totalrugbyleague.com**

SAILING

www.madforsailing.com

MAD FOR SAILING

ORIGIN UK
SPEED ✓✓✓
INFO ✓✓✓✓
EASE ✓✓✓✓

An informative and well laid out site covering all aspects of sailing both as a sport and as a hobby. There are some really good and well written articles and features such as a crew search facility and weather information.

www.bigblue.org.uk

PASSION FOR BOATING

ORIGIN UK	An interesting site devoted to boating and sailing or
SPEED ✓✓✓	just having fun on water. It has information on boat
INFO ✓✓✓✓	shows, buying a boat, a section for beginners, links
EASE ✓✓✓✓	and holidays too.

www.ukdinghyracing.com

UK DINGHY RACING

ORIGIN UK	Devoted mainly to this one aspect of sailing, it
SPEED ✓✓✓	covers the sport comprehensively and gives advice
INFO ✓✓✓✓	on buying and hosts links to auctions and specialist
EASE ✓✓✓✓	shops.

SKIING AND SNOWBOARDING

www.fis-ski.com

INTERNATIONAL SKI FEDERATION

ORIGIN US	Catch up on the news, the fastest times, the
SPEED ✓✓✓✓	rankings in all forms of skiing at this site. Very good
INFO ✓✓✓✓✓	background information and a live on line section
EASE ✓✓✓✓	enabling events to be monitored as they happen.

www.ski.co.uk

THE PLACE TO START – A SKI DIRECTORY

ORIGIN UK	Straightforward site, the information in the direc-
SPEED ✓✓✓	tory is useful and the recommended sites are rated.
INFO ✓✓✓✓	The sections are holidays, travel, weather, resorts,
EASE ✓✓✓✓	snowboarding, gear, fanatics and specialist services.

www.1ski.com

COMPLETE ONLINE SKIING SERVICE

ORIGIN UK
SPEED ✓✓✓
INFO ✓✓✓✓✓
VALUE ✓✓✓
EASE ✓✓✓✓

With a huge number of holidays, live snow reports, tips on technique and equipment and the ultimate guide featuring over 750 resorts, it's difficult to go wrong. The site is well laid out and easy to use. There's a good events calendar too.

Other good ski and snowboarding sites:
www.ifyouski.com – comprehensive skiing site that has a very good holiday booking service with lots of deals.
www.iglu.com – holiday specialists with lots of variety and offers.
www.mountainzone.com – great for features, articles and ski adventurers.
www.skiclub.co.uk – Ski Club of Great Britain has an attractive site with lots of information and links.
www.natives.co.uk – aimed at ski workers, there's info on conditions, ski resorts, a good job section, where to stay and links to other cool sites all wrapped up on a very nicely designed site.

www.boardtheworld.com

SNOWBOARDING

ORIGIN UK
SPEED ✓✓✓
INFO ✓✓✓✓
EASE ✓✓✓✓

Masses of information and links covering the world of snowboarding, the site is well designed and doesn't seem to miss out any aspect of the sport.

See also:
www.snowboarSnowboardinguk.co.uk - forums and snowboarding chat.
www.legendsboardriders.com - online shop for snowboarders.

www.board-it.com - links and information for
  snowboarders.
www.dryslope.co.uk - a good magazine for dry
  slope snowboarders.

SNOOKER

www.embassysnooker.com

WORLD CHAMPIONSHIPS

ORIGIN	UK	An overview of the world championships from their
SPEED	✓✓✓	sponsor, the site is comprehensive and there are
INFO	✓✓✓✓	good features such as a hall of fame, rankings and a
VALUE	✓✓✓	look behind the scenes. See also the informative
EASE	✓✓✓✓	www.worldsnooker.com which is run by the games

governing body.

TENNIS AND RACQUET SPORTS

Tennis

www.lta.org.uk

LAWN TENNIS ASSOCIATION

ORIGIN	UK	An excellent and attractively designed all-year
SPEED	✓✓✓	tennis information site run by the Lawn Tennis
INFO	✓✓✓✓	Association, it has information on the players,
VALUE	✓✓✓	rankings and tournament news, as well as details on
EASE	✓✓✓✓	clubs and coaching courses. There's also an online

tennis shop where you can buy merchandise and
equipment. See also www.atptour.com which gives
a less UK biased view of the game, with excellent
sections on the players, tournaments and rankings.

www.wimbledon.org

THE OFFICIAL WIMBLEDON SITE

ORIGIN UK	Very impressive, there's a great deal here and not
SPEED ✓✓	just in June, but you need to be patient. Apart from
INFO ✓✓✓✓	the information you'd expect, you can download
VALUE ✓✓	screensavers, visit the online museum and eventually
EASE ✓✓✓✓	see videos of past matches. The shop is expensive.

Other tennis sites worth a look:

www.cliffrichardtennis.org – excellent site aimed at
encouraging children to take up the game.

www.pwp.com – a comprehensive tennis and
racquet sport related store.

www.racquet-zone.co.uk – a good racquet shop.

www.tennis.com – good magazine, with gear guides,
tips and hot news.

www.tennisnews.com – the latest news updated
daily and e-mailed to you.

Badminton

www.badmintonuk.ndo.co.uk

BRITISH BADMINTON

ORIGIN UK	A clear, easy-to-use site packed with information
SPEED ✓✓✓	about badminton, how ladders work, directory of
INFO ✓✓✓✓	coaches, club directory, rules, but not much news on
EASE ✓✓✓✓	the game. For that go to **www.baofe.co.uk** the site

of the Badminton Association of England, also try
www.intbadfed.org home of the International
Badminton Federation.

Squash

www.squashplayer.co.uk

WORLD OF SQUASH AT YOUR FINGERTIPS

ORIGIN UK
SPEED ✓✓✓✓
INFO ✓✓✓✓✓
EASE ✓✓✓✓✓

A really comprehensive round up of the game, with links galore and a great news section, there's also a section for the UK, which has club details and the latest news. See also www.worldsquash.org for a good site on what's going on worldwide.

Table tennis

www.ettu.org

EUROPEAN TABLE TENNIS UNION

ORIGIN UK
SPEED ✓✓✓
INFO ✓✓✓✓
EASE ✓✓✓✓

Find out about the ETTU, its rankings, competition details and results plus a section devoted to world table tennis links. See also www.ittf.com which gives a worldview.

WATER SPORTS AND SWIMMING

www.swimnews.com

SWIMMING NEWS

ORIGIN UK
SPEED ✓✓✓✓
INFO ✓✓✓✓
EASE ✓✓✓✓

It's up-to-date and offers a wide coverage of news, with other features such as rankings, events calendar, shopping and competition analysis.

Other good swimming sites:

www.swimxtreme.com – for entertaining chat, advice and articles.

www.pullbuoy.co.uk – good site that covers the UK scene, you can find unusual features such as a job finder and time converter.

www.coldswell.co.uk

ULTIMATE GUIDE FOR SURFING THE UK COAST

ORIGIN UK
SPEED ✓✓✓
INFO ✓✓✓✓
EASE ✓✓✓✓

Includes forecasts for weather and surf, satellite images, live surf web cams from around the world and a complete directory of surfing web sites.

See also:
www.surfcall.co.uk – slightly odd site but useful for regional information.
www.surfstation.co.uk – for links, shopping and surf speak.

www.2xs.co.uk

WINDSURFING THE UK

ORIGIN UK
SPEED ✓✓✓
INFO ✓✓✓✓
EASE ✓✓✓✓

Where to go windsurfing, plus tips and the latest sports news, shopping, weather information and advice.

www.waterski.com

WORLD OF WATER SKIING

ORIGIN US
SPEED ✓✓✓
INFO ✓✓✓✓
EASE ✓✓✓✓

An American site which features information about the sport, how to compete, news, tips, equipment and where to ski.

See also:
www.waterski-az.co.uk – news and information for the UK.
www.waterski-uk.co.uk – links and information on niche forms of the sport.

www.scubauk.co.uk

SCUBA UK

ORIGIN	UK
SPEED	✓✓✓✓
INFO	✓✓✓✓
EASE	✓✓✓✓

A large directory site with lots of links to all the sites you'd associate with scuba diving, there are sections on travel, cave diving, product reviews and you can submit your best photos for the gallery. Good design too.

See also:
www.padi.com – the place to start when you want to learn to dive.
www.ukdiving.co.uk – a good resource site with the latest news and links.

SPORTS CLOTHES AND MERCHANDISE

www.sweatband.com

SHOP BY SPORT

ORIGIN	UK
SPEED	✓✓✓✓
INFO	✓✓✓✓
VALUE	✓✓✓✓
EASE	✓✓✓✓

A wide-ranging shop that supplies equipment for many sports, but it's especially good for tennis, rugby and cricket. Delivery costs depend on the weight of your parcel.

www.kitbag.com

SPORTS FASHION

ORIGIN	UK
SPEED	✓✓✓
INFO	✓✓✓✓
VALUE	✓✓✓✓
EASE	✓✓✓✓

Football kits and gear galore from new to retro; covers cricket and rugby too. Costs on delivery vary according to order. Also offers shopping by brand and a news service.

www.sportspages.co.uk

TAKING SPORT SERIOUSLY

ORIGIN UK	Book and video specialists, concentrating on sport,
SPEED ✓✓✓✓	they offer a wide range at OK prices, even signed
INFO ✓✓✓✓	copies. Great for that one thing you've been unable to
VALUE ✓✓	find. See also **www.sportonline.uk.com** who specialise
EASE ✓✓✓✓	in the same area, but with some good offers.

www.sportonline.uk.com

SPORT TO YOUR DOOR

ORIGIN UK	Similar to Sportspages but with less range; however,
SPEED ✓✓✓	they have better offers especially on DVD and video.
INFO ✓✓✓✓	For once you do get decent sized pictures of the
VALUE ✓✓✓✓	products.
EASE ✓✓✓✓	

www.sportsworld.co.uk

SPORT TRAVEL

ORIGIN UK	Specialists in making travel arrangements to
SPEED ✓✓✓✓	sporting events; at this site you can book tickets
INFO ✓✓✓✓	and find out about future events. The site is a little
VALUE ✓✓✓	temperamental though and not that easy to use.
EASE ✓✓	

Stationery

www.stationerystore.co.uk

STATIONERY STORE

ORIGIN UK	A well designed and easy-to-use stationery store
SPEED ✓✓✓	supplying everything from paperclips to office
INFO ✓✓✓	machinery. There are also sections on electronics
VALUE ✓✓✓✓	and lots of offers. Delivery is free for orders over
EASE ✓✓✓✓	£40, £4 if below that.

For other stationery stores try:

www.staples.co.uk – still no online store, it's now
promised in 2003, but you can order a catalogue.

www.office-world.co.uk – Office World is still
promising a service 'soon'. You can print off an
order form and fax or e-mail it to them though;
delivery is next day and free if you spend over
£30.

www.whsmith.co.uk/stationery – another good
W.H.Smith site with some offers and multi-buys
but a limited range which does include some of
their fashion stationery.

www.greenstat.co.uk
GREEN STATIONERY

ORIGIN UK
SPEED ✓✓✓
INFO ✓✓✓
VALUE ✓✓✓
EASE ✓✓

Green as in environmentally friendly, they supply a
wide range of recycled paper products and desk
accessories. It's unsophisticated with delivery costs
being well hidden and you have to go through an
annoying process of making a note of product code
numbers for your order form. It's got good links to
other environmentally friendly businesses.

Student Sites

*There's masses of information for students on the Net. Here are
some sites worth checking out. The links are generally very good,
so if the topic isn't covered here, it should be easy to track down.*

Universities and colleges

www.ucas.co.uk

THE UNIVERSITY STARTING BLOCK

ORIGIN UK
SPEED ✓✓✓
INFO ✓✓✓✓✓
EASE ✓✓✓✓

A comprehensive site listing all the courses at British universities with entry profiles. You can view the directory online and order your UCAS handbook and application form. If you've already applied, you can view your application online. There are links to all the universities plus really good links to related sites. There is good advice too. If you want to study abroad you can try finding a course through **www.edunet.com**

www.nusonline.co.uk

STUDENTS UNITE

ORIGIN UK
SPEED ✓✓✓✓
INFO ✓✓✓✓
EASE ✓✓✓

Lots of relevant news and views for students on this really good looking site. You need to register to get assess to their discounts directory and special offers. Once in, you can send e-cards and use their mail and storage facilities too.

Working abroad

www.gapyear.com

COMPLETE GUIDE TO TAKING A YEAR OUT

ORIGIN UK
SPEED ✓✓✓✓
INFO ✓✓✓✓✓
EASE ✓✓✓✓

Whether you fancy helping out in the forests of Brazil or teaching in Europe you'll find information and opportunities here. There's loads of advice, past experiences to get you tempted, chat, bulletin boards, competitions and you can subscribe to their magazine (an old-fashioned paper one).

www.payaway.co.uk
FIND A JOB ABROAD OR WORKING HOLIDAY

ORIGIN UK
SPEED ✓✓✓✓
INFO ✓✓✓✓✓
EASE ✓✓✓✓

A great starting place for anyone who wants to work abroad. There is a magazine, reports from travellers and you can register with their online jobs service. They've missed nothing out in their links section from embassies to travel health.

Discount cards

www.istc.org
INTERNATIONAL STUDENT TRAVEL CONFEDERATION

ORIGIN UK
SPEED ✓✓✓
INFO ✓✓✓✓✓
EASE ✓✓✓

Get your student and youth discount card as well as info on working and studying abroad. Also help with such things as railpasses, phonecards, ISTC registered travel agents worldwide, plus e-mail, voice mail and fax messaging. For a European youth card for discounts within the EU go to the cool **www.euro26.org**

Magazines

www.studentuk.com
STUDENT LIFE

ORIGIN UK
SPEED ✓✓✓
INFO ✓✓✓✓✓
EASE ✓✓✓✓

A good-looking, useful and generally well-written students' magazine featuring news, music and film reviews, going out, chat, even articles on science and politics. There's also some excellent advice on subjects such as gap years, accommodation and finance. It's worth checking out **www.ragmag.co.uk** who continue the tradition of rag week all the time, and is a noticeboard and a source for all things good. **www.anythingstudent.com** is also worth a look, it covers just about everything although it could be more fun.

Teenagers

Here's a small selection of the best sites that are aimed at teenagers. Many of the most hyped sites are just heavily disguised marketing and sales operations, treat these with scepticism and enjoy the best, which are done for the love of it. We've also indicated the sort of age group that the magazines are aimed at. We should add our thanks to all those people who wrote to us suggesting sites for this section.

Teenage magazines

www.4degreez.com
INTERACTIVE COMMUNITY

ORIGIN US	A friendly and entertaining site with reviews, poetry,
SPEED ✓✓✓✓	jokes, polls and links to other related sites. You have
INFO ✓✓✓✓	to become a member to get the best out of it though.
EASE ✓✓✓✓	*15 plus*

www.alloy.com
ALLOY MAGAZINE

ORIGIN UK	On the face of it this is great, it's got loads of
SPEED ✓✓✓	sections on everything from personal advice to
INFO ✓✓✓✓	shopping. But with too many adverts, it all seems
VALUE ✓	to be geared to getting your name for marketing
EASE ✓✓✓	purposes and selling stuff. *13 plus*

www.bbc.co.uk/so
SO

ORIGIN UK	The BBC have done a great job with the colourful
SPEED ✓✓✓	*So* mag, it's got really excellent stuff such as quizzes,
INFO ✓✓✓✓✓	music, problems, interviews, fashion, weird, links
EASE ✓✓✓✓	and a chat section. There are also some brilliant
	competitions, prizes and fun articles too. *10 plus*

www.cheekfreak.com

FOR THE FREAK IN ALL OF US

ORIGIN US
SPEED ✓✓✓✓
INFO ✓✓✓✓
EASE ✓✓✓✓

Best for stories, online diaries and free downloads. It's got chat sections, message boards and a search engine. They deserve a medal for the pranks section, which is brilliant. *13 plus*

www.cyberteens.com

CONNECT TO CYBERTEENS

ORIGIN UK
SPEED ✓✓✓✓
INFO ✓✓✓✓
VALUE ✓✓
EASE ✓✓✓✓

One of the most hyped sites aimed at teenagers, it contains a very good selection of games, news, links and a creativity section where you can send your art and poems. Don't bother with the shop, which was still being re-designed at time of writing, but on previous visits it was expensive, as is the credit card they offer. *13 plus*

www.globalgang.org.uk

WORLD NEWS, GAMES, GOSSIP AND FUN

ORIGIN UK
SPEED ✓✓✓
INFO ✓✓✓✓
EASE ✓✓✓

See what the rest of the world gets up to at Global Gang. You can find out what kids in other countries like to eat, what toys they play with, chat to them or play games. Lastly you get to find out how you can help those kids less fortunate than yourself. *10 plus*

www.kidsonline.co.uk

BLUE JAM

ORIGIN UK
SPEED ✓✓✓
INFO ✓✓✓✓
EASE ✓✓✓✓

Blue Jam is good; it has games, reviews, event listings, links and competitions, but it's not updated all that regularly. There's also a good advice section and a version for younger kids too. *10 plus*

www.thesite.org.uk

THE SITE

ORIGIN UK
SPEED ✓✓✓✓
INFO ✓✓✓✓
EASE ✓✓✓✓

This site offers advice on a range of subjects: careers, relationships, drugs, sex, money, legal issues and so on. Aimed largely at 15 to 24 year olds, it's well laid out and very informative. *15 plus*

www.teentoday.co.uk

FOR TEENAGERS BY TEENAGERS

ORIGIN UK
SPEED ✓✓✓✓
INFO ✓✓✓✓✓
EASE ✓✓✓✓

Get your free e-zine mailed to you daily or just visit the site which has much more; games, chat, news, entertainment, free downloads, ringtones and message boards. It's well designed and genuinely good with not too much advertising. *12 plus*

www.dubit.co.uk

GAMES, ARTICLES – THE LOT

ORIGIN UK
SPEED ✓✓✓
INFO ✓✓✓✓
EASE ✓✓✓✓

Dubit combines 3-D graphics with chat, games, video, music and animations in a fun and interactive way. It's a completely different approach to the normal teen magazine. It needs a little patience but it's worth it in the end. *13 plus*

www.girland.com

GIRL AND...

ORIGIN UK
SPEED ✓✓✓
INFO ✓✓✓✓
EASE ✓✓✓✓

An excellent, really attractive and well put together site aimed at teenage girls, it has chat forums, news and lots of features, but you have to register and pay a small sum to be part of it. Having said that it has won loads of awards and the environment is safe. *11 plus*

http://goosehead.com

COUNTER CULTURE PROGRAMMING

ORIGIN US
SPEED ✓✓✓
INFO ✓✓✓✓✓
EASE ✓✓✓✓

A great teen magazine site with brilliant graphics and lots to do from homework help, chat, horoscopes and all the important things in life like games and web soap – whatever. *13 plus*

www.mirabilis.com

ICQ – I SEEK YOU

ORIGIN UK
SPEED ✓✓✓
INFO ✓✓✓✓
EASE ✓✓

Not so easy for the very young but there's lots here and it's quick. A good site to use combined with a mobile phone, it has lots of features such as chat, games, money advice, music and lurve. *13 plus*

www.terrifichick.com

A FORUM FOR TEENAGE GIRLS

ORIGIN US
SPEED ✓✓✓
INFO ✓✓✓✓✓
EASE ✓✓✓✓

Recommended by Sherry, one of our readers, this excellent site has loads of advice, articles, although at the time of writing the message boards are being worked on and the site hasn't been updated recently. *13 plus*. See also **www.missminx.com** which was being updated when we last visited.

Directories

www.beritsbest.com

SITES FOR CHILDREN

ORIGIN US
SPEED ✓✓✓
INFO ✓✓✓✓✓
EASE ✓✓✓✓

Over 1,000 sites in this directory split into six major categories, fun, things to do, nature, serious stuff (homework), chat and surfing. Each site is rated for speed and content and you can suggest new sites as well. Another similar site to Berits is **www.kids-space.org**, which has some really cute graphics and a better search facility.

www.teensites.org

WEB DIRECTORY FOR TEENS

ORIGIN US	A huge directory of sites covering loads of subjects
SPEED ✓✓✓	of interest to teenagers. It's biased to the USA, but if
INFO ✓✓✓✓✓	you don't mind that, then it should have everything
EASE ✓✓✓✓	you need.

Telecommunications

In this section there's information on ADSL and computer-related communications, where to go to buy mobiles, get the best out of them and even have a little fun with them. For phone numbers see the section entitled 'Finding Someone' on page 136.

ADSL/broadband

Asymmetric Digital Subscriber Line (ADSL) is a technology for transmitting digital information at a high bandwidth on existing phone lines to homes and businesses. It enables you to access the Internet many times faster than with conventional phone lines. Unfortunately, access to broadband is limited and its introduction slower than in other parts of the world.

www.btopenworld.com

BRITISH TELECOM

ORIGIN UK	Here you can establish whether you are in line to get
SPEED ✓✓✓	access to broadband and more or less when. There
INFO ✓✓✓	are details of the various BT packages, other suppli-
EASE ✓✓✓✓	ers and also information for business users too.

www.adsluk.co.uk

ADSL ALL YOU NEED TO KNOW

ORIGIN UK
SPEED ✓✓✓✓
INFO ✓✓✓
VALUE ✓✓
EASE ✓✓✓✓✓

Informative and regularly updated, find out all the latest news and commentary as well as a good explanation of what you get for your money. Also check out www.bigpipes.org.uk which is a chat forum and newsletter with all the latest information on ADSL.

See also:
www.ntlhome.com/broadband – supplies most of the UK.
www.telewest.co.uk – supplies selected parts of the UK.
www.theregister.co.uk – the latest telecom and broadband news.
www.ispreview.co.uk/broadband.shtml – informative pages from the excellent ISP review.

Mobile phones

www.carphonewarehouse.com

CHOOSING THE RIGHT MOBILE

ORIGIN UK
SPEED ✓✓✓✓
INFO ✓✓✓✓
VALUE ✓✓✓✓
EASE ✓✓✓✓

You need to take your time to find the best tariff using their calculator, then take advantage of the numerous offers. Excellent pictures, details of the phones and the information is unbiased. There's an online encyclopaedia devoted to mobile phone terminology, a shop that also sells handheld PCs and delivery is free too. You can download a wide range of new phone ring tones, from classical to the latest pop tunes.

Another good site is www.miahtelecom.co.uk who, apart from good offers, have an easy-to-use tariff calculator. It's also worth checking out www.reviewbooth.com who review all models of phone.

www.mobileedge.co.uk
MOBILE INFORMATION

ORIGIN UK
SPEED ✓✓✓✓
INFO ✓✓✓✓
VALUE ✓✓✓
EASE ✓✓✓✓

A really well-designed site with help on buying the right mobile, it also offers information on health and mobiles, links and contact numbers, pre-pay deals, global networks, ring tones, shop and much more.

www.yourmobile.com
NEW RING TUNES FOR YOUR PHONE

ORIGIN UK
SPEED ✓✓✓
INFO ✓✓✓✓
VALUE ✓✓✓✓
EASE ✓✓✓✓

There are several hundred tunes, icons and logos that you can download on to your mobile using text messaging and most are free. See also www.toneylogo.co.uk and also www.onmymob.com who offer hundreds of free ringtones and logos.

Here's where to find the major phone operators:
www.orange.co.uk
www.vodafone.co.uk (www.vizzavi.co.uk for their WAP service)
www.t-mobile.co.uk
www.virginmobile.com
www.o2.co.uk

www.genie.co.uk
WAP PHONES MADE USEFUL

ORIGIN UK
SPEED ✓✓✓✓
INFO ✓✓✓✓✓
VALUE ✓✓✓✓
EASE ✓✓✓✓

A huge site with loads of information on what you can do if you've got a WAP phone, including how to get gossip, results and news. The site is well laid out, there are competitions, news, offers and you can download ring tones and logos.

Other WAP sites and what they do:

www.2thumbswap.com – large site with lots of WAP information and an especially good downloads section and good explanations too.

www.anywhereyougo.com – excellent for the latest news and developments, good links and information too.

www.wapaw.com – another directory site, with over 2,000 sites listed.

www.wapsight.com – excellent WAP news site.

www.wirelessgames.com – the best place to find games to play on your WAP phone.

www.bluetooth.com

AFTER WAP COMES BLUETOOTH

ORIGIN US	A superb official Microsoft site devoted to Bluetooth
SPEED ✓✓✓✓	technology which is supposed to come into its own
INFO ✓✓✓✓	soon. Whether it does or not is still open to question
EASE ✓✓✓✓	but here's where you can find out about it.

www.chatlist.com/faces.html

TEXT MESSAGING

ORIGIN UK	Confused about your emoticons? %-) Here's a list of
SPEED ✓✓✓✓	several thousand for you to choose from.
INFO ✓✓✓✓	
EASE ✓✓✓	

www.iobox.com

SMS MESSAGING FROM A PC

ORIGIN UK
SPEED ✓✓✓
INFO ✓✓✓✓
EASE ✓✓✓✓

Get tired of typing messages on your mobile, now you can do it from a PC. You get some free credits when you join up, from then on you can purchase them. Prices start at 1 credit for 6p, but it depends on what service you use, sending an icon costs 20 credits, for example. You can also play games, send e-cards, shop and much more, especially if you have a WAP phone. There are also masses of logos and ringtones from which to choose.

www.mediaring.com

PC TO PHONE COMMUNICATION

ORIGIN US
SPEED ✓✓✓
INFO ✓✓✓✓
VALUE ✓✓✓
EASE ✓✓✓✓

Media Ring offer a PC to phone service through their My Voiz technology. This enables users to communicate at a much lower cost than phone to phone, it's especially useful if you use the phone a lot.

www.coverfrenzy.com

DESIGN YOUR OWN PHONE COVER

ORIGIN US
SPEED ✓✓✓
INFO ✓✓✓✓
VALUE ✓✓✓
EASE ✓✓✓✓

You can use one of their images or one of your own to create a unique phone cover, however it costs £18.50. It's available for a wide range of Nokia phones but their range of options is expanding not only to phones but apparently to hairdryers too.

Television

TV channels, listings and your favourite soap operas are all here - some have great sites, others are pretty naff, especially when you consider they're in the entertainment business.

www.itc.org.uk

INDEPENDENT TELEVISION COMMISSION

ORIGIN UK	The ITC issues the licences that allow commercial
SPEED ✓✓✓✓	TV stations to broadcast and ensures fair play on
INFO ✓✓✓✓	advertising, so if you have a complaint about
EASE ✓✓✓✓	commercial TV then go here first.

Channels

www.bbc.co.uk

THE UK'S MOST POPULAR WEB SITE

ORIGIN UK	The BBC site deserves a special feature, it is huge
SPEED ✓✓✓	with over 300 sections and it can be quite daunting.
INFO ✓✓✓✓✓	This review only scrapes the surface. It has sections
VALUE ✓✓✓	covering everything from business to the weather
EASE ✓✓✓✓	and there are also regional sections, a web guide, as

well as tips on how to use the Internet and you can subscribe to a newsletter.

Their shopping site has been suspended, but you can also obtain full radio and TV listings by signing up to their ISP **www.beeb.net**

www.itv.co.uk

ITV NETWORK

ORIGIN UK	ITV has a pretty straightforward site with links to
SPEED ✓✓✓	all the major programs, topics and categories, their
INFO ✓✓✓	related web sites and a 'what's on' guide, plus a few
EASE ✓✓✓✓	extras such as quizzes.

www.citv.co.uk
CHILDREN'S ITV

ORIGIN UK
SPEED ✓✓
INFO ✓✓✓✓
EASE ✓✓✓

A bright and breezy site that features competitions, chat, safe surfing, features on the programs including all the favourite characters and much more. You need to join to get the best out of it though, and because there's so much on the site, it can be a little slow.

www.channel4.co.uk
CHANNEL 4

ORIGIN UK
SPEED ✓✓✓✓
INFO ✓✓✓✓
EASE ✓✓✓

A cool design with details of programmes and links to specific web pages on the best-known ones. There are also links to other initiatives such as Filmfour and the 4learning programme.

www.channel5.co.uk
CHANNEL 5

ORIGIN UK
SPEED ✓✓✓
INFO ✓✓✓✓
EASE ✓✓✓✓

Similar to Channel 4 except it's better designed and has more in the way of games, shopping and competitions. It's also a bit clearer and easier to find your way around.

www.sky.com
SKY TV

ORIGIN UK
SPEED ✓✓✓
INFO ✓✓✓✓✓
EASE ✓✓✓✓

A front page that sells the dish and its benefits then links to their sport, news and 'what's on' sites.

www.nicktv.co.uk
NICKELODEON

ORIGIN UK
SPEED ✓✓✓
INFO ✓✓✓✓
EASE ✓✓✓✓

Bright doesn't do this site justice, you need sunglasses! It's got info on all the top programmes plus games and quizzes.

www.sausagenet.co.uk

CULT AND CLASSIC TV

ORIGIN UK
SPEED ✓✓✓✓
INFO ✓✓✓✓
VALUE ✓✓✓
EASE ✓✓✓✓

An outstanding nostalgia site devoted to popular children's TV programs from the last 40 years. You can download theme tunes or buy related merchandise via the excellent links directory.

TV review and listings sites

www.digiguide.co.uk

THE DOWNLOADABLE GUIDE

ORIGIN UK
SPEED ✓✓✓
INFO ✓✓✓✓✓
VALUE ✓✓✓
EASE ✓✓✓✓✓

If you have Sky digital you'll be familiar with this guide, it follows a similar format, although you can customise it. Simply download the program and you get 14 days forward programming for up to 200 channels, masses of links and background information. You then need to access the site for updates. It costs £6.99 per year.

www.radiotimes.beeb.com

THE RADIO TIMES

ORIGIN UK
SPEED ✓✓✓
INFO ✓✓✓✓✓
EASE ✓✓✓✓

Excellent listings e-zine with a good search facility for looking up programme details, plus competitions, links and a cinema guide. There are also sections on the best-loved TV genres – children's, sci-fi, soaps and so on. See also www.teletext.co.uk/tvplus which is a far cry from the listings you get via your television.

Soaps

www.brookside.com

THE OFFICIAL BROOKSIDE WEB SITE

ORIGIN UK
SPEED ✓✓
INFO ✓✓✓✓
VALUE ✓✓✓
EASE ✓✓✓✓

You'll get the latest information, gossip or storyline with loads of background info on the cast. There are competitions and you can shop for Brookie merchandise. With the new animated version you can download clips and take a virtual tour, but be patient and the sound effects are really annoying. There are also links to related programs.

www.corrie.net

CORONATION STREET BY ITS FANS

ORIGIN UK
SPEED ✓✓✓✓
INFO ✓✓✓✓✓
EASE ✓✓✓✓

Corrie was formed in 1999 from several fan's sites and has no connection with Granada, the site is written by volunteer fans who have contributed articles, updates and biographies. There are five key sections. One for Corrie newbies (are there any?) with a history of the Street; a catch up with the story section; what's up and coming; profiles on the key characters; a chat section where you can gossip about the goings on. For another fan's eye view try out www.csvu.net

www.coronationstreet.co.uk

THE OFFICIAL CORONATION STREET

ORIGIN UK
SPEED ✓✓✓
INFO ✓✓✓✓
VALUE ✓✓
EASE ✓✓✓✓

This is the official site and it's split into several sections including 'breaking news', chat, storylines, a shop plus topical links. There's also a good archives section and games and quizzes to play.

www.carlton.com/crossroads

THE OFFICIAL CROSSROADS SITE

ORIGIN UK
SPEED ✓✓✓
INFO ✓✓✓✓
EASE ✓✓✓✓

Its back and this is a good site with all the latest gossip and intrigue for true Crossroads fans new and old.

www.dawsons-creek.com

DAWSONS CREEK

ORIGIN UK
SPEED ✓✓✓
INFO ✓✓✓✓✓
EASE ✓✓✓✓

Everything is here, storylines, interviews, chat and feedback all packaged on a good looking web site.

www.emmerdale.co.uk

THE OFFICIAL EMMERDALE SITE

ORIGIN UK
SPEED ✓✓✓✓
INFO ✓✓✓✓
EASE ✓✓✓✓

Updated to a more modern style, you can get the latest gossip, play games, read interviews with the stars or just chat.

www.emmerdale.clara.net

THE UNOFFICIAL EMMERDALE SITE

ORIGIN UK
SPEED ✓✓✓✓
INFO ✓✓✓✓
EASE ✓✓✓✓

A basic but effective site run by a true fan with a much less fussy approach than the official site, it is divided up into sections in which you can see things such as future plotlines – spoilers. There are links to other Emmerdale fan sites, a weekly poll, a message board and you can send an e-card.

www.bbc.co.uk/eastenders

THE OFFICIAL EASTENDERS PAGE

ORIGIN UK
SPEED ✓✓✓
INFO ✓✓✓✓✓
EASE ✓✓✓✓✓

A page from the massive BBC site, it's split into several sections: catch up on the latest stories and hints on future storylines; play games and competitions; get pictures of the stars; vote in their latest poll; reminisce and visit the 'classic clips' section; take a virtual tour and view Albert Square with the Walford Cam.

www.familyaffairs.co.uk

FAMILY AFFAIRS UNOFFICIAL

ORIGIN UK
SPEED ✓✓✓
INFO ✓✓✓✓✓
EASE ✓✓✓✓

A massive site dedicated to the goings on in Charnham, you can download whole episodes if you like, otherwise there's the usual collection of interviews, stories and pictures.

www.summerbay.co.uk

STREWTH, IT'S A HOME AND AWAY SITE

ORIGIN UK
SPEED ✓✓✓
INFO ✓✓✓✓✓
EASE ✓✓✓

As you'd expect, a bright and breezy site, in which you can learn all the facts about the characters that inhabit Summer Bay. There is also loads in the way of things to do but due to time pressure it's not being updated, so see also **www.homeandaway.org** and **http://homeandaway.i7.com.au** which is the official site.

www.hollyoaks.com

THE OFFICIAL HOLLYOAKS WEB SITE

ORIGIN UK
SPEED ✓✓✓
INFO ✓✓✓✓✓
EASE ✓✓✓✓✓

A very cool site with lots on it, you can subscribe to the fortnightly newsletter; peek behind the scenes; catch up on the latest news; chat with fellow fans. There's also the expected photos and downloads to be had.

www.baxendale.u-net.com/ramsayst

NEIGHBOURS WORLD-WIDE FANPAGES

ORIGIN UK
SPEED ✓✓✓
INFO ✓✓✓✓✓
EASE ✓✓✓✓

You can also get them at **www.ramsay-street.co.uk** This is a labour of love by the fans of Neighbours, it has everything you need: storylines past, present and future; info on all the characters; clips from some episodes; complete discographies of the singing stars; and access to all the related web sites through the links page. Unfortunately, you can't buy Neighbours merchandise from the site.

www.soapweb.co.uk
THE LATEST SOAP NEWS

ORIGIN UK
SPEED ✓✓✓✓
INFO ✓✓✓✓✓
EASE ✓✓✓✓

Can't be bothered with visiting each site separately? Then try Soap Web. Here you can keep up-to-date on all the soaps, even the Australian and American ones.

www.bbc.co.uk/radio4/archers/
THE ARCHERS

ORIGIN UK
SPEED ✓✓✓✓
INFO ✓✓✓✓✓
EASE ✓✓✓✓

OK so it's not strictly TV but we couldn't think were else this should go. It's a great site with all the information and background you'd wish for including the ability to listen to the last episode and catch up on previous ones.

Theatre

Here's a great selection of sites that will appeal to theatre goers everywhere.

www.whatsonstage.com
HOME OF BRITISH THEATRE

ORIGIN UK
SPEED ✓✓✓✓
INFO ✓✓✓✓✓
VALUE ✓✓✓
EASE ✓✓✓✓

A really strong site with masses of news and reviews to browse through plus a very good search facility and booking service (through a third party), a real theatre buff's delight.

www.aloud.com
ONLINE TICKET SEARCH

ORIGIN UK
SPEED ✓✓✓✓
INFO ✓✓✓✓
VALUE ✓✓✓
EASE ✓✓✓✓

You can search by venue, location or by artist, it's fast and pretty comprehensive and there's a hot events section – it mainly covers music and festivals, nowadays though it's good for comedy. The review section is good and you can buy tickets.

www.theatrenet.com

THE ENTERTAINMENT CENTRE

ORIGIN UK
SPEED ✓✓✓
INFO ✓✓✓✓✓
VALUE ✓✓✓
EASE ✓✓✓

Get the latest news, catch the new shows and, if you join the club, there are discounts on tickets for theatre, concerts, sporting events and holidays. You can also search their archives for information on past productions and learn how to become a theatre angel.

www.uktw.co.uk

UK THEATRE WEB

ORIGIN UK
SPEED ✓✓✓✓
INFO ✓✓✓✓
VALUE ✓✓✓
EASE ✓✓✓✓

A cheerful site offering all the usual information on theatre plus amateur dramatics, jobs, chat, competitions and just gossip.

www.rsc.org.uk

THE ROYAL SHAKESPEARE COMPANY

ORIGIN UK
SPEED ✓✓✓
INFO ✓✓✓✓
EASE ✓✓✓

Get all the news as well as information on performances and tours. You can book tickets online although it's via a third party site.

www.reallyuseful.com

ANDREW LLOYD WEBBER

ORIGIN UK
SPEED ✓✓✓
INFO ✓✓✓✓✓
EASE ✓✓✓✓

At this attractive, hi-tech site you can watch video and listen to top audio clips, download screen savers and wallpaper, take part in competitions and chat. There's also a good kids' section plus details on the shows.

www.nt-online.org

THE NATIONAL

ORIGIN UK
SPEED ✓✓✓✓
INFO ✓✓✓✓✓
EASE ✓✓✓✓

Excellent for details of their shows and forthcoming plays with tour information added. You can't buy tickets online, but you can e-mail or fax for them.

www.officiallondontheatre.co.uk

SOCIETY OF LONDON THEATRES

ORIGIN UK	The latest news, a show finder service and hot tick-
SPEED ✓✓✓✓	ets are just a few of the services available at this
INFO ✓✓✓✓✓	great site. You can also get a theatreland map, half
VALUE ✓✓✓	price tickets and they'll even fax you a seating plan.
EASE ✓✓✓✓	See also www.thisislondon.co.uk who have a good
	theatre section.

To book online try the following sites:
www.ticketmaster.co.uk
www.londontheatretickets.com
www.uktickets.co.uk
www.lastminute.com

Travel and Holidays

Travel is the biggest growth area on the Internet, from holidays to insurance to local guides. If you're buying, then it definitely pays to shop around and try several sites, but be careful, it's amazing how fast the best deals are being snapped up. You may find that you still spend time on the phone, but the sites are constantly improving.

Starting out

www.abtanet.com

ABTA

ORIGIN UK	Make sure that the travel agent you choose is a
SPEED ✓✓✓✓	member of the Association of British Travel Agents
INFO ✓✓✓✓	as then you're covered if they go bust halfway
EASE ✓✓✓✓	

through your holiday. All members are listed and there's a great search facility with links for you to start the ball rolling. See also the Air Travellers Licensing home page **www.atol.org.uk** which is part of the Civil Aviation site.

www.brochurebank.co.uk

BROCHURES DELIVERED TO YOUR HOME

ORIGIN UK
SPEED ✓✓✓✓✓
INFO ✓✓✓✓
EASE ✓✓✓✓✓

Holiday brochures from over 150 companies can be selected then delivered to your home, free of charge. The selection process is easy and the site is fast. Delivery is by second class post.

Travel information and tips

www.fco.gov.uk/travel

ADVICE FROM THE FOREIGN OFFICE

ORIGIN UK
SPEED ✓✓✓✓
INFO ✓✓✓✓✓
EASE ✓✓✓

Before you go, get general advice, safety or visa information. Just select a country and you get a run-down of all the issues that are likely to affect you when you go there, from terrorism to health.

For more travel safety information go to:
www.cdc.gov/travel – official American site giving sensible health information worldwide.
www.tripprep.com – country-by-country risk assessment covering health, safety and politics; it can be a little out of date so check with the foreign office as well.
www.etravel.org – masses of tips to browse through from book reviews to flying advice and weather updates.

> **www.tips4trips.com** – all the tips come from well-meaning travellers and are categorised under sections such as pre-planning, what and how to pack, travelling for the disabled, for women, for men or with children.
>
> **www.1000traveltips.org** – tips from the very well travelled Koen De Boeck and friends.

www.travel-news.org

TRAVEL NEWS ORGANISATION

ORIGIN UK
SPEED ✓✓✓
INFO ✓✓✓✓
EASE ✓✓✓

A good, travel magazine aimed at British travellers packed with the latest news and information, as well as destination reports and event listings. There are also links to airlines, special offers and specialist holidays.

www.guardian.co.uk/travel

FROM THE GUARDIAN NEWSPAPER

ORIGIN UK
SPEED ✓✓✓✓
INFO ✓✓✓✓✓
EASE ✓✓✓✓

A good reflection of the excellent *Guardian's* weekly travel section with guides, information and inspiration throughout, there's also the latest news and links to sites with offers plus extra features such as audio guides and articles on parts of the UK.

www.vtourist.com

THE VIRTUAL TOURIST

ORIGIN UK
SPEED ✓✓✓
INFO ✓✓✓✓
EASE ✓✓✓

Explore destinations in a unique and fun way. Travellers describe their experiences, share photos, make recommendations and give tips so others benefit from their experience. See also **www.travel-library.com** which is less entertaining but combines recommendation with hard facts very well.

www.budgettravel.com

BUDGET TRAVEL

ORIGIN UK
SPEED ✓✓✓✓
INFO ✓✓✓✓
EASE ✓✓✓

Masses of links and information for the budget traveller plus advice on how to travel on the cheap. It can be difficult to navigate but the information is very good.

Travel services and information

www.xe.net/currency

ONLINE CURRENCY CONVERTER

ORIGIN US
SPEED ✓✓✓✓✓
INFO ✓✓✓✓✓
EASE ✓✓✓✓✓

The Universal Currency Converter could not be easier to use, just select the currency you have, then the one you want to convert it to, press the button and you have your answer in seconds. See also www.oanda.com and www.x-rates.com/calculator.html

www.taxfree.se

GLOBAL REFUND

ORIGIN UK
SPEED ✓✓
INFO ✓✓✓✓✓
EASE ✓✓✓

Find out how to make the most out of tax-free shopping at this very useful web site.

www.webofculture.com/worldsmart/gestures.html

GESTURES OF THE WORLD

ORIGIN UK
SPEED ✓✓✓
INFO ✓✓✓✓
EASE ✓✓✓✓

Country-by-country, what gestures mean, what not to do and what's best to do, all in a concise format. Be warned, that you have to go through a really laborious registration process to get the information.

www.whatsonwhen.com

WORLD-WIDE EVENTS GUIDE

ORIGIN UK
SPEED ✓✓
INFO ✓✓✓✓
EASE ✓✓✓✓

An easy-to-use site with information on every type of event you can think of from major festivals to village fêtes.

www.ukpa.gov.uk

UK PASSPORTS

ORIGIN UK
SPEED ✓✓✓
INFO ✓✓✓✓
EASE ✓✓✓✓

Pre-apply for your passport online and get tips on how to get the best passport photo amongst other very useful information.

www.hmce.gov.uk

HM CUSTOMS AND EXCISE

ORIGIN UK
SPEED ✓✓✓✓
INFO ✓✓✓✓
EASE ✓✓✓✓

All you need to know about visiting the UK, exporting and importing and the regulations surrounding what you can bring in.

Travel insurance

www.travelinsuranceclub.co.uk

AWARD WINNING TRAVEL INSURANCE CLUB

ORIGIN UK
SPEED ✓✓✓✓
INFO ✓✓✓✓
VALUE ✓✓✓✓
EASE ✓✓✓

Unfortunately there isn't one site for collating travel insurance yet, it's a question of shopping around. These sites make a good starting point offering a range of policies for backpackers, family and business travel.

All these companies offer flexibility and good value:
www.columbusdirect.co.uk – good information, nice, but fiddly web site and competitive prices.
www.costout.co.uk – did well in a recent Which? survey.
www.direct-travel.co.uk – nice design and some good offers too, online quotes.

www.jameshampden.co.uk – wide range of policies, straightforward and hassle free.

www.underthesun.co.uk – good for annual and six monthly policies.

www.worldwideinsure.com – good selection of policies, instant online cover.

Travel shops

www.expedia.co.uk

THE COMPLETE SERVICE

ORIGIN US/UK
SPEED ✓✓✓✓
INFO ✓✓✓✓✓
VALUE ✓✓✓
EASE ✓✓✓✓

This is the UK arm of Microsoft's very successful online travel agency. It offers a huge array of holidays, flights and associated services, for personal or business use, nearly all bookable online. Its easy and quicker than most, and there are some excellent offers too. Not the trendiest but it's a good first stop. As with all the big operators, you have to register. They've also got sections on travel insurance, mapping, guides, ferries and hotels.

www.lastminute.com

DO SOMETHING LAST MINUTE

ORIGIN UK
SPEED ✓✓✓
INFO ✓✓✓✓
VALUE ✓✓✓✓
EASE ✓✓✓✓

Last Minute has an excellent reputation not just as a travel agent, but as a good shopping site too. For travellers there are comprehensive sections on hotels, holidays and flights, all with really good prices. There is also a superb London restaurant guide and a general entertainment section. Mostly, you can book online, but a hotline is available.

www.thomascook.com

THE WIDEST RANGE OF PACKAGE HOLIDAYS

ORIGIN UK
SPEED ✓✓✓✓
INFO ✓✓✓✓
VALUE ✓✓✓✓
EASE ✓✓✓✓

This site is easy to use and well laid out and, with over 2 million package holidays to chose from, you should be able to find something to your liking. You can also browse the online guide for ideas or search for cheap flights or holiday deals. Again you have to call the hotline to book.

www.e-bookers.com

FLIGHTBOOKERS

ORIGIN UK
SPEED ✓✓✓✓
INFO ✓✓✓✓✓
VALUE ✓✓✓✓
EASE ✓✓✓✓

Acclaimed travel agents specialising in getting good flight deals, but also good for holidays, special offers and insurance.

www.unmissable.com

UNMISSABLE HOLIDAYS

ORIGIN UK
SPEED ✓✓✓✓
INFO ✓✓✓✓
VALUE ✓✓✓
EASE ✓✓✓✓

An unusual holiday store dedicated to the sale of extraordinary, exclusive, exceptional and exhilarating experiences, and it succeeds – just visit for inspiration. It covers events as well, but whatever the holiday or trip you're looking for it's a great place to go if you want something different.

www.travel.world.co.uk

FOR ALL YOUR TRAVEL REQUIREMENTS

ORIGIN UK
SPEED ✓✓✓
INFO ✓✓✓✓✓
EASE ✓✓✓

A massive, comprehensive site, it basically includes most available travel brochures with links to the relevant travel agent. It concentrates on Europe, so there are very few American sites, but provides links to hotels, specialist holidays, cruises, self-catering and airlines. For a more global view go to www.globalpassage.com who offer 15,000 web sites to browse, and www.its.net which has turned itself into a web design company, fortunately they kept the directory which has 40 categories.

www.holidayauctions.net

BID FOR YOUR HOLIDAY

ORIGIN UK	Some amazing bargains are available from these
SPEED ✓✓✓	auction sites – you bid in the same way a normal
INFO ✓✓✓✓	online auction works. It's fully bonded and if you
VALUE ✓✓✓✓	hit a problem call their hotline. They also sell
EASE ✓✓✓✓	conventional holidays.

www.uk.mytravel.com

SEARCH FOR THE RIGHT DEAL

ORIGIN UK	This site has got an excellent search engine that
SPEED ✓✓✓	enables you to find a bargain or just the right holi-
INFO ✓✓✓✓	day, there are also good offers and the late escapes
VALUE ✓✓✓✓	holiday auction site.
EASE ✓✓✓✓	

www.priceline.co.uk

LET SOMEONE ELSE DO THE WORK

ORIGIN UK	You could leave it to someone else to do the travel
SPEED ✓✓✓	searching for you, here you provide details of the
INFO ✓✓✓✓	trip you want and how much you're willing to pay,
VALUE ✓✓✓✓	then they try to find a deal that will match your
EASE ✓✓✓✓	requirements. If you're flexible about timing then

there are some great offers. They cover flights, hotels and car hire. Another site to try is www.myownprice.com both this site and Priceline want your credit card details before you agree to any transaction so you may feel more comfortable using a more traditional route.

Here's a selection of well-proven and independent online travel agents – the choice is yours.

www.aito.co.uk – offers and information from the Association of Independent Tour Operators, excellent for the unusual.

www.balesworldwide.com – for something special, tailor-made holidays to the exotic parts of the world; hi-tech site is excellent but no online booking.

www.bargainholidays.com – probably the best for quick breaks, excellent for late availability offers.

www.beachtowel.co.uk – good all-round site from an independent travel agent who is ABTA and ATOL covered. 0800 013 1300.

www.escaperoutes.com – the travel section of *Red Magazine*, basically following the articles as they appear in the mag, but worth a look.

www.divechannel.co.uk – excellent site specialising in diving holidays and travel

www.firstchoice.co.uk – bargains from First Choice holidays see also the sister site found at **www.travelchoice.co.uk** – discounts for online booking.

www.firstresort.com – a good all-rounder with some good deals and a price promise, owned by Thomsons – 0870 055 6300.

www.golfbreaks.com – a travel agent specialising in holidays for golfing nuts.

www.gvillage.co.uk – specialising in independent travellers and students with some great deals and adventure holidays to the world's most interesting places, excellent round the world trip planner.

www.holidayextras.co.uk – good for parking, airport hotels, airport lounges and getting to airports by public transport.

www.holiday.co.uk – good deals on package holidays from a very well designed site.

www.lunn-poly.co.uk – updating the site at time of writing.

www.opodo.co.uk – slick newcomer from some of the major airlines, worth checking out for flight offers.

www.packageholidays.co.uk – late bargain holidays and flights from over 130 tour operators including Thomson, Sunworld, Airtours and specialist agents.

www.teletext.co.uk/holidays – much better than browsing the TV, you can now get all those offers on one easy-to-use site. There is also lots of useful travel information to help you on your way.

www.travelagents.co.uk – another all-rounder, nothing special but competent.

www.travelcareonline.com – loads of deals and honest information from the UK's largest independent.

www.travelfinder.co.uk – lots of options and great bargains at this simple-to-use site.

www.travelocity.com – one of the oldest online travel agents; it's similar to Expedia and there's a reward scheme too. The trip expert facility is a fun planning tool.

www.wtd.com – good comprehensive site but you have to register before using it, so why bother when you can use all these other sites?

www.webweekends.co.uk – specialists in weekend breaks both in the UK and abroad.

Airline and flight sites

www.cheapflights.co.uk

NOTHING BUT CHEAP FLIGHTS

ORIGIN UK
SPEED ✓✓✓✓
INFO ✓✓✓✓✓
VALUE ✓✓✓✓✓
EASE ✓✓✓

You don't need to register here to explore the great offers available from this site; you still need to phone some of the travel agents or airlines listed to get your deal though and some of the prices quoted seem magically to disappear once you've clicked on the link. Having said that, there are obviously some great deals to be had.

www.netflights.com

THE AIRLINE NETWORK

ORIGIN UK
SPEED ✓✓✓
INFO ✓✓✓✓
VALUE ✓✓✓✓
EASE ✓✓✓

Discount deals on over 100 airlines worldwide make The Airline Network worth checking out for their flight offers page alone. It's good for flights from regional airports. They also do all the traditional travel agent things and there are some good holiday bargains too.

www.deckchair.com

RELAX WITH DECKCHAIR

ORIGIN UK
SPEED ✓✓✓
INFO ✓✓✓✓✓
VALUE ✓✓✓✓
EASE ✓✓✓

A much improved site where you can get some good flight bargains as well as plan the rest of your holiday.

For more cheap flight deals try these sites:
www.bargainflights.com - good search facility and plenty of offers, but you need to be patient.
www.easyjet.co.uk - great for a limited number of destinations, particularly good for UK flights.
www.gofly.com - limited to selected airports but some excellent offers for Western Europe.

www.ryanair.com – very good for Ireland, northern
Europe, Italy and France. Clear and easy-to-use
web site, massive discounts.

www.buzzaway.com – clear and simple to use for
low cost flying in France, Germany and Spain.

www.travelselect.com – good flight selection and
lots of different options available at this very
flexible site.

Airport and airline information

www.worldairportguide.com

WHAT ARE THE WORLD'S AIRPORTS REALLY LIKE?

ORIGIN GERMANY
SPEED ✓✓
INFO ✓✓✓✓
EASE ✓✓✓✓

It seems that no matter how out of the way, this
guide has details on every airport – how to get there,
where to park, facilities, key phone numbers and a
map. There are also guides on cities, resorts and
even world weather.

www.baa.co.uk

BRITISH AIRPORT AUTHORITY

ORIGIN UK
SPEED ✓✓✓
INFO ✓✓✓✓
VALUE ✓✓✓✓
EASE ✓✓✓✓

Details on all the major UK airports that are run by
the BAA, you get all the essential information plus
flight data, weather and shopping information.

www.airlinequality.com

RANKING THE AIRLINES

ORIGIN UK
SPEED ✓✓✓✓
INFO ✓✓✓✓
EASE ✓✓✓✓

An independent ranking of all the world's airlines
and their services, see who's the best and the worst
and why. Each airline is rated using a number of
stars (up to 5) on criteria such as seat quality, catering and staff.

The key airlines:
www.aerlingus.ie – good easy to use site.
www.airfrance.co.uk – plenty of offers.
www.airindia.com – good offers and travel
information and destination guide.
www.britishairways.co.uk – easy to use, efficient site.
www.emirates.com – no frills design and flight
booking facilities.
www.flybmi.com – British Midland, good offers for
European destinations.
www.cathaypacific.com – comprehensive flight
service and guide.
www.virgin-atlantic.com – good online booking
facility with some offers.
www.klm.com – good design with lots of offers.
www.lufthansa.co.uk – masses of information and
express booking.
www.quantas.com – straightforward booking facility.
www.ual.com – United Airlines offers a good all
round service for this site.

Hotels and places to stay

www.hotelguide.com
COMPREHENSIVE

ORIGIN UK	With services available in eight languages and
SPEED ✓✓✓✓	specialist sections such as golfing breaks, this site
INFO ✓✓✓✓✓	ranks among the best for finding the right hotel. It
VALUE ✓✓✓✓	lists around 65,000 at time of writing.
EASE ✓✓✓✓	

www.from-a-z.com
A–Z OF HOTELS

ORIGIN UK	A well-designed British site with over 15,000 hotels
SPEED ✓✓✓✓	to choose from in the UK, Eire and France and a
INFO ✓✓✓✓	further 40,000 worldwide, it's quick and easy to use
VALUE ✓✓✓	and there's online booking available plus plenty of
EASE ✓✓✓	special discounts.

Other good hotel directory and booking sites:

www.all-hotels.co.uk – another directory of 60,000 hotels with lots of options, American bias.

www.best-inn.co.uk – 60,000 hotels listed but very good for London and links to specialist accommodation.

www.holidayleaders.com – if you need a villa or want self catering.

www.jamesvillas.co.uk – over 500 villas in the Med.

www.laterooms.co.uk – easy to use directory featuring unsold hotel rooms at great prices.

www.openworld.co.uk – a collection of links to hotel sites, just use the interactive world map.

www.placestostay.com – another with an interactive map, you drill down until you find the place you want to stay, then you get a list of hotels, a description, price and online reservation service.

Travel guides

www.mytravelguide.com

ONLINE TRAVEL GUIDES

ORIGIN US	A general American travel site that offers a good
SPEED ✓✓✓	overview of most countries, with points of interest, a
INFO ✓✓✓✓✓	currency converter, very good interactive mapping
EASE ✓✓✓	and live web cams too. You need to become a
	member to get the best out of it though.

www.lonelyplanet.com

LONELY PLANET GUIDES

ORIGIN UK	A superb travel site, aimed at the independent trav-
SPEED ✓✓✓✓✓	eller, but with great information for everyone. Get a
INFO ✓✓✓✓✓	review on most world destinations or pick a theme
VALUE ✓✓✓✓	and go with that; leave a message on the thorn tree;
EASE ✓✓✓✓✓	

find out the latest news by country; get health reports; read about the travel experiences of others - what's the real story? Maybe the best service is the eKno system which is a combined phone, e-mail and answer machine which offers a great way to stay in touch when you're in the back of beyond.

http://travel.roughguides.com
ROUGH GUIDES

ORIGIN UK	Lively reviews on a huge number of places - some
SPEED ✓✓✓✓	14,000; general travel information, share your travel
INFO ✓✓✓✓✓	thoughts with other travellers, or buy a guide.
VALUE ✓✓✓	Excellent for links and you can get some good deals
EASE ✓✓✓✓	via the site.

www.fodors.com
FODOR'S GUIDES

ORIGIN US	These guides give an American perspective, but
SPEED ✓✓✓✓	there is a huge amount of information on each
INFO ✓✓✓✓✓	destination. The site is well laid out and easy to use.
EASE ✓✓✓	

http://kasbah.com
WORLD'S LARGEST TRAVEL GUIDE

ORIGIN UK	Clear information, stacks of links and a good search
SPEED ✓✓✓✓	engine should mean that you will find the low down
INFO ✓✓✓✓	on most destinations. The highlights on each desti-
EASE ✓✓✓✓	nation are useful and the 'Global Travel Toolbox'

provides info, telecommunications, maps, currency and more. Unfortunately, some of the site's links were not working when we visited.

www.packback.com

PACKBACK TRAVEL GUIDE

ORIGIN UK — A good looking and useful site with an independent
SPEED ✓✓✓ — travel guide, a growing membership and a reputa-
INFO ✓✓✓✓ — tion for quality reviews. It includes a discussion
VALUE ✓✓✓ — forum, travel tools and flight booking.
EASE ✓✓✓✓

www.gorp.com

FOR THE GREAT OUTDOORS

ORIGIN US — A great title, Gorp is dedicated to adventure, whether
SPEED ✓✓✓ — it be hiking, mountaineering, fishing, snow sports or
INFO ✓✓✓✓✓ — riding the rapids. It has an American bias, but is full
EASE ✓✓✓ — of relevant good advice, links and information.

www.timeout.com

TIME OUT GUIDE

ORIGIN UK — A slick site with destination guides covering many
SPEED ✓✓✓✓ — European cites and some further afield such as New
INFO ✓✓✓✓ — York and Sydney. Not surprisingly, it's outstanding
EASE ✓✓✓✓ — for London and you can also book tickets and buy
books via other retailers.

www.bradmans.com

BRADMAN'S FOR BUSINESS TRAVELLERS

ORIGIN US — A really excellent city guide with none of your fancy
SPEED ✓✓✓✓ — graphics, just a straightforward listing of countries
INFO ✓✓✓✓✓ — and sensible information on each one, includes tips
EASE ✓✓✓✓ — on orienting yourself in the city and restaurant
reviews.

Other global guides worth checking out are:
www.worldinformation.com - not specifically a travel
   guide but there is a mountain of information on the
   world's countries, their culture and advice about
   how to deal with issues like corruption.

www.officialtravelinfo.com - a directory covering
the world's official tourism sites.

http//:about.com/travel – a comprehensive travel
directory from About.com

Online maps and route finders

www.mappy.co.uk

START HERE

ORIGIN UK
SPEED ✓✓✓
INFO ✓✓✓✓✓
EASE ✓✓✓✓

Mappy has a great-looking site which is easy-to-use
and has lots of added features such as a personal
mapping service where you can store the maps
you use most. The route finder is OK, doesn't use
postcodes but business users can fill in their mileage
allowance and Mappy will calculate how much you
should claim.

www.mapblast.com

IT'S A BLAST!

ORIGIN US
SPEED ✓✓✓
INFO ✓✓✓✓✓
EASE ✓✓✓✓

Get detailed maps and information on virtually
anywhere. It has a superb, probably the best, route
finder.

www.multimap.com

GREAT BRITAIN

ORIGIN UK
SPEED ✓✓✓
INFO ✓✓✓✓✓
EASE ✓✓✓✓✓

Outstanding design, easy to use, excellent for the UK,
you can search using postcodes, London street names,
place names or Ordnance Survey grid references.

See also:

www.easymap.co.uk – superb interactive map of the
UK, easy to use and up-to-date but prone to some
eccentric route taking.

http://maps.expedia.co.uk – limited to the US, France, Germany and the UK for detailed maps – modest route finder.

www.mapquest.com – find out the best way to get from A to B in Europe or America, not always as detailed as you'd like, but easy to use and you can customise your map or route plan.

www.mapsonus.com – it's notoriously difficult to find your way around America, but using the route planner you should minimise your risk of getting lost.

www.viamichelin.com – a good all-round travel site with an improved route finder service which is OK.

www.ordsvy.gov.uk – a good site with mapping for sale but the interactive mapping was suspended at time of writing.

www.stanfords.co.uk – travel book and map specialists.

www.theaa.co.uk

AUTOMOBILE ASSOCIATION

ORIGIN UK
SPEED ✓✓✓✓
INFO ✓✓✓✓✓
EASE ✓✓✓✓

A superb site that is divided into four key sections: breakdown cover, route planning and traffic information, hotel guide and booking, in addition, help with buying a car. There is also information on insurance and other financial help.

www.rac.co.uk

GET AHEAD WITH THE RAC

ORIGIN UK
SPEED ✓✓✓
INFO ✓✓✓✓✓
EASE ✓✓✓✓

Great for UK traffic reports and has a very reliable route planner, which seems to be very busy and slow at peak times. There's also a good section on finding the right place to stay, and lots of help if you want to buy a car.

Destinations

Here's an alphabetical list of countries and regions to help you research your chosen destination and plan your holiday.

www.antor.com

ASSOCIATION OF NATIONAL TOURIST OFFICES

ORIGIN UK	A useful starting point for information about the 90
SPEED ✓✓✓✓	or so countries that are members of the association.
INFO ✓✓✓✓	It also has very good links to key tourism sites. See
EASE ✓✓✓✓	also www.officialtravelinfo.com

www.embassyworld.com

EMBASSIES AROUND THE GLOBE

ORIGIN US	Pick two countries one for 'whose embassy', one for
SPEED ✓✓✓✓	'in what location', press go and up pops the details
INFO ✓✓✓✓	on the embassy with contact and essential informa-
EASE ✓✓✓✓✓	tion.

A

www.africaonline.com

AFRICA

ORIGIN S AFRICA	Exhaustive site covering news, information and
SPEED ✓✓✓✓✓	travel in Africa, with very good features and articles.
INFO ✓✓✓✓✓	
EASE ✓✓✓✓	

See also:
www.africaguide.com – detailed country-by-country guides, discussion forums, shopping, culture and a travelogue feature make this site a good first stop.
www.backpackafrica.com – excellent site for back-packers with over 400 links and advice on where to go and what to see.

www.ecoafrica.com – tailor-made safaris with the emphasis on eco-tourism.

http://i-cias.com – excellent information site covering North Africa.

www.onsafari.com – good advice on what sort of safari is right for you.

www.phakawe.demon.co.uk – safaris in Botswana and Namibia.

www.travelinafrica.co.za – budget travel in Southern Africa.

www.vintageafrica.com – awesome safaris and destinations from this specialist travel agent, who will tailor-make holidays if requested.

www.wildnetafrica.net – an excellent travel and information portal for safaris to south and southeast Africa.

www.arab.net

RESOURCE FOR THE ARAB WORLD

ORIGIN **SAUDI ARABIA**	A wide ranging site covering North Africa and the Middle East with excellent country guides. See also http://I-cias.com
SPEED ✓✓✓✓	
INFO ✓✓✓✓	
EASE ✓✓✓✓	

www.turisme.ad

ANDORRA

ORIGIN ANDORRA	A nice little site extolling the many virtues of this tiny country.
SPEED ✓✓✓✓	
INFO ✓✓✓✓	
EASE ✓✓✓✓	

www.argentour.com

ARGENTINA

ORIGIN **ARGENTINA**	Outstanding travel site with video clips, regional information, history and slide shows of the major cities, even a section on how to tango.
SPEED ✓✓✓✓	
INFO ✓✓✓✓	
EASE ✓✓✓✓	

www.asiatour.com

ASIA

ORIGIN PHILIPPINES	Good travel information on all Asian countries. See also www.accomasia.com which concentrates mainly on the Far East.
SPEED ✓✓✓	
INFO ✓✓✓✓	
EASE ✓✓✓✓	

www.austria-tourism.at

AUSTRIA

ORIGIN AUSTRIA	An excellent site covering all you need to know about the country, with information on skiing and summer holidays too.
SPEED ✓✓✓	
INFO ✓✓✓✓	
EASE ✓✓✓✓	

www.australia.com

DISCOVER AUSTRALIA

ORIGIN AUSTRALIA	The Australian Tourist Commission offer a good and informative site that gives lots of facts about the country, the people, lifestyle and what you can expect when you visit.
SPEED ✓✓✓✓	
INFO ✓✓✓✓✓	
EASE ✓✓✓✓	

See also:

www.ansett.com.au – one of the world's top rated airlines with some good deals and flight prices from Australia only.

www.wilmap.com.au – excellent for Australian maps and links.

www.travelaustralia.com.au – informative site, good for regional information.

B

www.indo.com

BALI ONLINE

ORIGIN INDONESIA
SPEED ✓✓✓
INFO ✓✓✓✓
EASE ✓✓✓

Concentrating on Bali and its top hotels, but there's also plenty of information on the rest of Indonesia as well as links to other Asian sites.

www.trabel.com

BELGIUM

ORIGIN BELGIUM
SPEED ✓✓✓✓
INFO ✓✓✓✓
EASE ✓✓✓✓

The Belgium Travel Network offers a site packed with information about the country and its key towns and cities. You can get information on hotels, travelling, an airport guide, flight information and there's also a good links page. See also the well-designed **www.belgium-tourism.net**

www.brazil.com

BRAZIL

ORIGIN BRAZIL
SPEED ✓✓✓
INFO ✓✓✓✓
EASE ✓✓✓✓

A straightforward, no-nonsense guide, travelogue and listing site for Brazil that also contains information on hotels and resorts. See also **www.brazilinfo.com** and the excellent site for the Brazilian embassy in London **www.brazil.org.uk**

C

www.travelcanada.ca

EXPLORE CANADA

ORIGIN CANADA
SPEED ✓✓✓✓
INFO ✓✓✓✓✓
EASE ✓✓✓✓

Did you know that the glass floor at the top of the world's tallest freestanding structure could support the weight of 14 large hippos? Find out much more at this wide-ranging and attractive site, from touring to city guides. See also www.canadian-affair.com who offer some excellent low cost flights and tours, and for the outdoor experience of the country go to www.out-there.com

www.turq.com

CARIBBEAN

ORIGIN US
SPEED ✓✓✓
INFO ✓✓✓✓✓
EASE ✓✓✓✓

All you need to organise a great holiday in the Caribbean. There's information on flights, hotels, cruises, a travel guide and trip reports to the islands, all on a well presented and easy-to-use site.

See also:
www.caribtourism.com – for lots of information.
www.caribbeansupersite.com – good information.
www.nanana.com/caribbean.html – masses of links.
www.caribbeandreams.co.uk – UK travel agent
    specialising in the Caribbean.

www.chinatour.com

INFORMATION CHINA

ORIGIN CHINA
SPEED ✓✓✓✓
INFO ✓✓✓✓
EASE ✓✓✓✓

A comprehensive site stuffed with data on China: where to go and stay, how to get there and what to see, maps and visa application information. See also the China Travel System at www.chinats.com who have a good looking and very polite site where you can book hotels and tours, get travel information and chat to others who've experienced China. For Hong Kong go to **www.discoverhongkong.com**

www.croatia.hr

CROATIA

ORIGIN CROATIA	An excellent site covering the country and its virtues
SPEED ✓✓✓✓	with sections on events, attractions, background,
INFO ✓✓✓✓✓	accommodation and an all round travel guide.
EASE ✓✓✓✓	

www.cubanculture.com

CUBA

ORIGIN US	A fast, easy-to-use site with the basic information
SPEED ✓✓✓✓	about Cuba and its heritage. There are lots of useful
INFO ✓✓✓✓	links too.
EASE ✓✓✓✓	

www.cyprustourism.org

CYPRUS

ORIGIN CYPRUS	A pretty basic site about the country, well the Greek
SPEED ✓✓✓✓	run bit anyway.
INFO ✓✓✓	
EASE ✓✓✓	

www.czech-tourism.com

CZECH REPUBLIC

ORIGIN CZECHOSLOVAKIA	A good directory site providing information and
SPEED ✓✓✓✓	links in 15 categories from business to the weather
INFO ✓✓✓✓	including tour operators and a country guide.
EASE ✓✓✓✓	

D

www.visitdenmark.com

DENMARK

ORIGIN DENMARK
SPEED ✓✓✓✓
INFO ✓✓✓✓
EASE ✓✓✓✓

The official Danish tourist board site where you can get links to book a holiday and all the advice and information you'd expect from a well-run and efficient looking site. See also **www.woco.dk** for an excellent site on Copenhagen.

E

www.egyptvoyager.com

LAND OF THE PHARAOHS

ORIGIN EGYPT
SPEED ✓✓✓✓
INFO ✓✓✓✓✓
EASE ✓✓✓✓

A superb site with games, snippets of interesting information, in-depth articles and a great photo gallery. You could be forgiven for forgetting that its primary function is to sell holidays - you can even get a lesson on hieroglyphics. See also the more conventional **http://touregypt.net**, which is very comprehensive.

www.eurotrip.com

BACKPACKING EUROPE

ORIGIN UK
SPEED ✓✓✓✓
INFO ✓✓✓✓✓
EASE ✓✓✓✓

Student and independent European travel with in-depth information, facts, reviews, articles, discussion, live reports, links and travel advice on a good looking and well-designed site. See also **www.backpackeurope.com**

www.eurocamp.co.uk

SELF-CATERING EUROPE

ORIGIN UK	The leading self-catering company with over 170
SPEED ✓✓✓✓	holiday parks in 9 countries. Here you can find
INFO ✓✓✓✓	details of the accommodation and book a holiday
EASE ✓✓✓✓	and there are some bargains too.

www.europeaninternet.com/centraleurope

CENTRAL EUROPE ONLINE

ORIGIN EUROPE	A messy news-based site with comprehensive
SPEED ✓✓✓✓	information on the region. You can get travel
INFO ✓✓✓✓	information and airline tickets via the links sections.
EASE ✓✓✓	

www.visiteurope.com

EUROPEAN TRAVEL COMMISSION

ORIGIN US	A site aimed at Americans to encourage them to visit
SPEED ✓✓✓✓	Europe, it's informative and there's a section for
INFO ✓✓✓✓✓	each country.
EASE ✓✓✓✓	

F

www.franceway.com

VOILA LA FRANCE!

ORIGIN FRANCE	Excellent site giving an overview of French culture,
SPEED ✓✓✓✓	history, facts and figures, and of course, how to
INFO ✓✓✓✓✓	book a holiday. You can also sign up for the
EASE ✓✓✓✓	newsletter.

See also:
www.francetourism.com - the official French
   Government Tourist Office site for the US; great
   information for the UK too.

www.franceguide.com – official French Government
Tourist Office portal site.

www.vive-la-france.org – very comprehensive and
good fun

www.magicparis.com – good Paris guide with some
offers.

www.justparis.co.uk – details on how to get there
and hotels when you've arrived.

G

www.germany-tourism.de

GERMANY – WUNDERBAR

ORIGIN GERMANY	As much information as you can handle with good
SPEED ✓✓	features on the key destinations, excellent interactive
INFO ✓✓✓✓✓	mapping and links to related sites. For further
EASE ✓✓✓✓	information try www.germany-info.org

www.gibraltar.gi/tourism

GIBRALTAR – THE ROCK

ORIGIN GIBRALTAR	A good site devoted to the area with sections on the
SPEED ✓✓✓✓	sights plus travel information.
INFO ✓✓✓✓	
EASE ✓✓✓✓	

www.gnto.gr

GREEK NATIONAL TOURIST ORGANISATION

ORIGIN GREECE	An attractive site with the official word on travelling
SPEED ✓✓✓✓	in Greece, with a good travel guide and information
INFO ✓✓✓	for business travellers plus accommodation, advice
EASE ✓✓✓✓	and details on what you can get up to.

See also:

www.gogreece.com – a search engine devoted to all things Greek.

www.gtpnet.com – the Greek Travel Pages with the latest ferry schedules for island hoppers.

www.agn.gr – holidays, information and travel on the Aegean, the site has a good interactive map with lots of features. Aimed at US audience.

www.travel-greece.com – masses of links to everything about holidaying in Greece.

www.greekisland.co.uk – an entertaining and personal view of the Greek islands with over 200 links.

www.culture.gr – excellent site covering Greek culture and its legends.

H

www.holland.com

HOLLAND IS FULL OF SURPRISES

ORIGIN HOLLAND
SPEED ✓✓✓✓
INFO ✓✓✓✓✓
EASE ✓✓✓✓

Very professional site offering a mass of tourist information and advice on how to have a great time when you visit. There are sections on how to get there, what type of holiday will suit you and city guides.

I

www.iceland.org

ICELAND

ORIGIN ICELAND	Official site of the Icelandic Foreign Service with a
SPEED ✓✓✓✓	wealth of information about the country, the people
INFO ✓✓✓✓	and its history. It's easy to navigate and there are
EASE ✓✓✓✓	good links to related sites. See also

www.iceland.com and www.icetourist.is both of
which are more tourism oriented.

www.indiatouristoffice.org

INDIAN TOURIST OFFICE UK

ORIGIN UK	Essential tourist information and advice as well as
SPEED ✓✓✓✓	cultural and historical background on the country
INFO ✓✓✓✓	and its diverse regions. It has a massive hotel data-
EASE ✓✓✓✓	base as well.

www.indiamart.com

INDIA TRAVEL PROMOTION NETWORK

ORIGIN UK	Basically a shopping site with diverse information
SPEED ✓✓✓✓	including travel, hotels, timetables, wildlife,
INFO ✓✓✓✓✓	worship, trekking, heritage and general tourism.
EASE ✓✓✓✓	It's well organised and easy to use.

See also:
www.india-travel.com - a really strong travel site
   with lots of information and guidance as well as
   essential links.
www.rrindia.com - another good information site
   offering tour itineraries and hotel booking.
www.mapsofindia.com - an excellent site with maps
   of the country and a rail timetable and route
   planner.

www.**indianrailways.com** - passenger information and timetables of the largest rail network in the world.

www.**indiatraveltimes.com** - great for links and the latest news.

www.**partnershiptravel.co.uk** - specialist Indian travel agent.

www.**tourismindonesia.com**

INDONESIA

ORIGIN INDONESIA	A very good overview of the country and its people, with lots of useful information about travelling there and a good links section.
SPEED ✓✓✓✓	
INFO ✓✓✓✓	
EASE ✓✓✓✓	

www.**shamrock.org**

IRELAND

ORIGIN IRELAND	Wide-ranging site giving you the best of Ireland. Aimed at the American market, it really sells the country well with good links to other related sites.
SPEED ✓✓✓✓	
INFO ✓✓✓✓	
EASE ✓✓✓✓	

See also:

www.**iol.ie/~discover** – a good A–Z travel guide with lots of links.

www.**ireland.travel.ie** – the very good official Irish Tourist Board site.

www.**camping-ireland.ie** – over 100 parks listed for caravanning and camping.

www.**12travel.co.uk** – Irish holiday specialists with lots of holiday options.

www.goisrael.com

ISRAEL

ORIGIN ISRAEL	Excellent site with information on the country, its
SPEED ✓✓✓	sights and sites, how to get there and how to organ-
INFO ✓✓✓✓	ise a tour. There's also the latest information on 'the
EASE ✓✓✓✓	troubles' there from the official tourist board. See
	also www.infotour.co.il and www.e-israel.com

www.italytour.com

VIRTUAL TOUR OF ITALY

ORIGIN ITALY	Good looking, stylish and cool, this site is essentially
SPEED ✓✓✓	a search engine and directory but a very good one.
INFO ✓✓✓✓	
EASE ✓✓✓✓	

See also:

www.emmeti.it – slightly eccentric site with bags of good information, although it takes a while to find it. Very good for hotels, regional info and museums.

www.initaly.com – another eccentric site but generally well organised, informative and useful.

www.travel.it – a messy information site but you can book online.

www.itwg.com – Italian hotel reservations with online booking.

www.enit.it – from the Italian State Tourist board another wacky site but useful nonetheless.

J

www.jnto.go.jp

JAPAN

ORIGIN JAPAN
SPEED ✓✓
INFO ✓✓✓✓✓
EASE ✓✓✓✓

This excellent site is the work of the Japanese Tourist Association. There's a guide to each region, the food, shopping and travel info with advice on how to get the best out of your visit.

See also:
www.embjapan.org.uk – Japanese Embassy site, useful but not that up-to-date.
www.jaltour.co.uk – travel agents specialising in Japan.
www.japan-guide.com – comprehensive information site about Japan with links, culture notes, shopping and a hotel finder.

www.see-jordan.com

JORDAN

ORIGIN JORDAN
SPEED ✓✓✓
INFO ✓✓✓✓
EASE ✓✓✓✓

An attractive and interesting site from the Jordanian tourist board, very cultural and informative with good links and a photo gallery.

K

www.visit-kenya.com

KENYA

ORIGIN KENYA
SPEED ✓✓✓
INFO ✓✓✓✓
EASE ✓✓✓✓

A slightly amateurish site with links and information on travelling in Kenya. There are sections on Nairobi and the coast as well as the expected safari information.

See also:

www.kenya-wildlife-service.org – dedicated to preserving the wildlife of Kenya.

www.kenyaweb.com – a good portal site on all things Kenyan.

www.kenya.com – undergoing a re-vamp but much promised.

L

www.lata.org

LATIN AMERICA

ORIGIN UK	The Latin American Trade Association's text-based
SPEED ✓✓✓✓	site has a good country-by-country guide to the
INFO ✓✓✓✓✓	region plus links and general information.
EASE ✓✓✓✓	See also **www.latinamericatraveler.com** and

www.travellatinamerica.com and the sites listed under South America.

www.lebanon.com

THE LEBANON

ORIGIN LEBANON	The Lebanon is going through a resurgence and
SPEED ✓✓✓	is successfully rebuilding itself. Here you can find
INFO ✓✓✓✓✓	all the resources you need to organise a visit and
EASE ✓✓✓✓	see its many attractions. Also try the official

www.lebanon-tourism.gov.lb

M

www.malaysianet.net

MALAYSIA

ORIGIN MALAYSIA
SPEED ✓✓✓
INFO ✓✓✓✓
EASE ✓✓✓✓

Great for hotels in particular but you'll also find flight information and hidden away is a pretty good travel guide to the country. For air travel info see also www.malaysiaair.com

www.visitmaldives.com

MALDIVES

ORIGIN MALDIVES
SPEED ✓✓✓✓
INFO ✓✓✓✓
EASE ✓✓✓✓

A good overview of the islands and all the options available to tourists with links and a section on the capital Male, plus resort information.

www.visitmalta.com

MALTA

ORIGIN MALTA
SPEED ✓✓✓
INFO ✓✓✓✓
EASE ✓✓✓✓

A text-heavy but informative site about this beautiful island, with good details on accommodation and interactive mapping.

www.tourbymexico.com

MEXICO

ORIGIN US
SPEED ✓✓✓
INFO ✓✓✓✓
EASE ✓✓✓

A basic site, but there is a travel guide to Mexico plus information on tours, hotels, health, tips, links and sights to see. See also the bright and breezy European gateway into Mexico www.mexicanwave.com/travel

http://i-cias.com/morocco

MOROCCO

ORIGIN MOROCCO
SPEED ✓✓✓
INFO ✓✓✓✓
EASE ✓✓✓

A dense and detailed site about Morocco with over 650 articles and 900 photos covering cultural, musical and town by town information. See also www.morocco.com

www.mideasttravelnet.com

MIDDLE EAST TRAVEL NETWORK

ORIGIN US	A well-organised site concentrating on North Africa
SPEED ✓✓✓	and the Middle East. It's easy to use, targeted
INFO ✓✓✓✓✓	slightly towards business visitors, but still very
EASE ✓✓✓✓	informative for holidaymakers or independent
	travellers. See also **http://i-cias.com**

N

www.nepal.com

NEPAL AND THE HIMALAYAS

ORIGIN US	A beautifully presented site showing Nepal in its
SPEED ✓✓✓	best light. Business, sport, culture and travel all have
INFO ✓✓✓✓	sections and it's a good browse too. The travel
EASE ✓✓✓	section is not that comprehensive, it has a basic
	guide, lots about Everest and access to the useful
	Sherpa magazine. See also the specialist tour
	company **www.trans-himalaya.ndirect.co.uk** and
	also **www.rrindia.com/nepal.html**

www.purenz.com

NEW ZEALAND

ORIGIN NEW ZEALAND	A good looking and informative site about the
SPEED ✓✓✓✓	country with a section devoted to recollections
INFO ✓✓✓✓	and recommendations from people who've visited.
EASE ✓✓✓✓	See also the comprehensive **www.nz.com** and
	www.newzealand.com

www.visitnorway.com

NORWAY

ORIGIN	NORWAY
SPEED	✓✓✓✓
INFO	✓✓✓✓
EASE	✓✓✓✓

The official site of the Norwegian Tourist Board offers a good overview of what you can get up to when you're there, from adventure holidays to lounging around in the midnight sun to cruising the coast. See also **www.norway.org** which is the Norwegian Embassy's site.

P

www.tourism.gov.pk

PAKISTAN

ORIGIN	PAKISTAN
SPEED	✓✓✓
INFO	✓✓✓✓
EASE	✓✓✓✓

A pretty lightweight site but it has all the basic information and a good set of links with a travel guide built in. See also **www.pak.org** which is a very comprehensive portal site.

www.portugal-web.com

PORTUGAL

ORIGIN	PORTUGAL
SPEED	✓✓✓✓
INFO	✓✓✓✓
EASE	✓✓✓✓

A complete overview of the country including business as well as tourism with good regional information, news and links to other related sites.

See also:
www.thealgarve.net – all you need to know about the Algarve.
www.portugal.com – a news and shopping site with a good travel section.
www.portugal.org – well designed information site with a good travel section.

R

www.russia-travel.com

RUSSIA

ORIGIN RUSSIA
SPEED ✓✓✓✓
INFO ✓✓✓✓✓
EASE ✓✓✓✓

The official guide to travel in Russia with good information on excursions, accommodation, flights and trains, there's even a slide show, plus historical facts and travel tips. See also **www.themoscowtimes.com/travel** who offer a more traditional approach.

S

www.sey.net

SEYCHELLES, PARADISE — PERIOD

ORIGIN US
SPEED ✓✓✓✓
INFO ✓✓✓✓
EASE ✓✓✓✓

A good all-round overview of the Seychelles with background information on the major islands and activities, there's also links to travel agents. The slower **www.seychelles.uk.com** is also informative and geared to a British audience.

www.sg

SINGAPORE

ORIGIN SINGAPORE
SPEED ✓✓✓✓
INFO ✓✓✓✓
EASE ✓✓✓✓

The shortest URL in the book brings up one of the most detailed and comprehensive sites – all you need to know about the country and its people.

http://satourweb.satour.com/

SOUTH AFRICA

ORIGIN SOUTH AFRICA
SPEED ✓✓
INFO ✓✓✓✓
EASE ✓✓✓✓

Official tourist site with masses of information about the country and how you can set yourself up for the perfect visit with suggested itineraries.

See also www.gardenroute.org.za which is excellent, and www.southafrica.com/travel

www.southamericanexperience.co.uk

SOUTH AMERICA

ORIGIN UK
SPEED ✓✓✓
INFO ✓✓✓✓
EASE ✓✓✓

Specialists on South America are hard to come by, but at this site you can get tailor-made tours to suit you plus some scant information on the countries and special offers. See also www.adventure-life.com and www.gosouthamerica.about.com both are very informative and are good for links. Check out the listings under Latin America too.

www.tourspain.es

TOURIST OFFICE OF SPAIN

ORIGIN SPAIN
SPEED ✓✓✓✓
INFO ✓✓✓✓
EASE ✓✓✓✓

A colourful and award-winning web site that really makes you want to visit Spain. Very good for an overview.

You could also try any of these listed below:
www.red2000.com – a colourful travel guide, with a good search instrument!
www.okspain.org – nice all round information and travel site.
www.costaguide.com – your Costa del Sol companion, lots of information.
www.iberia.com – Iberian airlines site, with helpful advice and offers.
www.majorca.com – great site about the island.

www.lankadirectory.com

SRI LANKA

ORIGIN SRI LANKA
SPEED ✓✓✓
INFO ✓✓✓✓✓
EASE ✓✓✓✓

An excellent news and directory site with good links to specialist tour operators; the travel page is split into tourist guides, attractions, hotels and accommodation. There's also advice on the political troubles in the north of the island. See also **www.lanka.net**

www.sverigeturism.se/smorgasbord

SWEDEN

ORIGIN SWEDEN
SPEED ✓✓✓✓
INFO ✓✓✓✓
EASE ✓✓✓✓

The largest source of information in English on Sweden. It's essentially a directory site but there are sections on culture, history and a tourist guide. For more details of Sweden's cities see the very good **http://cityguide.se** and **www.visit-sweden.com** and also **www.sweden.com**

www.switzerlandtourism.ch

SWITZERLAND

ORIGIN SWITZERLAND
SPEED ✓✓✓✓
INFO ✓✓✓✓✓
EASE ✓✓✓✓

An excellent overview of the country with the latest new, travel information, snow reports and links, see also **www.vci-switzerland.com**

T

www.tanzania-web.com

TANZANIA

ORIGIN TANZANIA
SPEED ✓✓✓✓
INFO ✓✓✓✓
EASE ✓✓✓✓

Find your way round Tanzania with its wonderful scenery, Mount Kilimanjaro, safaris and resorts with this very good and comprehensive online guide from the official tourist board. See also **www.zanzibar.net**

www.thailand.com/travel/

THAILAND

ORIGIN THAILAND
SPEED ✓✓✓✓
INFO ✓✓✓✓
EASE ✓✓✓✓

Another excellent portal site, which acts as a gateway to a mass of travel and tourism resources. It covers some of South East Asia too and it has a good search facility. **www.tourismthailand.org** is the official tourist board site and is very informative, as is **www.nectec.or.th/thailand/**.

www.turkey.com

YOUR WINDOW ON TURKEY

ORIGIN US
SPEED ✓✓✓✓
INFO ✓✓✓✓
EASE ✓✓✓✓

A very well constructed site covering business, tourism, sport, culture and shopping. There's a great deal in terms of advice, tips, maps, but not much in-depth info. For that use the links or go to **www.exploreturkey.com** which is a good travel guide and **www.turkishembassy-london.com** for the official line.

U

www.uae.org.ae

UNITED ARAB EMIRATES

ORIGIN UAE
SPEED ✓✓✓✓
INFO ✓✓✓✓
EASE ✓✓✓✓

A useful guide to the seven states that make up the UAE, it carries historical information as well as the usual travel guide stuff. See also **www.godubai.com**

www.usatourism.com

USA

ORIGIN US
SPEED ✓✓✓✓
INFO ✓✓✓✓
EASE ✓✓✓

A state-by-state guide to the USA, just click on the interactive map and you get put through to the relevant state site. See also **www.areaguides.net** which is very detailed.

See also:

www.seeamerica.org – an excellent portal to American travel sites.

www.amtrak.com – rail schedules and fares across America.

www.greyhound.com – coach and bus schedules, but you can't buy tickets online from outside the US.

www.disneyworld.com – all you need to know about the world's number one theme park.

www.gohawaii.com – great site for checking out Hawaii and it's many attractions.

www.usahotelguide.com – reserve your room in any one of 50,000 hotels across the USA.

www.americanadventures.com – great site devoted to budget adventure tours.

V

www.vietnamtourism.com

VIETNAM

ORIGIN US	Vietnam is the hot destination apparently, here's the
SPEED ✓✓✓✓	official tourism site which is informative and good
INFO ✓✓✓✓	for links.
EASE ✓✓✓	

Travel in Britain

www.visitbritain.com

HOME OF THE BRITISH TOURIST AUTHORITY

ORIGIN UK	Selling Britain using a holiday ideas-led site with
SPEED ✓✓✓	lots of help for the visitor, maps, background stories,
INFO ✓✓✓✓✓	images, entertainment, culture, activities and a
EASE ✓✓✓✓	planner. There's also a very helpful set of links.

www.informationbritain.co.uk

HOLIDAY INFORMATION

ORIGIN UK
SPEED ✓✓✓
INFO ✓✓✓✓✓
EASE ✓✓✓✓

Where to stay and where to go with an overview of all the UK's main tourist attractions, counties and regions; it has good cross-referencing and links to the major destinations.

www.atuk.co.uk

UK TRAVEL AND TOURIST GUIDE

ORIGIN UK
SPEED ✓✓✓
INFO ✓✓✓✓✓
EASE ✓✓✓

A good county-by-county guide come directory, with plenty of links and extras such as web cams, awards, weather, site of the day and competitions. It's very good if you want something unusual, but it's a bit unclear whether they rate the activity or the web site. For another good links directory see **www.enjoybritain.com** who concentrate solely on travel.

www.sightseeing.co.uk

SIGHT-SEEING MADE EASY

ORIGIN UK
SPEED ✓✓✓✓
INFO ✓✓✓✓
EASE ✓✓✓✓✓

A good looking and very useful site if you're looking for something to do. Just type in what you want to see and where you are, then up pops a listing giving basic information on each attraction, how far it is to get there, entrance fee and a map. One slight criticism: would be better if there was more background information on each attraction.

www.ukholidaybreaks.co.uk

FIND YOUR PERFECT HOTEL

ORIGIN UK
SPEED ✓✓✓✓
INFO ✓✓✓✓
EASE ✓✓✓✓

A directory of hotels in the UK, you find the one you want by drilling down through a series of maps or select by category. It's easy although results are a bit hit and miss, but it claims to use the latest technology to find just the right break for you.

See also:
www.ukguide.org – well-organised directory with a
   UK and a London guide plus mapping.
www.e-street.com – excellent overview of a dozen or
   so English and Irish cities
www.aboutbritain.com – attractive, well laid out
   and comprehensive UK guide.
www.travelbritain.com – a modest directory site.

www.knowhere.co.uk

THE USER'S GUIDE TO BRITAIN

ORIGIN UK
SPEED ✓✓✓✓
INFO ✓✓✓✓✓
EASE ✓✓✓✓

An unconventional 'tourist guide' which gives a warts-and-all account of over 1,000 places in Britain; it's very irreverent and if you are squeamish or a bit sensitive, then they have a good list of links to proper tourist sites.

For separate countries and regions see also:
www.travelengland.org.uk – nice online guide to
   everything English, places to visit and accommodation.
www.aboutscotland.com – excellent site with information on a broad range of accommodation and
   sights to see, it's fast too.
www.scotland.com – nicely illustrated site with a
   good overview of the country.

www.scotland-info.co.uk – very good online guidebook, covering Scotland by area; it's quite slow but the information is very good.

www.holidays-in-wales.co.uk – holidays in the Welsh countryside with limited online booking, with a good overview of the country.

www.data-wales.co.uk – not so much a tourist site, but excellent for history and culture and quite funny too.

www.discovernorthernireland.com – Northern Ireland Tourist Board has an attractive site showing the best that the region has to offer. It has a virtual tour, holiday planner, accommodation, guides, links and special offers. See also **www.nidirectory.co.uk**

www.jerseyhols.com – good looking site with lots of information and info on where to stay and what to do, see also **www.jersey.com** who have a very slick site.

www.guernseytouristboard.com – slightly dodgy site but there's all the information you need on Guernsey.

www.alderney.net – a good looking site devoted to the third largest Channel Island.

www.sark.info – a lively site with all the information you need plus online booking for ferries.

www.visitorkney.com – from the Orkney Tourist Board a very informative and appealing site. See also **www.orknet.com**

www.visitshetland.com – a definite green theme to this site devoted to Shetland, highlighting its outdoor life and spirit of adventure.

www.visithebrides.com – a light and airy site with links and information relating to the islands. See also **www.hebrides.com** which offers beautiful photography.

www.isle-of-man.com – learn all about this unique island with help on where to stay and, of course, background on the famous TT races.

www.isle-of-wight-tourism.gov.uk – hi-tech site with lots of information on the isle and details about holidaying there, you can even have last minute breaks sent to your mobile.

www.simplyscilly.co.uk – specialists in travel to the Scilly islands with info on how to get there and what to do.

www.londontown.com – very comprehensive survival and holiday guide rolled into one, with sections on restaurants, hotels, attractions and offers. It is quite slow.

www.londonhotelreservations.com – some good deals on London hotels.

Things to do in Britain

www.virgin.net/daysout

FIND A GOOD DAY OUT

ORIGIN UK
SPEED ✓✓
INFO ✓✓✓✓✓
EASE ✓✓✓✓✓

If you can put up with the adverts, Virgin's days out page is well worth a visit if you're stuck for something to do. There's plenty of information on the sights and there's a 'days out finder service' for when you're really stuck. There are also links to related and useful sites. See also the exhaustive **www.daysoutuk.com** who list over 7,000 attractions and 10,000 events countrywide and offer discounts on over 500 venues.

www.gardenvisit.com

GO TO A GARDEN

ORIGIN UK
SPEED ✓✓✓✓
INFO ✓✓✓✓
EASE ✓✓✓✓

A basic text-based site, which lists some 1,000 of the UK's gardens open to the public, giving details of each, how to get there and how they rate. It also covers the USA and Europe and there's also an excellent overview of garden history.

www.nationaltrust.org.uk

PLACES OF HISTORIC INTEREST AND BEAUTY

ORIGIN UK
SPEED ✓✓✓✓
INFO ✓✓✓✓✓
EASE ✓✓✓✓✓

The National Trust's site has an excellent overview of their activities and the properties they own. There is a very good search facility and up-to-date information to help with your visit. See also English Heritage site at **www.english-heritage.org.uk** which is excellent.

www.goodbeachguide.co.uk

THE BEST BEACHES

ORIGIN UK
SPEED ✓✓✓✓
INFO ✓✓✓✓
EASE ✓✓✓✓

From the Marine Conservation Society you can find out which are Britain's worst and best beaches. It's set out regionally and the site is updated regularly.

What to do with the kids

www.kidsnet.co.uk

WHAT'S ON AND WHERE?

ORIGIN UK
SPEED ✓✓✓✓
INFO ✓✓✓✓
EASE ✓✓✓✓

Strong design and ease-of-use make this site stand out, aligned with a comprehensive database of places and attractions. Also has cinema listings, games and book search facilities which all add to the general excellence. Good links list too.

For more ideas try:

www.kidstravel.co.uk – nice design but comparatively little content, still some good ideas and travelling tips for parents though biased to England.

www.planit4kids.com – covers seven major areas of the country centred on the major cites, the linked sites are excellent with plenty to see and do, on top of all the information you need for a great day out. They plan to rollout internationally.

www.xkeys.co.uk – specialist in residential camps for children of all ages, excellent web site with lots of information and references.

Holiday cottages

www.preferedplaces.co.uk
HOLIDAY COTTAGE SEARCH

ORIGIN UK
SPEED ✓✓✓
INFO ✓✓✓✓
EASE ✓✓✓✓

A good place to start looking for a holiday cottage in the UK, Ireland or in France or Portugal, with an easy-to-use search engine. It offers lots of different types of accommodation to suit all types.

See also:

www.cottagesdirect.com – click on the interactive map and away you go.

www.hidays.co.uk – claims over 16,000 cottages in the UK, Ireland and France.

www.hideaways.co.uk – great for the south of England.

www.holidayrentals4you.com – a wide range of properties to rent in UK, USA and Europe.

www.oas.co.uk/ukcottages/ – some 450 cottages available throughout the UK.

www.nationaltrust.org.uk/cottages/ – holiday cottages with a difference.

Cycling and touring

The following are mostly UK specialists, but some cover further afield too.

www.ctc.org.uk

WORKING FOR CYCLING

ORIGIN UK
SPEED ✓✓✓
INFO ✓✓✓✓✓
EASE ✓✓✓✓

The CTC have a great travel section with routes, tours, offers, links and directories, it's a great place to start your search for the perfect cycling holiday.

Also check out:

www.nationalcyclenetwork.co.uk – details of the National Cycle Network and how to make the best use of it.

www.bikemagic.com – go to the travel pages for an excellent section where Bike Magic have got partners who'll supply flight deals for cyclists or rail travel and holidays.

www.bicycle-beano.co.uk – Bicycle Beano have a good site covering cycling holidays in Wales and the borders.

www.byways-breaks.co.uk – nice looking site, Byways Breaks arrange cycling and walking holidays in the Shropshire and Cheshire countryside.

www.scotcycle.co.uk – Scottish Cycling Holidays are specialists in cycling holidays in Scotland obviously. Nice site too.

www.rough-tracks.co.uk – wide range of active adventure holidays from beginners to experts.

www.biketours.co.uk – a very good selection of biking tours through Europe and further afield.

Camping and caravanning

Many of the sites listed specialise in Britain but some have information on camp sites abroad too.

www.camp-sites.co.uk

FIND A SITE

ORIGIN UK	Excellent regional listing of the UK's campsites with
SPEED ✓✓✓✓	comprehensive details on each site and links to other
INFO ✓✓✓✓	related directories.
EASE ✓✓✓✓	

See also:

www.camping-and-leisure.co.uk – lots of links and classified ads.

www.eurocampindependent.co.uk – excellent site if you want to go camping in Europe, some special offers and you can chat about your experiences too.

www.keycamp.co.uk – European specialist with a choice of 120 sites in eight countries.

www.pjcamping.co.uk – exhaustive selection of tents and camping equipment for sale, good info but no online ordering.

www.caravan.co.uk

THE CARAVAN CLUB

ORIGIN UK	Huge listing of sites, advice and practical help
SPEED ✓✓✓✓	with details of over 200 sites and some 3,000
INFO ✓✓✓✓	other certified locations where you can park up.
EASE ✓✓✓✓	There's also a European service, you can join the
	club on site and request any of the fifty or so
	leaflets they publish.

See also:

http://camping.uk-directory.com – a good regional sites directory, with retailing links, caravans for sale and conservation information.

www.caravan-sitefinder.co.uk – listing of over 1,000 caravan sites, with background information on a wide range of topics.

Waterways

www.britishwaterways.co.uk
BRITISH WATERWAYS

ORIGIN UK
SPEED ✓✓✓✓
INFO ✓✓✓✓✓
EASE ✓✓✓✓

This organisation is responsible for maintaining a large part of Britain's waterways and this excellent site details their work and contains interactive mapping of the routes with a great deal of background information and events listings and history.

See also:

www.waterways.org.uk – Inland Waterways Association site, dedicated to keeping canals open and you can find out about their organised activities too.

www.canalroutes.com – a roots and routes history of Britain's canals in a regional directory, a labour of love.

www.canals.co.uk – the biggest canal-related shop on the Internet, mainly videos, maps and books.

www.hoseasons.co.uk – great site from the specialists in boating holidays, you can book online too.

www.blakes.co.uk – another boating holiday specialist.

Adventure and activity

www.activitiesonline.co.uk

ULTIMATE RESOURCE FOR LEISURE PURSUITS

ORIGIN UK	A directory of adventure and activity holiday
SPEED ✓✓✓✓	specialists covering everything from extreme sports
INFO ✓✓✓✓	to gardening. You get a description of the activity,
EASE ✓✓✓	then a list of relevant sites.

www.sportbreak.co.uk

THE SPORTS BREAK DIRECTORY

ORIGIN UK	A good directory, apart from sports it covers all
SPEED ✓✓✓✓	activity holidays including leisure breaks, health
INFO ✓✓✓✓	clubs, even stag and hen parties. It's easy to use and
EASE ✓✓✓	the information is well put over.

Other adventure holiday sites:

www.activityholsni.co.uk – activity holidays in
Northern Ireland have a great site and lots to do.

www.activitywales.co.uk – break out and discover
the real Wales with Activity Wales. Use this well-
constructed site to suss out which activities to try.

www.activity-scotland.co.uk – lots of things to do in
here, nice regional guide as well.

www.adventure.uk.com – Adventure International
are experienced adventure holiday specialists
based in Bude, Cornwall.

www.adventureholiday.com – ProAdventure
specialise in activity holidays in North Wales.

www.leisurepursuits.com – one of the largest sports
tour operators and travel agents.

www.pgl.co.uk/holidays – adventure holidays for
kids - great site too.

www.mtn.co.uk – mountaineering, hillwalking and trekking – excellent site with all the information you're likely to need.

www.trailplus.com – the ultimate adventure, offering lifestyle experiences, adventure camps and much more.

Walking and rambling

www.ramblers.org.uk

THE RAMBLERS' ASSOCIATION

ORIGIN UK
SPEED ✓✓
INFO ✓✓✓✓
EASE ✓✓✓✓

News, strong views and plenty of advice on offer here, where you can find out about the Association's activities and even join a campaign. There are features on events and details of the *Rambler* magazine, shopping and holidays.

www.walkingbritain.co.uk

BRITISH WALKS

ORIGIN UK
SPEED ✓✓
INFO ✓✓✓✓✓
EASE ✓✓✓✓

Some 2,000 pages of information about walking in Britain, it mainly covers the national parks but it is expanding to include less well-known areas. They provide decent route maps and photos to guide you. There's also a list of handy links and a good photo gallery.

www.onedayhikes.com

WHERE DO YOU WANT TO HIKE TODAY?

ORIGIN US
SPEED ✓✓✓
INFO ✓✓✓✓✓
EASE ✓✓✓✓

A great site, which is basically a directory of hikes that you can complete in a day, it's not just for the UK either, it covers the whole world. There's excellent information on each hike plus pictures and you get the chance to win a digital camera if you send in a report of a hike you've done and it gets accepted.

For more sites for hikers try:

www.ramblersholidays.co.uk – Ramblers Holidays
   specialise in escorted rambling holidays.

www.bwf-ivv.org.uk – the British Walking
   Federation organise a wide range of activities and
   you can find out about them here.

www.gelert.com – equipment for sale, a good looking site well worth a visit.

Train, coach and ferry journeys

www.pti.org.uk

PUBLIC TRANSPORT INFORMATION

ORIGIN UK	An incredibly useful site if you're a frequent user of
SPEED ✓✓✓	public transport or if you're using it to go some-
INFO ✓✓✓✓✓	where you're not familiar with. It categorises all the
EASE ✓✓✓✓	major forms of public transport and lists for each

area useful numbers, timetables, web sites and
interactive mapping to help you. It also includes
routes to Europe and Ireland.

www.kizoom.co.uk

TRAVEL SERVICE TO YOUR PHONE

ORIGIN UK	Good quality travel information to your mobile
SPEED ✓✓✓	phone sounds great and this is a very well set up and
INFO ✓✓✓	easy-to-use site. Unfortunately, it only works with a
EASE ✓✓✓	limited number of WAP phones, so if you've one of

those you're in luck.

www.travelfusion.com

THE TRAVEL COMPARISON PORTAL

ORIGIN UK	A brilliant idea – pick a journey then compare
SPEED ✓✓✓	whether it would be best to go by coach, car, ferry
INFO ✓✓✓✓✓	or by air. It's simple to use and you can compare by
EASE ✓✓✓✓	price or speed. It then connects you with the right

operator if you want to book.

Railways

www.railtrack.co.uk

FOR TRAIN TIMES

ORIGIN UK
SPEED ✓✓✓
INFO ✓✓✓✓✓
EASE ✓✓✓

Go to the travel section and type in the start point and destination then Railtrack will tell you the time of the next train. It's very easy to use and a must for all rail travellers. You can also get travel news and information about Railtrack; there are no details of rail fares.

www.nationalrail.co.uk

NATIONAL RAIL

ORIGIN UK
SPEED ✓✓✓
INFO ✓✓✓✓✓
EASE ✓✓✓✓

National Rail's site has all the latest information, timetables and links you need to plan a rail journey. It's very comprehensive with up-to-the-minute information on what's going on.

www.thetrainline.com

BUY TRAIN TICKETS

ORIGIN UK
SPEED ✓✓✓
INFO ✓✓✓✓✓
VALUE ✓✓✓✓
EASE ✓✓✓✓

You have to log in first but you can book a ticket for train travel, whether business or leisure, (except sleeper, Motorail, Eurostar and ferry services). They have an up-to-date timetable and the tickets will be sent or you can collect. See also the fast working **www.qjump.co.uk**, which is similar. At both these sites there are a bewildering number of options and prices, a little help with what each ticket type and their relative costs wouldn't go amiss.

See also:
www.eurail.com – details of the Eurailticket, information and prices, but you can't buy online.
www.eurostar.co.uk – online booking plus timetables and offers.

www.thetube.com

LONDON UNDERGROUND

ORIGIN UK
SPEED ✓✓✓
INFO ✓✓✓✓✓
EASE ✓✓✓✓

An excellent and informative site from London Underground with lots of features, articles on visiting London and links to related sites. There's a good journey planner and tube maps too. See also the Tube Planner at **www.tubeplanner.com** which is a straightforward, easy-to-use journey planner.

Coaches

www.gobycoach.com

BOOK COACH TICKETS

ORIGIN UK
SPEED ✓✓✓
INFO ✓✓✓✓✓
VALUE ✓✓✓✓
EASE ✓✓✓

Organise your journey with this easy-to-use web site from National Express, and then book the tickets. Also offers an airport service, transport to events and tours. See also **www.stagecoachbus.com** where you can find information about Stagecoach services and buy tickets.

Ferries

www.ferrybooker.com

BOOK YOUR CROSSING

ORIGIN UK
SPEED ✓✓✓
INFO ✓✓✓✓✓
VALUE ✓✓✓
EASE ✓✓✓✓

The best ferry site for a wide range of information on crossing times featuring a large number of routes. There is help with planning, special offers, channel tunnel ticket booking and they offer holiday breaks too.

See also:
www.brittany-ferries.co.uk – crossings to France and Spain with online booking and special offers, also cruises and holidays.
www.dfdsseaways.co.uk – details and offers on Scandinavian routes.

www.drive-alive.com – motoring holiday specialists who get good rates on channel crossings as part of their package.

www.ferry.co.uk – great offers on selected crossings.

www.ferrysavers.co.uk – wide range of offers and a good selection of crossings at good prices, you can book online and they offer a price promise too.

www.hoverspeed.com – online booking and all the information you need to make the fastest channel and Irish Sea crossings.

www.irishferries.ie – excellent magazine-style site where amongst all the features you can find timetables and book tickets.

www.posl.com – P&O Stena Line with online booking, details of sailings and offers.

www.seafrance.com – bookings and information on their Calais-Dover service plus some special offers.

Car hire

It's probably best to go to a price comparison site before going to one of the car hire companies, that way you should get the best prices. One of the best is to be found at **www.priceline.co.uk**

www.holidaycars.co.uk

WORLD-WIDE CAR HIRE

ORIGIN UK	Over 3,000 car hire locations throughout the world
SPEED ✓✓✓	means that this site is well worth a visit on your
INFO ✓✓✓✓	quest, you can get an instant online quote and you
VALUE ✓✓✓	can book too. Very good for the USA. See also
EASE ✓✓✓✓	Holiday Autos who have a similar site at

www.holidayautos.co.uk and also the competitive www.pelicancarhire.co.uk who specialise in Europe.

Cruises

www.whatcruise.co.uk
WHAT CRUISE?

ORIGIN UK
SPEED ✓✓✓✓
INFO ✓✓✓✓✓
VALUE ✓✓✓
EASE ✓✓✓✓

Check out the best cruises, look for the best prices and get information on what to do on board. You can browse the site by region, by line and by ship and there's lots of tips and advice.

www.cruiseinformationservice.co.uk
CRUISE INFO

ORIGIN UK
SPEED ✓✓✓✓
INFO ✓✓✓✓
EASE ✓✓✓✓

A trade site put together to encourage people to take cruise holidays. There's an introduction to cruising, information on the cruise lines, a magazine and links to useful sites. There's also information on how to book and what sort of cruise is right for you.

Utilities

Get the best prices on you gas, electricity and water and find out what the big suppliers are up to as well.

www.ofgem.gov.uk
GAS AND ELECTRICITY SUPPLIER WATCHDOG

ORIGIN UK
SPEED ✓✓✓✓
INFO ✓✓✓✓✓
EASE ✓✓✓✓✓

Data on the suppliers and companies providing comparison information makes for interesting reading. There's also background on how bills are made up, complaints and how energy reaches your home. Excellent.

www.buy.co.uk
CUT YOUR BILLS – COMPARE PRICES

ORIGIN	UK
SPEED	✓✓✓✓✓
INFO	✓✓✓✓
VALUE	✓✓✓✓✓
EASE	✓✓✓✓✓

Take a few minutes to check the prices of the key utilities and see whether you can save on your current bills, its easy and quick. It also covers phones and loans, and there's also access to *Which?* Magazine's energy reports. See also www.servista.com which is easy-to-use and well designed, while www.uswitch.com and www.unravelit.com have signed up to OFGEM's code of conduct on price comparison information.

Electricity and gas

Here are the main energy sites, who owns them at time of writing and the highlights of the site.

www.amerada.co.uk – one of the best value suppliers with an excellent site, you can even switch to them online.

www.british-energy.com – one of the largest electricity providers with a good-looking but not very useful site.

www.centrica.co.uk – owners of British Gas and the AA, this site aims to give information about the group.

www.txuenergi.co.uk – formerly www.easternenergy.co.uk – good service, helpful, much improved.

www.esb.ie – good-looking site from an Irish supplier with online sign up available.

www.gas.co.uk – comprehensive service from British gas with account viewing.

www.hydro.co.uk – Scottish Hydro Electric has one of the sites most oriented to its customers.

www.innogy.com – good-looking site from this new
company with useful features and not much help
in the customer care centre.

www.london-electricity.co.uk – straightforward but
slow.

www.mep.co.uk – the old Midland supplier, really a
corporate site.

www.nationalgrid.com/uk – the National Grid, the
Railtrack of power.

www.nie.co.uk – Northern Ireland Electricity with
customer information on their service the rest is
fairly corporate.

www.npower.com – nicely designed site with online
application.

www.powergen.co.uk – Powergen has a neat site
with calculators and a switching service.

www.scottish-southern.co.uk – owner of Swalec, site
aimed at shareholders.

www.swalec.co.uk – Swalec, good house move
planner.

www.yeg.co.uk – Yorkshire Electric has a nice, helpful site – soon to be part of Innogy.

www.transco.uk.com

FOR GAS LEAKS

ORIGIN UK	Transco doesn't sell gas, but maintains the 24-hour
SPEED ✓✓✓✓	emergency service for stopping gas leaks –
INFO ✓✓✓	call 0800 111 999 to report one.
EASE ✓✓✓✓	

www.corgi-gas.com

COUNCIL OF REGISTERED GAS INSTALLERS

ORIGIN UK	CORGI is the gas industry watchdog; the site has
SPEED ✓✓✓✓	advice on gas installation and where to find a fitter
INFO ✓✓✓✓	or repairman.
EASE ✓✓✓✓	

www.calorgas.co.uk
CALOR GAS

ORIGIN	UK
SPEED	✓✓✓✓
INFO	✓✓✓✓
VALUE	✓✓✓
EASE	✓✓✓✓

Information on your nearest stockists, how best to use Calor gas and Autogas, there's also corporate background and customer services too. You can also order it online with payment collected on delivery.

Water

www.open.gov.uk/ofwat/index.htm
OFFICE OF WATER SERVICES

ORIGIN	UK
SPEED	✓✓✓✓
INFO	✓✓✓✓
VALUE	✓✓✓
EASE	✓✓✓✓

A very poor effort, especially when compared to the OFGEM counterparts site, however, you can find out about what they do and you can contact them for advice.

The following are the main water company sites:

www.nww.co.uk – United Utilities, once North West Water has a well-designed site with help, information and good advice for consumers, with online access to your account. They now supply electricity too.

www.severntrent.co.uk – well it's got the share price, which is nice.

www.swwater.co.uk – lots of information and good advice, bill paying online.

www.wessexwater.plc.uk – good site with bill paying facilities and information, even which reservoirs you can fish in.

www.nwl.co.uk – nice lifestyle site with leisure information and bill paying.

www.thameswater.co.uk – good information and advice.

The Weather

www.met-office.gov.uk

EXCELLING IN WEATHER SERVICES

ORIGIN UK
SPEED ✓✓✓
INFO ✓✓✓✓
EASE ✓✓✓✓

Comprehensive information on Britain's favourite topic of conversation, easy to use, in four sections with interactive maps – world weather and world weather news, UK weather headlines and flash weather warnings. There's also a good selection of links and a mobile phone service.

www.bbc.co.uk/weather

ANOTHER WINNER FROM THE BBC

ORIGIN UK
SPEED ✓✓✓✓
INFO ✓✓✓✓✓
EASE ✓✓✓✓

Another page from the BBC site, it gives up-to-the-minute forecasts, and is very clear and concise. It features: 5-day forecasts by town, city or post code; specialist reports such as ski resorts, pollution, sun index; world weather and the shipping forecast. There's also a section dedicated to articles on various aspects of the weather and details on making the weather forecast programme. For more information about the weather, the Weather Channel has a very good site on www.weather.com this is geared to the USA, but has some really good articles and features. For regional UK links try the very basic but informative UK weather information site www.weather.org.uk and www.uk-weather.co.uk, which is good for links.

www.weatherimages.org

SEE THE WORLD'S WEATHER – LIVE

ORIGIN US	Weatherimages is compiled by a true weather fan.
SPEED ✓✓✓	Split into twenty or so areas of interest, there is
INFO ✓✓✓✓	plenty of information and there's loads to see. The
EASE ✓✓✓✓	best feature is the network of weather cams from
	which you can see the best and worst of the world's
	weather.

Web Cameras

One of the most fascinating aspects of the Internet is the ability to tap into some CCTV or specially set up web cameras from all around the world. Some sites may contain adult material.

www.camcentral.com

WEB CAM CENTRAL

ORIGIN US	An excellent selection of cameras, chosen for quality
SPEED ✓✓✓	rather than quantity; the wildlife ones are very good
INFO ✓✓✓✓	in particular but there's a good search facility too.
EASE ✓✓✓	See also www.webcamworld.com which is a big
	directory of webcams and www.webcam-index.com
	which lists some 500 sites from around the world.

Web Site Design

As it's pretty expensive to get a site designed and built professionally, there's been an explosion in the number of books, software and sites dedicated to helping people put their own sites together. These web sites will help enormously and take you through the world of Hypertext Markup Language, Java and Flash.

http://hotwired.lycos.com/webmonkey

THE WEB MONKEY

ORIGIN US
SPEED ✓✓✓✓
INFO ✓✓✓✓✓
EASE ✓✓✓✓

A superb resource for all web designers of all skill levels providing everything from basic tutorials to articles from professional designers. The 'How to' library is brilliant and, as you'd expect, the site design is excellent too. See also **www.htmlgoodies.com** who also offer tutorials and lots of tips for those times when things don't go quite the way you want them to.

www.codebeach.com

CODE BEACH

ORIGIN US
SPEED ✓✓✓✓
INFO ✓✓✓✓
EASE ✓✓✓

Code Beach describe their site as 'your complete guide to free and open source code for ASP, C++, ColdFusion, Java, JavaScript, Palm, Perl, PHP, and Visual Basic' and it is. Each language has a section with tutorials, downloads and links for you to get your head around it all.

Other essential sites:
www.blogger.com – a free web publishing tool.
www.cutandpastescripts.com – a great time saving tool where you can literally cut and paste bits of essential computer graphics.

www.dreamweaver.com – home of one of the leading pieces of web creation software, here you can download a trial version, get lots of information and more downloads to improve your site.

www.flashkit.com – animate your site, give it life here.

www.homepagetools.com – a really strong resource of tools and services you can add to your site once you're up and running.

http://webdeveloper.earthweb.com/webjs – you're going to need this site, it's a great source of those helpful little java programs you find on most sites. Why write your own when you can download one for free.

www.jimtools.com – OK, you're site is up and running, now promote it. This site tells you how, with lots of tips and a program that will send your new URL to lots of search engines.

www.port41.com – manage and update your website the simple way.

www.spinwave.com – free software to ensure that the pictures you choose fit the site, and load quickly and efficiently too.

www.thecounter.com – find out who visits your site and how often.

www.ultimateresources.co.uk – advice and information on how to make money from your site.

www.useit.com – great place to go for advice from a bone-fide web design guru.

Web Site Guides and Directories

If you can't find the site you're looking for in this book then rather than use a search engine, check out one of these web site directories.

www.just35.com

FIND IT THE EASY WAY

ORIGIN UK
SPEED ✓✓✓
INFO ✓✓✓✓✓
EASE ✓✓✓

A very good directory site which is well categorised (maximum 35 sites in each category) and easy to use with each site reviewed and rated. You can also get the latest news and personalise the site.

www.uk250.co.uk

OVER 12,000 SITES IN 250 CATEGORIES

ORIGIN UK
SPEED ✓✓✓
INFO ✓✓✓✓✓
EASE ✓✓✓

Heavily advertised and hyped though this site has been, many people seem to think that it consists of just the top 250 sites, but it's actually a very comprehensive database of Britain's most important and useful '.co.uks' and '.coms'. The sites listed are not reviewed but a one-liner gives a brief description of what they are about. Desperately needs a good search facility.

www.thegoodwebguide.co.uk

GOOD WEB GUIDE

ORIGIN UK
SPEED ✓✓✓✓
INFO ✓✓✓✓
VALUE ✓✓
EASE ✓✓✓✓

The best web sites in several key categories are comprehensively reviewed but you have to subscribe (£30 per annum) or buy the related book (subscription then free to that subject area) to get the best out of it. It's a good site and the books are good (if a little expensive), but the problem for the Good Web Guide team is that you can get all the information at reduced cost elsewhere.

http://cool.infi.net

THE COOLEST SITES

ORIGIN US
SPEED ✓✓✓
INFO ✓✓✓✓
EASE ✓✓✓

Vote for the coolest sites and find out which are considered the best. This has got very commercial now, so lots of deals and adverts get in the way.

www.ukdirectory.co.uk

DEFINITIVE GUIDES TO BRITISH SITES

ORIGIN UK
SPEED ✓✓✓✓
INFO ✓✓✓✓✓
EASE ✓✓✓✓

A massive database of web sites conveniently categorised into sixteen sections, it is mainly geared to business, but there's leisure too. They don't review, but there are brief explanations provided by the site owners.

www.bored.com

IF YOU'RE BORED

ORIGIN US
SPEED ✓✓✓✓
INFO ✓✓✓✓
EASE ✓✓✓

Basically a directory of unusual and humorous sites to occupy you when you've nothing better to do, it's quite entertaining really.

Weddings

www.confetti.co.uk

YOUR INTERACTIVE WEDDING GUIDE

ORIGIN UK
SPEED ✓✓✓✓
INFO ✓✓✓✓✓
VALUE ✓✓✓
EASE ✓✓✓✓

A good looking and busy site, designed to help you through every stage of your wedding with information for all participants. There are gift guides, planning tools, advice, a supplier directory and a shop. They don't miss much.

www.wedding-service.co.uk
UK'S LARGEST WEDDING AND BRIDE DIRECTORY

ORIGIN UK
SPEED ✓✓✓
INFO ✓✓✓✓✓
EASE ✓✓✓

A huge list of suppliers, service providers and information by region, everything from balloons to speechwriters are listed. The site is not that easy on the eye and it takes a little while to find what you want.

www.all-about-weddings.co.uk
INFORMATION ABOUT GETTING MARRIED IN THE UK

ORIGIN UK
SPEED ✓✓✓
INFO ✓✓✓✓✓
VALUE ✓✓✓
EASE ✓✓✓✓

Excellent for basic information about planning weddings from the ceremony to the reception; it also has a good set of links to related and specialist supplier sites, a travel section and a shop. It's all wrapped up in suitably matrimonial design with love hearts flowing across the screen as you browse.

Other good sites for weddings:

www.bridalplanner.com – well designed and wide ranging, including advice and real life stories plus print off checklists and planners.

www.bridesuk.net – excellent site from *Brides* magazine; get all the latest in bridal fashion and a guide to where to go on honeymoon.

www.hitched.co.uk – another good all-rounder with the added feature of a discussion forum where you can swap wedding stories.

www.pronuptia.co.uk – details of the range and stores, not much else.

www.webwedding.co.uk – lots of expert advice and inspiration, a bit slow though.

www.weddingguide.co.uk – clean looking site with shop, directory and advice plus a good search facility.

www.weddings.co.uk – another good site with free
wedding planning software, follow a bride-to-be
as she keeps a diary of the countdown to the big
day.

www.lastnightoffreedom.co.uk – everything you
need to organise your stag or hen night.

www.partydomain.co.uk – if you want to organise
your own party then this is the site for you.

www.allstretchedout.co.uk – luxury limousine hire.

Women

The following are a few sites of particular interest to women.

www.cabinet-office.gov.uk/womens-unit
THE WOMEN'S UNIT AT NO 10

ORIGIN UK
SPEED ✓✓✓
INFO ✓✓✓✓
EASE ✓✓✓✓

The Government's Women's Unit 'provides a
two-way voice between Government and the women
of the UK'. Politics aside, the site provides useful
information on how government policies impact
on women's lives, covering hot topics such as
encouraging women to become more involved in
public life, balancing work and family, domestic
violence, money, health and equal opportunities.
Worth visiting for the useful links. For the UN
go to www.un.org/womenwatch

www.working-options.co.uk

PART-TIME RECRUITMENT

ORIGIN UK
SPEED ✓✓✓
INFO ✓✓✓
EASE ✓✓✓✓

Founded by two professional mothers unable to find stimulating part-time work, this site is devoted to finding such jobs for others. Register and they will try to match your skills with employers looking for part-time workers. For a similar site send your cv to Flexecutive at **www.resourceconnection.co.uk**

www.flametree.co.uk

INSPIRING SOLUTIONS TO BALANCE YOUR LIFE

ORIGIN UK
SPEED ✓✓✓✓
INFO ✓✓✓✓
EASE ✓✓✓✓

This former magazine site now acts as a specialist consultancy 'working with organisations to respond effectively to the work-life challenge'. If your company needs to improve their flexibility, visit this site.

Magazines

www.handbag.com

THE ISP FOR WOMEN

ORIGIN UK
SPEED ✓✓✓✓
INFO ✓✓✓✓✓
VALUE ✓✓✓
EASE ✓✓✓✓

Described as the most useful place on the Internet for British women, Handbag lives up to that with a mass of information written in an informal style and aimed at helping you get through life. There's shopping and competitions too. For some it's a little too commercial though.

www.ivillage.co.uk

WHERE WOMEN FIND ANSWERS

ORIGIN UK
SPEED ✓✓✓✓
INFO ✓✓✓✓✓
EASE ✓✓✓✓

All the sections you'd expect in a women's magazine, the difference here is that they are trying to create a community with a range of message boards, advice, a good section on work, even a dating service.

Other general women's e-zines and portals:
www.icircle.co.uk – part of the Freeserve network calling itself the Women's Channel.
www.newwomanonline.co.uk – good representation of the magazine, particularly liked the lunchbox with daily distractions.
www.cybergrrl.com – a good American women's e-zine.
www.allthatwomenwant.com – a portal site which offers links to sites covering a vast range of topics. It needs a search engine though.

www.e-women.com

THE MULTICULTURAL WOMEN'S PORTAL

ORIGIN UK
SPEED ✓✓
INFO ✓✓✓✓
EASE ✓✓✓✓

E-women aims to provide women world-wide with features and links which are relevant to their lives. There are lots of women's magazine-type features, a good range of forums, a shopping directory but less serious comment than when previously visited.

www.winmagazine.org

WOMEN'S INTERNATIONAL NET

ORIGIN UK
SPEED ✓✓✓
INFO ✓✓✓✓
EASE ✓✓✓✓

This is an online magazine devoted to bringing together women from all over the world for dialogue and mutual understanding, furthering the knowledge of women's issues and featuring new writing talent. Some of the writing is excellent, but it can be a little earnest.

www.aviva.org

INTERNATIONAL FEMINIST WEBZINE

ORIGIN UK
SPEED ✓✓✓✓
INFO ✓✓✓✓
EASE ✓✓✓✓

If you want information on the political and social issues facing women all over the world, this site has plenty of factual articles, details of meetings and loads of links. There is a nice section on International women's art too.

www.webgrrls.com

WOMEN'S TECH KNOWLEDGE CONNECTION

ORIGIN US
SPEED ✓✓✓✓
INFO ✓✓✓✓
EASE ✓✓✓

Although this site is very American, it offers a great deal of practical information on topics such as careers and technology.

Women's health

Below are a few excellent sources of information on women's health issues, for more general health sites see page 209 and don't rely on websites, see a doctor if you are unwell.

www.womens-health.com

EMPOWERING WOMEN THROUGH KNOWLEDGE

ORIGIN US
SPEED ✓✓✓✓
INFO ✓✓✓✓✓
EASE ✓✓✓✓

A truly comprehensive look at women's health issues with clear, high quality information. The personal assessments provide a range of linked questionnaires to help you make a self-diagnosis and/or assess you risk of contracting heart disease or osteoporosis for instance. There are good links, a good search engine, although the newsletter was written in 1999!

www.healthywomen.org

EDUCATING WOMEN ABOUT THEMSELVES

ORIGIN US
SPEED ✓✓✓✓
INFO ✓✓✓✓✓
EASE ✓✓

The layout doesn't do justice to the quality of information on the site provided by the American-based National Women's Health Resource Center. Go to the 'health center' and use the pull-down menu to select a topic such as breast cancer, acupuncture or menopause. The aim is to provide women with good information to help them make informed decisions about their health.

www.womens-health.co.uk

OBS AND GYNAE EXPLAINED

ORIGIN UK
SPEED ✓✓✓✓
INFO ✓✓✓✓
EASE ✓✓✓

A good starting point for information on obstetrics and gynaecology including pregnancy, infertility, complications and investigations. Has a good search facility and useful links.

www.fpa.org.uk

FAMILY PLANNING

ORIGIN UK
SPEED ✓✓✓✓
INFO ✓✓✓✓✓
EASE ✓✓✓✓

A really comprehensive web site from the Family Planning Association with information on all aspects of birth control written in a clear and helpful style. There is a useful page entitled 'I need help now' plus good links. For a more campaigning approach, try **www.mariestopes.org.uk** for a rundown on contraception choices and information on related topics such as health screening. You can even arrange for him to have a vasectomy online.

Leisure

www.journeywoman.com

PREMIER TRAVEL RESOURCE FOR WOMEN

ORIGIN US
SPEED ✓✓✓
INFO ✓✓✓✓✓
VALUE ✓✓✓
EASE ✓✓✓✓

Dedicated to ensuring safe travel for women, registering gets you access to the free newsletter plus lots of advice, guidance and tips from women who've travelled, traveller's tales and health warnings.

www.womengamers.com

BECAUSE WOMEN DO PLAY

ORIGIN US
SPEED ✓✓✓✓
INFO ✓✓✓✓
EASE ✓✓✓✓

The aim is to provide a selection of reviews and games geared specifically to a female audience (although it doesn't stop this being an enjoyable site for men to visit). It has up-to-the-minute reviews, really well-written articles, lots of content and high quality design.

www.wsf.org.uk

WOMEN'S SPORT FOUNDATION

ORIGIN UK
SPEED ✓✓✓✓
INFO ✓✓✓✓
EASE ✓✓✓✓

The voice of women's sport is committed to improving and promoting opportunities for women and girls in sport at every level. It does this by lobbying and raising the awareness of the importance of women in sport to the organisers and governing bodies. Here you can find out how to get involved or get help.

Index